To Belize
Xmas: 1995
12/21 to 12/30

4-95
30th anniv.

S0-CCJ-203

Adventure Guide to
Belize

KAREN + ROG...
HAPPY ANNIVERSARY...
YOUR YEARS TOGETHER
HAVE BEEN ONE ADVENTURE
AFTER ANOTHER! MORE GOOD
MANY MORE
JOURNEYS
AHEAD! DON'T
EVER FORGET TO
COME HOME!
LOVE...
CHARLIE + BONNIE

Harry S. Pariser

HUNTER
PUBLISHING, INC

Hunter Publishing, Inc.
300 Raritan Center Parkway
Edison NJ 08818
(908) 225 1900
Fax (908) 417-0482

ISBN 1-55650-647-3

3rd Edition © 1995 Hunter Publishing, Inc.

Acknowledgments

Thanks go out to my publisher Michael Hunter and his staff, mapmakers Joyce Huber and Kim André, as well as the following individuals for their help and advice: Ellen and Shawn, Fernando Cruz, John and Lea Young, Susan Vesala, Michelle Longsworth, Kevin Gonzalez, Lori Reed, Jacqueline Tipton, Kitty Fox, Fallet Young, Heidi, Johnny Grief, Luke Ramirez, Norris Hall, the Novelo brothers, Tim Boys, Don Penlon, Cynthia Robin, Diana Lozano, Richie Woods, Wade Bevier, Dr. Arlen Chase, Therese Rath, Phyllis Cayetano, Benjamin Nicholas, Glenn Crawford, Sue E. Williams, Ben Ruoti, Fernando Cruz, Galvin Nell, Desmond Leslie, Anne Floiss, Abel Novelo, Mrs. James Novelo, Lucen at Z-Line, Mary Jo Prost, Eugenio Ah, Jeff Medina, Donna M. Koehnen, Halina Gagne, Dorothy Beveridge, Caroline Ramclam, Ms. Joy Vernon, Rosanna Palma, Yvonne and Alfredo Villoria, Chet, Donna Marshall, John and Carolyn Carr, Meb Cutlack, Katie Stevens, Rosanna Palma, Thomas P. Rackowski, Melissa Johnson, Kathy Schaulfler, John & Lea Young, Rosita Arvigo, Bob and Nestora Jones, Michael A. Panton, Manuel Hoare, David Keleher, Donnan B. Runkel, Bart and Suzi Mickler, Ernesto Sacqui, Ellen MacCrae, Susan Scott, Man Man, Therese Rath, Dave Henson, Nelson Feinstein, Ralph Young, Carlson Tuttle, Meg White, Jack Chivers, Miguel Herrera, Rosa Castro, Alistair King, and Franziska and Nickie Nicholson. Thanks also go to my mother who always worries about me, as well as to many others.

Cover Photo: *French Angelfish*, Hal Beral/Photo Network.
All others by author.

Contents

List of Maps

Abbreviations

AID – agency for international development
a/c – air conditioned
BZ$ – Belizean dollars (US$1=BZ$2)
C. – century
d – double
OW – one way
PG – Punta Gorda
PUP – People's United Party
pp – per person
pn – per night
RT – round trip
Rte. – route
s – single
UDP – United Democratic party

Other Books by Harry S. Pariser from Hunter

Jamaica: A Visitor's Guide (ISBN 1-55650-536-1)
Adventure Guide to Barbados (ISBN 1-55650-277-X)
Adventure Guide to Costa Rica (ISBN 1-55650-598-1)
Adventure Guide to the Dominican Republic (ISBN 1-55650-629-5)
Adventure Guide to Puerto Rico (ISBN 1-55650-628-7)
Adventure Guide to the Virgin Islands (ISBN 1-55650-597-3)

About the Author

Harry S. Pariser was born in Pittsburgh and grew up in a small town in southwestern Pennsylvania. After graduating from Boston University in 1975, Harry hitched and camped his way through Europe, traveled down the Nile by steamer, and by train through Sudan. After visiting Uganda, Rwanda, and Tanzania, he traveled by passenger ship from Mombasa to Bombay, and then on through Asia before settling down in Kyoto, Japan, where he studied Japanese and ceramics. Using Japan as a base, he trekked to the vicinity of Mt. Everest in Nepal, taking tramp steamers to remote Indonesian islands like Adonara, Timor, Sulawesi, and Ternate, and visiting rural parts of China. He returned to the US in 1984, via the Caribbean, where he researched two travel guides: *Guide to Jamaica* and *Guide to Puerto Rico and the Virgin Islands*, the first editions of which were published in 1986. Returning to Japan in 1986, he lived in the city of Kagoshima at the southern tip of Kyushu. During that year and part of the next, he taught English and wrote for *The Japan Times*. He currently lives in San Francisco. Besides traveling and writing, his other pursuits include printmaking, painting, cooking, backpacking, and listening to music – especially jazz, salsa, and African pop.

A Note About Prices

Many prices are listed in Belizean dollars (BZ$). To convert to US dollars, divide by two. Prices quoted are subject to fluctuation and should be used only as a guideline. A 6% hotel tax and 10% service charge may be added to your hotel bill; check with the hotel in question. Credit cards may be subject to as much as a 5% surcharge. Establishments for which no prices are listed are classified as follows: *inexpensive* (under US$30), *moderate* (US$31- 50), *expensive* (over US$50 s or d), and *luxury* (over $100). If calling or faxing Belize, be sure to leave off the zero preceding the prefix. For example, dial 011-501-6-23232 instead of 06-23232.

We Love to Get Mail!

In today's world, things change so rapidly that it's impossible to keep up with everything that's happening in any one place. Travel books are like automobiles: they require fine tuning and frequent overhauls if they are to stay in top condition. We need input from readers so that we can continue to provide the best, most current information available. Please write to let us know about any inaccuracies, new information, or misleading suggestions. Although we try to make our maps as accurate as possible, errors can occur. If you have suggestions for improvement or places that should be included, please let us know.

We especially appreciate letters from female travelers, local residents, and hikers and outdoor enthusiasts. We also like hearing from experts in the field as well as from local hotel owners and individuals wishing to accommodate visitors from abroad. Send your comments to Harry S. Pariser, c/o Hunter Publishing, 300 Raritan Center Parkway, Edison NJ 08818. Fax 908 417 0482.

Reader's Response Form

The Adventure Guide to Belize

I found your book:

Your book could be improved by:

The best places I stayed in were (explain why):

I found the best food at:

Some good and bad experiences I had were:

Will you return to Belize?   If so, where do you plan to go?

If not, why not?

I purchased this book at:

Please include any other comments on a separate sheet and mail completed form to Harry S. Pariser, c/o Hunter Publishing, 300 Raritan Center Parkway, Edison, NJ 08818 USA.

Introduction

 Caribbean yet Central American, Belize is a cultural potpourri. Among its many treasures are the hemisphere's longest coral reef, hundreds of sandy offshore islands, 250 varieties of wild orchids, 500 species of birds, cats and other wildlife, and innumerable Maya ruins – many still unexplored. Set in an isthmus renowned for population density, Belize, a small nation, also contains a small population (est. 225,000) relative to its size. The greater part of its territory is dominated either by the craggy Maya Mountains or lowland swamps. Both the small population and the nation's physical isolation have made the construction of roads a formidable task, and many parts of the nation remain inaccessible today. If you're looking for a large resort with a pristine white beach and attendants catering to your every need, then this is not the place for you. Belize is for the adventurous traveler – one willing to trade a measure of discomfort for an abundance of experience.

The Land

 THE BIG PICTURE: The Central American isthmus is the only region in the world which is both interoceanic and intercontinental. The region comprises seven nations: Belize, Guatemala, El Salvador, Honduras, Nicaragua, Costa Rica, and Panama. All except Belize are former members of the Spanish Empire and, although some contain large native American populations, they share a similar cultural base, which includes the Spanish language and the Catholic religion. Despite their surface similarities, each has evolved its own national character, making political union unlikely. To the region's north lies Mexico, to its south is the continent of South America, connected to the isthmus at Colombia.

GEOGRAPHY: Situated on the east coast of Central America, Belize is bounded by Mexico to the north and by Guatemala to the west and south. Approximately twice the size of Jamaica, Belize is the second smallest nation (after El Salvador) on the North and South American continent. Including the offshore cayes, its total area is 8,886 sq. miles, the size of Massachusetts. From the Honda River in the north to the River Sarstoon in the south, the nation is

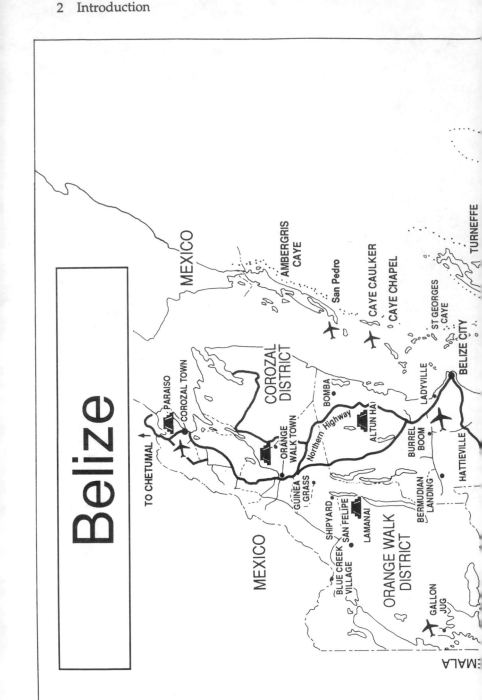

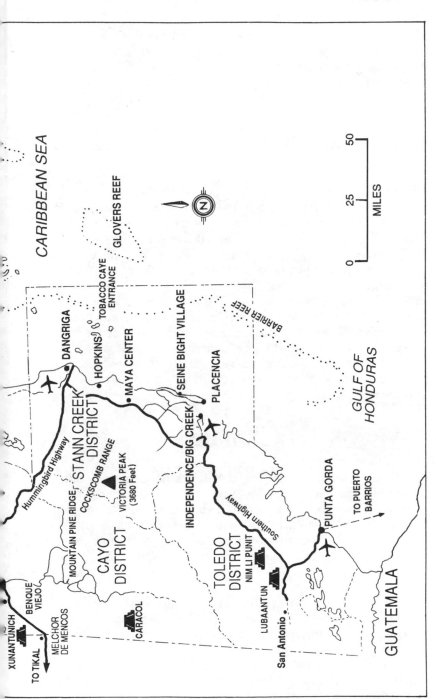

174 miles long and is widest (68 miles) between Belize City and Benque Viejo. While quartz and granite rocks predominate in the Maya range, the northern plain as well as parts of the south and west are formed from limestone, which has dissolved to form fertile soil. The Maya Mountains to the south fall away precipitously near the coast. Although 70% of the total area is covered by hills, the remainder is coastal plain. The low-lying plain to the north is swampy near the coast but rises to a slight plateau in the west.

RIVERS: Once forming a crucial link in the nation's communication system, rivers are among the most arresting geographical features. The northernmost Río Hondo delineates the border with Mexico; the New River runs parallel to it 10 miles to the south. Both flow east into Chetumal Bay. Once known as the Old River, the Belize River begins in the southwestern hills, flows to the north, and then turns towards the Caribbean. Navigable for at least 120 miles, it has numerous tributaries. The shorter Sibún River runs to its south and reaches the sea approximately 10 miles south of Belize City. Unlike those in the north, the southern rivers are short and steep, extending from the Maya Mountains to the east or southeast where they empty into the sea. Few can be navigated and their rapids pose a natural obstacle. This difficulty is one of the reasons that the northern part of the country was colonized first.

Climate

As holds true for the rest of Central America, Belize has a delightful climate. Its mild, subtropical weather varies little throughout the year, with most of the variation in temperatures coming from differences in elevation. Rain, which usually consists of short showers, is most likely to occur from June or July through the end of November; the driest months are February and March, extending up to May.

RAINFALL: This varies greatly from year to year. While Corozal receives an average of 40 inches annually, Punta Gorda may get as much as 160. Monthly averages also vary widely from year to year. While it might rain as little as 12 inches in Punta Gorda one month, 36 inches might fall that same month the following year. Obviously, this is problematic for farming. Northers are frontal storms which arrive during the winter months from Dec. to March. They bring several days of *chubascos* (thunderstorms). Another phenomenon is the *mauger* (pronounced "magah") season which is a period of dry, calm weather with still winds and a generally oppressive, stagnant atmosphere characterized by dry heat and biting insects. It usually lasts for a week or more during August.

TEMPERATURES: In Belize City these vary between 50° and 95°F and average out at 79°-80°F. While temperatures in the Cayo District may reach 100°F in the shade during April or May, it may be cooler here than in Belize City during the winter months. The worst humidity is found on the coastal strip between Belize City and Punta Gorda, but coastal breezes tend to cool down the same area.

Average Belize City Temperature (°F)/Rainfall Guide (inches)

	Jan.	Feb.	Mar.	Apr.	May	Jun.	Jul.	Aug.	Sep.	Oct.	Nov.	Dec.
Low	66	68	69	75	75	73	73	72	72	72	68	68
High	84	84	86	88	88	90	90	90	90	90	82	82

SEASONS: There is a clearly demarcated dry and wet season throughout the country, but with considerable differences in its length between north and south. While the dry season lasts for four months from Feb. to May in the north, it may last only for the month of March in areas of the extreme south, such as the Toledo District.

HURRICANES: One unfortunate characteristic of Belize's climate is its tendency toward hurricanes. These low-pressure zones are serious business and should not be taken lightly. Where the majority of structures are poorly built, property damage from hurricanes may run into the hundreds of millions of dollars. A hurricane begins as a relatively small tropical storm, known as a cyclone when its winds reach a velocity of 39 mph. At 74 mph it is upgraded to hurricane status, with winds of up to 200 mph and ranging in size from 60-1,000 miles in diameter. A small hurricane releases energy equivalent to the explosions of six atomic bombs per second. A hurricane may be compared to an enormous hovering engine that uses the moist air and water of the tropics as fuel, carried hither and thither by prevailing air currents – generally eastern trade winds which intensify as they move across warm ocean waters. When cooler, drier air infiltrates as it heads north, the hurricane begins to die, cut off from the life-sustaining ocean currents that have nourished it from infancy. Routes and patterns are unpredictable. As for their frequency: "June – too soon; July –

stand by; August – it must; September – remember." So goes the old rhyme. But hurricanes are not confined to July and August. Hurricanes forming in Aug. and Sept. typically last for two weeks, while those that form in June, July, Oct., and Nov. (many of which originate in the Caribbean and the Gulf of Mexico) generally last only seven days. Approximately 70% of all hurricanes (known as Cabo Verde types) originate as embryonic storms coming from the west coast of Africa. Fortunately though, they are comparatively rarer here than in the Caribbean islands and the southern US. Since record-keeping began, a number of hurricanes have wreaked havoc here. Some of the earliest of these were in 1785, 1805, and 1813. The hurricane of 1931 caused considerable damage to Belize City and killed 150. Punta Gorda was devastated in 1945 and Corozal was nearly wiped off the map a decade later. The most serious of a series, 1961's Hurricane Hattie persuaded the government to build Belmopan, a new capital set 50 miles inland. Hurricane Fifi hit the northern cane fields hard in 1978.

Flora and Fauna

 One of the things that makes Belize such a spectacular destination is its natural beauty – better preserved here than in other Central American countries. Belize still has 80% of its forests intact, as compared with only 2% in similarly-sized El Salvador. Sixteen tracts, comprising 30% of the total land area, have been designated national reserves in which only selective logging is permitted. Additional land has been placed in national parks.

NATURE WATCHING: Don't be disappointed if you fail to see any animals; the dense underbrush frequently makes viewing difficult. In addition the biomass of the rainforests is 99.9% plants so animals are definitely in the minority. Many of the smaller animals are strictly nocturnal and others are wary of humans. Some animals, however, are highly visible. These include the active monkeys, peccaries, and coatis. Only by attuning yourself to its rhythms, can you truly experience the rainforest's wonders. **opportunities:** One alternative to winging it is a tour. See "nature tours" under "practicalities." The best way to see wildlife is to stay in a lodge near the tropical forest or to camp within the forest itself. The latter, while preferable, requires equipment and adequate preparation.

Plant Life

Plants abound in the fertile valleys filled with citrus, bananas, and cacao; there is a marked contrast between these valleys and the outlying mangrove swamps or the pine ridges and tropical forest. Although approximately 90% of the land is forested, trees disguise the acid, infertile soils. While the mixed hardwood forests may contain some 700 species of trees, only 15-20 of them have any marketable value. Some of these are the ziricote, rosewood, mahogany, and cedar as well as secondary trees such as the mayflower and the Santa María, the most important timber tree in the central plateau. The comparatively small area of land that is suitable for agriculture is in the least accessible region.

Things You Can Do to Save the Forests

• *Start at home.* Much of North America's old growth forest is under threat from the timber industry. It is unrealistic to expect nations like Belize, Brazil, and Costa Rica to save their forests if the US and Canada cut theirs down. In particular, the government-subsidized rape of the US National Forests and the destruction of British Columbia's old growth must be halted.

• *Visit the rainforests.* Showing an interest reinforces a sense of pride in the forests among local people. When you return, tell your friends and relatives about what you've seen.

• *Boycott tropical products.* Don't purchase imported tropical birds, snakes, or animal hides. Avoid buying products made of teak, mahogany, or other tropical woods unless you are **positive** that it comes from tree farms and not from virgin rainforest. Encourage retailers to question the source of their products.

• *Organize.* If you live in a major city such as New York, there is likely to be an environmental organization for which you can volunteer. If not, start your own! For maximum effectiveness, coordinate your efforts with groups operating in tropical nations.

• *Educate yourself.* The most important hope for the human race is education. Read as much as you can, see as much as you can, and write to your political leaders and to newspapers. Inform people about what you have seen.

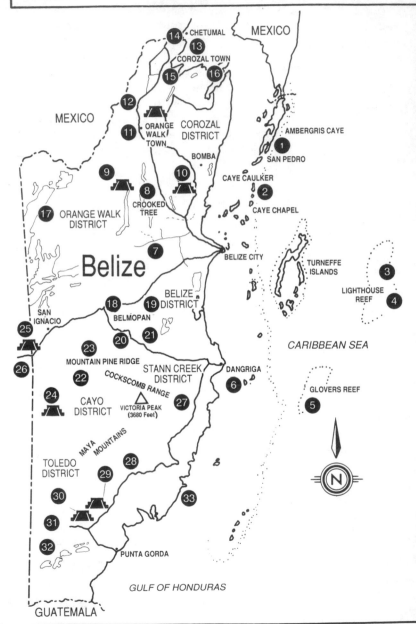

Major Archaeological Sites, Reserves,

National Parks & Natural Wonders

The Cayes

1. Hol Chan Reserve
2. Proposed Siwa-ban Reserve and Caye Caulker Reef Reserve
3. Great Blue Hole
4. Half Moon Caye National Monument
5. Glovers Reef Reserve
6. Proposed South Water Caye/ Tobacco Cay Reserve

The North

7. The Bermudian Landing Community Baboon Sanctuary
8. Crooked Tree Wildlife Sanctuary/ Chau Hiix
9. Lamanai Archaeological Reserve
10. Altun Ha
11. Cuello
12. Nohmul
13. Santa Rita
14. Four Miles Lagoon
15. Cerros
16. Shipstern Wildlife Reserve
17. Rio Bravo Conservation Area/ La Milpa

The West

18. Guanacaste Park
19. Belize Zoo/Monkey Bay Wildlife Sanctuary
20. Blue Hole/St. Herman's Cave
21. Five Blues Lake National Park
22. Mountain Pine Ridge Forest Reserve
23. Hidden Valley Falls
24. Caracol
25. Xunantunich
26. To Melchor, Tikal, Flores (Guatemala)

The South

27. Cockscomb Jaguar Reserve
28. Bladen Blanch Nature Reserve
29. Nim Li Punit
30. Lubaantun
31. Uxbenka
32. Pusilheá
33. Monkey River

The Rainforests

 Containing the planet's most complex ecosystem, rainforests have a richer animal and plant life than any other type of forest. Unlike other areas in which living organisms face conflicts with a hostile climate, in the rainforest organisms struggle for survival against each other. Since the climate has been stable in this region for some 60 million years, each being – whether plant, animal, insect, or microbe – has been able to develop its specialized niche. Rainforests occur in regions without marked seasonal variation and which commonly receive more than 70 inches of rain annually.

VARIETIES: There is no single "true rainforest," and forest botanists have varying definitions of the term. It can be argued that there are about 30 types including such categories as semi-deciduous forests, tropical evergreen alluvial forests, and evergreen lowland forests – each of which is subdividable into three or four more categories. **Equatorial evergreen rainforests** comprise two thirds of the total. As one moves away from the equator on either side, the forests develop marked wet and dry seasons. **Cloud forest** is another name for montane rainforest which is characterized by heavy rainfall and persistent condensation due to the upward deflection of moisture-laden air currents by mountains. Trees here are typically short and gnarled. The so-called **elfin woodland** is marked by the presence of extremely stunted moss-covered trees. Rainforests without as much rain, **tropical dry forests** once covered Pacific coastal lowlands stretching from Panama to Mexico, comprising an area the size of France. Today, they have shrunk to a mere 2% of that area and only part of this is under protection. None of these last three types of forest are found in Belize. In addition to rainforests which generally contain Santa María, mahogany, guanacaste, and other woods, Belize has large tracts of pine forest – known as **"pine ridge"** – which are mixed pine, oak, palm, calabash, and other trees. **"Broken ridge"** is pine mixed with many other trees. These generally grow in sandy soil. **"Cohune ridge"** is dominated by cohune palms and the soil is more fertile.

LAYERS: Life in the rainforest is highly stratified in vertical layers. The upper canopy layer contains animals which are mainly herbaceous and, in Belize, have prehensile tails. They rarely descend to earth. Typically more than a hundred feet in height, these canopy trees lack the girth associated with tall trees of the temperate forest, perhaps because there are fewer strong winds to combat and each tree must compete with the others for sunlight. The next lower layer is filled with small trees, lianas, and epiphytes. Some are parasitic, others use trees solely for support purposes. The ground surface layer is littered with branches, twigs, and foliage. Most animals here live on insects and fruit; others are carnivorous. Contrary to popular opinion the ground cover is thick only where sunlight penetrates sufficiently to allow it. The extensive root system of the trees and associated fungi (*mycorrhizae*) form a thick mat which holds thin topsoils in place when it rains. If these are cut, the soil will wash away: the steeper the slope, the faster the rate of runoff. As the sun beats down on the soil, sometimes baking it hard as a sidewalk, the crucial fungal mat and other organic life die off. It may take hundreds of years to replace important nutrients through rainfall, and the forests may never recover.

INTERACTIONS: As the name implies, rainforests receive ample precipitation, which promotes a rich variety of vegetation, to which animals and insects must adapt. Lowland rainforests receive at least 100 inches. Although some rainforests see almost no rain during certain parts of the year, they are generally cloaked in clouds from which they draw moisture. The high level of plant-animal interaction – taking forms such as predation, parasitism, hyperparasitism, symbiosis, and mutualism in Biologyspeak – is believed to be one major factor promoting diversity. The interactions are innumerable and highly complex: strangler figs steal sunlight from canopy trees; wasps may pollinate figs; bats and birds transport seeds and pollinate flowers. When a species of bird, for example, becomes rare or extinct, it may have an effect on a tree which depends solely upon it to distribute its seeds. There is no such thing as self-sufficiency in a rainforest; all life depends upon its cohabitants for survival.

BIODIVERSITY: Those who are unfamiliar with the rainforest tend to undervalue it. Tropical deforestation is one of the great tragedies of our time. We are far from cataloging the species inhabiting the rainforests, and when the forests are cut down, these will be lost forever. More than 70% of the plants known to produce compounds with anti-cancerous properties are tropical, and there may be many cures waiting to be found. One survey of Costa Rican plants found that 15% had potential as anti-cancer agents. Cures for malaria and dysentery have been found in the forests. Louis XIV was cured of amoebic dysentery by ipecac, a South American plant that remains the most effective cure. Cortisone and diosgenin, the active agents in birth control pills, were developed from

Guatemalan and Mexican wild yams. These are some of the 3,000 plants that tribal peoples use worldwide as contraceptives. Continued research could yield yet other methods of birth control. Shaman Pharmaceuticals is one company working to develop useful drugs based on rainforest products. Not all rainforest products are medicinal. Rice, corn, and most spices – including vanilla, the unripe fermented stick-like fruits of the Central American orchid *Vanilla fragrans* – are also medicinal. Other products native people have extracted from the rainforest include latex, resins, starch, sugar, thatch, dyes, and fatty oils. The rainforest also acts as a genetic pool, and when disease strikes a monocrop such as bananas, it's possible to hybridize it with rainforest varieties to see if this produces an immunity to pests or fungus.

GREENERY AND GREENHOUSE: Biodiversity is only one of many reasons to preserve the forest. Rainforests also act as watersheds, and cutting can result in flooding as well as increased aridity. This is because much rain is produced through the transpiration of trees, which helps keep the air saturated with moisture. Although it is commonly believed that rainforests produce most of the earth's oxygen, in fact there is an equilibrium between the amount mature forests consume through the decay of organic matter and the amount they produce via photosynthesis. However, many scientists believe that widespread burning of tropical forests releases large amounts of carbon dioxide. The amount of carbon dioxide in the atmosphere has risen by 15% in the past century (with about half of this occurring since 1958), and forest clearance may account for half of that gain. Since carbon dioxide along with other atmospheric elements traps heat that would otherwise escape into space, this means that temperatures may rise worldwide. Rainfall patterns would change and ocean levels would rise as the polar ice packs melt. In many areas, deforestation has already had an adverse effect on the environment. Although many uncertainties remain about the "greenhouse effect," one certainty is that by the time the effects are apparent, they will be irreversible.

FATE OF THE FORESTS: Just a few thousand years ago, a belt of rainforests, covering some five billion acres (14% of the planet's surface) stretched around the equator. Wherever there was sufficient rainfall and high enough temperatures there was or is rainforest. Over half that total area has now been destroyed, much of it in the past couple of hundred years, with the rate accelerating after the end of WWII. Squatters and logging continue to cause deforestation throughout the region. At current rates, much of the remaining forest will vanish by the end of the century. One reason for the expansion into the forests is the need for land resulting from the concentration of arable land in a few hands. For example, in El Salvador fewer than 2,000 families control 40% of the land. Another motivation is the desire to secure control over an area by one group or another. Cattle ranching, logging, mining, and industry are other reasons to cut the forests. Forests do not recover quickly. Depending how much has been cut, recovery may take from centuries to eternity.

EDUCATING YOURSELF: Don't miss an opportunity to visit the rainforest while you are in Belize. When you return home, one of the best organizations to join is **Rainforest Action Network** (☎ 415-398-4404, fax 398-2732). Write Ste. 700, 450 Sansome, San Francisco, CA 94111. Another is **Earth Island Institute** (☎ 415-788-3666, fax 788-7324) which was founded by longtime environmental activist David Brower. Write Ste. 28, 300 Broadway, San Francisco, CA 94133. A third is the **Rainforest Alliance** (☎ 212-941-1900, fax 941-4986). Write 270 Lafayette St., #512, NY, NY 10012. **Greenpeace** (☎ 202-462-1177) also has a rainforest program. Write 1436 U St. NW, Washington, DC 20009. Other, specifically Belize-oriented organizations are listed under "foundations" in the Practicalities section. A number of books about the rainforest can be found in the booklist at the back of this book. If you want to inform yourself about the state of Noth America's National Forests, join the **Native Forest Council** (PO Box 2171, Eugene, OR 97402). A donation of $25 or more gives you a subscription to their informative newspaper, the *Forest Voice*. If you're planning a visit to the Pacific Northwest and would like a guided tour, **Ancient Forest Adventures** offers both resort-based trips and less expensive backpacking trips. Call Mary Vogel at (503) 385-8633 or write AFA, 16 NW Kansas Ave., Bend, OR 97701-1202.

Trees and Tropical Vegetation

The hallmark of the rainforest is diversity, and trees are no exception to that rule. While temperate forests contain only an average of four species per acre, tropical forests may have from 20 to 86. Rainforest trees often have shallow root systems and they may be physically supported by basal buttressing or silt roots. These root systems are bound together in mutually beneficial relationships with the lowly fungi. If you look carefully, you can spot a link between the white threads of fungi, decomposing a leaf or fruit, with the rootlet of a tree. Fungi are able to recycle 20 times as much

Common Misperceptions About Rainforests

• Rainforests are not "the lungs of the planet." Mature trees produce as much oxygen as they consume. The danger in destroying rainforests lies with the effects on rainfall, flooding, and global warming from increased carbon dioxide being released into the atmosphere.

• The rainforests are not bursting with colorful plants, wild orchids, and animals. The overwhelming color is green; flowers are few; and the animal you're most likely to encounter is the ant.

• Rainforests are not a renewable resource. It is impossible to cut trees without destroying plants and affecting the environment.

• Rainforests are not merely a source of wood. There are other values associated with them which must be considered.

• Once damaged, rainforest does not simply grow back as it once was. It may take centuries for the complex ecosystem to regenerate. Reforestation cannot restore the environment.

• Despite its verdant appearance, rainforest soil may not be fertile. Most of the nutrients are contained in the biomass.

• There is no need to "manage" a rainforest. They've been doing just fine for eons on their own. Everything in the rainforest is recycled, and anything removed has an effect.

• "Selective" cutting has detrimental consequences because it affects the surrounding soil quality and weakens the forest as the strongest specimens are removed. No way has yet been found to exploit a rainforest so that all species are preserved.

• One "endangered" species cannot be effectively protected without safeguarding its ecosystem. Botanical gardens or seed banks cannot save important species. There are too many such species, seeds have too short a lifespan, and the species depend upon animals for their lifecycle equilibrium.

• Any reduction in consumption of tropical hardwoods will not preserve rainforests. The only effective method is to protect the forests in reserves and parks. The forests are falling at too fast a rate for any other methods to be effective.

potassium and phosphorus to a tree as it will lose in the rains. The rainforest's high humidity and relatively uniform temperatures allow fungi to flourish. Perhaps in a largely unsuccessful evolutionary attempt by nature to avoid the burden of stranglers and other plants, the trees are generally smooth barked.

Tree **buttresses** are triangular when viewed from the side and in cross-section resemble an irregular two-, five-, or occasionally up to 10-armed star. They function much like the guy ropes on a tent: hitting them with the blunt side of a machete will produce a "bong" showing that they are under tension. There are three types of buttresses: plank (resembling giant wedges), flying (of the stilt-root type), and serpentine – often looped or undulating from side to side: these extend some distance from the tree. Many trees possess buttresses of more than one type. A special characteristic of rainforest trees are the **drip-tip leaves** which are elongated at the end by an inch. This allows them to shed water after a shower more quickly and resume assimilating and transpiring. A further advantage is that the quick passage of water may also act to deter the growth of mosses and lichen. Another feature of tropical trees is **cauliflory** or flowering from the trunk. Southeast Asian examples of fruit produced in this fashion include jackfruit and durian.

VARIETIES: Banak is called *sangre palo* in Spanish after the dark red sap that exudes from its bark when wounded. The *yemeri* or **white mahogany** is another variety. **Black poison wood** *(chechem)* is also called Honduras walnut. The name comes from its caustic sap. Oak and Caribbean pine are found in the higher elevations of the Mountain Pine Ridge area of the Cayo District. Its milk will blister your skin. The **white poison wood** is much less toxic. **Sapodilla** – which provides chicle, the white resinous latex used to manufacture chewing gum – and mahogany dominate the deciduous forests of the north. The fronds of the **cohune** *(coroso)* palm have traditionally been used for thatch and the leaf stems for the sides of houses, for table tops and for beds. Its name is thought to derive from its testicle-shaped nuts *(cojone* is testicle in Spanish). Oil is obtained from the nuts and food from the heart of the "cabbage." In order to harvest the oil, the kernels are extracted and added to a pot of water; the oil slowly floats to the top. The oil has been used for cooking, as massage oil, and for making laundry soap. The nuts have even been used for tobacco pipes: men would bore a hole and put a stem on them. During WWI, the nuts were harvested extensively by the British, who used them to make charcoal filters for their gas masks. Shavings from the stem can be used on wounds as a coagulant which will stave off infection. The

Maya have always believed that where these trees grow the soil is more fertile than anywhere else, and cohune ridge is common near archaeological sites. Another famous tree is the **ceiba** which the Maya have believed is a "tree of life" because it separates heaven and earth and has a long life. It's noted for its eye-catching "plank" root buttresses. The silky fibers surrounding the seed in its fruit have given it the English name of silk cotton tree. The bark of the **craboo** tree is used as a cure for dysentery; a dessert and a rum can be made from its berry-like fruit. Popularly known in Spanish as the *Indio desnudo* ("naked Indian") and in English as the "tourist tree," the **gumbo limbo** utilizes chloroplasts under its orange bark in order to continue synthesizing during the months from Nov. to May when it is leafless. Known locally as the "tubroose," the **guanacaste** or ear fruit receives its English name from the unique shape of its fruits. These trees require an enclosed, noncompetitive tropical forest in order to thrive. The **cashew**, the center of a festival held in Crooked Tree, is called the "Devil's fruit" because it's said that the Devil made it and forgot to put the fruit inside.

EPIPHYTES AND BROMELIADS: Taken from the Greek words meaning "upon plants," epiphytes provide the luxuriant verdancy commonly associated with rainforests. Although they may be found in temperate and drier tropical forests as well, the combination of rain and warmth unique to the rainforest help them flourish here. Treetop life has many advantages. Birds and bats arrive to pollinate and deposit nutrient-rich dung, and their seeds are likely to be dispersed by the wind. But water may be harder to come by and evaporation is a problem, so many bromeliads have evolved tanks to hold up to two gallons of water. Don't make the mistake of thinking that these plants are parasitic. Although they are unwelcome guests, most do not feed on their hosts. Generally, they arrive in the form of tiny dustlike seeds which establish themselves on moss or lichen. Minute epiphytes residing on leaf surfaces, epiphylls (algae, liverworts, lichens, and mosses) are generally found on lower plants. Named after Swedish botanist Olaf Bromel, **bromeliads** are ground-dwelling epiphytes, the most famous of which is the pineapple.

ORCHIDS: Belize's extraordinary natural wealth includes some 250 varieties of orchids. Not all are epiphytic and the ones who are generally possess thicker leaves and keep their stomata – tiny pores on their leaves which absorb carbon dioxide – shut during the day, utilizing a metabolic process to store carbon dioxide for the next day's use. Nearly all orchids are pollinated by insects or hummingbirds, and many may only be pollinated by a single specific one. Aside from their aesthetic value, orchids are of little economic importance. Once thought to have medicinal properties, this has proven largely false and not a single species is currently used in modern medicine. Their only valuable product is vanilla, an extract obtained from the cured unripened pods of various species belonging to the genus *Vanilla*. Orchids were named by Dioscorides, a Greek physician who, noting the similarity of its tubers to male genitals, named the species "*orches*."

VINES AND COMPANY: Woody (vines, lianas, and bush ropes) and herbacaous climbers help give the rainforest its tropical quality. Using trees as trellises, vines crawl up from the ground to reach the light. Scramblers grow in gaps in the rainforest. Over 90% of **liana** species are found in the tropics where they commonly grow as long as 230 ft. and as wide as six in. or more. Lianas twist themselves around the tree and extend tendrils or hooks to secure themselves. Like vines, they drop their shaded understory leaves as they reach maturity. In order to guard against damage from kinking as trees sway, lianas have evolved bends, coils, and twists. The longest lianas are rattans – one of the rainforest's harvestable products – which may grow to more than 500 ft. In addition to closing the canopy, thus stabilizing the microclimate, lianas also offer protection to animals such as sloths. Sleeping in a mass of lianas, sloths tie in to a tensile network of vines that will alert them to the presence of an arboreal predator.

STRANGLER FIGS: Beginning life as epiphytes, some species of *Ficus* and *Clusia* send down woody, clasping roots that wind themselves around the trunk as they extend into the earth. As the roots grow in size, they meld into a trunk which surrounds the tree. These "strangler figs" most likely kill the tree not through strangulation but by robbing it of canopy space. They can grow in the ruins of buildings as well. Strangler figs are often the only trees left in an otherwise cleared tract of forest. There is little incentive to use their poor quality wood, and their spreading branches provide shade. The holes, cracks, twists, and turns in its trunk host geckos, anoles, ants, stingless bees, scorpions, and other life – each inhabiting its ecological niche. Bats, birds, and other fruit eaters flock around the trees, attracting ornithologists in the process. Even peccaries and other ground dwellers arrive to share in the bounty that falls to the ground. These creatures all help distribute its seeds when they defecate.

MANGROVES: Mangrove (*mangle* in Spanish) forests are found along the coasts and on the cayes; these water-rooted trees serve as a marine habitat which shelters sponges, corals, oysters, and other members of the marine community around its roots – organisms which in turn attract a variety of other sealife. Some species live out their lives in the shelter of the mangroves, and many fish use them as a shelter or feeding ground; lobsters use the mangrove environs as a nursery for their young. Above the water level, they shelter seabirds and are important nesting sites. Their organic detritus, exported to the reef by the tides, is consumed by its inhabitants, providing the base of an extensive food web. Mangroves also dampen high waves and winds generated by tropical storms. By trapping silt in their roots and catching leaves and other debris which decompose to form soil, the red mangroves act as land builders. Eventually, the red mangroves kill themselves off, building up enough soil for the black and white mangroves to take over. Meanwhile, the red mangroves have sent out progeny in the form of floating seedlings – bottom-heavy youngsters that grow on the tree until reaching six inches to a foot in length. If they drop in shallow water, the seeds touch bottom and implant themselves. In deeper water they stay afloat and, crossing a shoal, drag until they lodge. Named after their light-colored bark, the white mangroves are highly salt tolerant. If growing in a swampy area, they produce pneumatophores, root system extensions which grow vertically to a height that allows them to stay above the water during flooding or tides and carry on gaseous exchange. Producing a useful wood, the black mangrove also puts out pneumatophores. Smaller than the others, the buttonwood is not a true mangrove but is found on the coasts where no other varieties occur. Belize is the only nation that maintains 90% of its coastal mangroves. Although mangroves are theoretically protected by law in Belize, they are endangered by the activities of marauding developers. Vast tracts are being removed in the areas under development along the Northern and Western Highways near Belize City. Hopefully, the burgeoning "eco-tourism" industry will not result in further mangrove destruction.

OTHERS: A free-floating aquatic perennial, the water hyacinth (*jacinto de agua*) has spread during this century from its South American homeland to become one of the most troublesome and widespread aquatic weeds. Represented in Belize by numerous species, the heliconia (*platanillo*), famous worldwide as an ornamental, lends its bizarre color and shape to the tropical landscape. By producing nectar both deep in their flowers (for bees and hummingbirds) and also at nectaries on petals, stems, and leaves (for aggressive ants and wasps), passion flowers provide themselves with both pollination and protection.

Animal Life

 As with the plants, the Animal Kingdom is also wonderfully diverse. Many of the indigenous species are in danger of extinction, largely from loss of their traditional habitats through deforestation. Sea turtles, though, are threatened by often-illegal overhunting and a viral disease. The panoply of wild Belizean species includes manatees, ocelots, deer, coatis, coyotes, jaguars, margays, peccaries, tapirs, and howler and spider monkeys. Unlike their temperate counterparts, they are relatively difficult to spot. You need to have a keen eye, to keep still, and – best of all – to have a local friend or guide along. A fascinating book to peruse before your arrival is *Costa Rican Natural History*, edited by the eminent biologist and conservationist Daniel Janzen. While it includes many species not found in Belize, it is an invaluable reference nevertheless. Another superb book is *Neotropical Rainforest Mammals: A Field Guide* by Louise H. Emmons.

Mammals

PRIMATES: New World monkeys differ from their Old World monkey and ape cousins in many respects. Their noses have wide-apart, sideward-pointing nostrils as opposed to close-set, down-

---

Belizean Animal Names

Alligator – crocodile
Ant bear, Antsbear – anteater
Antelop – deer
Baboon – howler monkey
Bamboo chicken – iguana
Bush dog – tayra
Dilly – armadillo
Fillymingo – jabiru stork
Georgie Bull – northern jacana
Gibnut – agouti
Hilari – jaguarundi

Honeybear – kinkajou
Mountain cow – Baird's tapir
Nightwalker – kinkajou
Polecat – skunk
Quash – coati
Red tiger – puma
Tiger – jaguar
Tommygoff – fer-de-lance
Warrie, warree – peccary
Water dog – otter
Wowla – boa constrictor

ward-pointing ones; they are primarily arboreal; and they show a greater geographical variation in color patterns.

Actually sounding more like a "growler" than a howler, the sounds of the **black howler monkey** ("baboon," *saraguate*) reverberate up to several miles away. The unusual sound results from a special bone in its throat which acts as an amplifier. There are numerous local explanations as to why howlers roar, such as when it is going to rain and when other animals are feeding. Actually, they react to loud noises and to rain. They roar more frequently at midday. The cacophonous howling begins with an accelerating series of low-pitched grunts by the male which metamorphose into long, deep roars; the females join the fun with higher-pitched roars. Another unique characteristic of the howler is its prehensile tail, which features a dermatoglyph or fingerprint. Living in groups of up to 20 led by a senior male, they dine on flowers, fruits, and tender leaves. Howlers are entirely black, except for a pale-colored fringed mantle on their sides. Their robust shoulders contrast with comparatively diminutive hindquarters. If you should see a colony, don't get underneath: A favorite pastime is to urinate on *homo sapiens*! Another species, the gold mantled howler is thought to occur here but has not been documented.

Moving rapidly through the trees, the black-handed **spider monkey** ("monkey," *mono araña*) has a very complex language and lives in bands of about 20 which frequently subdivide into smaller groupings.

RACCOON FAMILY: Omnivorous, solitary, nocturnal, crafty, and clean, the **raccoon** *(mapache)* will dine on anything from frogs and fish to fruit and vegetables. Its nimble cousin the mischievous and sociable white-nosed **coati** ("quash" or *pizote*) hunts at dawn and dusk – resting in treetops or in hollow trunks the rest of the time. The term coati-mundi refers only to solitary coatis, adult males over two years old. Mainly nocturnal, the gregarious **kinkajou** ("nightwalker," *mico de noche, micoleon*) dines on small animals, birds, eggs, and honey. It has short and wooly fur, large soulful eyes, small ears, and a long prehensile tail. This tail is used as an anchor as it moves from tree to tree. During the day, the kinkajou naps in a tree hollow. Smaller and lacking a prehensile tail, the **olingo** or pale-faced kinkajou, is a close relative. Actively agile, they journey high in the rainforest canopy. A third related species is the **cacomistle**, a nocturnal and solitary tawny-brown creature which barks and has a tail longer than its head and body.

WEASEL FAMILY: With attractive, short and thick but soft fur, the long-tailed **weasel's** *(comadreja's)* slim frame allows it to slither into the burrows of mice. It also dines on rabbits, birds, and reptiles. It is a nervous, nocturnal, and solitary creature; you are unlikely to catch more than a glimpse of one. The **grison** ("bush dog," *huron, grisón*) resembles a large weasel with extremely short legs and tail and with a long neck and back. Perhaps the nation's least popular mammal, the striped hog-nosed **skunk** ("polecat," *zorro hediondo*) is probably better left unseen and unsmelled. Although it is not a true rainforest creature, it is sometimes found there. An excellent swimmer, the southern river **otter** ("waterdog," *nutria, perro de agua*) eats fish, shrimp, and turtles. On land, this graceful creature waddles awkwardly. In danger of extinction, they have been protected by law in Belize since 1974. Resembling a lanky mink with a long-haired tail, the **tayra** or bush dog *(tolumuco)* feeds on grubs, bird nests, fruit, eggs, and chicken or goat meat; it resides in an underground burrow.

CAT FAMILY: The principal predator in rainforests worldwide, cats have a physique that suits their killer lifestyle. Their teeth are designed for killing and meat eating, while their excellent sight and hearing, strong shoulders, and sharp claws come in handy when going after game. Some are territorial, most are solitary, and all prey on anything that comes their way – from large insects to small mammals. The best time to see them is after nightfall when they take to trails and their bright eyeshine makes them visible. Should you come across a den with kittens, leave them alone. They have not been abandoned: the mother has gone off to search for food.

The graceful, nocturnal and diurnal "king of the tropical rainforest," the **jaguar** ("tiger," tigre) is this hemisphere's largest cat; it may reach six feet long and three feet high at shoulder level. It will dine on peccaries, deer, monkeys, sloths, and even fish. The only large, spotted cats in the Americas, jaguars are easily identifiable. You might hear them roar at night – a series of hoarse, deep grunts. Although an encounter is extremely unlikely, it is fraught with danger. If you should see a jaguar, walk toward it, shout and clap your hands. If you run, it may pursue you, which could have unfortunate consequences!

Sometimes called a cougar or mountain lion, the **puma** ("red tiger") ranks second in terms of size. Slightly smaller than a jaguar, it has an unspotted tan or dark brown hide, a leaner, more low-slung frame, and a longer, thicker tail. It is the only large, uniformly colored cat. Although pumas may tag along behind humans out of curiosity, few attacks on *homo sapiens* have ever been documented.

Resembling a miniaturized jaguar, the **ocelot** *(manigordo)* feeds on anything from rabbits to insects. Unlike a jaguar, it has stripes and not spots on its neck. It captures game on the ground and may be encountered walking on man-made trails at night. A smaller, similar version of the ocelot, the **tiger cat** *(tigrillo)* has a combination of spots and stripes. Ranging from 33.5 to 51 in., it may weigh up to 22 lbs. Rarely sighted, it survives in the Tortuguero, Santa Rosa, and Corcovado national parks, the Reserva Forestal Río Macho, and on the lower slopes of the Cordillera Talamanca. More solitary and nocturnal than the ocelot, the **margay** *(mandu, tigrillito, maimselle)* is the size of a large house cat. Weighing 6.6-11 lbs., it has a somewhat bushy tail which runs well over half the extended length of its head and black-spotted body. It may easily be confused with an ocelot.

With unspotted blackish-brown or chestnut-to-red fur, the **jaguarundi** ("hilari," *onca*) has a small flattened head, long sleek body, short legs – all of which make it appear to be a cross between a cat and a weasel.

MARSUPIALS: Five-toed, **opossums** have short legs, long tails, large and delicate ears, and their first hindfoot toe functions as an opposable "thumb" which is used to clutch thin branches for climbing. Born only eight days after fertilization, opossum infants follow a trail of their mother's saliva from the cloaca to her pouch, where they secure themselves to their mother's nipples for the next 60 days. These malodorous creatures – which feed on small animals and fruits – enjoy rolling in fresh dung. When handled, they are aggressive, defecating and squirting evil-smelling urine with a twist of their tail. The four species of opossum *(zorro)* found here are the common, common grey four-eyed, woolly, and regular. Arboreal, the *zorro* is a nocturnal omnivore. The wooly mouse and slatey slender mouse opossums *(zorra, zorricí)* are also found.

EDENTATAS: Indigenous to the Americas, the name of this order – which includes anteaters, sloths, and armadillos – refers to the few teeth found in the latter two and their complete absence in the anteaters. They represent the last remnant of an order that evolved during the period when South America was an isolated island continent. Sloths and anteaters are both arboreal, soft furred creatures.

Possessing a prehensile tail and a long retractile tongue, the strictly nocturnal **silky anteater** ("antsbear," pigmy silky, *tapacara*) breaks open ant and termite nests to feed. The best way to find one is to gaze into clumps of lianas up to 33 ft. above the jungle floor for something resembling a golden tennis ball, which is in reality a sleeping anteater. Another species is the **banded or lesser anteater** (*tamandua, oso jaceta, oso hormiguero*), distinguished by the black V-shaped mark across its back, resembling a vest worn backwards. The **northern tamandua** (*oso mielero*) is black-vested and nocturnal. During the day, you will see them accompanied by a dense halo of flies and mosquitoes, which they brush away with a forepaw. The **giant anteater** (*oso caballo*) is a large shaggy creature that ambles about on its knuckles.

Mainly nocturnal insect-eaters, **armadillos** ("dillys") are protected by banded and bony plates separated by soft skin – which permits the creature to bend. Resembling trotting windup toys, armadillos may run right into you. Their burrows can be recognized by the smooth, dome-shaped roof. Each litter conceived in the burrow is a set of four identical quadruplets hatched from a single egg. The nine-banded long-nosed armadillo (*cusuco*) dines on beetles, ants, termites, fungi, berries, slugs, centipedes, millipedes, and other such exotic cuisine. Chiefly nocturnal, it is the most commonly seen variety. The rare northern naked-tail armadillo (*armado de zopilote*) walks about on the tips of its foreclaws. It is slow-moving; you might see no more than its naked tail disappearing under a log.

PERISODACTYLES: This group, which includes horses and the African and Asian rhinoceros, is characterized by two unmatched or unequal hoof-covered toes. One of the Americas' most corpulent mammals and the rainforest's largest terrestrial mammal, the **Baird's tapir** (*danto, danta*) weighs as much as 550 lbs. and may grow six feet long and up to three feet high. Dining on seeds, leaves, twigs, and fruit, a tapir devotes 90% of its waking time to foraging for food because the microorganisms that live in its stomach and that digest its plant material through fermentation are not very efficient. Its excellent hearing and sense of smell compensate for this ungainly creature's poor eyesight. Solitary, nocturnal, and marsh-dwelling, it bolts when frightened – flattening everything in its wake! Despite the fact that they are the mammalian equivalent of the all-terrain vehicle, tapirs are shy creatures and difficult to see. However, hunters can easily locate them through dogs and calls, and their meat is considered a delicacy.

PECCARIES AND DEER: These are the two families of Artiocactyla (even-toed hoofed animals) found in the rainforest. Resembling a gigantic pig, the **collared peccary** ("wari," *saino* or *javelina* after its spear-like tusks) lives in a group of two to 15, whose members recognize each other by their pungent, musky body odor resembling chicken soup or cheese. It may be identified by a faint but nevertheless distinct collar of pale yellow hairs running from its lower cheek down to the top of its shoulder. Peccaries are most often found at salt licks or mud wallows. Another species is the *cariblanco* or **white-lipped peccary**. Generally black in the rainforest environs, it may also be brownish or red. There's always at least a sprinkling of white hair on its jaws and body and some are even snow white. Feeding in large herds on fruits, palm nuts, or similar fodder, white-lipped peccaries cover a large area daily, leaving the ground churned and pocked in their wake. The noise coming from large groups (tooth clacking, screaming, bellowing) has given them a greatly exaggerated reputation for aggressiveness. They generally retreat in the face of humans, although one might rumble past without seeing you.

Male deer have antlers which are shed and regrown annually. The **white-tailed deer** ("deer," *venado, venado cola blanco*) are identical but smaller than the white-tailed deer found in the US. Not rainforest animals, they are generally found out in the open. Another variety is the **red brocket deer** ("antelop," *cabra de monte*). Its tapered shape is ideal for pushing through rainforest. Diurnal and solitary, it feeds on fallen fruits, flowers, and other vegetation.

MANATEES: Popularly known as the sea cow, the manatee *(manatí)* has been sighted in Tortuguero on rare occasions. Once ranging from South America up to North Carolina, their numbers have dwindled dramatically. They move along the ocean floor (at a maximum pace of six mph) searching for food, surfacing every four or five minutes to breathe. Surprisingly, as the manatee's nearest living relative is the elephant, the creature was thought to be the model for the legend of the mermaid – perhaps because of the mother's habit of sheltering her offspring with her flipper as the infant feeds. Weighing between 400 and 1,300 lbs., the pudgy creature is covered with finely wrinkled grey or brown skin decorated with barnacles and algae; it may reach 12 ft. in length. Although to you they might appear ugly with their small eyes, thick lips, bristly muzzles, and wrinkled necks, they are affectionate with one another, kissing and sometimes swimming flipper-to-flipper. Dwelling in lagoons and in brackish water, they may eat as much as 100 lbs. of aquatic vegetables per day. Strictly vegetarian, their only enemy is man, who has hunted them for their hide, oil, and meat. Belizeans have widely and incorrectly believed that manatee flesh holds special properties and comes in a variety of flavors. In other localities, their tough hides were used in machine belting and in high pressure hoses. Although community education may be the key to stopping hunting, propellor blades of motor boats continue to slaughter manatees accidentally, and the careless use of herbicides is also a threat.

RODENTS: The trademark of rodents is their sharp and versatile front incisors. Supported by several different complex systems of jaw and muscle structures, the incisors may be used to slice, dig, pry, and cut. Some can even fell trees and kill animals. These differences allow them to be separated into three groups: squirrel-like *(Sciuoromorpha)*, cavy-like *(Caviomorpha)*, and mouselike *(Myomorpha)*. By far the most diverse order of mammals, rodents number some 1,750 species worldwide – nearly equals the 2,300 other species of mammals.

Omnivorous, **squirrels** found in the rainforest may feed on palm nuts as well as fruits, insects, fungi, and even leaves, bark, and flowers. The red-tailed squirrel *(ardilla roja, ardilla chisa)* is widespread in some parts and may commonly be observed scurrying up a tree. Other species include the variegated squirrel, Deppe's squirrel, Richmond's squirrel, the Central American dwarf squirrel, and the montane squirrel.

Long-legged creatures with feet like hooves, bristly hair, and strong jaws, the cavy-like rodents all have four toes on their front feet. Residing near rivers and active during the day, the edgy brown-colored Central American **agouti** ("gibnut," *guatusa*) eats tender shoots, fruits, and seeds. Diurnal and largely solitary, they are frequently seen in protected areas, especially in late afternoon. Newborn young stay apart in their own burrow; mama calls them out for nursing and care. Living in a burrow, its cousin, the nocturnal and largely solitary **paca** ("gibnut," *tepezcuintle*) is larger and twice as heavy, with horizontal rows of cream-colored spots along its flanks and a piglike body.

A clumsy vegetarian covered with short, strong, and rigid quills, the skinny prehensile-tailed **porcupine** *(puercoespín)* forages at night for fruits and seeds. Its barb-tipped spines detach readily, and work their way inward in the flesh of an attacker. Rothschild's porcupine is entirely spiney and mostly black. The spines of the Mexican hairy porcupine are largely covered with dark fur. Another common rodent is the **gopher** *(taltusa)*.

RABBITS: Dwelling in thickets and forests, cottontail **rabbits** *(conejos)* eat grass and tree bark; they may have up to five litters per year. The only other species found is the Brazilian, which is smaller, reddish, and has only a small tail.

BATS: Bats are the most important animals – in terms of sheer number of species – in most Western Hemisphere rainforests. The only flying animals, bats have wings made of amazingly elastic skin which contracts rather than folds when they are closed. Emitting largely ultrasonic high-frequency sounds through their nose or mouth, bats plot their route by calibrating distances to solid objects based on returning echoes. Contrary to popular belief, they will not become tangled in your hair nor will they bite except in self-defense. In addition to consuming humongous quantities of insects, bats benefit the environment through pollination of many important plants and through seed dispersal. Some feed on nectar, others on frogs, others on fish, and still others on sleeping birds and lizards. Hiding out in cave harems guarded by a single male, the short-tailed fruit bat *(murciélago)* flies out at night. It resides in the rainforest understory and is an important seed disperser.

The infamous vampire bat *(vampiro)* also lives in Belize. Stealthily landing on a horse or cow, it makes an incision, a process which may take up to 20 minutes, and – exuding an anticoagulant – proceeds to lap up the blood. The vampire may run and hop with agility on all fours, using its thickened thumb as a foot. Its feces contain a fungus which causes histoplasmosis, a debilitating disease.

The fishing or bulldog bat *(murciélago pescador)* skims the water as it flies and feeds on insects and fish, which it grasps with its enormous feet. Nectar-feeding or long-tongued bats are important pollinators, often attracted by plants with large flowers and musky odors which open at night.

Reptiles and Amphibians

TURTLES: Belize has a wide variety. The **hickatee**, a river turtle, spends its entire life in the water and may weigh up to 50 lbs. Because it is becoming rarer and rarer, restrictions have been placed on its capture and a closed season has been instituted May 1-31. Green and leatherback turtles may not be captured between April 1 and Oct. 31. Medium-sized, with a total length of about a meter and weighing around 400 lbs., the large-finned, herbivorous **green turtle** *(tortuga blanca* or *tortuga verde)* lays eggs every two to three years, storming the beaches in massive groups termed *barricadas*. It is readily identifiable by its short rounded head. One of the smallest sea turtles at 35 in. or less in length, the **hawksbill** *(tortuga* *carey)* has a spindle-shaped shell and weighs around 220 lbs. Because of its tortoise shell – a brown translucent layer of corneous gelatin that covers it and peels off the shell when processed – it has been pursued and slaughtered throughout the world. It feeds largely on sponges and seaweed. Worldwide demand for its shell, which sells for a fortune in Japan, appears to have condemned it to extinction. Sales of its meat or any product taken from it are illegal in Belize. Owing to its large bird-jawed head, twice the size of the green turtle's, the short-finned **loggerhead turtle** ("lagra," *tortuga cabezona*) rarely reaches more than four feet. It dines on sea urchins, jellyfish, starfish, and crabs, but is threatened with extinction from coastal development, egg gathering, and hunting by raccoons. Black, with very narrow fins, the **leatherback's** name comes from the leathery hide which covers its back in lieu of a shell. Reaching up to six ft. in length and weighing as much as 1,500 lbs., the leatherback's chief predator has always been the poacher.

FROGS AND TOADS: The glands of the **marine toad** *(bufo marinus)* contain toxins. Don't try to pick one up: it'll urinate on you! The predominantly nocturnal marine toad exercises control over its paratoid gland and directs its poison in a fine spray, one that can prove fatal to dogs and cats that pick it up in their mouths. If you carry it around, it will be likely to defend itself by urinating. An equal-opportunity eater, it will consume anything from wasps to dog and cat food set out for pets. With bright, leaf-green dorsum, creamy-white throat and belly, orange hands and feet, dark blue side markings, and blood-red irises *(rana calzonudo)* the gaudy leaf frog, is Central America's most colorful.

LIZARDS: The basilisk ("cock malakka") is sometimes called the "Jesus Christ lizard" because, while fleeing predators or pursuing prey, it may dart across the surface of a stream, balancing with its tail. It resembles a miniature sailfin dinosaur. You'll undoubtedly see one of these lowland dwellers scurrying across your path. There are also a wide variety of **anoles,** small sit-and-wait predators that North Americans mistakenly call chameleons. The territorial, primarily vegetarian **iguana** ("bamboo chicken") has a drab red coloration and black bars along its back. The iguana population is decreasing because of the Belizean practice of eating pregnant females. There's also the prevalent misconception that iguana eggs serve as an aphrodisiac. In order to escape predators, it will jump into the water and can stay below for as much as a half-hour without needing to surface. The scaly iguana ("wishy-nilly") is distinguishable from its cousin by a large scale on the side of the head slightly below and behind the rear angle of the lower jaw, as well as by its green coloration and longer tail. Other lizards include the **skink** and the **spiny lizard**. The two species of crocodilians (termed "alligators" locally) are the **Morelet's crocodile**, which reaches only eight feet in length, and the larger **American crocodile**, both of which reside in many lowland swamps and slow-moving streams.

SNAKES: Of the 54 species, only nine are poisonous. Most infamous is the "**yellow-jawed tommy goff**" (fer-de-lance, *terciopelo* in Spanish) – colored olive green to dark brown, with yellow, V-shaped markings along the sides. It may also be grey or brownish, with a lateral pattern of darker, black-edged triangles running down its back. Reaching lengths of 6.5 ft. or more, this lowland-dwelling snake dines on mammals, especially opossums, with an occasional bird thrown in for variety. Hatching in litters of around 75, the young have yellow-tipped prehensile tails. The "tomigoff" (or "tommy goff") is both extremely poisonous and aggressive, chasing its victim and striking repeatedly. It will attack with little provocation. Biting only if provoked, the small **coral snake** (*coralillo*) comes in three varieties. The most common is the Atlantic coral snake, found thoughout the country; it can be identified by its stripes – alternating bands of red and black, with the black often trimmed with yellow and the red scales individually tipped with black, creating a speckled effect. Undoubtedly the most unusual snake is the "**two snakes in one**." Combining the markings of the poisonous coral snake and a nonpoisonous variety, it has a black head and then a few inches of coral snake markings: red, cream, and black. Its body then enlarges and the coloring changes to olive brown; the underside markings change from the smooth pink of the coral snake to the brown snake's yellowish cream. It is thought that it sticks only its head out of a hole in order to confuse predators. Climber par excellence, the large, nonvenomous *wowla* (boa constrictor) devours everything from lizards to dogs. After striking its prey, the *wowla* coils around it. It then locates the head and swallows the prey whole. Other varieties of Belizean snakes include the **coachwhip** or Central American whipsnake, the spotted **rat snake**, the Belize *cativeo* or **black water snake**, the **speckled racer**, the **Cohune Ridge tommygoff**, and the grey and green **vine snakes**.

Birds

 Belize is one of the world's birdwatching paradises. There are over 500 species of birds – a population which includes warblers, thrushes, mockingbirds, hummingbirds, wrens, banana birds, cowbirds, blackbirds, grackles, vireos, tanagers, finches, woodpeckers, nighthawks, anis, cuckoos, trogons, macaws, parrots, vireos, toucans, vultures, hawks, swifts, swallows, flycatchers, pigeons, doves, wild turkeys, kingfishers, acorn and other woodpeckers, cormorants, herons, and sooty terns.

WHERE TO FIND BIRDS: One of the reason birdwatchers flock to Belize is the number and variety of its species. Even if you aren't a diehard, be sure to bring binoculars. Everyone has a favorite spot. It may be around your hotel or at a nature preserve. The parks and reserves are sure bets. Birdwatchers will want to pick up a copy of either *Peterson's Field Guide to the Birds of Mexico* or *The Birds of Costa Rica* by F. Gary Stiles and Alexander Skutch, which also applies to this area. These are the most authoritative guides available.

SEA BIRDS: Distinctive for its huge bill, slow flight, and clumsy diving, the **brown pelican** is a prominent inhabitant of the coast and cays. The nearly jet black **frigate bird** *(rabihorcado magno)* swoops ominously overhead, occasionally veering down to the water to make a capture. The female is identifiable by her white breast. The six varieties of **terns** include the sooty tern and the royal tern. The **laughing gull** has a black head, a white body and tail, and grey wings. Others include the **brown booby** and the rare **red-footed booby**, which nests on Half Moon Cay. The booby's name is said to have come from the Spanish word *bobo*, which means "dunce" – an apt description as, unlike other species, they make no attempt to defend their eggs or young from frigate birds or other intruders.

BIRDS WITH CHARACTER: Sporting gaudy pink plumage, the **roseate spoonbill** features a strangely-shaped beak which is broader at its tip than at its stem. Its Spanish name of *chocolatera* is after the wood spoon used in cacao processing. The bill's function is to scoop up unwitting marine life. A favorite local bird is the **pauraque** ("who-you"), to which many legends have attached themselves. It is maintained that if someone picks up a "who-you" egg, they cannot put it down without breaking it, and that the eggs can never be consumed in a fire. If someone has a ticklish emotional relationship, it's said that they've picked up a "who-you" egg. The enormous **king vulture** ("King John Crow," *rey de zopilote*) has creamy white and black on its wings and a head with splotches of red, orange, yellow, purple, and black accompanied by a bright orange caruncle; its bulging white eyes are ringed in red. The **northern jacana** ("Georgie Bull") hops gracefully from lily pad to lily pad in search of prey; it's colored cinnamon-red with a bright yellow forehead shield on its black head and yellow-green patches on its wings. Largest and most powerful of the eagles of Central America, the **harpy eagle** may approach speeds of 50 mph. The **blue-crowned motmot** numbers among the most beautiful of the birds. Because it sometimes appears to move like a band conductor beating time, it has been called the "time bird." First arriving in the New World from Africa around 1877, the **cattle egret** or common white heron *(garcilla bueyara)* follows cattle and dines on the insects sent scurrying as the beasts meander. Thriving in deforested territory, the sedentary **roadside hawk** *(gavilán)* preys on lizards, snakes, rodents, and large insects. Dark colored antbirds or **ovenbirds** *(hormigueros)* are best seen on solitary excursions; they follow army ant columns and eat insects frightened by them. Related to the oriole and the grackle, the omnivorous **Montezuma** *oropendola* is mostly black with yellow outer tail feathers. The female constructs her sagging saclike nests on the ends of tree branches. One of the most splendid birds is the elegant and graceful **vermilion flycatcher**.

TOUCANS: The **keel-billed toucan** ("bill bird"), the largest in Central America, is the national bird. One of the forest's largest fruit eaters, its trademarks are its piercing call and colorful, six-colored bill and body. Thought to frighten off enemies, its bill has the feel of laminated balsa wood with the serrated edges of a stainless steel paring knife. With a partially lemon-yellow colored face and chest, its eyes are ringed by greenish skin; the area below its tail is colored cadmium red, and its legs and feet are iridescent blue! Generally feeding on the fruit of large trees, it rips off a chunk with its beak, flips it into the air, and catches it in its bill. The two other species found in Belize are the **collared aracari** and the **emerald toucanet**.

TROGONS: Sedate, arboreal and spectacularly-plumed, the trogons are widely distributed in the warmer areas of both the Old and New Worlds. Of the 40 species of trogons found in the Americas, Belize has five: red, slatey-tailed, collared (yellow), vidaceous, and citreoline. The most spectacular trogon of all, the resplendent quetzal, is not found in Belize. Male trogons have glittering green, blue, or violet upper plumage and chests with posterior underparts of contrasting red, orange, or yellow. Females are duller with brown gray or slatey coloring, where males are green, but with underparts nearly as bright as the males.

THE SCARLET MACAW: One of the nation's most beautiful birds, you might see this spectacularly plumaged parrot flying overhead and sounding raucously. However, it now survives only in very remote areas. Its bright red orange plumage has touches of yellow and blue, and does not vary with age or between sexes. Scarlet macaws *(loras)* mate for life, which is one reason they are in danger of extinction. Another is their blackmarket value – up to US$500 per bird. Its relatives include seven varieties of parrots (white-fronted, red-lored, blue-crowned, yellow-lored, yellow-headed, brown-hooded, and white crowned) as well as the Aztec parakeet.

THE GREAT CURASSOW: An unforgettable resident of the forest, the 36-inch great curassow *(pavón grande, granadera)* can be seen on the forest floor. As large as hen turkeys, but more elegant, the curassows dress by sex: the males sport a black suit with a green glossy bib and white lower markings, plus a caruncle – a large bright-yellow knob over their beaks. Females can be either brown or reddish brown, but the head and neck are striated black and white. They lack the male's caruncle. Dining off the forest floor, the couple builds a nest about 30 feet up in a tree. This bird spends its days scratching the ground in search of fallen fruit and small animals. If frightened, it generally runs away, emitting high-pitched yips like a small dog.

JABIRU STORK: The Americas' largest flying bird, the jabiru stork *(fillymingo, turk, el rey de ellos)* stands up to five feet high and has a wingspan extending from nine to 12 feet. It is characterized by its all-white plumage, a black head, large and slightly upturned black bill, and a neck bordered at its base by a bright red band. Feeding in wetlands, they arrive in solitary pairs in Jan. and build their nesting platforms – which may be as much as 10 feet across. Its young are brownish-grey colored. Bordering on extinction, they are generally sighted around swamps and ponds where they feed on reptiles, fish, snails, frogs, and small mammals.

OTHERS: There are at least 21 varieties of hummingbirds, five types of swifts, and nine types of swallows. Of the 49 types of flycatchers, one of the most spectacular is the vermilion flycatcher. Other indigenous species of note include the Muscovy duck, an assortment of woodpeckers, the rufous-necked woodrail, the turkey vulture and its relatives, the red-caped manakin, the green kingfisher, the boat-billed heron, the bananaquit, the groove-billed ani, the five species of tinamou, the homely brown jay, the chestnut-collared swift, the rufous-tailed jacamar, the ruddy quail dove, the laughing falcon, the mangrove swallow, the ochre-bellied flycatcher, the white-fronted nunbird, the tropical screech owl, the spotted barbtail, the great-tailed grackle, western and spotted sandpipers, the variable seedeater, ruddy-tailed and common-tody flycatchers, the barred antshrike, the tropical kingbird, the wren-thrush, and the rufous-colored sparrow.

Insects

Insect life is both varied and abundant. Lest you be tempted to view insects as uninteresting, remember that they have been around for at least 400 million years, while butterflies are believed to have evolved around 200 million years ago during the Triassic.

BUTTERFLIES: All told there are some 700 species found in Belize. The nation's most beautiful butterfly, the **morpho** is common in forests from sea level on up. It has almost completely iridescent blue upper wings. The three species of **owl butterflies** have two glaring eyes on the underside of their wings. These may serve as mimicry to suggest a vertebrate or large, distasteful tree frog, or as target spots for predators, which allow the butterfly to escape relatively unscathed. Other species of note include the heliconids, many beautiful skippers, several swallowtails, and the sulfur butterfly. Butterfly lovers should be certain to visit the butterfly farm at Shipstern near Sarteneja as well as Fallen Stones Butterfly Ranch in the Toledo District. **lifestyle:** As they have no jaws, butterflies must take all nutrients in liquid form. They feed on water with mineral salts found in the earth, juice from decaying fruit, juices from carrion, honeydew secretions from aphids, and other such delicacies. While you may find them warming up in the sun or drinking water at mud banks, they rest on the undersides of leaves to protect themselves during rainstorms.

MEMORABLE VIEWING: The pencil-thin **helicopter damselfly** (*gallito azul*) beats each of its four wings independently, resembling a slow-motion windmill. Its wing movement renders it invisible to spiders, upon whom it launches a single attack burst, snipping and capturing the succulent abdomen as the rest falls. The pit-making ant lion (hormiga león) is actually the larval form of a beautiful fly similar to a damselfly. It spends its childhood digging a pit, heaping up loosened particles on its head and tossing them clear. Then, burying itself – only its jaws project – it awaits its prey. Any captured game has its contents sucked out and empty skin tossed out of the pit. After having stored up enough food to support its next incarnation, it enters a cocoon and then re-emerges as a sexually mature adult. A pretty good handful, the male **rhinoceros beetle** (cornizuelo) sports a long upward-curved horn, but the females are hornless; they are endangered by habitat destruction. The **frangipani sphinx** (oruga, falso coral) appears to mimic the coral snake, both with its bright yellow coloring and red orange head and in the way it thrashes back and forth when touched like the coral. It also bites viciously! With a color that harmonizes perfectly with the large branches and logs on which they rest, the machaca (peanut-head fulgaria, lantern fly) is one of Latin America's best-known insects. Its enormous hind-wing eye spots and lizard-shaped head are probably designed to confuse predators. If pestered it will release a fetid skunk-like spray or drum its head against a tree trunk. A popular Latin American folk saying maintains that if a young girl is stung by a machaca, she must have sex with her boyfriend within 24 hours or die. Other intriguing bugs include the tarantula and the paper wasp, the local version of the praying mantis.

ANTS: One resident of the rainforest you'll undoubtedly encounter is the ant. If you sit down, you may well have some unpleasant bites to contend with. Shake a bush and ants will scurry out. In many tracts, they may outweigh all of the vertebrates present. Commonly seen marching along a forest trail holding aloft cut pieces of leaves and flowers, **wee wee ants** (leaf cutting ants, farmer ants, zompopas) cut leaves into shreds, and carry them off to their nests where they then clear the leaves of unwanted fungal spores, chew the plant material, and mix it with a combination of saliva and excrement to cultivate a spongy, breadlike fungus (Rhozites gongylophora) on which they dine. This species of fungus no longer produces sexual spores and has come to rely solely upon the ants for propagation. Ranking among the largest and most complex societies in the world, each colony may have a million members, and each member has a role to play. The smallest tend to eggs and larvae, larger ones forage, and the still larger soldiers defend the nest. Watch them as they meet, stroke antennae, and exchange chemical cues. If you draw a thick line across their formation, they'll lose their scented track and become momentarily bewildered until the line is re-established. Thumping around the base of a nest with a machete will draw them out. Fertilized by males during swarming, a young queen begins a new colony by digging a tunnel and creating a royal chamber. Spitting out fungus from her own colony, she fertilizes it with fecal material. Laying eggs, she feeds the larvae on malformed eggs while fasting. In 40-60 days, the new workers emerge and begin work. All told, there are more than 200 species of leaf cutting ants.

Joined in a symbiotic relationship with the acacia tree, the **acacia ant** *(hormiga de cornizuelo)* wards off herbivores while the tree supplies the ants with nectar, protein and protection in return. The ants produce an alarm pheromone which can be smelled for some six ft. downwind. You can easily recognize these trees by their hollow swollen horns, resembling those of cattle.

Another example of mutualism is found between the *Azteca* or **cecropia ants** and their namesake. In order to ward off herbivores, the cecropia attracts the ants which it provides with specialized food: Beltian bodies, budlike leaflet tips which the ants harvest and use to nourish their larvae. These are raised inside the tree's hollowed-out thorns. In return, the ants defend the tree. Although stingless, they bite with their tough jaws and secrete caustic chemicals which they rub into bites.

Semi-nomadic **army ants** may travel in packs of up to 20 million members, sweeping in a continually-foraging 20-foot-wide front. They bring back bits of twigs, lichen, leaves and other insects to feed their queen; the detritus also feeds the roots of nearby plants. Their colonies regularly pass from stationary to nomadic phases every couple of weeks. A number of species – from birds to flies to millipedes – use the presence of army ants to help them feed.

TERMITES: Resembling gigantic wasps nests and found on trees, dark brown or black termite nests are a frequent feature of the forested landscape. Made of "carton," wood chewed up by workers and cemented with fecal "glue," the nest has a single reproductive king and queen commanding hordes of up to 100,000 attending workers and soldiers. Termites digest raw cellulose, a substance low in nutritional value, with the aid of protozoan symbiots dwelling in their guts. Camouflaging itself with bits and pieces of termite nest, the assassin bug *(reduvio)* preys at the entrance. In death as in life, termites contribute to the rainforest ecosystem. Their defecated roughage is a feast for fungi which also feed on their carcasses.

LOATHED BY HUMANS: Nearly invisible, **chiggers** *(coloradillas)* thrive in locations ranging from lowland cattle pastures to rainforests. A form of mite larva that inserts the tips of its well-developed mouthparts into your skin, a chigger loves to squeeze into protected places such as bra and belt lines and the genital area, where it bites and gleefully deposits a histamine which makes the surrounding area itch like hell for up to 10 days! Small gnats which favor the tender skin of the ears and neck, **no-see-ums** *(purrujas,* biting midges, sand fleas, sand flies) are almost invisible and are most active on warm days and windless evenings. Only the females bite humans. Their bites also last for days; sulfur powder will discourage them. They can be a problem out on the keys and on the coast. A breeze will keep them away, and they live and procreate only in mangrove swamp areas; they aren't found on sand-and-palm cayes. In the forest, you'll also find an abundance of **ticks** *(garrapatas).* With 20 body segments, the forest-floor **millipede** *(milpies)* is readily identifiable both by its movements and its dull whitish-yellow color. Its ability to curl up in a spiral and expel violently a solution of hydrogen cyanide and benzaldehyde as far as 12 inches discourages predators. Its relative, the **scorpion** *(alacrán, escorpión)* stings only in self-defense; scorpions are active at night when they prey on insects and spiders.

  flies: Biting flies can be a problem in season, and the most loathesome insect of all is the **botfly** *(Dermatobia hominis),* whose larvae (known locally as a "beefworm") matures inside flesh. An egg-laden female botfly captures a night-flying female mosquito and glues her eggs on to the mosquito before releasing it. When the mosquito bites, the host's body heat triggers an egg to hatch, fall off, and burrow in. Secreting an antibiotic into its burrow which staves off competing bacteria and fungi, the larva secures itself with two anal hooks; its spiracle pokes out of the tiny hole, and a small mound forms which will grow to the size of a goose egg before the mature larva falls out. Should you be unfortunate enough to fall prey to a larva – an extremely unlikely occurrence for the average visitor – you have three cures available. One is to use the acrid white sap of the *matatorsalo* (bot killer), which kills the larva but leaves the corpse intact. Another is to apply a piece of soft, raw meat to the top of the airhole. As the maggot must breathe, it burrows upward into the meat. At the Massachusetts General Hospital, physicians apply slices of raw, fatty bacon. A third cure is to apply a generous helping of Elmer's glue or cement to the hole; cover this with a circular patch of adhesive tape; seal this tape with a final application of glue. Squeeze out the dead larva the next morning. The only other alternative is to leave it to grow to maturity, giving you an opportunity to experience the transmogrification of part of yourself into another creature. It only hurts when the maggot squirms and if you swim, presumably because you are cutting off its air supply. Whatever you do, don't try to pull it out because it will burst. Part of its body will remain inside and will infect the area.

A biting fly is the hardy but hunchbacked black or **botlass fly.** These small and incredibly annoying flies silently zoom in on you and will feast on your hands and whatever else they can land on. **other nuisances:** Coming in a number of species, the mosquito *(zancudo)* needs no introduction, nor does the giant cockroach *(cucaracha)*. Finally, although they should not be a problem for visitors, Africanized "killer" bees are proving a menace; since their arrival in 1983, they have attacked more than 500 people, resulting in nine deaths.

Sealife

ECHINODERMATA: Combining the Greek words for *echinos* (hedgehog) and *derma* (skin), this large division of the animal kingdom includes sea urchins, sea cucumbers, and starfish. All share the ability to propel themselves with the help of tube "feet" or spines. Known by the scientific name *Astrospecten,* **starfish** *(estrella de mar)* are five-footed carnivorous inhabitants which use their modified "tube-feet" to burrow into the sea. Sluggish **sea cucumbers** ingest large quantities of sand, extract the organic matter, and excrete the rest. Crustaceans and fish reside in the larger specimens.

Avoid trampling on that armed knight of the underwater sand dunes, the **sea urchin.** Consisting of a semi-circular calcareous (calcium carbonate-built) shell, the sea urchin is protected by its brown, jointed barbs. It uses its mouth, situated and protected on its underside, to graze by scraping algae from rocks. Surprisingly to those uninitiated in its lore, sea urchins are considered a gastronomic delicacy in many countries. The ancient Greeks believed they held aphrodisiac and other properties beneficial to health. They are prized by the French and fetch four times the price of oysters in Paris. The Spanish consume them raw, boiled, in *gratinés,* or in soups. In Barbados they are termed "sea eggs," and the Japanese eat their guts raw as sushi. Although a disease in recent years has devastated the sea urchin population, they are making a comeback. **contact:** If a sea urchin spine breaks off inside your finger or toe, don't try to remove it: it's impossible! You might try the cure people use in New Guinea. Use a blunt object to mash up the spine inside your skin so that it will be absorbed naturally. Then dip your finger in urine; the ammonia helps to trigger the process of disintegration. It's best to apply triple-antibiotic salve. Avoiding contact is best. Sea urchins hide underneath corals, and wounds are often contracted when you lose your footing and scrape against one.

SPONGES: Found in the ocean depths, reddish or brown sponges are among the simplest forms of multicellular life and have been around for more than a half-billion years. They pump large amounts of water between their internal filters and extract plankton. There are numerous sizes, shapes, and colors, but they all can be recognized by their large, distinctive excurrent openings. Unlike other animals, they exhibit no reaction when disturbed.

CNIDARIANS: The members of this phylum – hydroids, anemones, corals, and jellyfish – are distingushed by their simple structure: a cup-shaped body terminating in a combination mouth-anus which, in turn, is encircled by tentacles. While hydroids and corals (covered later in this section) are colonial, jellyfish and anemones are individual. This phylum's name comes from another identifying characteristic: nematocysts, stinging capsules primarily used for defense and capturing prey. Growing in skeletal colonies resembling ferns or feathers, **hydroids** ("water form" in Greek) spend their youth as solitary medusas before settling down in old age. Some will sting, and the most famous hydroid is undoubtedly the floating Portuguese Man-Of-War; its stinging tentacles can be extended or retracted; wordwide, there have been reports of trailing tentacles reaching 50 feet! It belongs to the family of siphonophores, free-floating hydroid colonies which control their depth by means of a gas-filled float. The true **jellyfish** are identifiable by their domes, which vary in shape. Nematocysts reside in both the feeding tube and in their tentacles. Also known as sea wasps, **box jellies** can be identifed by their cuboidal dome, from each corner of which a single tentacle extends. Many of them can sting painfully; keep well away. If you should get stung by any of the above, get out of the water and peel off any tentacles. Avoid rubbing the injured area. Wash it with alcohol and apply meat tenderizer for five to 10 minutes. The jellyfish season is Aug. to Oct. Solitary bottom-dwellers, sea anemones are polyps which lack a skeleton and use their tentacles to stun prey and force them to their mouth. They often protect shrimp and crabs who, immune to their sting, reside right by them. Their tentacles may retract for protection when disturbed. One type of anemone lives in tubes buried in the murky muck or sand. Their tentacles only come out to play at night.

CRUSTACEANS: A class of arthropods, the largest phylum with more than two million species, crustaceans are distinguished by their jointed legs and complex skeleton. The decapods (named after their five pairs of legs) are the largest order of crustaceans. These include shrimp, crabs, and lobster. The **ghost crab** *(Ocypode)* abounds on the beaches, tunneling down beneath the sand and emerging to feed at night. Although it can survive for 48 hrs. without contacting water, it must return to the sea to moisten its gill chambers as well as to lay its eggs which hatch into planktonic larvae. The **hermit crab** carries a discarded mollusc shell in order to protect its vulnerable abdomen. As it grows, it must find a larger home, and you may see two struggling over the same shell.

OTHER UNDERWATER HAZARDS AND CURES: Not a true coral, **fire coral** mimics its appearance; it may appear in many forms and has the ability to encrust nearly anything and take its host's form. Generally colored mustard yellow to brown, it often has white finger-like tips. Its bite is quite painful. As with coral wounds, you should wash the affected area with soap and fresh water and apply a triple-antibiotic salve. Found on rocky or coral bottoms, **spotted scorpionfish** are well camouflaged so it's easy to step on them. Although the Caribbean species is non-lethal, their bite can be quite painful. Another cleverly camouflaged denizen of the deep, the **stingray** will whip its tail if stepped on – driving the serrated venomous spine into the offender. If this happens, see a doctor. Fuzzy creatures which have painful-when-touched defense mechanisms, **bristle worms** have glass-like bristles which may break off in the skin and be very painful. Apply tape to the skin and attempt to pull the bristles out; reduce the pain with rubbing alcohol. With a tendency to bite at things thrust at them, **moray eels** have a tight grip and can be difficult to dislodge. Once again, preventing bites is best. Always exercise caution before reaching into a crevice!

The Coral Reef Ecosystem

One of the least appreciated of the world's wonders is the coral reef. This is in part because little has been known about it until recent decades. One of the greatest opportunities the tropics offer is to explore this wondrous environment, one which in many ways goes beyond the limits of any wild fantasy conjured up in a science fiction novel. It is a delicate environment: the only geological feature fashioned by living creatures. Reefs throughout the world – which took millions of years to form – have already suffered adverse effects from human beings. Corals produce the calcium carbonate (limestone) responsible for the buildup of most offlying cays and islets as well as most of the sand on the beaches. Bearing the brunt of waves, they also conserve the shoreline. Although reefs began forming millenia ago, they are in a constant state of flux. Seemingly solid, they actually depend upon a delicate ecological balance to survive. Deforestation, dredging, temperature change, an increase or decrease in salinity, silt, or sewage discharge may kill them. Because temperature ranges must remain between 68° and 95°F, they are only found in the tropics and – because they require light to grow – only in shallow water. They are also intolerant of fresh water, and reefs can not survive where rivers empty into the sea.

THE CORAL POLYP: While corals are actually animals, botanists view them as being mostly plant, and geologists dub them "honorary" rocks. Acting more like plants than animals, corals survive through photosynthesis: the algae inside the coral polyps do the work while the polyps themselves secrete calcium carbonate and stick together for protection from waves and boring sponges.

Bearing a close structural resemblance to its relative the anemone, a polyp feeds at night by using the ring or rings of tentacles surrounding its mouth to capture prey (such as plankton) with nematocysts, small stinging darts.

The coral polyps appear able to survive in such packed surroundings through their symbiotic relationship with the algae present in their tissues: Coral polyps exhale carbon dioxide and the algae consume it, producing needed oxygen. Although only half of the world's coral species possess this symbiotic relationship with these single-celled captive species of dinoflagellates (*Gymnodinium microdriaticum*), these species – termed hermatypic corals – are the ones that build the reef. The nutritional benefits gained from their relationship with the algae enable them to grow a larger skeleton and to do so more rapidly than would otherwise be possible. Polyps have the ability to regulate the density of these cells in their tissues and can expel some of them in a spew of mucus should they multiply too quickly. Looking at coral, the brownish colored algal cells show through transparent tissues. When you see a coral garden through your mask, you are actually viewing a field of captive single-celled algae.

An added and vital but invisible component of the reef ecosystem is bacteria, micro-organisms which decompose and recycle all matter on which everything from worms to coral polyps feed. Inhabitants of the reef range from crabs to barnacles, sea squirts to multicolored tropical fish. Remarkably, the polyps themselves are consumed by only a small percentage of the reef's inabitants. They often contain high levels of toxic substances and are also thought to sting fish and other animals that attempt to consume them. Corals also retract their polyps during daylight hours when the fish can see them. Reefs originate as the polyps develop – the calcium secretions form a base as they grow. One polyp can have a 1,000-year lifespan.

CORAL TYPES: Corals may be divided into three groups. The hard or **stony corals** (such as staghorn, brain, star, or rose) secrete a limey skeleton. The **horny corals** (for example sea plumes, sea whips, sea fans, and gorgonians) have a supporting skeleton-like structure known as a gorgonin (after the head of Medusa). The shapes of these corals result from the fashion in which the polyps and their connecting tissues excrete calcium carbonate; there are over a thousand different patterns – one specific to each species. Each also has its own method of budding. Found in the Caribbean, giant elk-horn corals may contain over a million polyps and live for several hundred years or longer. The last category consists of the **soft corals**. While these too are colonies of polyps, their skeletons are composed of soft organic material, and their polyps always have eight tentacles instead of the six or multiples of six found in the stony corals. Unlike the hard corals, soft corals disintegrate after death and do not add to the reef's stony structure. Instead of depositing limestone crystals, they excrete a jelly-like matrix which is imbued with spicules (diminutive spikes) of stony material; the jelly-like substance gives these corals their flexibility. Sea fans and sea whips exhibit similar patterns. There are also false corals. One such type is the precious **black coral**. Prized by jewelers because its branches may be cleaned and polished to high gloss ebony-black, it resembles bushes of fine grey-black twigs. (Do not buy this jewelry because it contributes to reef destruction).

COMPETITION: To the snorkeler, the reef appears to be a peaceful haven. The reality is that, because the reef is a comparatively benign environment, the fiercest competition has developed here. Although the corals appears static to the onlooker, they are continually competing with each other for space. Some have developed sweeper tentacles which have an especially high concentration of stinging cells. Reaching out to a competing coral, they stick and execute it. Other species dispatch digestive filaments which eat the prey. Soft corals appear to leach out toxic chemicals called terpines to kill nearby organisms. Because predation is such a problem, two-thirds of reef species are toxic. Others hide in stony outcrops or have formed protective relationships with other organisms. The classic case is the banded clown fish. They live among sea anemones, whose stingers protect it. Cleaner fish protect themselves from larger fish by setting up stations at which they pick parasites off their carnivorous customers. Mimicking the coloration and shape of the feeder fish, the sabre-toothed blenny is a false cleaner fish which takes a chunk out of the larger fish and runs off!

CORAL LOVE AFFAIRS: Not prone to celibacy or sexual prudery, coral polyps reproduce sexually and asexually through budding, and a polyp joins together with thousands and even millions of its neighbors to form a coral. (In a few cases, only one polyp forms a single coral.) During sexual reproduction polyps release millions of their spermatozoa into the water. Many species are dimorphic – with both male and female coral. Some species have internal, others external fertilization. Still others have both male and female polyps. As larvae develop, their "mother" expels them and they float off to found a new coral colony.

EXPLORING REEFS: Coral reefs are extremely fragile environments. Much damage has been done to reefs worldwide through the carelessness of humans. Despite their size, reefs grow very slowly, and it can take decades or even hundreds of years to repair the effects of a few moments. Do nothing to provoke moray eels, which may retaliate when threatened. Watch out for fire corals – recognizeable by the white tips on their branches – which can inflict stings. In general, "look but don't touch" is the maxim to follow.

UNDERWATER FLORA: Most of the plants you see underwater are algae, primitive plants that can survive only underwater because they do not have the mechanisms to prevent themselves from drying out. Lacking roots, algae draw their minerals and water directly from the sea. Calcareous red algae, are very important for reef formation. Resembling rounded stones, they are 95% rock and only 5% living tissue. Plants returned to live in the sea, sea grasses are found in relatively shallow water in sandy and muddy bays and flats; they have roots and small flowers. One species, dubbed "turtle grass," provides feed for turtles. In addition, sea grasses help to stabilize the sea floor, maintain water clarity by trapping fine sediments from upland soil erosion, stave off beach erosion, and provide living space for numerous fish, crustaceans, and shellfish.

THE BARRIER REEF: Found off the coast, the hemisphere's second largest coral reef extends 180 miles from the tip of Mexico's Isla Mujeres to Sapodilla Caye in the Bay of Honduras. Much of its topography is spur and groove – coral ridges interspersed with deep trenches culminating in flat sand bottoms. The spur walls often have tunnels and overhangs. The diverse environments of this topography allow a diversity of marine life to coexist in relative proximity. In addition to some 230 fish species, there are also stingrays, eels, and innumerable other creatures. For more information about the reef and its islands see the "The Cayes and the Reef" section.

History

 When one visits contemporary Belize, it is difficult to imagine that it formed part of the Maya Empire for centuries longer than it has been colonized. While the Maya of today's Belize are not their direct descendants – having immigrated from Mexico and Guatemala – they still share some characteristics, such as tending their *milpas* in the traditional style. In contrast with other indigenous groups, which have scattered over Mexico and Central America, the Maya remain centered in Belize, the western parts of Guatemala and Honduras, and in Mexico's Yucatán and the states of Chiapas and Tabasco – an area which also encompasses all of their civilization's ruins. Of the three main areas of Maya civilization, Belize, Guatemala, and parts of Honduras enclose the area where the great ceremonial centers flourished. Their ruins have been covered by dense jungle since around 850 AD and it's amazing that, using only stone axes and wheel-less technology, they were able to tame the flourishing foliage and raise their remarkable cities. After the Maya came under the influence of Teotihuacán, a city-state in central Mexico from about 400 AD, indigenous Mayan architecture bloomed only in the lowlands. Around 800 AD, just as the culture – with the development of pottery figurines, jade carvings, and invention of the Maya calendar – was at its peak, things began to fall apart for unknown reasons. Note: For more information about the Maya and their world read the "Mundo Maya" appendix.

COLUMBUS AND COMPANY: On his fourth voyage in 1502 Columbus "discovered" the Bay of Honduras, a name derived from *Hondo*, the Spanish word for deep. A few years later Pinzón and Desolís reached the Gulf of Honduras. Sailing west to the Río Dulce, they then proceeded north along the Belize coast. Some other explorers followed suit, but interest in the area waned after the mid-16th C. A few missionaries ventured in thereafter. One of them had his clothes stolen by a band of Englishmen in 1677, the first recorded mention of English presence.

ENTER THE ENGLISH: As there are few written records, much of Belize's early years remain shrouded in mystery. The first recorded settlement was by the Providence Company, a settlement that landed in May 1631, and was terminated after the Spanish attacked in May 1641, capturing 400 of the colonists and sending the remainder fleeing elsewhere. Most of the legends about the early years mention one Peter Wallis or Willis, a Scottish buccaneer. Although there is no way to corroborate that Wallace ever so much as set foot in Belize, some accounts maintain that Belize derives from a corruption of his name. Other explanations are that the name derives from one of three Mayan words: either *belakin* (land towards the sea), *balitza* (land of the Itzá), or *beliz* (muddy waters). The third term appears to be the most appropriate and, thus, the likeliest explanation.

ENTER THE LOGCUTTERS: The timber industry began in the Yucatán during the second half of the 17th C. Up until that time the Spanish had monopolized the logwood trade in the Gulf of Campeche. Used in making dye manufacture, it was vital for dying woolen goods in the colors of grey, black, purple, and dark red. As the English buccaneers encountered more and more resistance on the sea, they learned about the value of logwood and began harvesting timber in the Yucatán, eking out a meager existence while fending off sandflies and mosquitoes. At first the English presence didn't bother the Spanish, but they had begun to attack by the 1680s. The first mention of Belize in print was in the accounts of a John Fingas in 1705, who described the area as "the river of Bullys where the English for the most part now load their logwood." On four occasions (in 1717, 1730, 1754, and 1779) Spanish attacks on the settlers forced loggers to leave, but they always returned. Concluded at the end of the Seven Years War in 1763, the Treaty of Paris gave the British the right to cut logwood but legitimized the Spanish claim to the territory. The Versailles Treaty (1783) and the Convention of London (1786) reinforced the rights of the "Baymen" while giving control of the area to Spain. The last attempt by the Spanish to expel the English took place off of St. George's Cay in 1798. While the Spaniards were forced out of Central America in the 1820s, the British failed to declare Belize a colony until 1862. The time gap spurred Guatemala to make claims on the territory, a conflict that has endured right up to the present. Because they could not control them for labor and because they regarded their slash-and-burn techniques as a threat to the timber reserve, the British forced out the indigenous Maya and brought in slaves as supplemental labor.

SLAVERY: Although slaves were used in Belize for harvesting timber rather than for producing plantation crops as elsewhere in the Americas, they were equally ill treated. The first mention of slavery in Belize comes in a Spanish missionary's 1724 account of a visit. A century later, some 1,500 Africans formed the body of a 2,300-person slave population. They had grown to a majority of the population by mid-18th C., and by the early 1800s they comprised approximately 75% of the population, with the rest consisting of whites (10%) and "free people of colour" (14%). Shortly prior to emancipation in 1838, the number of slaves had diminished to half the population, with the remainder being white (10%), along with freed blacks and mulattoes. Despite their minority status, the whites continually dominated both the economy and government. While logwood grew in clumps near the coast and could be cut with minimal labor, the growth of demand for mahogany necessitated more finances, land, and slaves. After 1770 approximately 80% of all slaves age 10 and over were woodcutters. The huntsmen found the trees, the axemen cut them, and cattlemen cared for the beasts of burden that pulled the logs to the river. Rafts brought the logs downriver. Other slaves served as domestic servants and in occupations such as blacksmiths, nurses, sailors, and bakers. Conditions were horrid and many revolted, committed suicide, or escaped to establish maroon colonies within Belize. Revolts took place in 1765, 1768, 1773, and in 1820. Free blacks and colored could not hold military commissions nor could they become jurors or magistrates. In order for them to qualify to vote in elections, they would have to own more property, and have lived in the area longer, than whites. In an effort to distinguish themselves from the slave population, the free colored shamelessly embraced the status quo, affirming their European-ness and their loyalty. During an era when their peers in other West Indian outposts were being granted equal rights, the Colonial Office threatened to shut down the Public Meeting, the Baymen's legislative assembly, unless it kept in line.

The "colored Subjects of Free Condition" were granted civil rights only on July 5, 1831. Slavery was abolished in 1833, but the Abolition Act required slaves to labor on for five years in a system of "apprenticeship" for free, and it compensated slaveowners for their losses. At the time of legal emancipation in 1838, Belize had become a stratifed, hierarchical society with gross institutionalized inequalities. The Crown had freely distributed land in the past to the white owners, but no lands were granted African-Americans after emancipation for fear that they might no longer be willing to labor for cheap wages.

THE SETTLER OLIGARCHY: Although, at the end of the 18th C., there was no official Crown control of the colony, but the "principal inhabitants" had passed the location laws in 1787, a series of resolutions granting themselves land to be classified as freehold private property. The economic shift during this era from logwood to mahogany also resulted in the concentration of land and power in the hands of an elite few. In the same year that the location laws were instituted, 12 individuals held 85% of the approximately 2,300 sq. miles made available under the 1786 treaty. In 1790 the 20 largest estates owned about half of the total slave population, and the ruling elite determined the price of logwood and mahogany, taxation rates, and the import trade – of great importance, as locals were forbidden from cultivating provisions locally. Their economic monopoly allowed them to dominate both the Public Meeting and the Magistracy. Political power was used to keep both other settlers and ex-slaves under their control. Belize came to have the same boom-bust price cycles common to other plantation economies but with an added twist: the boom of 1835-47 led to a severe depression because all of the easily accessible trees had been cut, including young growth. Costs rose as loggers had to move farther into the interior, and mahogany exports plummeted from 14 million feet in 1846 to 5.5 million feet in 1859 and down to 2.75 million feet in 1870 – a low for the century. Registered in 1859, the British Honduras Company became the colony's leading landowner, changing its name to Belize Estate and Produce Company in 1875. Based in Belize City, it owned roughly half of Belize's land and has remained a driving force in the economy ever since. Its supremacy eclipsed that of the settler elite and by 1881 the white settlers, predominantly male, had dropped to 1%. All of this came in the face of increasing governmental control over the country. Although Belize was not yet officially a colony, the superintendant took over the appointment magistrates in 1832. During this period the territory's status, ignored in official accords and treaties, remained vague. After the British were pressed by the US government to abandon the area, a formal constitution was introduced, along with a figurehead legislative assembly, while the colonial office pulling the strings. In 1862, British Honduras was formally declared a colony, and the legislature was replaced by an appointed Legislative Council in 1871. Meanwhile, Maya – fleeing to the area during the War of the Races period – had mounted rebellions against the British. A battle at Orange Walk in 1872 bested the Maya, who were subsequently herded into reservations. The 1900s heralded a change of perception among black Belizeans. The Ex-Servicemen's Riots in 1919, with veterans protesting the society's racism, marked the beginning of a growing political consciousness.

THE GREAT DEPRESSION: In the early 1930s, the contracts for chicle collection and for mahogany dwindled, causing massive unemployment. The hurricane of 1931 demolished Belize City, but the British response was late and inadequate. By 1933, the total value of imports and exports had dropped to a quarter of the 1929 level. In what proved to be the initiation of a broad social movement, a group calling itself the Unemployment Brigade marched through Belize City on Feb. 14, 1934 and presented its demands to the government. Others among the poor turned to the Governor who, in his humanistic beneficence, responded by offering work breaking stones at 10¢ per day and ordering a ration of poorly cooked rice served at the prison gates daily. Those demanding the dispensation of cash found a new leader in barber Antonio Soberanís Gomez (1897-1975). Putting the Unemployment Brigade's leaders in their place at a meeting on Mar. 16, 1934, Soberanís took over the movement. Biweekly meetings of his Laborers and Unemployed Association (LUA) attacked the establishment. All of this led to a riot in Belize City and a strike in Stann Creek by the year's end. After Soberanís was jailed under a new sedition act in Nov. 1935, factional infighting weakened the movement, and its power had diminished by the time of his release in Feb, 1936. The demonstrations had pressed the Governor to create relief work – over 200 miles of road were built – and to urge the institution of a semi-representative system of government. The April, 1935 constitution, while bringing back elections, included restrictions ensuring that working class Belizans could not qualify. LUA and the Citizens' Political Party endorsed black lawyer Arthur Balderamos and Creole chicle millionaire R. S. Turton, who led the opposition to the big business interests in the newly elected 1936 council.

THE 1940s-50s: The culmination of years of agitation, major labor reforms were passed during the 1940s as the newly-legalized labor unions grew in power. In 1947, George Cadle Price won election to the Belize City Council. Educated by Jesuits in the US, Price had served as Turton's personal secretary. Coming from a middle class background, Price widened his political base by appealing to both the labor and nationalist political factions. Running on a platform opposing immigration and import controls, Price triumphed in the 1947 election, riding into office on the massive sentiment generated against the proposed inclusion of British Honduras in the West Indian Federation. The devaluation of the British Honduras dollar on the last day of 1949 – coming after repeated denials by the British that they would devalue – sparked the organization of the People's United Party which coalesced its internal structure in 1950-54. The new party's success was largely due to the support extended by the General Worker's Union (GWU), whose organization formed the integral core of the new party. The imprisonment of two of the party's chief members (charged with sedition after they had refused to hang a portrait of the King) and the resignation of another left George Cadle Price in the saddle, and he comfortably secured a victory in the 1952 Belize City Council elections.

Universal suffrage was achieved only in 1954 when the constitution created a Legislative Assembly with nine elected members, three appointed members, and three unofficial appointed members. For nearly a year and a half prior to the election the government had supported the National Party (NP), an openly fanatical Anglophilic party backed by the Anglicans and Methodists as well as the upper classes. It charged the PUP with being pro-Guatemala, racist, practicing religious prejudice (i.e., being pro-Catholic), and with being communist. On election day a vote for the PUP had become a mandate for self-government and, with 12,274 people or nearly 70% of the electorate voting, the PUP secured 66.3% of the vote and eight of nine elective seats in the new Legislative Assembly. It continued to triumph in elections right through 1984. During these years it was a populist party, one whose strategies and policies were determined by an elite at the top rather than by the membership. In succeeding years, the party was plagued by factionalism and a tendency for the aging leadership to become increasingly removed from its constituency. Issues were often obscured by political deification and mudslinging.

After the GWU split off from the PUP in 1956, it created the National Independence Party (NIP); the PUP created the Christian Democratic Union, a new trade union. However, Price and the PUP triumphed in the 1957 elections, securing all nine elected seats. But later events served to shake the PUP. After Price met with the Guatemalan minister for discussions during constitutional talks in London at the end of that year, the British secretary of state denounced Price and broke off talks. Price was removed from the Executive Council because his actions were allegedly in conflict with his oath of loyalty to the Crown. Accusing Price in a radio broadcast of attempting to sell the colony to Guatemala, the governor brought in a British frigate from Jamaica. Price's partner Nicholas Pollard defected and formed the Christian Democratic Party (CDP); the two other opposition parties united under the National Independence Party (NIP). However, the colonial administration's tactics backfired: the PUP won 29 of 33 seats up for grabs in seven districts in Nov. 1958, and Price became mayor of Belize. The PUP continued its sweep through the next three consecutive national elections, winning all 18 seats in 1961, 16 in 1965, and 17 in 1969. The CDP was dissolved in 1961, and the NIP became a mere shadow of an opposition. The NIP split apart in 1969 when Dean Lindo left to form the People's Development Movement (PDM). Price called an election, and – although the parties hastily realigned – both were trounced. With the introduction of the ministerial system, Price became first minister in 1961 and premier in 1964.

THE NEW GENERATION: As the 60s wore on an increasingly radicalized, impatient generation began to emerge. Like the PUP of two decades before, they were unfairly labeled as racists and communists. Inspired by the example of the Black Power movement in the US, leaders like US-educated Evan Hyde and British-trained lawyers Said Musa and Assad Shoman organized meetings and demonstrations, and began breakfast programs for poor children as well as public education seminars on cultural and economic imperialism. Even though Hyde's United Black Association for Development (UBAD) and Musa's Political Action Committee (PAC) collaborated for a brief period in 1969, they soon parted ways as Musa and Shoman joined the radical wing of the PUP while Hyde began publishing *Amandala* and associated himself with the opposition parties. In the 1970s, the National Independence Party, the People's Development Movement, and the Liberal Party joined forces in the United Democratic Party (UDP). In the Oct. 1974 general election, the PUP won 51% of the vote with the opposition's coalition receiving 38%, giving them six out of the 18 seats. Although the PUP won 52% of the vote in the 1979 election, it continued to lose support, especially among the young voters. After the UDP won a landslide victory in the Belize City

Council elections of Dec. 1983, Prime Minister Rogers resigned, leaving Price with no clear successor within the PUP. A balance-of-payments crisis coupled with a deficit-ridden budget triggered the PUP's first electoral setback. Held in Dec. 1984, the election gave the UDP 53.3% of the vote. Humiliatingly, Price himself was defeated by the party's youngest candidate. Expelled from the PUP in 1985, rightists Louis Sylvestre and Fred Hunter formed the now-moribund Belize Popular Party (PPB) that same year. Two months after the party's formation, Briceno was convicted in North Carolina of drug smuggling and sentenced to a federal penitentiary. During the elections, the party, under leader Manuel Esquivel, had presented a platform espousing the need for foreign investment and private sector solutions for problems. One of the administration's more controversial policies was the sale of Belizean passports to foreign investors (mostly Hong Kong Chinese) in exchange for US$25,000 interest-free loans with a 10-year maturity. Campaigning on the slogan "Belizeans first" – a reference to the contention that the UDP had opened the door to foreign speculators while Belizeans were not benefiting from new investment projects – in the Aug. 1989 snap election, the PUP regained power by a small 5% margin in the 28-seat House of Representatives, and George Price once again assumed the role of Prime Minister.

THE 1990s: In the 1993 election, Manuel Esquivel and the UDP again resumed control, taking 16 of 29 seats. Although the PUP actually garnered more votes than the UDP, the UDP won one seat in Belize District by a single vote and two others by a mere eight votes. It is still too early to say which direction the Esquivel government will take.

Important Dates In Belizean History

1763: Signing of the Treaty of Paris permits the British to cut wood and export logwood while affirming Spanish sovereignty over the region.

1779: British settlers are attacked by Spaniards for the fourth time since 1717.

1783: Treaty of Versailles provides similar (although more limited) terms as the earlier treaty.

1786: Convention of London affirms rights of Baymen to cut wood but not to establish fortifications, plantations or government lands in Belize. First British Superintendent arrives.

1798: Spanish defeated by British in Battle of St. George's Caye.

1821: The Central American region declares independence from Spain.

1831: Civil rights granted to "Coloured Subjects of Free Condition."

1834: Slaves, who comprise less than half of the population, are emancipated.

1839: Central American federation falls apart. Guatemala asserts claim over Belize.

1840: British Government asserts that the Laws of England are in force in Belize. Formation of Executive Council which will assist superintendent.

1854: Formal constitution adopted which includes provision for Legislative Assembly.

1855: Regularization of legal system.

1859: Although Guatemala recognizes British sovereignty, it claims it signed treaty because both parties agreed to build road from Guatemala City to Caribbean coast.

1862: Colony of British Honduras officially established.

1871: British Honduras becomes a Crown colony under the Governor of Jamaica.

1884: British Honduras reestablished as separate colony.

1894: Riot by mahogany workers protesting conditions.

1919: Ex-Servicemens' Riot.

1931: Hurricane hits.

1934: Labourers and Unemployed Association (LUA) formed. Demonstrations and boycotts staged.

1936: New constitution includes election but bulk of electorate still disenfranchised by property, income, and literacy qualifications. Although Britain offers £50,000 towards building road, Guatemala demands £400,000.

1939: Establishment of the British Honduras Workers and Tradesman Union, forerunner of the General Workers' Union (1943).

1941: Mass meetings demand adult suffrage and right to elect govern-

1945: Guatemala lists "Belice" as its 45th department in its new constitution.

1950: People's United Party (PUP) formed. Women permitted to vote at 21 instead of 30.

1954: New constitution provides for universal adult suffrage as well as elected majority in legislative council.

1955: Although a semi-ministerial government is introduced, governor retains reserve powers. PUP sweeps elections, beginning a 30-year trend.

1958: National Independence party (NIP) formed, and PUP faces its first opposition.

1963: Breaking off negotiations, Guatemala threatens war.

1964: Belize granted control of local government, and Governor General appoints George Price as Premier.

1972: Breaking off negotiations again, Guatemala mobilizes troops at border, and Britain responds by sending several thousand troops along with naval fleet.

1973: Name changed to Belize and Belmopan declared to be capital.

1980: UN passes unanimous resolution demanding secure independence of Belize prior to 1981 session. Guatemala abstains.

1981: Promulgation of new constitution. Negotiations with Guatemala bring on riot and state of emergency in the country. Belize becomes fully independent member of Commonwealth, and Price becomes first Prime Minister. Belize joins UN and Non-Aligned Nations. US begins training Belize Defense Force.

1984: After a landslide victory, the UDP's Esquivel becomes Prime Minister. VOA transmitter installed in Punta Gorda.

1989: Price becomes Prime Minister again by narrow margin.

1991: Newly inaugurated Guatemalan President Serrano pronounces the end to his nation's claim on Belize.

1993: Esquivel again becomes Prime Minister.

1994: British troops depart Belize. Guatemalan government re-asserts its claim on Belize.

Government

 With one of the strongest democratic traditions in the Central American region, Belize remains among the most politically stable nations in the hemisphere. Although independent only since 1981, the nation's history of self government dates back to 1964. From that year up until independence, the British controlled only foreign affairs, defense, and international security. Belize is a constitutional monarchy and a member of the Commonwealth of Nations. The nation's foreign policy has been shaped through its close ties with Britain and, more recently, the United States.

POLITICAL STRUCTURE: Drafted a few months before independence in 1981 and ratified by the National Assembly, the Belizean Constitution defines governmental structure, identifies certain rights and freedoms for the individual, and defines specific, additional rights for citizens. Elections are held at intervals of five years or less; there is universal suffrage, and the voting age is 18. Represented by the Governor General, the Queen of England is the (mostly ceremonial) head of state. Appointed on Independence Day, the current Governor General is Dr. Minita Gordon. Called the National Assembly, the bicameral legislature is divided into a Senate and a House of Representatives. Comprising eight members appointed by the Governor General, the Senate is a body intended to reflect the elected political status in the lower chamber: five members are recommended by the Prime Minister, two by the leader of the opposition, and one selected by the Belize Advisory Council – a body put together by both the party in power and the opposition which advises the Governor General on such issues as the pardon of a convicted person. The Senate's chief function is to consider and pass laws sent to it by the House. It may either refuse to ratify legislation or send it back to the House supplemented by recommended amendments. The 28 members of the House (10 of whom are from Belize City) are elected for a term not to exceed five years. Selected either from the ranks of the House or from outside, the speaker – whose job is to serve as an impartial chairperson – is elected. The Governor General has the authority to dissolve the National Assembly, either on the recommendation of the Prime Minister or after a no confidence resolution has been passed by the House. Normally the leader of the party commanding a parliamentary majority, the Prime Minister selects the members of the cabinet who together form the executive branch. A government may be brought down by a no confidence vote in the House; this has yet to happen in Belize. The main problem with this system is that cabinet members are drawn solely from the National Assembly, which means that the executive and legislative branches are closely linked and that many able candidates for cabinet posts cannot be chosen. On the local level, there are six administrative districts (Belize, Cayo, Corozal, Orange Walk, Stann Creek, and Toledo) which are governed by locally elected seven-member town boards (with the exception of Belize City, which has a nine-member city council).

POLITICAL PARTIES: Belizean politics has always been more a question of personalities and the degree of stress placed on issues rather than an ideological battlefield. While the PUP is anti-communist, it has strong social-democratic elements and shows mixed feelings about US regional influence. Although the UDP is generally more conservative and pro-US than the PUP, it also recognized the Nicaraguan government and the People's Republic of China. The UDP espouses privatization and free market principles, while the PUP supports a mixed economy. Since the mid-1950s, the PUP has been largely dominated by George Cadle Price, a middle class Catholic Creole of ascetic character. The party has become increasingly centrist in recent years. Florencio Marin and Said Musa are the party leaders most likely to follow him in control. Founded in 1973, the ruling UDP combined three national parties: the National Independence Party (NIP), People's Development Movement (PDM), and the Liberal Party (LP). However, only the NIP could have been considered to be a true party before the merger. Coming from the Liberal Party, which had its origins in the Chamber of Commerce, Manuel Esquivel has led the UDP since 1984.

Economy

In order to understand the Belizean economy a number of factors must be taken into account. First of all, the nation's very small size and relatively small population have hampered industrial development. Incessant regional instability coupled with socio-cultural and political differences, have served as obstacles to development of a truly unified regional economic block. Secondly, Belize has always been a plantation economy with agricultural exports commanding chief importance. Finally, the same lack of industrial development that has hampered the economy in other ways has also made it necessary to import a large number of items from the "developed" world (the

US in particular), running up an enormous trade deficit in the process. Another factor to consider is the government's role as employer: about 5,000 work in the public sector.

size and survival: The Lilliputian size of its economy makes Belize more susceptible than most to the vagaries of international commerce. Rising fuel costs and shrinking sugar prices have, in recent years, played havoc. Low sugar prices caused the near-bankrupt government to apply for an emergency IMF loan in the 1980s. On the other hand the economy's small size means that even relatively modest amounts of foreign aid, tourism income, or remittances from abroad can balance the books. Belize currently has a substantial trade deficit (BZ$129.4 million in 1989). If informal trade with Mexico were factored in, the trade deficit would be quite a bit higher.

personal income: Income distribution is more equitable than in surrounding countries. GNP per capita hovers around US$2,000 pp, and for paid employees, who make up two-thirds of the labor force, it runs about US $6,000. Although there is no general minimum wage, those wage rates which are set range between US$1.25 and $2.50 ph. Shops must pay 63¢ per hour to their employees, while liquor stores are required to pay 75¢. Domestic servants in institutions are paid 63¢ per hour. While a skilled laborer may be paid US$2.50 per hour, a secretary earns US$700 a month. Employers with more than one employee between 14 and 65 must contribute to the Social Security system. Women are generally paid a quarter to a third less, even though they may be performing the exact same task. Unemployment (estimated at 15%) and underemployment (estimated at 35%) help keep wages low. Unions are nonexistent.

CLIMATE AND THE ECONOMY: Climatic factors have played an important role throughout the nation's economic history. The seasonality of rainfall affected the logging industry which depended on a dry season for felling and a wet one for floating the logs downriver to the sea for transport. The longer dry season in the north enabled mahogany cutters to work more months every year, and caused them to resist Spanish attempts to drive them further south. Its dependence upon the climate has made and continues to make the timber industry a high-risk investment. Many roads also become impassable during the rainy season, while variations in rainfall affect agricultural production.

TRADE WITH THE US: US recognition of British control over Belize prevented the covert and overt interventions which have characterized US relations with the rest of Central America. As trade and transport links improved, the market shifted from Britain to the US, to the point where by 1920 70% of all trade was with the US. In May 1976, the Belizean dollar was tied to its US counterpart at a two-to-one ratio. At present, over half of exports go to the US which, in turn, supplies more than a third of imports.

LIGHT INDUSTRY: Despite the passage of a series of Development Incentive Laws, manufacturing remains a minor economic sector, representing only 20% of the national income. The bulk of production is in agroindustry, which includes such activities as citrus extraction, feed manufacture, and flour milling. One of the largest manufacturing areas is the garment industry but, as the cloth and other materials utilized are all imported, the revenue it brings in is rather low, and both productivity and wages are uncompetitive with other Central American countries. High electricity rates are another problem: Belize hopes to develop hydropower or attract assembly plants to Santa Elena on the Mexican border where cheaper Mexican power can be utilized. Other small manufacturing concerns produce cigarettes, beer, soft drinks, matches, batteries, footwear, mattresses, furniture, and fertilizers. A newcomer on the manufacturing scene is Heritage Diskettes, a firm which commits a percentage of its profits to rainforest preservation. Plans to build a plant were announced in 1994.

MINING: The nation's first commercial mining operation, a dolomite extraction and processing plant, opened in Toledo in 1992. Dolomite is a carbonate sedimentary rock which is rich in magnesium and calcium; it's used as fertilizer by agro-industries throughout Central America and the Caribbean. Eventually, it's expected to generate BZ$4 million annually. The emphasis is on sustainable development: the environment is protected and there is little environmental impact caused by the mining. In 1993, Belize Natural Resources discovered an area off the coast potentially containing millions of barrels of oil. What impact this discovery will have on the economy and ecology of the country remains to be seen.

TOURISM: Ranking second to sugar production as a source of foreign exchange, tourism is becoming an increasingly integral part of the economy. Among Belize's attributes are its proximity to the Yucatán and the Tikal ruins in Guatemala, the widespread convertibility of the US dollar, use of the English language, and an abundant flora and fauna complemented by the largest barrier reef in the Americas just offshore. Recently, the nation has been focusing on "ecotourism," and Belize is the only country where the Minister of Tourism is also the Minister of the Environment.

Although much has been made of the benefits of tourism, particularly "eco-tourism," it commands more than its share of problems. The much-maligned backpacker or low-budget traveler stays in local accommodation and eats what is available in local restaurants, thus funneling money directly to the local economy. Package and upscale tourism is often paid for abroad and much of the money can and does stay there. Tourism necessitates expensive imports, as little is made locally in Belize and wages in the hotel industry are low, sometimes exploitatively so. Some hotels hire illegal immigrants from Honduras and Guatemala in order to cut costs. Regrettably, it can also attract both undesirable visitors and residents who have condescending attitudes towards locals. Another problem is the price of land, which has skyrocketed beyond the range of the average Belizean. In other words, the average Belizean may see few of the benefits from tourism.

Agriculture

In contrast with British and other nations' former colonies in the Americas, Belize has no tradition of large agricultural plantations operated with slave labor. Instead of harvesting cane or gathering cotton, Belizean slaves cut down logwood for shipment to Europe. After demand diminished for logwood, they cut mahogany and other hardwoods. Chicle, a gum extracted from the sapodilla tree used to make chewing gum, was another major export until it was superseded by the development of synthetics. Approximately 70% of the nation's trade comes from agriculture. Sugar accounted for 33% of export income in 1988; textiles came next with 22%, then citrus at 16%, bananas at 11%, seafood at 8%, lumber 3%, and vegetables at 3%. Out of 5.7 million acres, more than 2.2 million could be used for agriculture; the government has been attempting agricultural development and diversification during the past few decades.

PROBLEMS: Despite the immense agricultural potential, numerous serious obstacles stand in the way. The inconsistent rainfall creates problems. Although corn is usually planted between May and June and Nov. and Dec., the lowlands may flood in a really wet year or corn may wither on the hills during a hot one. Another impediment to agriculture is the ferocity of the insect population, which has done in many a foreign immigrant agricultural project. Still another reason for the neglect of agriculture in Belize stems from efforts by the post-abolition colonial power structure to control the former slaves by limiting access to land, a policy which is continued today. The Land Tax Ordinance passed in 1967 was a progressive piece of legislation. Unfortunately, the Belize Estate and Produce Company refused to pay the tax until it succeeded in exempting 1.23 million acres or 95% of its land. Despite attempts such as the Alien Landholding Ordinance, passed in 1973, most of the land remains undeveloped and in the hands of foreigners.

SUGARCANE: The nation's modern sugar industry began with the 1937 opening of a small factory at Pembroke Hall (now Libertad) in Corozal. It was supplied by foreign-owned estates. Purchased by the British corporation of Tate and Lyle in 1967, the firm enlarged the plant and opened another at Tower Hill near Orange Walk Town. With production of some 100,000 tons annually, more than 60,000 acres are now under cultivation. The bulk of that amount is controlled by small farmers who grow on less than six acres. The price of sugar has undergone sharp fluctuations and, as Belizeans have put it at times, "sugar is no longer sweet." In 1985 Tate and Lyle closed the Libertad plant and essentially handed over another plant to its employees, retaining only a 10% stake. Once comprising up to 60% of total export income, sugar exports today represent only about a third. Farmers receive approximately BZ$50 per ton of cane, of which BZ$20 is profit.

CITRUS: Second only to sugar as an export earner, the citrus industry produces orange and grapefruit concentrates in the Stann Creek District. Citrus exports, mostly comprising frozen orange juice concentrate shipped to the US, tripled in value between 1980 and 1990, when over 40,000 acres were under cultivation. Like agroindustries elsewhere, citrus production depends upon the brutal exploitation of migrant laborers, many of whom are undocumented workers from El Salvador and Guatemala. The better jobs are reserved for the Creoles and Garifuna.

One of the most controversial projects in the nation's brief history has involved citrus production. In Oct. 1985, the government facilitated the sale of 686,168 acres to US private investors for a bargain basement price: US$6 million for land valued at US$150-200 million. Sold by Belizean businessman Barry M. Bowen, the property constituted one-eighth of the nation's land area, a tract described as "the largest single piece of potentially arable land in the whole of Central America." Of the property, 50,000 acres were sold to Minute Maid, 50,000 acres to Houston tycoons Walter Mischer and Paul Howell, and 50,000 acres were retained by Bowen.

The remaining acreage was divided on a 30:30:40 basis between the three. It was both the largest single overseas investment in Belizean history and the largest single investment by a US company in a nation covered by the Caribbean Basin Initiative. Plans were for Coca Cola's juice subsidiary Minute Maid to establish a 5,000-acre nursery, which was to expand to 25,000 acres within seven years, quadrupling citrus exports in the short run. In addition to the government's violation of a 1973 ordinance outlawing the sale of more than 10 acres of rural land, it also agreed to grant Coca Cola a 15-year tax holiday and to construct roads and bridges in the area. After coming under attack both from environmentalists and from the Florida citrus lobby, Coca Cola reconsidered and now retains just 50,000 acres. In 1993 exports dropped to 2.8 million boxes, a decrease of about 22%.

citrus pests: Currently, the industry is gearing up for an invasion of the Tristeza virus, transmitted by the brown citrus aphid. Once infected, a tree's growth is stunted: its leaves will shrink and yellow, the peel of its fruits thickens, juice content diminishes, and honeycomb-like holes appear on its inside bark. Ultimately, the tree will die. Of the nation's 47,000 acres, 90% consist of sour oranges which are quite susceptible to the virus, and the highest impact is expected in the Stann Creek District; growers in the Cayo and Toledo Districts have already planted virus-tolerant trees. Originating in Asia, the virus arrived in South Africa and South America in the early part of this century. The plague has been moving up from South America since the 1980s (where it decimated more than six million acres in Venezuela). Belize and Honduras are expected to be hit hard soon. Although the virus has been in Belize since 1983, it has not had much impact because the brown citrus aphid, which spreads the virus, has not yet arrived. Reportedly, it is at the southern border of Honduras and is expected to move north. Another pest, the citrus leaf miner, has already appeared. Its larva sucks the sap from tree cells, stunting tree growth and fruit production. A native of Asia, the moth lays its eggs on the underside of leaves. It was first spotted in Dade County, FL last year and quickly spread across the US. It appeared in Belize in 1994 and is thought to have been introduced by someone who smuggled in a citrus or budwood tree.

BANANAS: Commencing in the late 19th C., production was ruined by Panama disease in the first part of the century. With British assistance during the 1960s, production began again, only to suffer severe hurricane damage in 1975 and 1978. Exports expanded through the 1980s. Before the construction of the port at Big

Creek, shipments had to be channelled through Puerto Cortéz, Honduras, an expensive arrangement. With the new port, which handles the ships of the United Brands British subsidiary Fyffes, things should go more smoothly. Producing only 11 tons per acre, Belize is less competitive than Costa Rica and Honduras, which produce 14 tons per acre. Production rose to 76.6 million pounds in 1993.

OTHER CROPS: These include rice, corn, red kidney beans, poultry, beef, and honey. One of the world's largest mango farms is located near Big Creek. Hershey's Belizean subsidiary operates a research farm. Grown organically, cacao produced by the Toledo Cocoa Growers Association (TCGA) is being sold to Green & Black's Whole Earth Foods in Britain. It is processed in France and marketed in Britain under the Maya Gold label. Its "Fairtrade" label indicates that a fair price has been paid for the product. The TCGA has contracted with the company to supply 15,000 tons during 1994-95.

nontraditionals: With Reagan's Caribbean Basin Initiative (CBI) having served to open up the US market for nontraditional agricultural exports, AID has funded crop diversification projects in Belize, mostly to little effect. The program is seen by small farmers as a failure because it does not guarantee markets. Although Belize imports 25% of its food, opposition from AID resulted in the temporary dissolution of a marketing board which guaranteed prices to farmers. While farmers producing nontraditionals for export receive credit and technical assistance, there is little aid offered for small farmers producing food for local consumption.

BELIZE BREEZE: Belize's most notable export is illegal: the ubiquitous and highly potent form of *cannabis sativa*. The US Drug Enforcement Agency (DEA) has alleged that Belize is the fourth largest marijuana supplier to the US (behind Colombia, Mexico, and Jamaica). With acreage under production quadrupling since 1982, estimates put the sale of ganja (marijuana) to the US at 1,100 metric tons, totalling a staggering retail value of US$300 million in 1986, surpassing the nation's GNP for that year and dwarfing the $36 million-a-year molasses and sugar industry! The US began funding an attack on the marijuana fields in recent years, however, and exports have greatly decreased. Threatened with the potential loss of some US$26 million in bilateral aid, the government began spraying fields with paraquat, a US-banned herbicide. Although the spraying destroyed 90% of the marijuana crop, it also led to a slip in the PUP's popularity. After complaints from farmers, they were reimbursed for crops accidentally sprayed, and paraquat was replaced with another pesticide, supposedly harmless glyphophosphate (marketed as "Roundup"). Sending over 300 police and soldiers into the marijuana fields in 1986, the government claimed to have destroyed more than 34 million plants in some 2,400 fields. Production in Belize has been sharply reduced but production in Guatemala has grown. At the same time, cocaine use has risen, and the country has become an important trans-shipment point. Society members at every level – from "base boys" to the police and politicians – are involved in this nasty but lucrative business. The people at the top of the pyramid have seldom been apprehended. This changed in 1994 when three officers were charged in Jan. with theft of 10 kg of coke, which had disappeared from the Eastern Division, and with the arrests of three prominent Belizeans at Dangriga in March for alleged cocaine smuggling. One problem in fighting drug abuse has been that the propogandists have failed to draw the important distinction between relatively harmless marijuana and potentially-deadly cocaine, while neglecting legal and well-advertised alcohol and tobacco – drugs which pose serious health threats.

FORESTRY: Cutting down trees was once the chief "industry" in Belize, until overcutting resulted in the depletion of reserves, to the point where a mahogany tree is a rare find today. While in 1950 forest products accounted for 85% of the value of total domestic exports, they had shrunk to only 1.8% in 1981.

FISHING: The fishing industry accounts for only a small part of agricultural production. There are now five fishing cooperatives, and fishermen are legally obliged to sell a proportion of their catch at controlled prices to the local market. Fish products have risen as a percentage of total export earnings largely as a result of a concentration on higher-priced lobsters and shrimp. One major investor in the shrimp farming industry is US-owned Maya Maricure Ltd. However, overfishing and out-of-season poaching has resulted in lowered catches, and conch and lobster are very likely to be either scarce or extinct in the future.

The People

 Belizean culture is truly polyglot. Given the small area, nowhere in the Americas will you find a more unusual blend. It is the only place where Maya have met English, African-American, and Garifuna (Black Carib) cultures. These social and ethnic groups differ greatly but have been united by the colonizer's monopoly on power. There is relatively little racial tension, and the nation lacks the class structure found in other former British colonies such as Jamaica.

SOCIAL STRATIFICATION: Determinants of class in early Belizean society were skin color and language. Rising to important positions and coming to own slaves themselves, Free Creoles looked down upon their darker brothers, causing resentment in turn. In the 19th C., a series of intricate divisions classed the "white" elite at the top, with soldiers, skilled craftsmen, house servants, and field laborers following in order.

SOCIAL CHARACTERISTICS: The contemptuous attitude towards physical labor, long considered to be demeaning, is one of the remaining legacies of colonialism. Consequently, unemployed woodcutters have refused to become farmers. Although both are equally backbreaking, a woodcutter contracts out his labor whereas a farmhand works for wages – a small but distinct difference. Other characteristic attitudes which may stem from the days of slavery include the exceeding politeness shown to employers and visitors and an unwillingness to say "no," substituting the word "maybe" or "possibly" instead. Instructions also tend to be carried out literally, allowing little space for flexibility.

POPULATION: The least populated independent nation on the American mainland, Belize has some 235,000 people. There are about 50,000 registered aliens in the country with an additional 10,000 or more estimated illegals. Although its overall population density is only 17 persons per sq. mile, the specific figure may range from seven (Toledo District) to 32 (Belize District). From about 1930, more than half have resided in the seven largest towns. In order of decreasing size these are: Belize City, Orange Walk Town, Corozal Town, Dangriga, San Ignacio, Benque Viejo, Punta Gorda, and San Pedro. Despite a net emigration from Belize in this century, its population has more than doubled between 1945 and 1985. Accounting for the increase are a longer life expectancy, coupled with a dramatically declining infant mortality rate (from 190/thousand in the 1930s to 20/thousand in the 1980s). Approximately 46% of all Belizeans are aged 14 or younger, and the birth rate is 39 per thousand. Among women aged 15-19, the birth rate is 137 per thousand, contrasting with 99 for Costa Rica, 100 for Jamaica, and 104 for the Dominican Republic. A survey conducted by the World Health Organization and the Pan American Health Organization ranked illegal abortions (no legal abortions are permitted) as the leading cause of death for women nationwide.

A growing problem in Belize is the breakdown of the traditional family, which has been brought about through emigration, poverty, and the emergence of single-family households. Emigration has frequently left children in the hands of elderly relatives who were incapable of properly supervising them. There are now large numbers of rootless teenagers who lack skills and education; a gang culture is growing, as is child abuse and neglect.

THE MAYA: The nation's only indigenous group, the Maya re-entered the country during the British colonial era. Today, there are three groups (Yucateco, Mopanero, and Kekchí), each speaking a distinct dialect. Although granted land in the Toledo District, they were not confined there and have also settled in the districts of Orange Walk and Corozal; in Cayo District **Mopan Maya** live in Succoths near Benque Viejo and Yucatecans reside in San Antonio. While the largely deculturated **Yucatec Maya** emigrated during the 1850s from the Yucatán in order to escape the Caste Wars, the Mopan arrived from the town of San Luis in Guatemala's Petén to settle in southern Belize in 1886.

Residing in the villages of San Miguel, San Antonio, and Crique Sarco near Punta Gorda, the **Kekchí** are the least acculturated of the three. Fleeing from the Veracruz area of Guatemala in the 1870s and 1880s in order to avoid exploitation by German coffee growers, their largest settlement is in San Pedro Colombia. Today, because they continue to live in relatively remote areas, they remain less assimilated than other ethnic groups.

In addition to raising cattle and pigs, the Maya still practice shifting cultivations on one- to 10-acre plots of land, cultivating small crops of maize, black beans, and tobacco. Those who are not farmers are generally chicle tappers. Modernization and the outside influences that come with it threaten the traditional Maya lifestyle; another threat comes from the activities of evangelical Christians. Some groups have gone so far as to prohibit converts from participating in *fajina*, the communal tradition of cleaning and maintaining the village.

THE CREOLES: Introduced as slaves sent in to help with the timber harvest, the first African-Americans quickly outnumbered their former owners. They were joined in 1817 by 500 men from the all-black 5th West India Regiment who were given land grants and temporary visas along with transport to Belize. Their families arrived the next year. During the 1830s, captured slave ship inmates were permitted to settle. The high frequency of racial intermarriage created the Creoles who now dominate the civil service. Two-thirds of all Creoles reside in Belize District, which is for the most part a Creole settlement.

MESTIZOS: These are Maya with some Spanish blood. They arrived after the War of the Races, which broke out in the Yucatán during 1848. By 1859 an estimated 12-15,000 refugees had arrived. After the conflict's conclusion in 1874, more than 8,000 of the refugees chose to remain. Settling largely upon the River Hondo along the nation's northern border, they worked as logcutters and farmers. Their most important contribution was the introduction of sugar cane which came to form the basis for a thriving industry. Today found largely in the Corozal and Orange Walk districts, their presence has resulted in a large number of bilingual Belizeans.

THE GARINAGU (GARIFUNA PEOPLE): This ethnic group (also known as the Black Caribs) has been living in Central America since 1797. Its presence and origin are quirks of history. In 1675 a sailing vessel with a cargo of slaves ran aground off the miniscule island of Becquia near St.Vincent in the Caribbean's easternmost rim. At this time the island was inhabited by the Calinago, whom the Spanish called Carib, meaning "cannibal." Intermarriage with the indigenous Caribs gave birth to this unique group. Later, they spread to St. Vincent, an island already populated by runaways from Barbados. Under the leadership of Chattoyer in 1795, they rebelled and were deported to the islands of Roatan and Bonacca in the Bay of Honduras, where they still live today. Some migrated to the mainland, and they first came to Belize in the early 1800s as smugglers, carrying contraband British goods into Honduras. Some began to stay on to labor in the mahogany harvest. In 1832, after participating in an unsuccessful governmental overthrow in Spanish Honduras, large numbers settled permanently in Punta Gorda and later in Dangriga (Stann Creek Town), Hopkins, Seine Bight, and Barranco. Treated by the British as squatters, they were ordered in 1857 to obtain leases from the Crown or face losing their land along with any property. The Crown's land ordinance of 1872 set up Garifuna reservations as well as Maya ones. Prevented from owning their own land, they were valued for their labor. Rarely intermarrying with outsiders, even with those residing in the same town, the Garinagu possess a hodgepodge of Carib, African, and Spanish ideas and values. They are difficult for the outsider to identify by appearance alone but can be recognized by their Hispanic surnames. Traditionally, they have been fisherman but are more and more turning to farming – an occupation they once deemed only appropriate for women. While their tongue is basically Carib, their music and dance are largely African: their *wanaraqua* – a group of costumed dancers and drummers which appear during the Christmas season – is the equivalent of the John Canoe spectaculars found elsewhere in the Caribbean. They also retain other customs such as the *dugu*, a week-long healing ritual, during which a female shaman goes into a trance and talks to the dead. (See "Religion"). Despite the fact that the Garinagu have become more integrated through the years, the urbanized Creole still finds it difficult to accept them. The Garinagu, in turn, have often clashed with the African-Americans, whom they regard as having "diluted" their racial purity. Today, however, they are leaving their self-enforced isolation and many have entered the mainstream. Many are now schoolteachers.

THE EAST INDIANS: In 1857, the Sepoys – a group of British-trained and -equipped Indian soldiers – mutinied in New Delhi, massacring thousands of British residents before the rebellion could be put down. About 1,000 of the unfortunates who had come to their assistance were sent to British Honduras to labor in the Corozal District's sugarcane fields. Today, their highly acculturated descendants reside in areas such as Calcutta in Corozal District. Although they are culturally distinguished from their Creole neighbors only by a few traditional foods, there are a number of more recent immigrants (mostly shopkeepers) who contrast more markedly.

THE CHINESE: In the early 1860s, the mahogany reserves in British Honduras were running low, and simultaneously demand was dropping because of the introduction of iron and steel in the shipbuilding industry. The need to diversify the nation's economic base led to the establishment of an immigration fund in 1864. Through the fund, a group of Chinese laborers was brought over in 1865. Although they initially met with a hearty and curious welcome, the newcomers encountered resentment in the *mestizo*-settled areas where they were first sent. The *mestizo*s could not understand why Chinese had been brought in rather than encouraging immigration from neighboring countries. The Chinese were moved from the Corozal to the Toledo District the following year, and no others followed. By 1868, of the 474 who arrived, only 211 remained. Although their survivors still live mostly in Belize City and in Punta Gorda, the majority of today's Chinese population stems from immigration that has occurred since the 1920s. For many, Belize is a stepping stone to Canada: they arrive, work hard, save some money, and move on.

EUROPEANS AND NORTH AMERICANS: Caucasians are referred to as *backras*, a term deriving from their "raw backs." Most of the white folks in Belize these days come from Europe or North America. Strangely enough, the first US immigrants to arrive were Confederates fleeing a defeated South. Given land grants in the Toledo District, they started large sugar plantations near Punta Gorda. Among them were former army officers, ministers, and doctors. All had been attracted by a New Orleans Immigration Company. In the face of sugar price drops and the 1868 cholera epidemic, many returned home. Those remaining introduced the banana industry. Their children were sent back to the South to be educated, where they frequently stayed on, and the community gradually disintegrated. In 1879 around 450 Italians arrived from Guatemala and were granted land near Manatee. Belize has one of the world's highest per capita quotas of Peace Corps volunteers. Although they are a significant source of foreign exchange, they have in the past been accused of taking scarce jobs, involving themselves in areas felt to be best reserved for nationals, and of being improperly used by the Belizean government as a source of free labor. There are also a large number of Lebanese expatriates ("Syrians") who, in the best Phoenician tradition, now number among the nation's most prosperous businessmen.

THE MENNONITES: Members of this conservative religious sect have had a memorable impact on Belize. Named for Dutch priest Menno Simons, the Mennonites were one of the Anabaptist sects to emerge during the Radical Reformation of 16th C. Northern Europe. Their refusal to serve in the army made them unpopular with governments, who forced them to move on. From Frisia in the Netherlands they moved to Switzerland to Prussia (E Germany) and then to Canada in 1863. Over the decades their numbers were supplemented by others fleeing the aftermath of upheavals in the Soviet Union. They became disaffected with prairie life after the Canadian government imposed a heavy tax burden because they refused to send their children to public school. Invited to come to

Mexico, thousands emigrated to the Chihuahua and Durango states during the 1920s. They found themselves cramped after a few decades, and 3,000 relocated to Belize in 1959. Purchasing a 100,000-acre stretch along the River Hondo, they built a road from the Blue Creek settlement to Orange Walk. Additional settlements were later founded at Spanish Lookout and at Shipyard. Isolating themselves from the local community, they market farm products including eggs and vegetables.

The Mennonites have become split into two camps: modernist or progressive and traditionalists. Progressives believe that the church should participate in the world, and they may use all manner of vehicles, power tools, machinery, and electricity. Traditionalists, on the other hand, believe that contact with modern ways contaminates their faith's purity. As traditionalists do not believe in engines, all work and transport are accomplished with horses. Even though they have not traditionally sought converts, progressives have spread the faith among the Garifuna and Maya communities, and today there are 28 different types of Mennonites. In 1973, many of the stricter Mennonites – finding the jungle too tough for hand cultivation – departed for Bolivia where they found more suitable land as well as freedom from price controls. Today, the Mennonites are a common sight in many of the nation's towns, many Belizeans consume Mennonite-grown vegetables, and their furniture can be seen in many homes.

EDUCATION: The Church of England founded the nation's first public school, and the vast majority of the nation's schools are operated by churches (largely Catholics, Anglicans, and Methodists). The government subsidizes church salaries and the Catholic Church runs some 60% of the schools. Despite the fact that primary education is free, only some 80% of children are enrolled in school and only about 55% complete the first eight years. Fewer Belizeans still graduate from high school and only a tiny elite continue on to college. The government administers the Belize School of Agriculture, the School of Nursing, and the Belize College of Arts, Sciences, and Technology, as well as the Belize Technical College Sixth Form. St. John's Sixth Form is privately operated.

Religion

Any visitor to Belize will soon discern the importance of religion. Churches abound, even in small villages, and the country practically grinds to a halt during the Christmas and Easter seasons. While the majority are Catholics, evangelicals are playing an increasingly prominent role, and there are a small number of Jews, Muslims, and Ba'hais.

CATHOLICISM: Although today the majority of the population are Catholics, the religion was slow to take hold initially. Mullins River was the first and only Catholic community. With the influx of *mestizos* during the War of the Races, the church grew a thousand-fold. Two Jesuit priests, arriving in 1851, built the first Catholic Church at Corozal Town, followed by another in Orange Walk. Arriving in Jan. 1883, six Sisters of Mercy established the first convent as well as a girls' school. The Jesuits established St. John's College, a high school, in 1887. Belize became a Catholic bishopric in 1956. Many Maya have also become Catholics, but the majority are little more than nominal members. The religion is now a national institution which cuts across ethnic lines. Although he never left the airport grounds, the 1983 visit by Pope John Paul II was a national event, and he was received by heads of the Anglican and Methodist Churches as well as by his own bishops.

PROTESTANTS: The first Church of England (Anglican) was established in Feb. 1777, and Central America's first Anglican Church, St. John's Cathedral, was constructed with government funding. It served for state as well as secular functions, but only the white elite attended, and it remained the white folks' religion until the late 1820s. The Baptists and the Methodists ("Methodizzies" as the locals contemptuously termed them) arrived and helped the ex-slaves make the transition from slavery to freedom through instruction in English and other means. The first Baptist church was established in 1822, followed by a Wesleyan Methodist church in 1825. The first Seventh Day Adventists arrived in 1891, and they built their first church in 1932. Other sects include a Scottish Presbyterian congregation, the Salvation Army, and the Nazarenes. Today, the most influential sects with the strongest memberships are these evangelical fundamentalists, one of the most important post-independence phenomena. Unlike Catholicism, which has made its peace with local customs and beliefs, evangelicals have declared war on indigenous beliefs, even on such practices as the

Indian custom of sacrificing pigs before planting. Religion has served to reinforce existing class divisions: while East Indian Muslims are hated by evangelicals, evangelicals in turn are looked down upon by other Christians. Among the Maya, the large variety of denominations and sects has tended to undermine community unity.

DUGU: This is the religion of the Garifuna people, a system of beliefs which has the same name as its major ceremony. Not only does *dugu* coexist with Catholicism, Catholic masses are held on the first Friday of the month in Dangriga's temple. *Dugu* revolves around the shaman *(buye)*. *Buyes* do not choose their position; they are chosen. The Garinagu believe that the dead are always with us. A *dugu* may be held owing to an illness in a family or simply because it is time. The many phases of the ritual include food offerings, dance, and prayer. It all culminates in the *awisahdi*, a farewell ritual. An expensive and complex affair, the preparation for a *dugu* may take up to 15 months.

RASTAFARIANISM: You may see these colorful Belizeans sporting dreadlocks in the towns and on the cayes. Originating in Jamaica during the 1930s, the Rasta creed has been diffused worldwide with the popularity of reggae music. Most simply explained, Rastas believe blacks to be the reincarnation of the ancient Israelites and the late Haile Selassie to be their king. Rastafarians have traditionally avoided meat or chicken, leather goods, and tobacco. In Belize many followers have been dubbed "Rastaphonians." The main thing that they have in common with real Rastas are the now-fashionable dreadlocks and a penchant for smoking marijuana. For more information on Rastafarianism see *Jamaica: A Visitor's Guide* (Hunter Publishing, 1993) by Harry S. Pariser or Leonard Barrett's *The Rastafarians* (Beacon Press, 1977).

OBEAH: In contrast with other areas of the Caribbean, *obeah* never put down strong roots in Belize. Today, few Belizeans are active practitioners. Over the centuries many deaths have been blamed upon *obeah-men* who are said to have used a black doll made from a stocking stuffed with dark chicken feathers and held together with black thread and pins. It is then buried under the victim's doorstep. *Obeah-men* are also believed to be able to affect crops, love affairs, and business enterprises.

COMMON SUPERSTITIONS: Although educated Belizans may deride *obeah*, many still fear a certain species of black butterfly which is commonly believed to bring either bad luck or an early death. Others wear *obeah* charms and cross their shoes in front of the bed in order to deter evil spirits during sleep. Mayan-derived superstitions are also prevalent; many of them are a mix of Mayan, European, and African beliefs. Portents of a family member's coming death include dreams of breaking a water jug, of floating on air, of a black bull attempting to enter one's house, and of having a tooth pulled. Dreaming of red tomatoes foretells the death of an infant. Placing gourds filled with food in the doorway is believed to ward off sickness brought by dwarves. One may not give away burning wooden embers lest one's turkeys die. Eggs laid on Friday, considered to be an unlucky day, will not hatch. Saturday and Monday are lucky days. In the past, Maya would buy lottery tickets on Saturday and get married only on Mondays. There are stories of ceramic statues, spirited away from their ceremonial resting places, magically returning under their own power. Weather omens are also common. If cornhusks are thin, the winter will be mild; if swallows fly low overhead, it will rain.

SPIRITS AND CREATURES: Perhaps because nature is so alive here, the air seems lush with spirits. The *Greasy Man* and the *Ashi de Pompi* both live in foresaken dwellings (the *Ashi* in burned houses) and stir at night, taking pleasure in scaring the bejeezus out of locals. The most infamous mythological creatures are the *Duendes* (Spanish for "dwarf"). According to reported sightings, *Duendes* are up to four feet tall with flat, yellowish faces, long arms and heavy shoulders, their bodies covered with thick, short brown hair. They are reported to carry away dogs on occasion, leaving deep, pointed-heel footprints behind. Maya bas reliefs do depict pairs of nude dwarves sporting what appear to be either banana fronds or sombreros on their heads. If you should encounter one of these creatures on a jungle trail, be sure to give him the traditional greeting: with your thumb concealed in your palm, salute him with the backside of your hand. The reason for this is simple: *Duendes* are four-fingered and are reportedly jealous of anyone possessing five! While they are capable of vile and despicable acts, they are also said to perform miracles. If they take possession of you, you will go insane, but you will acquire instant proficiency in your chosen musical instrument. A far more dreadful creature is the *Sisimito* or *Sisemite*, a gigantic and powerful hairy beast said to tear men to pieces and carry off their wives. They allegedly have been known to kidnap small children in the hopes of learning how to talk, and they make piles of twigs in an effort to start a fire, an art unknown to them. If they come across the embers of a campfire, it is said that they will sit transfixed until the embers grow cold and then they eat them. While a man who looks into their eyes is said to die within a month, a woman doing so will live a longer life as a result. A *Sisimito* has no thumbs and his feet point backward. Should one see you, just jump behind a bush. Puzzled as to where you've gone, he'll glance around, see his own footprints, and then take off in that direction. Another creature is the *Ixtabay*. She is always spied sitting in a tree combing her hair. Descending to walk above the surface of the ground, she hypnotizes onlookers, who follow her into the bush and go insane. Those who survive the encounter and make it home die a few days later.

Festivals and Events

On each of the official holidays most government and professional offices, some banks, and many stores are closed. During Easter and Christmas weeks, the entire country nearly shuts down completely.

BARON BLISS DAY: On March 9th the death of this somewhat eccentric British baron with a Portuguese title is commemorated by a formal ceremony at his tomb followed by fishing and sailing regattas. Arriving to fish off the coast in 1926, Henry Edward Ernest Victor Bliss fell ill from food poisoning and died before ever stepping ashore. Also known as "the "Fourth Baron Bliss of the former Kingdom of Portugal," Bliss was born in England's Buck-

Official Holidays
Holidays are now movable. For example, if Baron Bliss Day falls on a Wed., it will be celebrated on the preceding Mon.

Jan. 1	New Year's Day
March 9	Baron Bliss Day
April	Easter (three days or more)
May 1	Labor Day
May 24	Commonwealth Day
Sept. 10	National Day
Sept. 21	Independence Day
Oct. 12	Columbus Day
Nov. 19	Garifuna Settlement Day
Dec. 25	Christmas
Dec. 26	Boxing Day

ingham County. Falling in love with the country through the friendly people that he encountered aboard his yacht, he left the bulk of his estate to the colony – a sum which came to BZ$1.6 million (in today's money) after estate taxes. He stipulated that an annual regatta be held in his name, that the bequest be used only on capital projects and that all buildings costing £500 or more must bear his name. Money could not be spent on recurrent expenditures (such as salaries and utilities), and no churches or schools (save vocational or agricultural training) could be built. The money was used to found the Bliss Trust (which has been used to build the Bliss Institute), roads and markets, cricket fields, improve water supplies, and purchase the land on which to build Belmopan. The latest project was the Punta Gorda Multi-purpose Center. The Trust currently has around BZ$4 million, the majority of which is invested in UK Treasury notes and fixed deposits in Belizean banks.

NATIONAL DAY: Commemorating the Battle of St. George's Caye (on Sept. 10, 1798) in which the British defeated a Spanish armada, this holiday is spread over an entire week and includes religious services and carnival celebrations. A parade takes place in Belize City on the 10th. This identification by the upper class Creoles with a British victory seems a curious phenomenon to the outsider.

NATIONAL INDEPENDENCE DAY: Commemorating the nation's independence on Sept. 21, 1981, this nationwide celebration includes a variety of food, music, and cultural activities.

GARIFUNA SETTLEMENT DAY: On Nov. 19, the Garinagu celebrate their legendary arrival from Roatan. Drumming, dancing, and feasting enliven Dangriga. If you think you know what partying is, after participating in this event, you'll realize you hadn't a clue!

OTHERS: Many of the Maya still follow their traditional beliefs and customs, including corn planting and harvesting festivals. In the Mopan Maya village of San José Succotz near San Ignacio, the big fiestas are St. Joseph (March 19) and the Holy Cross (May 3), when the local dances – "Hog Head," "Mañanitas," "Quinceaños," and "El Baile de los Mestizos" – are all performed to the accompaniment of marimbas. In the Toledo District, San Antonio has revived its deer dance, which takes place around Sept. 25. In some localities (such as San Antonio), an effigy of Judas is tied to a tree and then shot by firing squad as part of the Easter celebrations. At Christmas, the traditional Cortez dance held in the village of San

Miguel in Toledo District tells the story of the Spanish arrival; the masks and costumes originate in Guatemala. See these local customs and celebrations while you can: intolerant, hard-sell evangelical Christianity may well render them extinct in the coming decades.

Food and Drink

 While Belize may not have one of world's most innovative cuisines, it is hearty and appetizing. And there are a variety of restaurants large and small. International cuisine is scarce outside of the resort areas, but Chinese food (or an imitation thereof) can generally be found just about everywhere. Small settlements such as Burrell Boom or Hopkins often have a local family that cooks for visitors. Ask around.

TYPICAL FARE: The staple dish is rice and beans cooked with coconut milk. The less-tasty stewed beans (whole or refried) and rice – with the rice and beans served separately rather than blended – is also popular. Both are generally served with meat, chicken, or fish on the side along with some semblance of a salad. Eggs are also available everywhere; a fried egg is a "drop egg." Traditionally cooked in pots above an open fire, game meat – consisting of either gibnut (paca), armadillo, or brocket deer – is largely a thing of the past. Most of today's Belizans thrive on chicken, beef and imported ham. But game is still served up to tourists, including the Queen of England, who dined to her delight on gibnut (the "royal rat") during her visit. Steak and fried chicken, served with rice or French fries, are also common menu items. *Tortillas* (thin wheat or corn pancakes) are an important side dish. *Tamalitos*, steamed ground corn cakes wrapped in corn stalks, are found in Indian areas. Vegetables are seldom served in most local restaurants. About as much as you get is a bit of coleslaw or a piece of tomato. One reason is their extremely high price: green bell peppers, for example, can sell for BZ$3.50/lb. The reason for the high price is that many are imported from Mexico. Another factor is that there is no local custom of eating vegetables. You'll find this to be true throughout Central America.

SEAFOOD: Chinese restaurants around the world often feature seafood, but in Belize this is not usually the case. Fish is generally more expensive than chicken. Specialties include the local spiny lobster, red snapper, conch fritters, and shrimp. Avoid turtle steak at all costs and shun restaurants serving it. Don't eat conch or lobster when the seasons are closed: Mar. 15 to July 14 (lobster) and July 1 to Sept. 30 (conch).

FOREIGN FOOD: Although often bland, Chinese restaurants are found throughout the land. The quality varies from gourmet to grease galore, but the bulk of them feature the same menu: egg foo young, chop suey, rice and beans, and steak and sandwiches. You may want to ask them to leave out the monosodium glutamate, MSG, a Japanese flavoring derived from soy that, along with corn-starch, ruins the quality and flavor of traditional Chinese cuisine. As one recent Chinese emigrant puts it, "there are no good condiments here. If you want good Chinese cooking, you have to go to Hong Kong or China." Other nationalities have opened restaurants in both Belize City and in San Ignacio. Many Mexican and Guatemalan snacks are served as well.

SNACKS: *Tamales* are ground corn and chicken wrapped in plantain leaves; they are traditionally served at Christmas. *Empanadas* are corn turnovers filled with cheese, beans, or meat and potatoes. *Plátanos* (plantains) are large banana-like grains which must be fried or baked. They are often sliced and fried like potato chips. A *gacho* is a flour tortilla stuffed with cheese and beans and with tomato sauce on top. A *great dog* is a hot dog sausage with coleslaw in a tortilla. A *sabute* is a fried corn pancake topped with shredded baked chicken, tomato, and cabbage. A *full house* is a baked *burrito* with chicken, cheese, and beans. *Panades* are deep fried cornmeal patties stuffed with fish. *Chirmale* is a beef, pork, or chicken stew with eggs and corn. *Relleno* is almost the same but with chicken or pork.

TAXES AND TIPS: There are no taxes on food. When dining at small restaurants, locals almost never leave a tip; you can do as you like. At larger, more formal establishments, a 10% tip is customary.

ALCOHOL: Drinking is a very popular activity, second to or possibly surpassing churchgoing, and many males would rather drink than eat. One reason for this is the excellent, locally brewed beer and rum which are sold in stores, restaurants, and bars. Some stores will let you drink on the premises, others not; the sign on the storefront indicates their status. Prices in local bars and small stores are virtually identical. Selling for BZ$2.25 a 10 oz. bottle and up, Belikin is the nation's sole beer. Its stranglehold on distribution drove competitor Crown out of business. Belikin also has a larger-sized (and more expensive) premium brand, and markets a superb stout which some may prefer to the beer. Imported brews are twice the price because of the tax. Caribbean-style brewed rum comes in two varieties: dark and light. The nation's rum is popular – so much so that Belize is the only rum-producing nation that does not export because its entire output is consumed locally! *Rum-popo* is made by mixing rum with condensed milk and sometimes egg. Another popular concoction is a mix of the local Tropical Brandy with regular milk in a 50-50 ratio.

SOFT DRINKS: Colored sugared water is enormously popular in Belize; imbibers will find a choice selection practically everywhere. Brands include Sprite, Fanta, Pepsi, 7 Up, Coke, and Club Soda. Milk is available in supermarkets. Known in Jamaica as Irish Moss, a local specialty drink is *Seaweed* which is made by blending agar, milk, sugar, and alcohol. It's most commonly found in Belize City.

TOBACCO: Nicotine junkies can choose their poison from several local brands, including the popular Independence, which makes you just the opposite. If you wish to cut down or quit, Belize is an excellent place, as single cigarettes are sold for 10¢ each or "three for a shilling."

DINING OUT: If you're only into fine dining, it's better not to leave Belize City or San Pedro unless you're traveling to a resort. However, if you pass up local eateries, you'll also miss some of the best food and hospitality the nation has to offer. The so-called "jungle lodges" generally have good food. You'll get more vegetables and varied cuisine, but you'll also pay substantially more than the average for the privilege – about what you'd pay in the US or even more.

BUDGET DINING: You'll find no lack of places to eat: there are a number of local restaurants in every town and most are in this book. Ask locals for recommendations. Expect to spend BZ$6-12 per meal. It's always best to ask the price of food before ordering. Australian butter and Dutch cheese are imported staples available at affordable prices.

TIPS FOR VEGETARIANS: This is most definitely a carnivorous society so the more you are able to bend or compromise your principles, the easier time you'll have. If you're a vegan (non-dairy product user), unless you're cooking all of your own food, you will find it even more difficult. But the local fruits may be your salvation. The local rice and beans is a good staple, but it can get monotonous after a while, and (as noted above) Belizeans don't eat many vegetables owing both to their scarcity and their high cost. Also try Chinese restaurants which do use more vegetables. If you eat fish, you should be aware that locals eat it fried and that it may have been fried in lard or in the same oil as chicken or pork. Cheese sandwiches will serve you well in a pinch. If you eat a lot of nuts, plan on bringing your own because those available locally are expensive. The same goes for dried fruits such as raisins. More well-heeled visitors will have fewer problems, as the more expensive lodges will cater to vegetarians and have the ability to cook tasty and wholesome food. **note:** Places serving vegetarian food are frequently listed in the text.

Sports and Recreation

 While Belize is best known for diving and snorkeling, the range of sports is increasing as the nation expands and tourism increases. Spectator sports are coming of age in Belize with the 1995 opening of the new National Stadium in Belize City.

Water Sports

BEACHES AND SWIMMING: Truth be told, if you're expecting fantastic beaches, forget it! The barrier reef apparently tends to interefere with beach formation, and some beaches (as on San Pedro) have been subject to erosion, partially caused by dredging of sand for construction. In many places the water is too shallow for swimming: on Caye Caulker, for example, you have to go to The Cut, a river-like divide which cut off the northern part of the island during the last hurricane. The best beach, hands down, is on the Placencia Peninsula, but even this is only a narrow strip of sand.

SAILING: With a nearly 200-mile stretch of reef-sheltered coastline, Belize is a sailor's paradise, and its potential remains so untapped that you are unlikely to see more than a few other sailboats during your stay. Based on Moho Caye, **Sail Belize** has charters with rates from US$1,000 pw on up. For information contact a travel agent or call 02-45798 in Belize City.

SCUBA AND SNORKELING: With the hemisphere's longest coral reef lying just off the nation's coast, Belize is a great place to do either. The drop-offs from the atolls are spectacular, and the variety of dive sites is seemingly endless. Although equipment is available, serious snorkelers and divers will want to bring their own snorkeling and diving equipment; you can leave it at your hotel in Belize City while you travel around the interior. Resorts generally supply weights and tanks, but you may need to bring the rest. Check with the specific resort if you have questions. Don't forget to bring your NAUI or PADI card; certification is also available. **snorkeling tips:** Wear a tee-shirt to protect your back from the sun's lethal rays, snorkel only on the outer side of the reef wall on low-wind or calm days, bring your own equipment or at least a mask you feel comfortable with (especially if you require a prescription mask), and don't worry about sharks – it's extremely unlikely that you'll see one. If you're using a kayak, it's a good idea to tie a line to it and carry it around when snorkeling.

dive spots: Found outside the reef at 50-100-foot depths, immense canyons have been formed by large coral ridges rising upward from a downward-sloping sandy bottom. Filled with caves and tunnels, these canyons swarm with life, including snapper, grouper, nurse sharks, and – on occasion – hammerhead and blacktip sharks. Barracuda, schools of spotted eagle rays, manta rays, and schools of amber jack can also be found in the reef's vicinity. The nation's most spectacular dive location is The Great Blue Hole in Lighthouse Reef. An almost perfect circle 1000 feet in diameter, its interior walls plummet 412 feet – an almost straight descent for the first 125 feet. At the bottom is a majestic underwater cathedral containing columns, archways, and alcoves. It is a huge cave with 12- to 15-foot stalactites hanging from the ceiling. Another wonderful area is the Hol Chan Marine Reserve. There are other spectacular dives in the same area, off Glover's Reef, and in the Turneffe Islands Atoll.

diving: This is a paradise for divers. Visibility in the Caribbean ranges from 50 to 100 feet. Since the water temperature is around 80°F, a wet suit is needed only for protection against coral outcrops. As the reef is only a few feet deep and about a half-mile offshore, dives are easy and economical on the tanks. Expect to pay around $35 and up for a single tank dive or $45 and up for a two-tank dive. Most hotels will require certification for participation in dives or to rent equipment. Hotels such as San Pedro's Coral Beach Hotel and Dive Club offer instruction for beginners, and the shallow, still waters surrounding the cayes are an ideal place to practice. Shops with equipment rental and tours are also located on Moho Caye, Caye Caulker, Caye Chapel, St. George's Cay, and on Glover's Reef. There's a decompression chamber on San Pedro which is funded by a tax on tank refills.

WIND SURFING: Rentals are available from most resorts, but the sport remains underdeveloped here.

ANGLING AND DEEP-SEA FISHING: There's a wide and wonderful variety of fish. Sailfish and marlin visit the exterior of the Barrier Reef in spring and fall. Trolling and bottom fishing along the reef can reap grouper, mackeral, amberjack, crevalle, barracuda, and snapper. While barracuda, permit, jack, bonefish, snapper, bonito, wahoo, and tuna may be caught all year, January is best for grouper, February for snook, March for tarpon, snook, marlin, and sailfish. April is a good month for tarpon, snook, marlin, and sailfish; May for tarpon, snook, marlin, and sailfish; June for tarpon and sailfish; July for tarpon; November for tarpon and snook; and December for snook and grouper. **Angler Adventures** (☎ 203-434-9624, fax 203-434-8605, 800-628-1447; Box 872, Old Lyme, CT 06371) offers all-inclusive packages and represents a number of fishing lodges. Information on the major lodges is also included in the travel section. These include the Belize River Lodge, El Pescador, the Blue Marlin Lodge, and the Ranguana Lodge.

TUBING: This relatively new and undeveloped sport involves floating downriver in a giant inner tube. Trips can be arranged at Cayo District resorts, at Adventurous Belize, and at the Cockscomb Jaguar Preserve.

CAVING: This sport remains undeveloped and can be dangerous. There are a number of caves you can visit, including Chechem Hah and the Rio Frio caves in the Cayo District, St. Hernan's Cave near the Blue Hole, and the caves near Punta Gorda. The Chiquibul is the most extensive cave system, but it is difficult to reach.

KAYAKING: Reef-Link Kayaking (☎ 515-279-6699; ask for Sonna Newton) operates from Ranguana Caye off of Placencia. Write c/o S. Newton, 3806 Cottage Grove, Des Moines, IA 50311. They publish the informative and comprehensive *Belize by Kayak*, the only kayaking guide available. The **Slickrock Kayak Adventure Co.** (Box 1400, Moab, UT) offers trips, as do many resorts in the Cayo district. **Monkey River Expeditions** (☎ 206-660-7777, fax 206-938-0978; 1731 44th Av. SW, Ste. 100, Seattle, WA 98116) offers kayak trips to the reef around Placencia and up the Monkey River for about US$1,300; custom trips are also available. Another firm is **Island Expeditions** (☎ 604-325-7952, fax 604-325-7952; 368-916 W Broadway, Vancouver, BC, Canada V5Z 1K7) which has kayaking trips around Glovers Reef (where they have a base camp on Southwest Caye) and to other islands as well as the Blue Hole, plus rainforest expeditions (including trips to La Milpa and Río Bravo), and trips to Tikal. **Ecosummer Expeditions** has trips down the Crooked Tree Lagoon and out on the cayes including Lighthouse Reef. They combine kayaking with horseback riding, tubing, and interpretive hiking. In the US, call 800-688-8605 or 206-332-1000, or write 936 Peace Portal Dr., Blaine, WA 98231. In Canada call 604-669-7741, fax 604-669-3244, or write 1516 Duranleau St., Vancouver, BC. V6H 3S4. **Laughing Bird Adventures** (☎ 800-238-4467; Box 131, Olga, WA 98279) offers five- to 11-day trips from December through April in Belize (departing from Kitty's Place in Placencia) and in northern Honduras. Prices start from US$499. In addition to these operations, numerous lodges rent kayaks; these are generally noted in the text. **alternatives:** You can 1) bring your own kayak on top of your car or truck; 2) bring a foldable kayak which can be transported by air; 3) or rent a kayak. Foldable kayaks are easier to transport, but solid boats are easier to get in and out of for snorkeling and they are safer. When planning a kayak trip, remember to allow plenty of time. Safety is more important than distance covered.

HORSEBACK RIDING: Trips into the Mountain Pine Ridge are available with Banana Bank, Chaa Creek, du Plooys, Windy Hill Cottages, and Mountain Equestrian Trails – all of which are near San Ignacio.

Practicalities

WHO SHOULD COME: Belize is not the destination for everyone. If the least little sandfly bite or mosquito sting takes you aback, then Belize isn't the place for you, unless you confine yourself to San Pedro's must luxurious resorts. Much of mainland Belize is truly for the adventurous. But you'll find that the rewards more than repay you for any discomfort you may endure.

WHEN TO COME: This depends upon your motives for coming. The best time is definitely off-season, when rates for hotels plummet and there are few visitors to be found in the more popular spots. The rain is heaviest June through January, with the worst months are October and November. It can rain during the dry season as well, but squalls generally come and go. If weather is your concern, February through May are probably your best bets. If camping and hiking are important, the dry season would definitely be preferable. If you go to the more inaccessible or untouristed towns, parks, and reserves, crowds shouldn't be a problem no matter what the season! The time **not** to arrive is at Christmas and Easter, when Belizeans themselves go on holiday. Don't count on finding a hotel room in Placencia during Holy Week for example.

PLANNING EXPENSES: Expect to spend from US$25 pp, pd at a *minimum* for food and very spartan accommodations. Generally, you'll find yourself spending at least US$30 total and, depending upon your needs, probably more. If you're renting a car and staying in deluxe accomodations you can easily end up spending hundreds of dollars per day. Differences in price from top to bottom reflect facilities and comfort, so the more you can do without the cheaper you can travel. When staying in hotels, be sure to find out the total price including tax and service charge (which can boost the final price by 16% or more). The best way to cut down on expenses is to stay in one (relatively inexpensive) location for a time. Expect prices to be about the same as they are in the US, but much higher for imported items; Canadians will find Belize to be somewhat cheaper than their homeland. Finally, if a price is not posted, be sure to ask, so as to avoid later misunderstandings.

Belize Tourist Board Offices

United States
421 Seventh Ave.
Suite 701
NY NY 10001

☎ 212-563-6011; 800-624-0686; fax 563-6033

Mexico
PO Box 725
Plaza Caracol
Cancún, Quintana Roo
Mexico

☎ 00-52-988-30074

Germany
Bopserwaldstrasse 40G
70184 Stuttgart
Germany

☎/fax 0711/23 3947

Belize
83 North Front St.
Belize City
Belize, Central America

☎ 501-2-77213/73255; fax 2-77490

Arrival

BY AIR: The best way to get a deal on airfares is by shopping around. A good travel agent should seek out the lowest fare; if not, find another agent, or try doing it yourself. If there are no representative offices in your area, check the phone book. Most airlines have toll-free numbers. In these days of airline deregulation, fares change quickly so it's best to check the prices well before departure – and then again before you buy the ticket. The more flexible you can be about when you wish to depart and return, the easier it will be to find a bargain. Whether dealing with a travel agent or directly with the airlines, make sure that you let them know clearly what it is you want. Don't forget to check both the direct fare and the separate fares to the gateway city and then on to Belize City; there

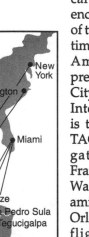

San Francisco
Los Angeles
New York
Washington
New Orleans
Houston
Miami
Mexico D.F.
Belize
Guatamala
San Salvador
San Pedro Sula
Tegucigalpa
Managua
Panama
San José

TACA
Routes

can be a price difference. Allow a minimum of two hours connecting time when scheduling. Among the carriers presently serving Belize City from the US, TACA International Airlines, is the most prominent. TACA flies from eight gateway cities: San Francisco, LA, Chicago, Washington, DC, Miami, Houston, and New Orleans. The latter three flights are nonstop. TACA provides excellent in-flight service, a choice of meals, and complimentary movies and cocktails. TACA now presides over a coalition of Central American airlines composed of Guatemala's AVIATECA, Costa Rica's LACSA, Nicaragua's NICA, and Panama's COPA. These airlines have integrated their routes and services, and currently offer the "Visit Central America Program" and the "Mayan Airpass" fares. These are specially priced and based on multiple destinations. Using "Visit Central America" coupons, you may use all six airlines and visit up to 16 locations in eight nations. The "Mayan Airpass" comprises the five nations of the Mundo Maya. For information and reservations call 800-535-8780. Continental flies nonstop from Houston. American Airlines flies daily from Dallas and out of its Miami hub. It is one of the most convenient airlines, with connecting flights to and from virtually every major city. **from Canada:** TACA has connecting flights. Call 800-263-4063 in Quebec; 800-263-4309 in Ontario; and 800-387-6209 in the other provinces. Also flying, with connections in Miami, are American and Continental. Charter flights from Calgary to Cancún run about C$500; it's a two-day bus ride from there to Belize City. **from the Caribbean:** Trans Jamaica flies to Belize City from Montego Bay, Kingston, and Grand Cayman. **from Cancún, Mexico:** A cheaper (but more troublesome) way to get to Belize is to take a charter flight into Cancún and then head by bus into Belize via Chetumal. **from Guatemala:** Aerovias flies from Guatemala City and Flores (near Tikal) and Tropic Air flies from Flores on demand. **from**

Honduras: West Caribbean Airways flies from La Ceiba and Roatan. **from Europe:** You must fly to Miami or another gateway city and make connections. **by bus:** Unless you have a damned hard ass and a hell of a lot of patience or plan on taking a month or so to complete the trip, this isn't really a viable alternative. It will cost you well under US$100 for the total fare from Texas or San Diego. From Guatemala City, you can take a bus to the border town of Melchor de Mencos. From Mexico, you can travel from Mérida to the border "duty free" town of Chetumal, Mexico. If you're changing buses in Mexico City, you need to take a taxi (around US$7) to TAPO, the bus terminal for the south.

BY CAR: It takes at least four days from Brownsville, TX to reach Chetumal Mexico and a minimum of five days from CA. When you arrive at the border. you'll have to surrender your Mexican Tourist Card and/or car papers. If you are asked to pay an "exit tax" here, it's an attempt to rip you off so decline to pay. If you've taken out Mexican auto insurance (for a rental car), have your policy officially stamped so that you'll be able to obtain a rebate for the days spent in Belize when you return the car. Be sure to get a temporary import permit from the customs official as well as mandatory auto insurance. The latter can be purchased at the restaurant across from the border station. One travel agent that can help you with travel to Mexico with your own car is **Sanborn's** (☎ 800-222-0158) in McAllen, TX. If you are intent upon driving, you may wish to purchase *Drive the Interamerican Highway to Mexico and Central America* which was published in 1992. To order send US$12.50 (plus $2.50 handling and shipping) to Interlink 209, PO Box 526770, Miami, FL 33152.

BY SEA: You can travel by sea from Guatemala; a ferry arrives in Punta Gorda twice a week from Puerto Barrios. For cruises, see page 84.

ARRIVING FROM MEXICO: From Chetumal you take a bus for Belize City. There's a stop at Mexican immigration and customs, and the bus then proceeds to the Belize side, where it waits for you to pass through both sides. You will be asked to show sufficient means of support for your stay in Belize. Imports of liquor and cigarettes are forbidden. Change money to Belizean dollars on the Belize side, where you may be able to negotiate a better-than-usual exchange rate if you have US dollars in cash.

ARRIVING FROM GUATEMALA: Ferries leave Puerto Barrios, Guatemala for Punta Gorda on Monday and Wednesday, with a return run on Tuesday and Friday. You can also fly to Belize City from Flores or Guatemala City (see above), and buses run regularly between Flores and Melchor on the border.

Internal Transport

 Belize is an easy country to travel in. Buses are reasonably plentiful, and charters are always available if you're willing to pay the fee. The best **map** is the "Traveller's Reference Map of Belize" published by ITMB Publishing of Vancouver. Fax 604-687-5925 or write 736A Granville St., Vancouver, BC V6Z 1G3 Canada. Essential if you're going off the beaten track, it should be available through your local bookstore. The tourist bureau in Belize City generally has copies on hand for sale, as does the gift shop in the Belize Biltmore.

BY AIR: Maya Airways and Tropic Air (026-2012, 800-422-3435) fly from Belize City's municipal airstrip, less than a mile from the city center, to San Pedro on Ambergris Caye, Independence/Big Creek (Placencia), Dangriga, Corozal, and Punta Gorda. Island Air also flies to San Pedro.

BY BUS: Buses run almost everywhere, though service can be scant – especially on Sunday. It's best along the roads leading to the borders with Mexico and Guatemala. In the case of Mexico (Chetumal), buses actually cross the border. Travel times anywhere within the country are reasonable; the longest run (approximately eight hrs.) is between Belize City and Punta Gorda. Because of the bad roads, travel with the smaller local bus companies can be trying. Since there may be only one bus on a route, a breakdown can take the entire route out of service. Buses are supplemented by trucks in some rural areas. Although the buses are relatively peaceful and uncrowded by Latin American standards, the driver may jack up the volume of his radio. Other passengers may compete, so that reggae may be in the front, rock in the back, and heavy metal in the center. Keep a close watch on your things while in transit. Baggage can be a problem. Although some buses may have storage below, many do not – including the local buses. Overhead racks inside won't hold large backpacks or suitcases; it's preferable to carry as little as possible. If you're planning to travel on weekends or during three-day holidays, it's advisable to obtain tickets in advance when possible.

BUS ROUTES: Buses run approximately every hour from Belize City to the nearer outlying towns and to Chetumal, Mexico. The bus companies are *Batty* (54 East Collet Canal, Belize City) and *Novelo* (19 West Collet Canal, Belize City). To Dangriga, south of Belize City, there are only four daily runs with *Z-Line* (Magazine Rd., Belize City), and there is generally only one run per day to Punta Gorda with the same line. There is only limited Sunday service. The quality of the vehicles ranges from the large buses used on the northern routes – including the luxury buses serving to Chetumal – to the geriatric Bluebirds found frequently in the countryside. Travel is faster on the better roads. But, on the rougher rural roads, fares and travel times escalate. You'll need to have patience! One problem is that buses to more remote areas may leave only once or a few times per day. Your hotel, and a bar or restaurant near the bus stop are all good sources of information on departures. Because schedules seldom change, the times in this book should be accurate. But, if you're on a tight schedule or have an early departure, you would do well to doublecheck.

BOATS AND FERRIES: There are regular but non-scheduled runs out to Caye Caulker and Ambergris Caye, and ferries operate between these two islands. Boats to other islands must be chartered – at rates ranging from BZ$100 to BZ$200. Once out on the cayes, you may wish to charter a boat to go fishing, snorkeling, or diving. Coastal runs are from Punta Gorda to Livingston and Puerto Barrios in Guatemala. Canoes may be rented in San Ignacio by the hour, day, or week. Other places to rent them are Placencia (to go on a Monkey River trip) and in Punta Gorda.

CRUISES: A number of cruise ships now call at Belize and **American Canadian Caribbean Lines** operates from Belize City to various cayes, including Ambergris, Goff Caye, South Water Caye, and Tobacco Caye, before continuing on to Livingston and other locations in Guatemala. Prices run from US$1,300 on up. For information and reservations call 800-556-7450 in the US and Canada, fax 401-247-0955, or write Box 368, Warren, RI 02885. In RI only, call 401-247-0955 collect. Sailing aboard the Ukrainian cruise ship m/v *Gruziya*, **OdessAmerica** offers seven-day "Mayan" cruises from Tampa to Playa del Carmen, Cozumel, Belize City, and Puerto Cortes with sidetrips to Copán and other sites. Prices range from US$1,300. Call 800-221-3254 or write 170 Old Country Rd.,

Mineola, NY 11501. **Special Expeditions** takes 80 passengers for a 13-day trip on its *Polaris* down the Caribbean Coast of Central America from Belize City as far south as Tortuguero National Park in Costa Rica and then continuing through the Panama Canal. Other stops include Lighthouse Reef, Nicaragua's Corn Islands, and Copán. Rates run from US$5,000, not including airfare. For more information call 800-762-0003, 212-765-7740, fax 212-265-3770, or write 720 Fifth Av., NY, NY 10019.

HITCHING: Owing to the lack of cars, hitchhiking is slow but very possible and a good way to pass the time while waiting for buses in the boonies. In some places, where there are no buses, it may save you a taxi fare. In the rural areas, Belizeans with cars are generally conscious of the transport situation and, although there may not be many vehicles, a high percentage of those that do pass will stop for you. If you get a ride with a truck that functions as a bus, you'll be expected to pay.

BY TAXI: Reasonably priced from BZ$4 for a short trip, cabs are meterless, with prices fixed by the local government. Be sure to agree on the price before getting into a cab. They are easily identified by their green plates. It will cost about US$100 to rent one for a day. Especially if you have a group of people, taxis can be a reasonable alternative to renting a car, but you should negotiate.

RENTING A CAR: Although renting a car may be a viable option for you, you should know exactly what you're getting into. You can use a valid US or international driver's license here for up to a year. A permit is necessary to drive a motorbike of up to 90cc. Cars may also be rented at the airport. Prices are very high – as much as US$130 per day including insurance! Per-mile charges are added, and gas is around US$2.25/gal. You can skirt these charges by renting a vehicle in Mexico and driving it across (see "by car" in the "getting there" section earlier). However, parts may not be available in the event of an accident or breakdown, and the car may have to be repatriated by towtruck. Don't rent a four-wheel-drive vehicle unless you really need it to get where you're going. As you should do everywhere, read the contract thoroughly – especially the fine print. Ask about unlimited mileage, free gas, late return penalties, and drop-off fees. Check the car over for dents and scratches and make sure that the agent notes any damage so you won't be charged later. You can reserve a car by sending a fax.

DRIVING: Of the 1,417 miles of roads, only 273 are paved – the rest are gravel and earth. While the Northern and Western Highways are paved two-lane roads, most of the others turn to muck after a rain. The worst roads are the ones which were once paved but no longer are. Although it is being improved, the Hummingbird Hwy. to Dangriga is one such case. The road from Dangriga south to Punta Gorda is unpaved, although it too is slated for eventual improvement. Drivers should pick up a copy of Emory King's *Driver's Guide to Beautiful Belize*. Road hazards at night include pedestrians, holes, and livestock. Four-wheel-drive vehicles, minibuses, or pickup trucks are *de rigueur* on some of these roads. As unleaded gas is unavailable, you may have to disconnect your catalytic converter. Good provisions for safe transport include spare tires, extra gasoline, a supply of water, plugs, points, electrical tape, belts, etc. Be sure to fill up at the main towns before heading out to the sticks where there may be no service stations. Most stations run from dawn to dusk. Bring a rag to wipe the inside windows in the rain. **insurance:** If you're bringing your own vehicle in, insurance is dispensed at a booth just across the border (closed on Sundays). Third party liablility insurance is mandatory; charges run around BZ$2 pd. However, this coverage is not comprehensive, so you'll be liable for **any** damage to the vehicle. Drivers license and registration are necessary for entry. Gas is around BZ$8 per gallon. Note: Traffic accidents are now one of the leading causes of death in Belize. Most accidents occur in and around Belize City.

Road Distances in Miles from Belize City	
Belmopan	52
Benque Viejo	81
Corozal	96
Dangriga	107
Dangriga (via New Road)	77
Guatemala border	82
Mango Creek	107
Maskall Village	39
Mexican border	103
Mountain Pine Ridge	80
Orange Walk	65
Placencia	150
Punta Gorda	202
San Ignacio	72
Xunantunich	81

RENTAL AGENCIES: These are listed under Belize City and other towns, where applicable.

BY BICYCLE: The major highways are easy cycling, and places like Altun Ha can be reached with a mountain bike. Although there's little traffic, backroads are preferable. Rocky roads can be challenging, however. Keep in mind that repairs and spare parts are generally found only in Belize City. There's no problem with cycling in the north, but you'll definitely want a mountain bike if headed south. It's usually possible to put your bike on top of a bus. **Tour de Caña** (Box 7292, Philadelphia, PA 19101, ☎ 215-222-1253) offers bicycle tours, as does The Touring Exchange (☎ 206-385-0667; Box 265, Pt. Townsend, WA 98368). **rentals:** These are becoming increasingly common. Mountain bikes can now be rented in San Ignacio and hotels such as the Victoria Resort in San Pedro include rentals in the room rates.

Tours

 One option for visitors without a great deal of time or with an urge to savor different experiences is a tour or excursion. Most of these include hotel pickup, meals, and dropoff in their pricing. The cost is typically about US$60/day. The advantage of tours is that you avoid crowded buses, you can cover a lot of territory, and your driver may be very informative. The disadvantages include the added expense, the isolation from locals, and the loss of flexibility. They do provide an easy way to visit many of the national parks, reserves, and wildlife refuges. In addition to those listed, hotels may offer their own tours for guests.

NATURE AND ADVENTURE TOURS: It's in to be green these days among tour operators. So many people have jumped into the business of "ecotourism" so fast that many can not deliver on their promises. You have to choose carefully. Local operators are listed in the text under each town or locality. Due to the high cost of gas and imported vehicles, bad roads, and the nation's relatively high standard of living, tours are an expensive way to see Belize. If you have more time than money, you can cut costs by making your own arrangements. In the case of Maya ruins, there's generally a care-taker on-site who will take you around. The Baboon Sanctuary has guides available, as does Crooked Tree. On the other hand, if you have little time to spare and want things to go like clockwork, many tour companies do an excellent job, and you can learn a great deal through a guide's expertise.

PACKAGE TOURS: As they say, all that glitters is not gold. This cliché may be old but it remains pertinent when it comes to package tours. If you want to have everything taken care of, then package tours are the way to go. However, they do have at least two distinct disadvantages: Most decisions have already been made for you, which takes much of the thrill out of traveling; and you are more likely to be put up in a large characterless hotel (where the tour operators can get quantity discounts), rather than in a small inn (where you can get quality treatment). So think twice before you sign up. Also read the fine print and see what's **really** included and what's not. Don't be taken in by useless freebies that gloss over the lack of paid meals, for example.

ENVIRONMENTAL AND ADVENTURE TOURS: If you're pressed for time, and convenience is more important than money, you may want to sign up for one of these. It's possible to get any package you want in the US. Billed as "An Opportunity for Postive Action," **Programme for Belize** (☎ 02-75616, fax 02-75635; Box 749, Belize City) offers six- to eight-day tours to the Rio Bravo Research Station. These are combined with visits to Placencia, Ambergris, Cayo, and sites in northern Belize; you can select the tour best suited for you or collect your own group and order a custom tour. Profits are reinvested in the development of the Rio Bravo Conservation and Management Area. Based in Belize, **The Divide Ltd.** (☎/fax 501-92-3452; General Delivery, Central Farm PO, Cayo) is a "Rainforest Resource Company" offering very special tours to the rainforests in the Chiquibul and Slate Creek Preserve areas. Trekking and rafting expeditions run from US$400 (three days, four nights). Some of the best nature expeditions are operated by **International Expeditions**, with all-inclusive tours departing from Miami. Call 1-800-633-4734 or write 1776 Independence Court, Birmingham, AL 35216. **Field Guides** (☎ 512-327-4953, fax 512-9231; Box 160723, Austin, TX 78716-0723) offers trips to Belize visiting Caye Caulker, Chan Chich, and other areas. Co-sponsored by the Siwa-ban Foundation based on Caye Caulker, the **American Littoral Society** (Highlands, NJ 07732, ☎ 908-291-0055) conducts an annual eight-day tour; five days are spent on Caye Caulker. Run by Jacqueline Tipton, a living legend within the coterie of Belize hoteliers, **Best of Belize and Beyond** (☎ 800-735-9520, 415-884-2325, fax 800-405-BEST, 415-884-2339; 31F Commercial Blvd., Novato, CA 94949) is one of the best-run travel agencies; they represent some of the nation's finest hotels and resorts, including many of those in San Pedro and San Ignacio. **Travel Belize Ltd.** (☎ 800-626-DIVE; 303-494-7797; 637-B South Broadway, Boulder, CO 80303) is a highly competent organization. They offer a variety of trips, including sea kayaking, mountain biking, rafting, and other packaged adventures. Another good company is **Magnum Belize** (☎ 800-447-2931, fax 218-847-0334; PO Box 1560, Detroit Lakes, MN 56502) which operates Captain Morgan's on Ambergris and represents some of Belize's most popular up-market lodges and hotels. Representing a number of fishing lodges, **Angler Adventures** (☎ 203-434-9624, fax 203-434-8605, 800-628-1447; Box 872, Old Lyme, CT 06371) offers all-inclusive packages. Specializing in adventure travel in Belize, **Island Expeditions** (☎ 604-325-7952, fax 604-325-7952; 368-916 W Broadway, Vancouver, BC, Canada V5Z 1K7) offers kayaking trips around Glovers Reef and the Blue Hole, rainforest expeditions (including trips to La Milpa and Río Bravo), and trips to Tikal. **Steppingstone Environmental Education Tours** (☎ 800-874-8784, 215-649-6895, fax 215-649-3428; Box 373, Narbeth, PA 19072) offers an "Archaeo-Astronomy" tour, to visit the cayes and Maya sites near San Ignacio, as well as conducting orchid and other tours. In addition to kayaking and tours incorporating kayaking, **Ecosummer Expeditions** operates a 22-day traverse across the Maya Mountains, a 15-day trek in their foothills, and a special tour for artists and photographers. In the US, call 800-688-8605 or 206-332-1000 or write 936 Peace Portal Dr., Blaine, WA 98231. In Canada call 604-669-7741, fax 604-669-3244, or write 1516 Duranleau St., Vancouver, BC. V6H 3S4. **FITS Equestrian** offers a horseback tour of Belize through Mountain Equestrian Trails; it also includes a stay in San Pedro. Call 800-666-FITS or 805-688-9494, fax 805-688-2943, or write 685 Lateen Rd., Solvang, CA 93463. **Laughing Heart Adventures** (☎ 800-541-1256, 916-629-3516; Box 699, Willow Creek, CA 95573) operates trips which include canoeing in the Cayo area as well as hiking. **Rothschild Travel Consultants** (☎ 800-359-0747, 212-662-4858, fax 212-749-6172; 900 West End Av., Ste. 1B, NY, NY 10025) represents a number of dive operators and resorts as well as San Ignacio lodges such as duPlooy's. Other companies include **Great Trips** (☎ 800-552-3419, 612-890-4405, 218-847-4441; 1616 W 139th St., Burnsville, MN 55337); **Ocean Connection** (☎ 800-365-6232, 713-996-7800; 211 E Parkwood, Ste. 108, Friendswood, TX 77546); **Belize Resorts** (☎ 800-333-3459, 305-595-3459; 10127 Sunset Drive, Miami, FL 33137); **International Zoological Expeditions** (☎ 800-548-5843; 508-655-1461; 210 Washington St., Sherborn, MA); **Massachusetts Audubon Society** (☎ 617-259-9500; 5 S Great Rd., Lincoln, MA 01773); **Mayan Adven-**

ture Tours (☎ 206-523-5309; PO Box 15204, Wedgewood Station, Seattle WA 98115); **Triton Tours** (☎ 800-426-0226, 504-464-7964; 1111 Veterans Blvd., Ste. 5, Kenner, LA 70062; and **Tropical Travel** (☎ 800-451-8017; 720 Worthshire, Houston, TX 77008).

in Canada: For Canadians, there are a number of operators. **Eco Summer Canada Expeditions** (☎ 604-669-7741; 1516 Duranleau St., Vancouver, BC V6H 3S4); **South American Tours** (☎ 416-234-9176; 4800 Dundas St. W, Ste. 206, Toronto, Ontario M9A 1B1); and **Winter Escapes** (☎ 204-636-2968; PO Box 429, Erikson MB R0J OPO).

In the **UK** contact **Journey Latin America** (☎ 01-747-3108; 16 Devonshire Rd., Chishire, London W4 2HD). There are also about 40 other tour companies. For a complete list check the *Travel Industry Sales Manual* available from the Belize Tourist Board.

DIVING AND FISHING BOAT TOURS: Various companies offer boat-based diving tours; fishing can be arranged as well. Trips are offered aboard the *Lucretia B* (write Boulder Scuba Tours, 1737 15th St., Boulder, CO 80302, ☎ 800-826-9834); the 40-ft. *Princess* (write Caribbean Charter Services, Box 752, Belize City. ☎ 02-45841); and the 75-ft. *Isla Mia* (write Rte. 3, Box 214A, Corpus Cristi, TX 78415, ☎ 512-854-247 or See and Sea, 50 Francisco St., San Francisco, CA 94133, ☎ 1-800-DIV-XPRT, 415-434-3400; call 02-45217 in Belize City). The 160-ft. yacht *Aquanaut Explorer* is a combination small cruise ship and dive boat; holding up to 40, it has a Jacuzzi and casino. Contact See and Sea, 50 Francisco St., San Francisco, CA 94133, ☎ 1-800-DIV-XPRT, or 415-434-3400. Others are *La Strega* (write *La Strega*, 4572 Telephone Rd., Ste. 913, Ventura, CA 93003; call 800-433-DIVE, 805-654-8100 in CA) or the *Aggressor*, a 100-ft. luxury yacht (write Aggressor Fleet Ltd., P.O. Drawer K, Morgan City, LA 70381, ☎ 800-348-2648, 504-385-2416, fax 504-384-0817, telex 784041.) The *Manta IV* is based on San Pedro. Call 800-468-0123 or write Box 450987, Sunrise, FL 33345. For information on the *Great Reef*, call 800-255-8503, 512-854-0247, or write Rt. 3, PO Box 214A, Corpus Cristi, TX 78415. For information on the *Ocean Spirit*, call 800-338-3483 or 504-586-8686. For the *Reef Roamer II*, call 800-433-7262, 504-385-2416, or (in Belize) 026-2151, fax 2180; write Out Island Divers, San Pedro, Ambergris. For the luxurious 120-ft. *Wave Dancer*, call 800-932-6237 or write Peter Hughes Diving, 1390 S Dixie Hwy., Coral Gables, FL 33146.

EDUCATIONAL TRIPS: The **School for Field Studies** (☎ 508-927-7777, fax 508-927-5127; 16 Broadway, Beverly, MA 0195-2096) offers a "Tropical River Ecology" course which is based at Possum Point on the Sittee River. The month-long course also includes a week stay at the jaguar sanctuary. Other courses may be available in the future. **The Divide Ltd.** (☎/fax 501-92-3452; General Delivery, Central Farm PO, Cayo) has rainforest workshops, co-sponsored by International Expeditions (☎ 800-633-4734) which are held at a tent camp in the Slate Creek Preserve. The program includes studies of conservation, biodiversity, life zones, symbiotic relationships, and other topics. Activities include horseback riding, trekking, and night walks. The price is US$665 for five nights and six days. **Maya Mountain Lodge** (☎ 092-2164, fax 092-2029; PO Box 46, San Ignacio) runs a number of educational summer workshops for elementary, junior high, and high school teachers and other interested parties. These include courses in rainforest ecology and Maya culture. Based in Costa Rica, the **Institute for Central American Development Studies** discusses issues such as agriculture, social justice, and refugees. They have internships in Belize. Write Institute for Central American Development Studies, Dept. 826, PO Box 025216, Miami, FL 33102-5216.

Accommodations

Belize has hundreds of hotels – everything from luxury resorts to simple inns. It all depends what you want, and what you want you can find. While prices are low compared to the Caribbean or the States, they're high for Central America – two to five times what you'll pay in Guatemala. Rooms with a private bath will run you a minimum of BZ$15 and are generally priced much higher. Budget travelers will want to avoid San Pedro and Belmopan. As the towns are small, it's easy to walk from hotel to hotel to check out the rooms. A 6% sales tax is added to your bill, and many tourist-oriented hotels and resorts add a 10% service charge as well. **making reservations:** Advance reservations should be made for the Christmas season. During the rest of the year, reservations are a good idea, but you generally can have your pick of rooms. Couples should state whether they prefer twin or double beds. Rooms with a shared bath down the hall are the least expensive. Remember that most tourist-oriented hotels give a 20-30% discount during the low season. If communicating with lodges or hotels directly, you may be able to get a discount even in the high season. The major resorts and hotels have three or four sets of rates: winter, summer, shoulder, and (sometimes) Christmas. **pricing:** For the reader's convenience, prices (generally inclusive of 5% tax and 10% service where applicable) are often listed in US dollars. They are subject to fluctuation and should be used only as a guideline. Wherever you go, there are likely to be one or more newer places not listed in this guide. Local hotels either charge double, or slightly less than double, the single price for a couple. Establishments for which no price is listed are classified as follows: *inexpensive* (under US$30), *moderate* (US$31-50), and *expensive* (over US$50 s or d). It's a good idea to get the current rates from the hotel before you arrive. **reservations:** Finally, while reservations may not be necessary for the large hotels except during the season, it would be prudent to reserve and send a deposit to the smaller establishments which do accept reservations so you can be certain of your booking. The least expensive hotels often do not take reservations. **checking in:** Be sure to read what you're signing. It's too late to complain once that 10% service charge – surprise, surprise – has been tacked on to your bill. Each hotel has its own policy on cancellations, service charges, and tipping, so don't make the mistake of thinking one and all are the same.

ON A BUDGET: Among the difficulties you might encounter are blaring TVs, clucking chickens, mosquitoes, spiders, and cockroaches. Some of the rooms are dimly lit. In spite of this, the smaller hotels offer a genuine Belizean experience, one which often brings you closer to the local people and their lives. Your neighbors will be ordinary, hardworking folks, and not wealthy tourists on holiday. If you try it, you'll find that you can survive quite well without a/c – a fan, or sometimes no fan, will suffice. And, once you adjust, everything else just falls into place.

SELECTING A RAINFOREST LODGE: As tourism in Belize has grown, so have the number of private reserves. It is becoming increasingly difficult to catalog the accommodations available, let alone evaluate them all. Practically everyone wants to jump on the "eco-tourism" bandwagon, some without really understanding what's involved.

Lodges are generally not for people on a tight budget. Costs run around $100 pp, pd for room and board, and this does not include transportation, a guide, horses, or other extras. If you can't afford this, you're better off hiking in a less frequented park or reserve. If you're staying in a cottage with a thatched roof, you can expect some insects in your room. There is no way to prevent this without zapping the entire jungle with pesticides, in which case the ecosystem you've come so far to experience would collapse. Think of it as part of the charm and consider that you are integrating yourself with your environment. After all, you have zillions of microorganisms continually squirming over you already, so what difference will a few larger ones make? Otherwise, arachnophobes and the like should stay only in well-screened conventional rooms, though even these may not be bug proof.

The lodges are generally not for those who are finicky about their accommodation. While most are well constructed and relatively new, the occasional bug will inevitably get into your room. If there *is* a generator, it will probably not run all night, and you won't be near a shopping mall or a boutique. At best there will be a small store in the lodge or in the village nearby.

The best way to select a lodge is by asking the right questions, i.e., those pertinent to you. Is there electricity? Hot water? What kind of food is served? Is it served buffet style, at a main table, or are guests waited on individually? Is there a choice of entrees? Do you serve wild game? Do you have a bar or is a BYOB policy in effect? Do you have caged animals? How close is the lodge to the main road? What is the fastest way to get there? How much does the transport cost? What's the least expensive way to get there? Do you have trips on horseback? Do you have night hikes? Do your prices include taxes and service charges? Do you have a biologist/naturalist on the premises? What is his or her nationality and professional background? Are guided hikes included in the price or are they additional? What other tours and excursions are available? Do you have interpretive trails? What type of forest is near your lodge? How's the birding?

These are some of the questions you may wish to ask. Depending upon your situation, you might come up with others. Some answers you'll find in this book; others not. Some details will have changed. Allow plenty of time for correspondence to and from the lodges. Many do not have direct telephones. Whenever possible, avoid travel agencies and deal with the lodges directly. This will save 15-20% and you'll get the lowdown from the horse's mouth.

Another alternative is to talk to friends who have recently returned or to travelers you meet while in the country. But make sure that you take stock of their differences in experience and outlook. A lodge that may appear "wild" to Sunday strollers may seem a bit too civilized for an avid backpacker. In any event, **do** write us and let us know your recommendations.

CAMPING: Although camping is not officially encouraged, you may be able to pitch a tent or sling a hammock in the coastal villages such as Placencia or Hopkins. Camping in San Pedro may be more difficult. In the San Ingacio environs, some ranches offer camping facilities. At Mountain Pine Forest Reserve camping is permitted only at the entrance and at Augustine. In the north, camping should be possible near the ruins of Altun Ha and Lamanai, at the Burrell Boom Baboon Sanctuary, and at the Crooked Tree Wildlife Reserve. Camping facilities in the south are limited to one place and Placencia, but a tent will allow you to explore the more remote villages and ruins. Avoid staying in pastures, which have ticks and chiggers. For kayakers, camping is often the only option, and a tent will be invaluable. If you decide to camp be sure that your things will be safe. Finally, be aware that you need permission to camp on any public land, including forest reserves. This must be obtained from the Ministry of Natural Resources (☎ 08-22037/72232).

Entertainment

 If you're expecting a flashy and glamorous nightlife, you're going to be disappointed: Belize lacks both the population and the income levels to support much in the way of clubs and concerts. Still, you'll be able to find plenty of bars, and even a place as small as San Ignacio has two discos with live bands. Occasionally you'll see posters for a *jumpup*, a Belizean dance. But much of the time you'll have to make your own entertainment.

MUSIC AND DANCE: Belize does have one fine steel band: The All Stars, an 11-member "music for the sake of music" group that appears infrequently. You can book them by calling 02-77348 (daytime) or 02-30866 (evenings) or write The All Stars Band, c/o 71 Pickstock St., Belize City. The best band to see if you have the chance is the Gil Harry Band. They specialize in Punta (Garifuna-influenced rock) and calypso.

   concerts: The National Arts Council holds occasional concerts at the renovated Bliss Cultural Center. Other concerts are held at Bird's Isle and at the stadium.

   recording artists: Many are based in Los Angeles and featured on Fresh Breeze Records (☎ 213-234-9159; 4309 S. Vermont Ave., LA, CA 90037). The label's most famous artist is Andy Palacio, whose most recent offering, a cassette single release, is *Samudi Guñou* (FBC 91599). Bella Caríb is an outstanding singer-songwriter whose best known song so far is "Bald Head Man," about the advantages of dating a "shinehead man." It was one of the most popular Belizean songs of 1991. Dubbed the "Queen of

Punta," Bella was born in Belize but raised in LA. Her most recent album, *Tropical Motions* (1992), includes the touching "Coming Home Belize," a song about her return to the land of her birth. Another artist is Pupa Curly, a Belizean dance hall-style reggae vocalist who combines Punta with rapid-fire vocals. In addition to the cassette single *Habinaha Whama* (FBR 91596), Pupa is also featured on the dance hall-style reggae compilation, *Belizean Girls*.

dance and theater: Founded in 1990, the **Belize Dance Company** is the nation's first modern dance company. Pieces are choreographed to the music of Olatunji, Black Uhuru, and Kitaro, ampng other local stars. There's also the fledgling **Belize Theatre Company.** It promises to re-introduce theater to a new generation of Belizeans.

Visas, Services, and Health

VISAS: American and Canadian citizens may enter with a passport and stay for 30 days. All visitors should note that they will be expected to show sufficient funds (around $30/day) and a return or onward ticket. **for other nationalities:** Citizens of the following nations do not require visas for stays of up to 30 days: Great Britain, Belgium, Spain, Denmark, Netherlands, Finland, France, Italy, Norway, Luxembourg. Liechtenstein, Iceland, Sweden, Switzerland, Mexico. All others should check with a British embassy or consulate regarding visa requirements.

EXTENDING YOUR VISA: Go to the Immigration Office (☎ 02-77273) in Belize City (115 Barrack Rd.) or to a police station in one of the major towns. An extension now costs BZ$25. Unfortunately, going to Guatemala or Mexico does not automatically guarantee that you will get another 30 days. Immigration officials have been known to give you only a few more days, in which event you'll have to travel to an office for an extension. Hopefully, this shortsighted policy will be eliminated.

SERVICES AND INFORMATION: Tourist information centers run by the Belize Tourist Board are at the airport and in Belize City (☎ 02-77213, 75812, fax 02-77490) at 83 North Front St. The latter is open weekdays 8 to noon and 1 to 5. Generally, they only give you what you ask for. Be sure to ask for the handy "Travel Industry Sales Manual," if available. For exploring the towns and ruins, they sell a good fold-out map for around BZ$8. They may also have the excellent ITMB map of Belize.

The Belize Information Service publishes *Belize Today*, a free and very informative monthly magazine. To subscribe, write PO Box 60, Belmopan, Cayo District.

LAUNDRY: Laundry services are generally available only in San Ignacio, San Pedro, and Belize City, but your hotel can usually arrange to do laundry or hook you up with a launderer. Otherwise be prepared to do it yourself.

TELEPHONE SERVICE: Belize has a very reliable phone system – one of the best in the region – but there are very few pay phones. While collect overseas calls can be made from your hotel, you may have to go to the local telephone office if you wish to pay. Belize Telecommunications Services, the main office (1 Church St., Belize City) is open from 8 AM to 9 PM daily. It costs BZ$3.20/min. to call the US (prefix 001) and BZ$6/min. to call Europe. Guatemalan calls must be prefaced with 00502. Branches in the major towns of each district are open 8-12, 1-4 and 8-12 on Saturday.

area codes: To call Belize the country code is 501; area codes are used when dialing from overseas except in the case of Belize City, where the (02) prefix is omitted. Area codes are as follows: (02) Belize City, (025) Ladyville, (026) San Pedro, (028) Burrell Boom, (03) Orange Walk, (04) Corozal, (05) Dangriga, (06) Independence/Placencia, (07) Punta Gorda, (08) Belmopan, (092) San Ignacio, (093) Benque Viejo. The number for local information is 110. To call Central America, dial 114; for other international calls, dial 115. AT&T USADirect can be reached by dialing 555. Finally,

Belizean Area Codes

	In Belize	From the US, dial
Belize City	02	011-501-2
Belmopan	08	011-501-8
Benque Viejo	093	011-501-93
Caye Caulker	022	011-501-22
Corozal	04	011-501-4
Dangriga	05	011-501-5
Guinea Grass	03	011-501-3
Independence	06	011-501-6
Ladyville	025	011-501-25
Orange Walk	03	011-501-3
Placencia	06	011-501-6
Punta Gorda	07	011-501-7
San Ignacio	092	011-501-92
San Pedro	026	011-501-26
Sarteneja	04	011-501-4
Spanish Lookout	08	011-501-8

where there is no pay phone available, there is generally a pay-by-time phone. Ask around.

calling from abroad: Direct dial service is available from both the US and Canada. To call, dial 011-501, drop the zero from the local prefix (for example the "0" from the "02" area code for Belize City).

POSTAL SERVICE: Window service at the General Post Office, near the Swing Bridge in Belize City, run from 8-noon and 1-5 weekdays and on Saturday. Other offices are located nationwide and are generally open weekdays from 8-noon and 1-5. Although there can be exceptions, mail generally takes about five days to the US, Canada, or Europe. Sea mail runs four to six weeks to North America. To ensure prompt delivery, mail from your hotel desk or a main post office and avoid enclosing anything other than a letter. If you send or receive a package you must pick it up at at the Special Package Office on Church St. You can have mail sent to you at your hotel or to Poste Restante, The Main Post Office, Belize City or any other town. If you have American Express traveler's checks or an Amex card, you can have mail sent c/o Belize Global Travel, 41 Albert St., Belize City.

FAXES: Faxes are growing in popularity; many hotels now have them.

BROADCASTING AND MEDIA: Founded in 1952 as Radio Belize, Radio One (834, 910, 930, 940 AM and 91.1 FM, 3.28 SW) transmits a wide variety of music in both English and Spanish, as well as limited programming in Garifuna and Mayan. It keeps all Belizeans informed of developments, and it even transmits personal emergency messages. Calling itself the "Caribbean beat in the heart of Central America," it joined the Commonwealth-Caribbean-Canada (CCC) broadcasting group in 1967. Another government-sponsored station is Friends (88.9 FM). Privately-owned Radio KREM is run by Evan X Hyde (editor of *Amandala*) and plays a lot of dance hall-style reggae. It also has "Aunt Grace" Coleman's family values and advice talk show on Thursday evenings. Premiering on the airwaves at the end of 1992, LOVE FM (95.1, 98.1 FM) plays music in the "adult contemporary" format. Television entered Belize with the introduction of dish antennas. Although there is no local broadcasting, two channels (7 and 9) rebroadcast a mishmash of US programming, together with local features (such as the government-produced "Belize All Over"); program schedules are found in the paper. Many places also have cable TV, and the world of Belizeans has opened up to the wonders of CNN, HBO, Chicago television, and the worst and most moronic dreck of American programs. Unfortunately, save for the Discovery Channel, no educational programs are broadcast, and the long-term effect of such low quality broadcasting can only be negative. One exception is "Lauren Da Mawnin," a Creole language show which is made by Belizeans for Belizeans. All issues save politics are covered; it's aired weekdays from 7:30 AM. Despite a broad range of newspapers, there is a dearth of quality. Name calling and accusations dominate the papers, and coverage of international issues ranges from scant to nonexistent. Of the four weekly newspapers, the largest is the *Belize Times*, the unoffical party paper of the People's United Party. An independent business-oriented weekly, *The Reporter* is supported by the conservative UDP, as is the the official *The People's Pulse*. The most politically independent newspaper and the best written is *Amandala*. The *San Pedro Sun* is the newpaper of Ambergris Caye; send US$40 to subscribe (26 issues) to Box 35, San Pedro, Ambergris. Other papers include the weekly official *Government Gazette*. The Government Information Service also publishes *Belize Today* monthly. The highly informative *Belize Review* edited by Meb Cutlack, is published monthly and focuses on "News, Views, and Ecotourism." (Subscribe for US$36 per year; send a check or money order to Belize Review, PO Box 1234, Belize City.) The quarterly color magazine *Belize Currents* has excellent articles about the nation; however, it also toes the line of the business interests who are responsible for its publication. Subscriptions are US$24 from *Belize Currents*, PO Box 24809-390, Houston, TX 77242. A newcomer on the scene, *Belize First* is published five times per year by Lan Sluder. It contains information on hotels, restaurants, history, real estate, and other topics. Subscription rates are US$19.50. Write Equator Travel Publications, 280 Beaverdam Rd., Chandler, NC 28715. Published by Joe Miller on San Pedro, *Belize Magazine* (Box 74, San Pedro) is a glossy magazine which has fantastic pictures and informative articles. Serious and leftist, the periodical *Spearhead* is published by SPEAR. Issued three times a year by the Belizean Studies Association at St. John's College, *Belizean Studies* publishes local research and writing. The US Embassy publishes the bi-monthly newsletter *Commercial Opportunities*. Cubola Publications is the local book publisher and is by far the nation's most professional publishing operation.

HEALTH: The water is safe to drink, and Belize is one of the most sanitary of the Central American nations. Take basic precautions, such as washing both your hands and pocketknife before peeling fruit. When visiting Guatemala or using water from an uncertain source, water purification tablets should be used. No immunizations are required, but you might want to catch up on your polio and tetanus injections. Also, a typhoid booster and an injection of immunoglobulin to stave off hepatitis are recommended for extensive mainland travel; ordinary visitors probably won't find these necessary. Malaria persists in the Punta Gorda district in the south, and if you are planning on spending an extended period of time in the area, it would be wise to take a malaria preventative such as Aralen. Start taking it two weeks before departure (two tablets per week). While public water is generally chlorinated, water supplied via "catchments" (cisterns which catch roof rain runoff) may not be. Health care is practically free to all comers, but equipment is antiquated. It's at its best in Belize City and very limited in rural areas. A new hospital in Belize City is slated to open in early 1995, and a new Dangriga Hospital is also planned. There are plenty of pharmacies around should you require medicine, but most medications are imported (largely from Europe and the US) and are expensive.

snakebite: In the extremely unlikely event you should be bitten by a snake, don't panic! Stay still and try to take note of its characteristics (size, color, pattern, and head shape). Nonpoisonous snake bites show two rows of teeth marks, but fang marks are lacking. Suck venom from the wound or push it out with your fingers and apply a loose tourniquet. Walk back to the field station.

protection against insects: Although scarce at higher altitudes, mosquitoes are prevelant in the lowlands. A mosquito net is a handy appurtenance, as are the mosquito coils (spirals) which keep the numbers down when you relax or sleep. Small shops will sell you one or two if that's all you need, but make sure you get a stand. Avoid inhaling the smoke. Try antihistamine cream, Euthrax, or Caladryl to help soothe bites. You have to watch for ticks when you undress because they may not be evident otherwise. If you pull one straight off, you risk leaving its pincers in your flesh. Hold a lighted match or cigarette to the bite and squeeze the area to extract it. Gasoline, kerosene, or alcohol will encourage the tick to come out. Repellents are ineffective against sand gnats; use antibiotic ointment and, as is the case with all bites, avoid scratching or risk infection. In summary, prevention is the best cure: take the precautions listed here, and wear adequate clothing.

Money and Shopping

MONEY: Monetary unit is the Belizean dollar, but transactions may be conducted in either currency so make sure which one you're dealing in. The current exchange rate is US$1= BZ$2, but you'll receive a slightly lower rate at the bank and an even lower rate at hotels. US cash is easily exchangeable at a two-for-one rate in shops, restaurants, and hotels in San Pedro, Ambergris Caye. To a lesser extent this is true all over. Don't change more than you have to because you lose on the rate when you change it back at the airport. Paper money is issued in notes of 1, 2, 5, 10, 20, 50 and 100 dollars; coins are 1, 5, 10, 25, and 50¢. Although 25¢ is sometimes referred to as a "shilling," the other coins are commonly referred to by their US names of nickel, dime, and quarter.

monetary history: The first settlers used any currency available, provoking endless squabbles over exchange rates. British colonial money from Jamaica predominated during the 18th C. The 19th C. saw an increase in local trade and a subsequent increase in Spanish American *pesos* and *reales*, while the California Gold Rush popularized American gold dollars. In 1887 the Guatemalan silver *peso* was declared legal tender, but the US dollar supplanted it in 1894. Founded by a group of local financiers, the Bank of British Honduras issued private "dollar" notes. The Currency Commission was created in 1937, and the British Honduras dollar was devalued on Dec. 31, 1949 following the lead of the British Pound. Since independence, the currency has been tied to the US dollar, and no devaluation is expected.

changing money: Although you are technically supposed to exchange all notes at the bank, US dollar notes are almost universally accepted at a two-to-one rate; many shops will change money for you and some will change travellers' checks. Most banks charge a service fee of 2% for travellers' checks. Currency other than US dollars, Canadian dollars, or pounds sterling can be exchanged only with difficulty. It would be wise to bring only US currency – including a generous supply of cash. Most banks are open from Monday to Thursday, 9 to 1 and Friday from 9 to 1 and 3 to 6. Although they will exchange travellers' checks, hotels generally will not accept personal checks except as a deposit for rooms. You can exchange your US$ upon departure at the airport (you'll lose 2-3%). You can also do so with moneychangers at the border.

CREDIT CARDS: Although there are a large number of establishments (mostly high-priced) accepting credit cards, don't make them your chief source of cash. Frequently, a 3-5% surcharge is added to your bill. At the American Express office you may be able to write a personal check to purchase travellers' checks in dollars if you have one of their credit cards. **note:** Be sure you investigate *all* of the charges before going this route.

SHOPPING: Opening hours vary but stores are generally open 8-4 from Mon. through Fri., with some stores closing from 12 to 1 in the afternoon. Most close down Wednesday and Saturday afternoons and are closed on Sundays. Some reopen from 7 to 9. Aside from the rather mundane local handicrafts, there isn't much to buy that can't be found cheaper (or at the same price) somewhere else. Many of the handicrafts are imported and then sold at inflated prices. As is the case with all luxury items, there's an import tax on photographic equipment and accessories, so bring your own. T-shirts (Belikin beer design, for example) make good souvenirs. Dr. Rosita Arvigo, of Ix Chel Farm fame, has marketed a line of "rainforest remedies" which consist of various tinctures. With attractively-packaged and expensive products, Rainforest Rescue pledges 6% of its gross proceeds to the Belize Audubon Society. Souvenirs you *won't* want to bring out are things fashioned from tortoise shell or black coral. You can also bring back a bottle of local rum or some of the less expensive items imported from Mexico or China. Hunks of useless Belizean chicle are also being marketed. They might be used for a paperweight or to manufacture your private line of chewing gum. A blend of habanero peppers, carrots, onions, and vinegar, Melinda's Pepper Sauce (regular and extra hot) is now exported. They also manufacture jams (60% fruit, cane sugar, molasses, lime juice), with guava, papaya, banana, mango, pineapple, orange, and mixed fruit. Avoid buying bootleg tapes. While it is tempting to do so, the quality isn't always good. In the case of Belizean artists, they are deprived of a royalty, and the originals can be purchased rather inexpensively at the Chamber of Commerce-run handicraft center on Fort St.

   market shopping: The towns all have their own markets, with the largest in Belize City. San Ignacio has a small market on Sat. mornings, and Melchor, across the border from Benque Viejo in Guatemala, has a fine market daily with good buys. Supermarkets are uniformly expensive, but they are good for the unusual souvenirs – hot sauce, papaya wine, matches, or what have you.

   stores: There are a few places you won't want to miss. The National Handicraft Center is on Fort St. in Belize City; it has an excellent selection of crafts, books, and tapes. Cottage Industries, 26 Albert St., sells crafts (mostly reed) made by Belizean women. Galeria Hicaco on Caye Caulker features a good selection of arts and crafts. The Garcia sisters in San Antonio near San Ignacio feature slate carvings in their museum shop, as does the Magana shop down the road and the crafts center next to the entrance to the Cockscomb Jaguar Reserve access road at Maya Center. Finally, Dem Dat's Doin has an impressive selection of box-framed large beetles and butterflies at their office near the Punta Gorda pier.

BARGAINING: Although most of the stores have fixed prices, you can bargain in some market stalls and with moneychangers at the borders.

AMERICAN CUSTOMS: Returning American citizens, under existing customs regulations, can lug back with them up to US$400 worth of duty-free goods, provided the stay abroad exceeds 48 hours and that no part of the allowance has been used during the past 30 days. Items sent by post may be included in this tally, thus allowing shoppers to ship or have shipped goods like glass and china. Over that amount, purchases are dutied at a flat 10% on the next $1,000. Above $1,400, duty applied will vary. Joint declarations are permissible for members of a family traveling together. Thus, a couple traveling with two children will be allowed up to $3,200 in duty-free goods. Undeclared gifts (one per day of up to $50 in value) may be sent to as many friends and relatives as you like. One fifth of liquor may be brought back as well as one carton of cigarettes. Plants in soil may not be brought to the US.

CANADIAN CUSTOMS: Canadian citizens may make an oral declaration four times per year to claim C$100 worth of exemptions, which may include 200 cigarettes, 50 cigars, two pounds of tobacco, 40 fl. oz. of alcohol, and 24 12-oz. cans/bottles of beer. In order to claim this exemption, Canadians must have been out of the country for at least 48 hours. A Canadian who's been away for at least seven days may make a written declaration once a year and claim C$300 worth of exemptions. After a trip of 48 hours or longer, Canadians receive a special duty rate of 20% on the value of goods up to C$300 in excess of the C$100 or C$300 exemption they claim. This excess cannot be applied to liquor or cigarettes. Goods claimed under the C$300 exemption may follow, but merchandise claimed under all other exemptions must be accompanied.

BRITISH CUSTOMS: Each person over the age of 17 may bring in one liter of alcohol or two of champagne, port, sherry or vermouth plus two liters of table wine; 200 cigarettes, 50 cigars, or 250 grams of tobacco; 250 cc of toilet water; 50 gms (two fluid ounces) of perfume; and up to £28 of other goods.

GERMAN CUSTOMS: Residents may bring back 200 cigarettes, 50 cigars, 100 cigarillos, or 250 grams of tobacco; two liters of alcoholic beverages not exceeding 44 proof or one liter of alcohol over 44 proof; two liters of wine; and up to DM300 of other items.

Life, Language, and Study

 LANGUAGE: Over half of all Belizeans speak English as their native language, and just under a third speak Spanish. Other native tongues include Garifuna, Maya (divided into Yucateco, Mopanero, and Kekchí dialects), and low German. About a third of all Belizeans are bilingual and a smaller percentage are trilingual. As English is both the language of school instruction and the official language, approximately 80% can speak English, and you should have no trouble communicating. Today's language combines King James English, West African words, and other foreign expressions in a blend delivered in a lilting sing-song which shows both Scottish and Irish influences. Antiquated words still in common use include "frocks" for dresses and "coaches" for automobiles. A meal is referred to as "tea." The Creole tongue is largely a result of combining African constructions and words with standard English. Because Belize also has a large Spanish-speaking population, the more Spanish you speak the better!

Belizean Proverbs

Barefoot-tea better than empty belly.
A meal without meat and/or cheese is better than nothing at all.

Blood falla vein.
"Blood follows vein." Relatives look out for each other; traits are inherited.

Blow your nose same place where you ketch you cold.
Ask your friends for help in times of trouble – especially if they were the ones who got you there.

Di olda di violin, di sweeta di music.
Older (more experienced) sexual partners are superior.

Falla-foot jumbie, you jump eena water.
"If you follow a ghost, you jump in the water." Follow others blindly and you'll get in trouble.

Fishaman neva say e fish 'tink.
"The fisherman never says his catch stinks." People don't like to criticize themselves.

Fos laugh no de laugh; las laugh the laugh.
"The first laugh is not the laugh; the last laugh is the laugh." He who laughs last laughs best.

If crab no waak, e no get fat; if e waak too much, e lose e claw.
New experiences, though necessary, can carry risks.

If you kyaa(n't) ketch Harry, ketch e shirt.
"If you can't catch Harry, catch his shirt." Take what you can get.

If you play with puppy o, e lick you most'.
Familiarity breeds contempt.

No change-i blaack daag for monkey.
"Don't exchange a black dog for a monkey." Things that may look similar can be quite different in reality.

Small axe fall big tree.
Size is not always the most important factor.

Too much rat no dig good hole.
Too many cooks spoil the broth.

Wen cockroach mek dance, e no invite fowl.
Hang out with unsavory characters and you're looking for trouble.

Wen puss no de, rat take place.
Mice play when the cat's away. Lack of authority brings anarchy.

Wen stone throw eena hag-pen, di hag weh squeal da di hog weh get hit.
"When a stone is thrown in the hog pen, the hog that squeals is the one that got hit." The guilty party is often the one that denies it the loudest.

Conduct

Call Me Belizean

Mister Visitor, don't call me
NATIVE
in my land;
Mister Foreigner, don't call me
LOCAL
in my Country;
Mister Tourist, don't call me
CITIZEN
in my home;

Mister Come Ya, don't call me
ANY FUNNY NAMES
yá da mi birth-place – Belize;
All you Mister Outsiders in Belize
Just don't call me names –
But instead, I appreciate you to
Call me Belizean – Love that!
or
Call me Balícina – Aba isieni!
or
Call me Beliceño – Con Amor!
"Cause me da fu yá – Belize!"

– *Luke Ramirez*

Keep in mind that Latin and other conservative cultural mores prevail here. Men and women alike tend to dress conservatively. If you want to be accepted and respected, dress respectably: skirts or slacks are appropriate attire for women in towns and villages. Women should wear shorts only in the resort areas. Bathing attire is unsuitable on main streets, as is any revealing female clothing. But, unlike other Central American nations, Belize does accept skimpy bathing suits on beaches. Business dress for men is a short-sleeved cotton or poplin shirt, or a *guayabera*. Formal wear often consists of bush jackets or long-sleeved embroidered *guayaberas*, rather than coat and tie. **hustlers:** Ever-present in Belize City are the calls of "Hey white boy/white chick! What's happening?" Sometimes these are Belizeans being genuinely friendly; at other times they want to a) sell you a piece of coral, b) change money, c) bum money, d) offer you a deal on a boat trip, e) offer you sex, f) sell you crack, cocaine, or marijuana. Don't let yourself be taken advantage of. **note:** The following activities are banned by law – removal and export of coral; unlicensed hunting; picking of orchids in forest reserves; removal of archaeological artifacts; spear fishing; overnight camping in any public place, including forest reserves unless you have Forestry Dept. permission. **drugs:** With the exception of alcohol, coffee, and tobacco, all drugs – from marijuana to cocaine – are treated as narcotics. No matter how many locals you see smoking in public, you may not receive the same tolerance from police, who positively revel in catching tourists. You can expect hundreds of dollars in fines and a few days in jail. If driving around the country, you may notice the occasional "Customs" checkpoint manned by police. They're looking for drugs, and there are no civil liberties in this regard; there's no such thing as illegal search and seizure on the part of the police! **tipping:** If a service charge is added to your restaurant bill, it's not necessary to leave a tip. Nor is it necessary in small, family-run restaurants. But in other eateries a 10-15% tip is expected. A doorman or porter should be tipped BZ$1-2. Taxi drivers do not require a tip unless they handle your baggage.

THEFT: Particularly in Belize City and in Orange Walk (the capital of the drug trade), this can be a problem. Nevertheless, you should be fine if you take adequate precautions. The very best prevention is being aware that you might be a victim. By all means avoid the slum areas of Belize City, don't flash money or possessions around and, in general, keep a low profile – avoid looking affluent. Keep track of your possessions; things like expensive sunglasses are very popular. Don't leave anything unattended on the beach. Avoid carrying anything in your back pockets. Women should carry purses that can be secured under their upper arm. Never, never leave anything in an unoccupied vehicle, not even in a trunk. Remember that locals who form sexual liaisons with foreigners often do so with pecuniary gain in mind. And, if you give one of them access to your hotel room, it can be a bit sticky when you have to go to the police and make a charge! It's useful to photocopy your passport and keep it separately, along with the numbers of your travellers' checks and any credit cards. A useful precaution is to secure unnecessary valuables in the hotel safe; a more effective precaution is to leave them at home. With an estimated 20-30 planeloads landing each month, Belize is a major transhipment point for cocaine from Colombia, and the drug has permeated Belizean society. Problem areas include Caye Caulker, Ambergris

Caye, Orange Walk, Dangriga, and Belize City. It should not affect you as long as you don't associate with the wrong people.

WOMEN TRAVELING ALONE: A large number of women come to Belize alone or in groups, and the attitudes of some of them (particularly in Caye Caulker) have led local males to assume that they are part of a woman's adventure in paradise. You should have no problems with men if you simply say "thanks, but no thanks." Part of the problem here is the influence of Western movies and television programs. Traveling will be a relatively hassle-free experience as long as you exude a certain amount of confidence.

TRAVELING WITH CHILDREN: Belize is as safe as anywhere for children. They are generally only charged half-fare to international destinations. Just take care that they are not overexposed to sun and get sufficient liquids. Remember to bring whatever special equipment you'll need. Disposable diapers and baby food are available but expensive. Be sure to inquire at your hotel as to extra charges for children and if they'll even be wanted. Finally, keep an eye on the kids while they're in the water. There are no lifeguards. Also, make sure that they apply sun protection.

ENVIRONMENTAL CONDUCT: Dispose of plastics properly. Remember that six pack rings, plastic bags, and fishing lines can cause injury or prove fatal to sea turtles, fish, and birds. Unable to regurgitate anything they swallow, turtles and other sea creatures may mistake plastic bags for jellyfish or choke on fishing lines. Birds may starve to death after becoming entangled in lines, nets, and plastic rings. Remember that the parks and reserves were created to preserve the environment so refrain from carrying off plants, rocks, animals, or other materials. Buying black coral jewelry supports reef destruction. If you're camping when kayaking on a small island, don't go to the bathroom on the island itself; instead, wade in the water to go. Ecology also revolves around food. Avoid eating lobster and conch out of season (Mar. 15 through July 14 for lobster; July 1 through Sept. 30 for conch), and try to avoid eating undersized lobster not of reproductive age. Finally, remember to treat nature with respect. Those interested in preserving the environment or in gaining a further appreciation would do well to contact the environmental organizations listed in this book.

UNDERSEA CONDUCT: Respect the natural environment. Take nothing and remember that corals are easily broken. Much damage has already been done to the reef by snorkelers either standing on coral or hanging onto outcroppings, and white patches of dead coral are clearly visible at locations such as Hol Chan Marine Reserve. Stony corals grow at the rate of less than half an inch per year, it can take decades to repair the desecration caused by a few minutes of carelessness. It's wise to keep well away just for your own protection: many corals will retaliate with stings and the sharp ridges can cause cuts that are slow to heal. In order to control your movement, make sure that you are properly weighted prior to your dive. Swim calmly and fluidly through the water and avoid dragging your console and/or octopus (secondary breathing device) behind you. While diving or snorkeling, resist the temptation to touch fish. Many fish (such as the porcupine) secrete a mucous coating which protects them from bacterial infection. Touching

Belize Dos and Don'ts

• Don't condescend to locals. Do treat the local people with the same respect you would like to receive yourself. Allow them the courtesy of answering at their own pace. Don't act as though there are no social problems in your country and make it clear that Western societies have their share of ills. Do try local food and patronize local restaurants. Don't be offended if Maya in remote villages stare at you.

• Don't make promises you can't or don't intend to keep. Don't make local children into beggars by acting like Santa Claus and dispensing gifts and money. Never pay for photos. In general, refrain from giving out money: it creates a cycle of dependency and creates more problems than it solves.

• Don't waste time lounging in your hotel. Do get around and explore. But don't try to do too much. Belize is not a place for rushing around. There's always the next visit.

• Don't dump your garbage at sea or litter in town. Do protect the environment and set a good example for others.

• Don't remove or injure any coral, spear fish, remove tropical fish, or annoy turtles or touch their eggs. Do not feed fish or disturb wildlife. Do visit archaeological sites but refrain from damaging them or moving anything.

them removes the coating and may result in infection and death for the fish. Also avoid feeding fish, which can disrupt the natural ecosystem. Spearfishing with scuba gear is illegal in Belize, and trigger-controlled spear guns are prohibited. If you're diving, be sure you have a realistic appraisal of your own abilities and pay attention to decompression and other factors. In short, look, listen, enjoy, but leave only bubbles.

BOATING CONDUCT: In addition to the behavior patterns detailed above, always exercise caution while anchoring a boat. Improperly anchoring in seagrass beds can destroy wide swathes of the grass, which takes a long time to recover. If there's no buoy available, the best place to anchor is a sandy spot where you create relatively little environmental impact. Tying your boat to mangroves can kill the trees, so it is acceptable to do so *only* during a storm. In order to help eliminate unnecessary discharge of oil, maintain the engine and keep the bilge clean. If you notice oil in your bilge, use oil-absorbent pads to soak it up. Be careful not to overfill the boat when fueling. Emulsions from petrochemical products stick to fish gills and suffocate them. Deposits in sediment impede the development of marine life. Detergents affect plankton and other organisms, which throws off the food chain. When you approach seagrass beds, slow down because your propellor could strike a sea turtle. Avoid maneuvering your boat too close to coral reefs. Striking the reef can damage both your boat and the reef. Avoid stirring up sand in shallow coral areas. The sand can be deposited in the coral and cause polyps to suffocate and die. If your boat has a sewage holding tank, empty it only at properly equipped marinas. Avoid using harsh chemicals such as ammonia and bleach while cleaning your boat; they pollute the water and kill marine life. Use environmentally safe cleaning products whenever possible. Boat owners should avoid paint containing lead, copper (which can make molluscs poisonous), mercury (highly toxic to fish and algae), or TBT. Finally, remember that a diver-down flag should be displayed while diving or snorkeling.

ARCHAEOLOGICAL THEFT: In spite of the fact that Belize has had laws on its books prohibiting the export of antiquities since 1929, smuggling has been a continual problem. Removing objects from their archaeological context severely diminishes their worth to an archaeologist because their relevance has a direct relation to their location. Throughout the world, much knowledge has been lost to us forever because of the activities of looters. Looting diminishes our cultural heritage. Never support such activities by purchasing artifacts, and never move anything you might see at an archaeological site.

Sadly, for the most part, those who plan and carry out these thefts are "respectable" US citizens who operate behind the scenes. Their positions in international business provide a veil behind which they can hide their illegal activities. It is also common to combine antiquity smuggling with drug smuggling. The actual looters are often poor farmers who are taken advantage of by middlemen. The middlemen sell the pieces in turn to North Americans for up to 10 times the initial purchase price. These buyers might then resell the object for as much as 100 times what they paid. The US, Switzerland, Japan, and Australia are the nations with the biggest trade in illegal artifacts. There are no laws on the books in these countries prohibiting this trade.

In Belize, an "antiquity" is a man-made object 150 years old or more. An "ancient monument" is any structure over a century old. Historic and colonial remains also qualify as artifacts. Individuals may possess antiquities as long as they are not taken out of the country and are registered with the Dept. of Archaeology. Antiquities may only be exported with a permit issued by the Minister of the Dept. of Archaeology.

Other Practicalities

WHAT TO TAKE: Bring as little as possible, i.e., bring what you need. It's easy just to wash clothes in the sink and thus save lugging around a week's laundry. Remember, simple is best. Set your priorities according to your needs. With a light pack or bag, you can breeze through from one region to another easily. Confining yourself to carry-on luggage also saves waiting at the airport. And, if a second bag of luggage gets lost, you at least have the essentials until it turns up. If you do pack a lot of clothes, you could leave things at your hotel and pick them up later. When packing, it's preferable to take dark, loose clothing. If you're going to wear shorts, make them long and loose. Be sure to bring plenty of reading material, especially if you're planning a vacation on the cayes.

protectives: Avon's Skin-So-Soft bath oil, when diluted 50% with water, has a reputation as an excellent sand flea repellent. Recent scientific tests, however, have failed to show any repellent effect in the laboratory. Sunscreen should have an 8-15 protection level or greater and should be purchased in the US. If you're going kayaking or intend to spend a lot of time in the sun and have sen-

What to Take

CLOTHING	OTHER ITEMS
socks and shoes	passport/identification
underwear	driver's license
sandals, thongs	travellers' checks
T-shirts, shirts (or blouses)	moneybelt
skirts/pants, shorts	address book
swimsuit	notebook
hat	Spanish-English dictionary
light jacket/sweater	pens/pencils
	books, maps
TOILETRIES	watch
soap	camera/film
shampoo	flashlight/batteries
towel, washcloth	snorkeling equipment
toothpaste/toothbrush	earplugs
comb/brush	compass
prescription medicines	extra glasses
chapstick/other essentials	umbrella/poncho
insect repellent	rubber boots
suntan lotion/sunscreen	laundry bag
shaving kit	laundry soap/detergent
small mirror	matches/lighter
toilet paper	frisbee/sports equipment
nail clippers	cooking supplies (if necessary)
hand lotion	

sitive skin, zinc oxide cream serves as an effective sunblock. When snorkeling, consider wearing a tee-shirt to avoid ending up with a raw back. A flashlight is essential; you might want to bring two, a larger one and one to fit in your handbag or daypack. Feminine hygiene items are rarely found outside of Belize City; bring a good supply. Likewise, all prescription medicines, creams, ointments, and other items should be brought with you.

others: Books are twice US prices so you'll also probably want to stock up before arrival. It's a good idea to have toilet paper with you, as the least expensive hotels and the park restrooms may not supply it. Film is very expensive, so be sure to bring a supply. Plastic trash bags and an assortment of different-sized baggies will also come in handy. High-topped rubber boots are an essential investment before or after your arrival. If you have unusually large feet, though, it would be a good idea to bring your own.

budget travel: If you're a budget traveler, you'll want to bring along earplugs, some rope for a clothesline, towel and washcloth, toilet paper, cup, small mirror, a universal plug for the sink, and a cotton sheet. A smaller pack is preferable because a large one will not fit on the overhead rack above the bus seats.

hikers and backpackers: If nature is your focus, you'll want to bring a rain parka, walking shoes or hiking boots, a day pack, canteen, hat, binoculars, and insect repellent, as well as a bird book or two. Loose cotton trousers are recommended; jeans take a long time to dry.

anglers: Necessities include sleeved shirts and pants, a wide-brimmed hat, and effective sun protection. For the southeast raingear is necessary, even during the dry season. Although lodges can generally arrange rentals, it's better to bring your own equipment. Bring a 20-lb. or stronger line for saltwater fishing.

MEASUREMENTS: The British system of weights and measure is used, but gasoline is sold by the American gallon. Belize operates on Central Standard Time. Electric current is 110 volts AC, but some hotels in the boonies may use 12 volt electricity supplied by generators. While some villages are without electricity, other villages (and resorts which have their own generators) have electricity only part of the day. **conversions:** A meter is equal to three feet and three inches. A kilometer equals .62 miles (about 5/9 of a mile), a square km is equal to about 3/8 of a square mile.

PHOTOGRAPHY: Film is expensive here so you might want to bring your own. Kodachrome KR 36, ASA 64, is the best all around slide film. For prints 100 or 200 ASA is preferred, while 1000 ASA is just the thing underwater. For underwater shots use a polarizing filter to cut down on glare; a flash should be used in deep water. Avoid photographs between 10 and 2 when there are harsh shadows. Photograph landscapes while keeping the sun to your rear. Set your camera a stop or a stop and a half down when photographing beaches in order to prevent overexposure from glare. A sunshade is a useful addition. Keep your camera and film out of the heat, and use silica gel packets to stave off mildew. If you're intending to shoot animals in their environments, the ideal would be to bring two camera bodies (loaded with ASA 64 and ASA 1000 film), along with 300 mm zoom and regular lenses. Animal photography is an antsy proposition owing to distances and dense vegetation. You can't hesitate or the animal may be gone! Replace your batteries before a trip or bring a spare set. Finally, remember not to subject your exposed film of ASA 400 or greater to the X-ray machines at the airport: hand-carry them through. Because local developing is very expensive and of generally poor quality, it's better to take your film home for developing.

National Parks and Nature Reserves in Belize

Name	Date Established	Acreage
Half Moon Caye Natural Monument	Mar. 1982	10,000
Crooked Tree Wildlife Sanctuary	Nov. 1984	16,000
Society Hall Nature Reserve	Nov. 1986	6,000
Cockscomb Basin Wildlife Sanctuary	Feb. 1986	102,000
Blue Hole National Park	Dec. 1986	600
Hol Chan Marine Reserve	May 1987	3,000
Guanacaste National Park	Apr. 1990	50
Bladen Bank Nature Reserve	June 1990	97,000
Five Blues Lake National Park	Apr. 1991	885
Laughing Bird Caye National Park	Nov. 1991	
Chiquibul National Park	Nov. 1991	200,000
Burdon Canal Nature Reserve	June 1992	6,000
Río Blanco National Park	Dec. 1992	100
Aguas Turbias National Park	Dec. 1992	8,950
Paynes Creek Nature Reserve	Dec. 1992	27,000
Temash/Sarstoon Nature Reserve	Dec. 1992	41,000
Monkey Bay Nature Reserve	Dec. 1992	2,250
Glovers Reef Marine Reserve	May 1993	

VISITING THE NATIONAL PARKS AND RESERVES: Many consider these treasures to be the nation's greatest attraction for visitors. However, they're universally difficult to get to if you don't have your own transportation, and, in many cases, you'll need your own food as well. One alternative to visiting on your own may be to visit the parks with a tour; see individual listings for information.

SEEING WILDLIFE: Because their survival mechanisms are geared to differing needs and circumstances, Belize's wildlife differs dramatically from that found on East Africa's open plains. While the latter depend upon strength, speed, and size, animals in Belize depend upon camouflage for survival. As a result, they are smaller and more difficult to see. If you're visiting the reserve on your own, with a group, or on a group tour, it is essential to maintain quiet. The quieter you are, the more you will see. Early morning and late afternoon are the best times for viewing wildlife. The best way to see wildlife, if you are really serious about it, is to camp. During the dry season, the animals come down to drink at waterholes during the early morning and late afternoon.

FOUNDATIONS: If you would like to help conservation in Belize, there are a number of organizations which welcome donations. The nation's foremost environmental association, the **Belize Audubon Society** (☎ 02-77369/78239, fax 02-78562; Box 1001, Belize City) supervises many of the nation's parks and reserves. One of its principal activities is environmental education. Foreign associate membership is US$25 per year and includes a subscription to their newsletter. **The Programme for Belize** (☎ 02-75616/7, 168 N Front St., Belize City) is devoted to purchasing land for environmental preservation. Memberships in **The Belize Zoo** are US$25 on up. Write The Belize Zoo, PO Box 474, Belize City, Belize. If you wish to take advantage of a tax deduction, you may send a check to Belize Zoo, c/o World Wildlife Fund-US, 12150 24th St. NW, Washington, DC 20037. Another worthy organization is the **Belize Center for Environmental Studies.** Tax deductible contributions can be sent to Belize Center, c/o "Project Lighthawk," PO Box 8163, Santa Fe, NM 87504. The **Siwa-ban Preserve** will preserve flora and fauna on the north end of Caye Caulker. To make a donation to the reserve, contact Ellen MacCrae at Galerie Hicaco on Caye Caulker or send a tax deductible donation to The Siwa-ban Foundation, 143 Anderson, San Francisco, CA. Established in 1993, The **Cubola New Art Foundation** promotes and develops Belizean artists in the fields of video, creative writing, crafts, performance arts, product design, music, and visual arts. For more information contact Cubola Publishing (☎ 093-2083) at 35 Elizabeth St., Benque Viejo. **Adopt An Acre** is an innovative program coordinated by the San Francisco Zoo, which purchases rainforest land; donors receive an "Honorary Deed" certificate. For $25 you get a half-acre parcel; $50 buys an acre, and so on. This is an ideal gift for someone who has absolutely everything. Write and make checks payable to Ecosystem Survival Plan, San Francisco Zoo, Adopt an Acre, 1 Zoo Road, San Francisco, CA 94132. Enclose $1.50 additional for postage and handling. Another worthy endeavor is the Belize Agroforestry Research Center, a project of the Tropical Conservation Foundation. Send contributions to The Tropical Conservation Foundation, 14 N Court St., Athens, Ohio 45701; $25 or more brings a subscription to the newsletter. For more information, write 209 Seneca Rd., Great Falls, VA 22066, call (703) 450-4160, or fax (703) 450-4170. The **La Ruta Maya Foundation** is dedicated to helping protect the environmental and cultural assets of the ancient Maya homelands. One of its projects is making replicas of Maya stelae including ones of Caracol. They also are offering scholarships to Central Americans, promoting parks, and working on sustainable tourism in Flores, Guatemala. For more information, write 209

Seneca Rd., Great Falls VA 22066 (☎ 703-450-4160, or fax 703-450-4170). **Earthwatch** is an organization that allows you to visit the country and to actively participate in valuable research at the same time. Volunteers contribute financially and receive an unusual experience at the same time. For more information, call (800) 776-0188. A very unusual organization working to change the face of world tourism is the **Ecotourism Society**. It publishes a set of guidelines for nature tour operators, a newsletter, and a number of other publications. Membership is $15 students, $35 ecotourists, $50 professional, and on up. For more information write Box 755, North Bennington, VT 05257. In Britain, **Tourism Concern** is an organization devoted to uniting British people who are concerned with the effects of tourism. It advocates tourism which will put long-term social and environmental health of areas affected in front of short-term pecuniary gain. For more information write Tourism Concern, Froebel College, Roehampton Lane, London SW15 5PU, UK or call 081-878-9053.

Belize City

Although it resembles the capital cities of former Anglo-African colonies and those of the West Indies, "Belize," as the city is popularly called, lacks their hustle and bustle. But, with around 25% of the total population, it's the chief commercial center and by far the busiest place you'll find. The city (pop. 47,000) overruns both sides of Haulover Creek – the name applied to the last four miles of the Belize River, a stretch along which cattle being transported to market were forced to cross.

Belize City still has the feel of the colonial seaport era. Never intended to be a permanent settlement, the town is located on a swamp without a good harbor; most of the town is pretty run down, with the majority of the houses set on piles above swampy ground. Now largely covered with landfill, its canal network once gave it the title of the "Venice of the Caribbean," and legend has it that the city is built on its former chief imports and exports: gin bottles and mahogany logs.

Belize City's location has proved to be a singularly unfortunate choice. Set on a peninsular stretch of coast a few inches below sea level amidst a mangrove swamp, its environs have served as a breeding ground for disease. The high water table has deterred the installation of an underground water supply and sewage system, and most homes depend upon rainfall for their water supply through "catchment" – cisterns which collect water rolling down galvanized iron roofs. The septic tanks are treated with chemicals and then spew their contents through open trenches that eventually empty into the ocean. This sewage provides sustenance for the hordes of hungry, government-protected catfish or "shittifish" – the catty colloquialism by which they are known – as well as the gar which live at the river's mouth. Back in town, you may experience the occasional passing nocturnal pesticide-spraying truck, with its noxious fumes intended to counter the mosquito population; shield yourself as best you can.

However, there are a few charming aspects. Along the city's streets, dilapidated houses are flanked by flowering pink, orange, and purple bougainvillea and red poinciana trees and you can see the sun-bleached white sails of schooners tied up along the banks of Haulover Creek. The names of this odoriferous town's 13 sections – such as Port Loyola, Mesopotamia, and the Barracks – literally reek of history, and the rather imaginative English phrases found on buildings provide endless entertainment for pedestrians.

Although the town has high humidity, the northeast tradewinds mitigate the steamy summer weather.

HISTORY: Belize City's roots lie with logwood. By the late 17th C, logwood was being cut in the area, and the town had its origins as a logging camp – a place where the Baymen (the white loggers) could return during the rains. Their houses once lined the sea front, while the houses of their slaves were grouped by ethnic origin and located on the south side of Haulover Creek. The locus of settlement moved here from St. George's Caye after a 1798 Spanish attack, and Belize City became the major export center for logwood and mahogany on the Bay of Honduras. British expatriates arrived in increasing numbers during the 19th C. and, as the "Scot's clique" took over the town, colonial-style wooden buildings proliferated along the shore. Arriving Anglican missionaries made the settlement a base for propagation, and the Anglican Cathedral was built in 1812 to serve a diocese that stretched all the way to Panama. Fires devastated the city in 1804, 1806, and 1856, during the same era that epidemics of yellow fever, cholera, and smallpox decimated the populace.

Belize City became the capital of the new colony of British Honduras in 1862. In 1919 returning soldiers rioted in town, protesting continuing racism and their status as second-class citizens. On Sept. 10, 1931, as the town was preoccupied with celebrating the anniversary of the Battle of St. George's Cay, a hurricane struck – flooding the town, destroying houses, and killing 1-2,000 – about 10% of the population. The subsequent neglect and squalor, coupled with an inadequate and tardy response from Britain, gave momentum to the independence movement. The decades following witnessed numerous rallies and marches.

In 1961 the city was devastated by Hurricane Hattie's 160 mph winds.They created a 14-foot tidal wave, killing 275 Belizeans and leaving 3,000 homeless. Damage was estimated at US$50 million. Despite the relocation of the capital to Belmopan after the hurricane, Belize City has continued to thrive.

ARRIVING BY AIR: The new terminal of Phillip Goldson International Airport, located at Ladyville just off the Northern Highway, is the size of just two departure gates in an average US airport. As you stand in line for customs, a drug-sniffing German shepherd is brought by. Customs officials here can be surly, and some delight in going through everything in your bag. Consult the small tourist information stand and obtain a card with the shuttle bus schedule (BZ$5, exact fare; ☎ 02-73977/77811). This antiquated school bus is still the best way to get to town, where it terminates at Belcan Bridge. As it generally leaves only once every one or two hours, it may or may not suit your schedule. From its terminal you may take another taxi to your hotel or walk into the central area in 15 minutes or so. Other alternatives from the airport are to share a taxi (BZ$30) or walk out to the main highway (two miles) and flag down a bus or truck. Domestic flights arrive and depart from the Municipal Airport, a BZ$5 taxi ride or a 40-minute walk.

ORIENTATION AND GETTING AROUND: The main streets are Regent (Front) and Albert (Back). The Haulover Creek divides the city into north and south halves. While the north area is more exclusive, the south is the commercial zone where offices, banks, and supermarkets are located. The foreshore area commands high prestige. The slum areas west of Regent and Albert Streets are dangerous at night. Most of the town is small enough to get around in on foot, but be sure to look where you're going as there are open sewers in the sidewalks. Buses are supposed to run each way once an hour; a ride is great for getting oriented – if you can find one of them that is! To the north are the exclusive areas: the fine houses of Kings Park, the more expensive hotels, and most of the embassies and consulates. The commercial district to the south features some expensive properties lining the foreshore – former residences of the elite. In the northern part of town, the recently-constructed Bel-China Bascule Bridge links Northside from Douglas Jones St. to the Southside from Vernon St.

The taxi fare for one passenger between any two points in Belize City is BZ$4. If you plan on making several stops, inform the driver and negotiate a price beforehand. The main taxi stand – which has some of the wildest gas guzzlers you'll ever see – is on Albert St. by Central Park. If you need to phone for a taxi, call Caribbean (☎ 02-72888), Imperial (02-72334), or Baldemar Varella (☎ 02-73600).

SIGHTS: Opened twice a day at approximately 5:30 AM and 6 PM so that larger vessels can pass through, the **Swing Bridge** connects the city's two main sections. In use since 1923, it was built in Liverpool, England and is the only manually-operated swing bridge still operating anywhere. During the operation, four men holding long poles turn a capstan which winches the bridge around until it's pointing towards the harbor mouth.

Originally built in 1820 on the site of another market and demolished in 1989, the current version of the **market** dates from 1991. It offers such culinary raw materials as brightly-colored fish,

Belize City

1. Paslow Building:
   General Post Office/
   Lands Dept. Office
2. Police Station
3. Supreme Court Building
4. Telephone Office
5. Bliss Institute
6. Tourist Office
7. Belize Tourism Industry
   Assoc. Office
8. City Market
9. Sea Side Guest House
10. Macy's Guest House
11. Pizza House
12. Dit's Cafe
13. St. John's Cathedral
14. Government House
15. Mom's
16. Baron Bliss Memorial/
    Ft. George Lighthouse
17. Ft. George Hotel
18. Memorial Park
19. Mexican Embassy
20. Belize Guest House
21. Prison
22. Belize Center for
    Environmental Studies
23. Municipal Airport
24. Farmer's Market
25. Bus stop for
    airport shuttle
26. Batty Bus Terminal
27. Venus/Z-Line Bus
    terminals
28. Novelo Bus terminal
29. Temporary market/
    Civic Center

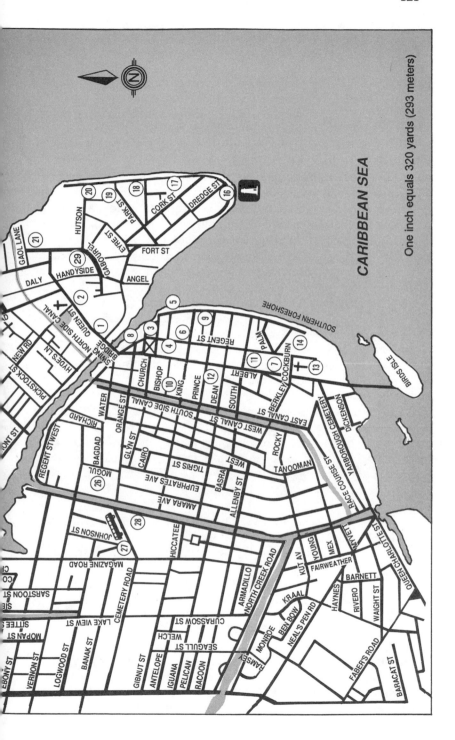

CARIBBEAN SEA

One inch equals 320 yards (293 meters)

live iguanas, and pitiful, upturned turtles, thrashing about help-lessly. Offshore, the catfish eagerly feast on whatever scraps and remains are tossed their way. Just past the market, the Mona Lisa Hotel was used as a set in the 1985 film version of Paul Theroux's novel *The Mosquito Coast*. The Swing Bridge area was also used in filming *The Dogs of War*. To the north of the Swing Bridge, the Pas-low Building – an enormous, somewhat dilapidated wooden structure – houses the post office on the first floor and other gov-ernment offices on the upper stories.

Running south from the Swing Bridge past the rotating Coca Cola clock, Albert (Back) St. hosts the main shopping area. With its wrought iron columns and red Georgian brick facade, the **Old Court House** complex, actually a group of former colonial admini-stration and court buildings, was finished in 1926, replacing an earlier building which had burnt down in 1918. Gov. Hart Bennett was helping extinguish the fire when the burning flagpole was cut down and fell on him. He later died of his injuries. A plaque com-memorates the fire. Each of its four clock faces stopped working at a different time. The Court House faces small **Redemption Park**, with its centerpiece a decorative but nonfunctional fountain. For-merly called Central Park, it was renamed on Dec. 31, 1991 when a bust was unveiled honoring labor leader Antonio Soberanís (see "History" under "Introduction").

Set a block or two behind the Court House on the waterfront, the **Bliss Institute** (open Mon. to Fri. 8:30-noon, 2-8; Sat 8:30-noon) resembles an aircraft control tower. It houses the National Arts Council which sponsors exhibitions, plays, and concerts. A sadly neglected group of stelae and altars from Caracol can be seen to the left of the entranceway. The National Library is now on Prin-cess Margaret Drive. There homesick Brits can find British news-papers.

Both Central America's oldest Anglican (Episcopalian) cathe-dral and one of the nation's oldest buildings, **St. John's Cathedral**, at the south end of Albert St, resembles a large English parish church. Construction commenced in 1812 using bricks brought over as ballast in ships. This is the only Anglican cathedral in the world outside England in which kings were crowned. Four Kings of the Mosquito Coast were crowned in the Cathedral between 1815 and 1845, each claiming title to the British protectorate which stretched along the eastern coasts of Honduras and Nicaragua. In order to cement their links with England, they also had their chil-dren baptized here. Inside, a plaque commemorates yellow fever victims. Named after the magistrate who owned the land, the Yar-borough Cemetery to the west of the Cathedral ran out of plots at the end of the 19th C. The cemetery was first used from 1781 to bury notables. Only later were the stiffs of ordinary folk welcomed, exhausting the space by 1870. At the southern end of Albert St. across the Yarborough Bridge, the Belize City Vaults, entombing 24 souls, now enclose a children's playground. After the closure of the Yarborough Cemetery, this vault method of burial was introduced by Gustav Von Olhaffen, a German officer who was the last corpse to be interred in the cemetery.

Set between the cathedral and the seafront at the southern end of Regent St. and also bordering on the Southern Foreshore, **Government House**, constructed between 1812 and 1814, was the Governor's official residence during the colonial era. Designed by British architect Christopher Wren, this elegant clapboard structure hosts official occasions and houses visiting royalty. The Prime Minister's office is also located in Government House.

Complete with a roller skating rink and concert area, **Bird's Isle**, right at the tail end of a strip of land, is attached to the mainland by a narrow wooden walkway. Many homes on Regent St. have a brick first floor and a second level of timber and shingle. Slaves were chained inside the brick sections when not at work. One example is Mrs. Thompson's House at the corner of Regent and Prince opposite the plumbing supply store. The home at the corner of Dean and Regent Streets dates from 1857.

FORT GEORGE AREA: This area received its name in 1803 after the small fort of the same name erected on a little swampy island. Losing importance after the West India Regiment moved on, the environs mutated into a fishing village, with a small bridge connecting it to the mainland. Privately leased in the 1920s, a strait separated it from town, and Key Hole Alley led to the bridge. The strait was filled in by the US-based Jefferson Construction Co. during 1922-24 at a cost of BZ$300 million. The island was fenced in by a concrete wall and, in tribute to the WWI dead, Memorial Park was built on the mound at the tip of the strip.

To the east, following along the shore, are the Custom House and adjacent wharves, the lighthouse, and the concrete tomb of Baron Bliss. Traversing the shoreline you come to the Ft. George Hotel and the neighboring Memorial Park, commemorating the WWI dead. Several of the well-preserved colonial mansions here are occupied by embassies and hotels. At the corner of Gabourel Lane and Hudson Street, is a colonial building that still houses a portion of the American Embassy. Originally built in New England, the house was taken apart and transported as ship's ballast to Belize, where it was reconstructed. Constructed in 1857, the Belize City Prison is located on Gabourel Lane and Gaol Lane. Overcrowded and without running water, it will eventually be replaced by a new facility along the Boom/Hattieville Rd. Up on Eve St., two traditional structures house the Belize City Hospital and Belize Center for Environmental Studies/Association for Belizean Archaeology.

THEFT AND CONDUCT: Although Belize City is becoming increasingly dangerous, you can be reasonably safe if you take adequate precautions. Walking alone at night may be asking for trouble. The most dangerous areas are the environs of Mesopotamia and King's Park, as well as the streets running over the South Side Canal near the bus station. Take a cab if arriving at night. Another dangerous area lies to the west of Regent and Albert Streets. Near the Big Apple, Hyde's Lane is a crack center, as is the alley between the Majestic Theatre and the Chon San II. The best way to avoid being hassled by hustlers is to shake your head and wag your finger if approached – although even this often doesn't work. In any case, don't let yourself be intimidated, because that's their game plan. The Belizeans you *want* to meet will not be ones who approach you in this fashion. Then there's the woman who comes around to hotels with a sob story: don't believe her. Avoid dealing with untrustworthy streetside moneychangers. Park your car in carparks at night for safety. Attractive women are simply inviting harassment if they wear too short skirts or revealing clothing. Don't make eye contact or answer taunts, such as, "Where is your husband?" Never wear expensive jewelry around town. Don't carry much money on your person, and try to keep on the main streets. The most recent crime wave is by thugs on bicycles, who grab gold chains, wallets, or cameras. Victims are Belizeans and tourists alike.

Belize City Practicalities

LUXURY ACCOMMODATIONS: Towering over the city, ultramodern **Radisson Ft. George Hotel** at 2 Marine Parade offers 70 rooms, a pool, and a roof deck with superb views. Paintings by Dangriga artist Benjamin Nicholas adorn the hotel. It has purchased the Holiday Inn Villa Belize across the street. Call 02-77400, fax 02-73820 or ☎ 800-552-3419, and 612-890-4405. In the US ☎ 800-44-UTELL. The 25-room **Chateau Caribbean** (☎ 02-30800) is at 6 Marine Parade. Its attractive ambience makes it popular with European visitors. Overlooking the mouth of the Belize River and only two blocks from town at 5 Southern Foreshore, the **Bellevue Hotel** (☎ 02-77051, fax 02-73253) has 42 a/c rooms with phones, an upstairs bar, and a disco. In the US ☎ 800-223-9815. Featuring a swimming pool, the gaudy 120-room **Ramada Royal Reef Hotel** (☎ 02-32670, fax 02-32660; PO Box 1248) opened along the sea at 2A South Park St. in 1991. It has two restaurants, a pool, marina, and meeting room. In the US ☎ 800-228-9898 or 800-444-4275 (for groups).

out of town: The **Best Western Biltmore Plaza** (☎ 02-32302, fax 02-32301; PO Box 959, Belize City; 800-528-1234 in the US and Canada – ask for "International Desk") is at Mile 3 on the Northern Hwy. This 90-room luxury hotel offers rooms with a choice of a/c or fans, TV, and radio. Other facilities include meeting halls, a pool and sunken pool bar, and a business center. Set on a secluded portion of the Belize River, the mahogany-constructed **Belize River Lodge** (☎ 025-2002, fax 025-2298; PO Box 459, Belize City) is set in a garden environment. Its four rooms can accommodate up to 16. Fishing is done from 18-foot skiffs. A seven-night/six-day all-inclusive fishing package is US$1,895, based on double occupancy; the single rate is US$2,232. The Lodge also operates three live-aboard vessels: 40-foot *The Permit*, 50-foot *Christy Ann*, and 52-foot *Blue Yonder*. Featuring a/c, the **Riverbend Resort** (☎ 025-2297; PO Box 48, Belize City) is at Mile 9½ in Ladyville.

houseboats: Definitely an unusual way to see Belize, **River Haven** (fax 02-32742; Box 78, Belize City) has floating 10-by-15 foot houseboats which hold up to four in two bedrooms. On board are CB and AM-FM radios, and a kitchenette. Prices run around BZ$1,200 pw or BZ$400 pd for a charter cruise with captain and lunch; shorter-term rentals are also available.

MODERATE ACCOMMODATIONS: The white-painted wooden Belize Guest House (☎ 02-77569) at 2 Hutson St. is just a few steps from the sea. There are wood-floored rooms with shared bath as well as two rooms with private bath. The large and comfortable wood-paneled living room has a comfortable couch and chairs, with cable TV. The coffee is complimentary. A good seafood restaurant and bar is downstairs. Ellen and Shawn are your hosts here, and guests are made to feel part of the family. If you're looking for snob appeal, glitz, and glamour, you've come to the wrong place. The atmosphere here is unpretentious and homey. You'll meet Major the dog, Pirate the parrot, and Savage the timid cat. Rates are from BZ$60 s and BZ$70 d (plus tax) with shared bath. One room with private bath can hold one person (BZ$70), two (BZ$90), three (BZ$110), or four (BZ$140) people. **Fort Street**

Restaurant and Guesthouse (☎ 02-30116, fax 02-78808) is at 4 Fort Street. Set in a restored colonial house, it's probably the classiest of the city's guest houses. Room rates are around BZ$90 s, BZ$120 d, BZ$150 t, and BZ$170 quad for rooms with shared bath and ceiling fans; tax is added, and breakfast is included. In the US, ☎ MAGNUM Belize at 800-240-FORT, fax 218-847-0334, or write Box 1560, Detroit Lakes, MN 56520. Set opposite the Radisson Fort George at 9 Cork St., **Colton House** (☎ 02-44666) is an intimate, family-run four-room guest house. Features here include complimentary coffee and access to a videotape library. Their one a/c room is luxury priced at around BZ$90 d plus tax. Other rooms start at BZ$60 s, BZ$70 d. There are plans to serve breakfast; it may now be available. Environmental videos are shown in the living room. The rooms are quite attractive, and Mr. Colton has a lot of singularly controversial opinions to share. Whether you agree with him or not, he's quite interesting to talk to. This place is best suited for serious, quiet types. Party animals should stay away. **Glenthorne Manor** (☎ 02-44212; PO Box 1278, Belize City), located at 27 Barracks Rd., offers a charming interior and attractively furnished, if small, rooms with high ceilings. The kitchen and refrigerator are available for use. Rates are from BZ$60 s and BZ$70 d with breakfast in season; tax and service are added. Group rates and church- and Peace Corps-affiliated discounts are available. The 12-room a/c **El Centro** (☎ 02-72413, fax 02-74553; PO Box 122, Belize City) is at 4 Bishop St. Offering a/c, cable TV, refrigerator, and conference facilities, the comfortable **Bakadeer Inn** (☎ 02-31400/323286/32363, fax 02-31963), 74 Cleghorn St., also includes breakfast in its rates. Rates are around BZ$100 s and BZ$110 d. They also offer motorbike, scooter, and bicycle rentals. The 22-room **Royal Orchid** (☎ 02-32783, fax 02-32789; PO Box 279, Belize City) is at 153 New Road (corner of Douglas). Rooms have a/c and fans, cable TV, and phones; there's a parking lot, restaurant, and meeting room. Rates are about BZ$90 s, BZ$110 d, plus BZ$20 for each additional person; children under 12 are free. **The Mopan Hotel** (☎ 02-77351/73356, fax 02-75383), 55 Regent St., is run by environmental activists, Jean and Tom Shaw. Ask them about Shawfields, their own nature reserve, which is still in the planning stage. The partially a/c 24-room **Golden Dragon Hotel** (☎ 02-72817/72067) is at 29 Queen St; it charges around BZ$37 s or d plus tax. Offering bed and breakfast, four-room **Alicia's Guest House** (☎ 02-75082) is at 8 Chapel Lane (corner of Dean St.). Featuring both partial a/c and a swimming pool as well as private baths, the **Bliss Hotel** (☎ 02-72552, 02-73310) is at 1 Water Lane. **New Archie's Hotel** (☎ 02-73303, fax 02-74159), at 74 Euphrates Ave., offers a choice of a/c or fans. **Venus** (☎ 02-77390/22132, PO Box 11482, Belize City) is at 2371 Magazine Rd. by the Venus Bus Station. **out of town:** The a/c **Rio-Haul Motel** (☎ 02-44859) is at Mile 5½ Northern Highway. The partially a/c **International Airport Hotel** (☎ 02-52150; PO Box 1253, Belize City) is, as you might suspect, near the airport. Located on Miami Rd., the 16-room partially a/c **Estell's Airport** (☎ 025-2282) is in Ladyville.

BUDGET AND LOW-BUDGET ACCOMMODATIONS: Plan on paying at least BZ$15 for the least expensive room. Other than price, one factor to consider is safety; the Fort George area is probably the safest. At 7 Eyre St., **Eyre St. Guest House** (☎ 02-77724) is one of the better low-priced guest houses. Rates range from BZ$30 s to BZ$45 d, with BZ$8 breakfasts. Another fine place to stay is the **Sea Side Guest House** (☎ 02-78339) at 3 Prince St. near the Swing Bridge. Manager Philip charges BZ$16 for a dorm bed, BZ$28 for a single, and BZ$38 for a double. There's a common area with tables, and breakfast can be ordered. Just one block from the Caye Caulker departure dock, **North Front Street Guest House** (☎ 02-77595) is at 124 North Front Street. The recently-remodeled rooms are BZ$15 s and BZ$25 d. Baths are shared. Nearby are **Bon Aventure** (☎ 02-44248) at No. 122 next door and **Dim's Mira Rio** (☎ 02-44970) across the street at No. 59. Its rooms all have a private bath. And don't overlook five-room **Bell's Hotel** (☎ 02-31023) at 140 North Front St., offering fans and shared bath. **Freddie's Guest House** (☎ 02-44396), 86 Eve St., has only three rooms but is secure and peaceful. Comfortable, quiet, and clean, **Marin's Travelodge** (☎ 02-45166) is at 6 Craig St. **Vinats Hotel**, 8 Gabourel Lane, is under the same management as Vinats Guest House, 59 Regent St. W.; the latter is in a less safe area. Equipped with fans and shared bath, six-room **America Hotel** (☎ 02-77384) is at 11 Dean St. Offering similar facilities, the **Annis Louise** (☎ 02-44670) is at 3 Freetown Road. Others include the **Belcove Hotel** (02-73054), 9 Regent St.; **Dianne's Hotel** at 65 George St; **Eden Sweet Hotel** (☎ 02-74043) at 137 Regent St. West; two-room **Isabel's Guest House** at 3 Albert St.; **Jane's Hotel** (☎ 02-44240) at 64 Barrack Rd.; **Simon Quan's "Luxury" Hotel** (☎ 02-45793) at 24-26 Queen St.; **Kitty's Travelodge** (☎ 02-44966) at 58 Daly St.; the 17-room **Las Palmeras Hotel** (☎ 02-73345, PO Box 299) at cor. George and Bishop Sts.; **Riverview Hotel** (☎ 02-73392), 25 Regent St.; **Violet's Hotel** (☎ 02-44171) at 41 Barrack Rd.; **R-B's Hotel** (☎ 02-30510) at 162 Freetown Rd.; **Fairweather Guest House** (☎ 02-72866) at 9 Rectory Lane; **The Taj Mahal Hotel** (☎ 02-72931) at 16 Albert St.; **The Gold Star Guest**

House (☎ 02-33160) at 114 New Rd. (it charges BZ$20 for rooms with a fan and shared bath). Don't try smoking pot in your room. The owner will call the fuzz, as he did on one British lad. **camping:** The only alternative is mainly for trailer vehicles. The **Caribbean Trailer Court** (☎ 02-45086), 5224 Barracks Rd., has RV and regular camping. It is a long way out of town, however, and security is poor.

DINING OUT: Four Fort Street has a pleasant atmosphere as well as unusual cuisine. Its Sunday brunch features everything from seafood quiche (BZ$18) to mosquito toast (French toast stuffed with cream cheese and served with fruit, BZ$12). Another swank bistro is **Chateau Caribbean**, 6 Marine Parade. Formal **Fort George Hotel** offers American and European cuisine in an a/c setting; its sister hotel, **The Villa**, across the road, also offers fine dining. **The Bellevue**, 5 Southern Foreshore, serves European food with an extensive wine list. Located at the corner of King St. and East Canal, the **Mexican Corner** offers escabeche, chimole, tacos, salbutes, and other dishes. Bring your own wine or beer, as only soft drinks are available. **The Barracks Restaurant and Bar**, 136 Barracks Rd., is at Barracks Green, a short taxi ride from town on the way to the Muncipal Airport. It serves lunch and dinner from Monday to Saturday; dinner only is served on Sunday. Set at 164 Newtown Barracks Rd., **The Grill** (☎ 02-45020) offers charcoal-grilled fish, chicken, and beef. In addition to gourmet fare, the **Ramada Royal Reef** also has a BZ$12 business lunch daily, except Wednesday. At 3580 Sittee St. near the Civic Center by the river, the **Red Roof Lounge** (☎ 02-77158) is open for dinner late, has live music, and offers "a personalized drink mixed by the reading of your psychic." At Mile 4½ on the Northern Hwy. facing the seafront, the **Privateer** bar and restaurant features live music on weekends.

BUDGET DINING: Reasonably-priced (BZ$10-18 for entrees) **Sea Rock** (☎ 02-34105) is an East Indian restaurant with wonderfully spiced vegetarian and other dishes ranging from vegetable *samosa to nan* to *biryani, tandoori,* and vegetable curries. Wall decor ranges from a tapestry of dogs playing pool to Indian batiks and a painting of a little white cat with roses. It's open daily from 11-10:30 except on Monday, when it opens at 6. Just around the corner, seedier and less expensive **Krishna's Fast Food** is a hole in the wall featuring BZ$3 breakfasts. Unique, unforgettable and reasonable, the **Ark Restaurant** is on the lower part of North Front St. at Gabourel Lane. Featured are Spanish dishes, lobster, pancakes, waffles, juices, and fish dishes, including séré, a traditional Garifuna fish and coconut milk soup rarely found in restaurants. All this comes with the accompaniment of a hissing radio blaring gospel programming and the companionship of a merry ex-marine. Located up from the Ark and resembling a metal aircraft hangar, the orange **Temporary Market** is your best bet for truly cheap food. Food stalls sell fried fish, fried bread, and beans for breakfast, as well as various meat dishes; lunches run about BZ$3.50. You can also buy Iron Man Seaweed drink. Reasonably priced and quite hospitable, the restaurant below the **Belize Guest House**, 2 Hutson St., specializes in seafood. At the Belize Commercial Center across the Swing Bridge and to the left, you'll find **Kadel's** on the second floor, which serves reasonably-priced Belizean-style food with lunchtime specials. **The Picadilly** at 35 Queen St. has reasonable prices, a/c interior and an outdoor patio with ceiling fans and an epiphyte collection suspended from metal grills. The most reasonably priced place for pizza (including slices), **Pizza House**, is on Albert St. near the BTIA office; it's closed Mondays. More expensive, **Buenas Pizzas** at 16 Albert St. features pizza and breakfast specials. One excellent place for local food is the **Black Orchid**, 48 Albert St., which is open daily from 9 AM-10 PM and Sunday from 9-5. If you want to eat fish, get there before noon. It consistently sells out. At 50 King St., **Dit's** offers pastries, patties, conch fritters, and conch and cowfoot soups on Friday and Saturday. Acclaimed by some as the best place to eat local food, **Macy's Cafe**, marked by a flickering sign at 18 Bishop St., is dark, with plenty of whirring fans and laminated placemats featuring fruit plates and flowers. Sadly, it also serves sea turtle. One of the few places where you can dine in an outdoor atmosphere, **G. G.'s Cafe & Patio** is at 2-B King St. Prices are low (except for fish), and fresh brewed coffee is served. **The Marlin** is at 11 Regent St. West. Featuring daily happy hour from 6 to 7 and live entertainment every Thursday from 5:30, it specializes in seafood. **Dominique and Rochelle's**, 161 George St., serves Belizean and American food. **Big Daddy's** on Pickstock St., (two blocks from North Front St.) serves good vegetarian food. **Hotel El Centro's** restaurant at 4 Bishop St. offers lunch specials for BZ$6-8. **Bel's Taco** is a hole-in-the-wall Mexican spot on Hyde's Lane. Very competitively priced, **Mom's** has long been a favorite with visitors and is the closest thing the city has to a hangout. It's open from 6 AM to 10 PM, Sunday through Friday. Mom's is newly located at 7145 Slaughterhouse Rd. near the Technical College. Owner Sue Williams now offers a Belizean-style salad bar and expanded gift shop in addition to her menu of inexpensive Belizean and other dishes, including burritos and a vegetarian plate. Opposite the technical school on Freetown Rd., **Trev's** features Jamaican-style food. Located across the street from Save U, where the Northern Highway comes into town, **Raoul's** offers Mexican and Belizean food.

CHINESE RESTAURANTS: There are so many Chinese restaurants in town that you could spend days visiting them all. Some give new meaning to the word kitsch. Dark and cool **Friendship Restaurant**, 2 King St., is decorated with Christmas lights. **Ping Woo** at Cinderella Square, curiously enough, has good rice and beans. **Chon Saan II**, opposite the Texaco station at 184 North Front St., has large servings of vegetables. Chinese videos show in the "dinning room." Also try the **Caribbean Restaurant**, 36 Regent St.; **New Archie's Restaurant**, 74 Euphrates Ave. (Dim Sum served on Sundays from 10-3); **Hong Kong Restaurant**, 50 Queen St.; **Golden Dragon**, 29 Queen St.; **New Chon Saan Restaurant**, 55 Euphrates Ave.; **Lotus Garden Restaurant**, 81 Cemetery Rd; **Tam Yi**, cor. Magazine Rd. and Vernon St.; and the **Ocean**, 96 Barracks Rd. at Pickstock St.

BAKERIES AND SNACKS: There are a number of bakeries around town, including one near the Environmental Center. The **Eve St. Mini Mart** sells cupcakes, cookies, and crackers. **Scoops** on the same street sells ice cream from BZ$1. Bananas and peanuts are sold near the Swing Bridge, and **Creamy Corner** on Albert St. is just across from the bridge. **Blue Bird**, 35 Albert St., has burgers, sandwiches, and tropical fruit drinks. **The Play Boy Restaurant** on King St. has good sandwiches. A number of other places are in this same area of town. Across from the Budget Store on North Front St., **Ding Ho** sells ice cream. The snack place **"Hello Amigo"** is opposite the Farmer's Market near the Belcan Bridge.

MARKET SHOPPING: Visit the **Temporary Market** which is where the inhabitants of the original market were moved "temporarily" when it was rebuilt. Here, in addition to the usual piles of vegetables, bunches of garlic, cabbages, greens, herbs, and spices are sold. There are also corked bottles of coconut oil and bottles of "honney." Rebuilt in 1991, the **Belize Commercial Center** stands next to the Swing Bridge. The original market dated from 1845 and the area was originally known as Mule Park because local vendors and farmers would tether their mules and buggies in front to be watered. Inside, besides vegetables and the like, you'll also find the Daiquiri Factory, which dispenses expensive (BZ$6-10) mixed drinks from machines which resemble front-loading washers. You can buy sexy panties at PJ's Modern Romance, and Laurine Chocolates sells pricey handmade chocolates. However, if you want atmosphere, you're better off at the Temporary Market. Hops and other items are sold at a small shop on the right-hand side of the Swing Bridge. Hops are claimed to "bringeth down women's courses, and expel urine." Also visit the **Farmer's Market** near the Belcan Bridge. For a good selection of alcohol try **Gonzalo Quinto & Sons**, 11 Queen St. Doubling as a sort of department store, **Brodies** is the largest supermarket. Sample average prices: 75¢/lb. for potatoes; 90¢/lb. for onions; 30¢/lb. for brown sugar; 75¢/lb. for rice; 85¢/lb. for cabbage; fresh eggs BZ$2.80/doz. (including tray); three apples for BZ$4.50; tomatoes for BZ$3.50/lb.; fresh milk, BZ$1.85/qt.; sliced bread, BZ$1/loaf; cassava bread, BZ$1.25/pkg.; ground steak, BZ$4.50/lb.; ground sirloin, BZ$5.30/lb; Rye Crisp crackers, BZ$5/8 oz.; 12 Nature Valley granola bars, BZ$10; Hershey's Cocoa, BZ$19/lb.; Taster's Choice instant coffee, BZ$10/4 oz.; grated parmesan cheese, BZ$4.15/3 oz.; McCormick Garlic powder, $3.50/1.3 oz; Baby Ruth bar, BZ$1.30; can of Diet Coke, BZ$1.25; bottle of Belikin beer, BZ$2.25; 12 oz. can of Old Milwaukee beer, BZ$4.50; 15 fl. oz. of Alberto VO5 Shampoo BZ$6.75; Crest toothpaste, BZ$6.30/6½ oz.; Kleenex tissues (250, 2 ply), BZ$8; Lightning Anise, BZ$9/750 ml; Ginger Wine, BZ$4.25/750 ml; Fandango Papaya and Banana Wines, BZ$5/bottle; Dewar's Scotch, BZ$33/750 ml.; Marlboro cigarettes, BZ$41/carton; Independence cigarettes, BZ$ 15.50/carton; Kodak 36 Gold 100, BZ$13; month's strip of Ovral contraceptives, BZ$4; one condom BZ$1.65; Deep Woods Off, BZ$7; Scotch tape 30½ yds. BZ$3.20; and patron saint votive candles from BZ$4.50.

ENTERTAINMENT: Evenings bring quiet to town. Along the seafront in the Ft. George area it's all quiet, with rustling palm leaves and gentle lapping surf – save for an occasional passing car blaring "LA Woman." The streets are nearly deserted on Sundays when the main distractions to your solitude will come from hustlers and religious radio and TV broadcasts. However, there are a number of places to go and boogie at night. The **Hard Rock Cafe** is just a block away from Mom's and near the theater. **The Bellevue**, 5 Southern Foreshore, has a disco on weekends. Popular with locals, the **Big Apple** (☎ 02-44758), 67 North Front St., features live bands. The **Red Roof Lounge** (☎ 02-77158), 3580 Sittee St. near the Civic Center by the river, has live bands. The **Lumba Yaad** is a popular eating, drinking, and dancing club. It's located along the Haulover Creek river bank just outside town on the Northern Higway. The nation's most famous brothel, **Raoul's Rose Garden**, is out on the way to the airport.

bars: The most happening place is the bar beneath the **Belize Guest House** at 2 Hutson St., where you can meet an incredible assortment of local characters – whether long-staying visitors, local transplants, or indigenous Belizeans. The Fort George has the **Paddle Lounge** where sports afficionadoes will find a wide-screen TV. Located at the southern end of Foreshore St., **Sea Breezes Bar** is a pleasant spot. **Dim's Mira Rio's** bar has a veranda overlooking the ocean and is a favorite with boat owners. Also try the **Pub**, 91 North Front St. Out of town, the Belize Biltmore Plaza has the **Squires Lounge**, which features (gasp! groan!) karaoke. Sing along to the insipid song of your choice.

concerts: The 5,000-seat **Belize City Civic Centre** has occasional events. Check the newspapers and watch for posters.

INFORMATION: The **Belize Tourist Bureau** (☎ 02- 77213/73255, fax 02-77490; PO Box 325, Belize City) is located at 83 North Front St., just a few blocks down from the Swing Bridge, past the PO and on the right. The **Belize Tourism Industry Association/BTIA** (☎ 02-78709/75717, fax 02-78710; Box 62) has its offices at 99 Albert St. The **Belize Center for Environmental Studies** (☎ 02-45545, PO Box 666) is at 55 Eve St., just north of the Fort George area. It has a library containing a large amount of information on Belize, which may be used with permission. The Economic/Commercial Section of the **US Embassy** (☎ 02-77161, PO Box 286, Belize City) dispenses handouts and information on trade and investment opportunites and procedures in Belize. The Commercial Library is open Monday to Friday, 8:30-noon, 1:30-4:30 and on Wednesday from 8:30 to noon. The **USAID Mission** (☎ 02-31066, PO Box 817, Belize City) has its office at the corner of Queen St. and Gabourel Lane. The offices of the **Belize Audubon Society** (☎ 02-34987/3504; PO Box 1001, Belize City) are in the Old Customs Bldg. at 12 Fort St.; it's readily identifiable by the toucan poster outside. Founded in Britain in 1989 with the intention of saving 250,000 acres of rainforest, the headquarters of the **Programme for Belize** (☎ 02-75616/7) are at 168 North Front St. Located at 63 Regent St., the **Chamber of Commerce** (☎ 02-73148/74394, fax 02-74984) offers a wealth of information on commercial opportunities in Belize. Selling a two-sheet 1:250,000 projection of the entire country, as well as 1:50,000 section maps, the **Lands Dept. Office** is on the second floor of the Paslow Building above the PO.

SERVICES: The **PO** is in the Paslow Bldg. on the Ft. George side of the Swing Bridge. It's open Monday to Thursday from 8:30 to noon and 1 to 4, closing at 5:30 on Friday. The parcel office is on Church St. just past Barclays Bank. **BTL's** office is also on Church St.; overseas and long distance calls can be made from here. First you must pay a deposit and the operator will dial the number. Although it's open daily from 8 AM to 9 PM, only collect calls can be made on Sundays. **TACA** (☎ 02-77257) is located in Belize Global Travel, 41 Albert St. At 13 Albert St., **Tropical Vision** will do faxes and photocopies. **The Belize Laundromat** (☎ 23-1117) at 7 Craig St. does laundry for BZ$10/load, and the **Belize City Dry Cleaners and Coin Laundry** (☎ 02-75153), 3 Dolphin St., offers delivery service. Film can be purchased at **Venus Photo**, Albert and Bishop Sts. **The Acupuncture Massage Center** (☎ 02-31834) is at 8 Craig St. Chinese newspapers may be purchased at the **Bolinas Shop**, 158 North Front St. **The Belize Country Club** (☎ 02-33779) is out on the Western Highway at Mile 8.5. It has horseback riding, a pool, a tennis court, and a "gymnastic" room. It's chiefly open on weekends.

HEALTH: Brodie's Pharmacy (☎ 27-7776, ext. 26) is the place to go for drugs. One medical practitioner recommended by the US Embassy is **Dr. Manuel Lizama** (☎ 02-45138) at 13 Handyside St., Belize City. **St. Francis Hospital** (☎ 02-77068), 28 Albert St., is a small private hospital. **Belize Medical Services** (☎ 02-30303/30098), 5791 St. Thomas St., is a prominent private clinic.

TRAVEL AND TOUR AGENCIES: Most tour agencies run packages to the following destinations, often in combination: Cockscomb, Mountain Pine Ridge, Baboon Sanctuary, Altun Ha, Xunantunich and Guanacaste Park, Lamanai, and Crooked Tree. Some also offer excursions to Tikal for a hefty US$2-300. Prices average US$60 for a day tour. Operated by the husband and wife team of Sarita and Lascelle Tillett, **S & L Guided Tours** (☎ 02-77593/evening 73062; PO Box 700, 91 North Front St., Belize City) offer the usual variety of trips. Their half-day tours to Altun Ha or the Baboon Sanctuary are a comparatively modest BZ$25. **Jal's Travel and Tours**, 148 North Front St., runs standard trips ranging from Bermudian Landing (BZ$25, half-day) to Mountain Pine Ridge/Xunantunich (BZ$60, full day). **Belize Mesoamerica** (☎ 02-73383; PO Box 1217, Belize City) offers a large number of tours including trips to all of the major ruins and reserves as well as reef trips and a "Manatee Experience." Their office is at 4 South Park St. At Mile 2½ along the Northern Highway, **Blackline** (☎ 02-44155) offers a similar "Manatee Magic" trip, river and reef tours, fishing excursions, and dive trips. Set in the Bellevue Hotel on 5 Southern Foreshore, **Maya Circuit Tours** (☎ 02-77051; PO Box 428, Belize City) offers hotel-and-tour packages with optional rental car. **Aerobel Ltd.** (☎ 02-72692/31938; 12 Douglas Jones St.) specializes in group package tours to destinations such as Tikal and Cancún. **Gilly's Personalized Inland Tours** (☎ 02-77630/77613; 31 Regent St.) features a range of trips from a walk along the Panti Trail to a visit to Lamanai. A full service travel agency, **Belize Global Travel** (☎ 02-77185/77363/77364) is at 41 Albert St. **Singing Woods Tours** (☎ 02-31070) is at 38 New Rd. The **Belcove Hotel** (02-73054), 9 Regent St., offers day trips to the reef at Gallows Point. **Seven Candles Cab Service** (☎ 02-31979, VHF 152.975; Box 820, Belize City) offers a/c charters including lunch to destinations such as Xunantunich, Altun Ha, the Baboon Sanctuary, Lamanai, Crooked Tree, and others. Other Belize City-based agencies include **Caribbean Holidays Ltd.** (☎ 02-73131/72593; 81 Albert St.), **Maya Land Tours** (☎ 02-30515; 64 Bella Vista), **Maya Mar Tours** (☎ 02-72262; PO Box 1234, Belize City), **Mayaworld Safaris** (☎ 02-31063; West Landivar or PO Box 997, Belize City), **Native Guide System** (☎ 02-75819/78247; 1 Water Lane or PO Box 1045, Belize City), **Oswald Gillett** (☎ 02-78736; 66 Dean and Euphrates Ave.), **Gilly's Inland Tours** (☎ 02-77630/77613; 31 Regent St.), **Melmish Mayan Tours** (☎ 02-45221; PO Box 934, Belize City), **Pancho's Guided Tours** (☎ 02-45554; 5747 Lizarraga Ave.), **Rosy Tours** (☎ 02-30341; 194 North Front St. or PO Box 1681, Belize City), **Royal Palm Travel Services** (☎ 025-2534; Belize International Airport), and **Thrifty Tours** (☎/fax 02-75491; PO Box 1678, Belize City).

DIVING: Contact Frank Bounting (brother of Mom's manager Sue Williams) at Belize Diving Services (PO Box 667, Belize City; ☎ 02-22143). He rents equipment and offers instruction and diving. At Mile 2½ along the Northern Highway, **Blackline** (☎ 02-44155) offers dive trips.

CAR RENTALS: Renting a car is quite an expensive proposition here so be sure to check around. **Crystal Auto Rental** (☎ 02-30921; Mile 1½ Northern Highway, is popular, as is **Budget** (☎ 02-32435/33986, fax 02-30237, 800-527-0700 in the US and Canada). Other agencies include **Avis** at the Ft. George Hotel (☎ 02-78637); **Lionel Gordon** (☎ 02-72184), 113 Amara Ave.; **Lewis** (☎ 02-74461), 23 Cemetery Rd.; **Maya World Safaris** (☎ 02-31584), West Landivar; **National** (☎ 02-31586), 126 Freetown Rd.; **Pancho's** (☎ 02-

45554), 5747 Lizarraga Ave.; and **Sutherland** (☎ 02-73582), 127 Neal Pen Rd. For the most current list check the yellow pages.

BIKE RENTALS: Located at the Bakadeer Inn, **Bike Belize** (☎ 02-31400, fax 02-31963) rents motorbikes, scooters, and bicycles.

EMBASSIES: The **US Embassy** (☎ 02-77161) is at 20 Gabourel Lane. **Mexico** (☎ 02-45367), at 20 Park St. near the Belize Guest House, issues tourist cards the same day. **El Salvador** (☎ 02-44318) is at 120 New Road. **Honduras** (☎ 02-45899) is at 91 North Front St.

EVENTS AND FESTIVALS: There are three important holidays. On March 9th the death of the somewhat eccentric British baron with a Portuguese title, Baron Bliss, is commemorated by a formal ceremony at his tomb followed by fishing and sailing regattas. The holiday commemorating the Battle of St. George's Caye (on Sept. 10, 1798) is spread over an entire week and includes religious services and carnival celebrations. A parade takes place in Belize City on the 10th. Commemorating the nation's independence on Sept. 21, 1981, National Independence Day includes a variety of food, music, and cultural activities.

CRAFTS AND SHOPPING: Most businesses are open from 8 to noon and from 1 to 4; some reopen from 7 to 9. The entire city closes down on Sunday. The shops are generally small. Compared to Guatemala, Belize does not have an impressive variety of crafts, but Belize City is a good place to shop for what is available. On the Ft. George side of Fort St. across from the Audubon and Maya offices in the old TACA warehouse next to the BDF Maritime Wing, the **National Handicraft Center** is a great place to shop. They have an excellent selection of cassette tapes (BZ$12) by local artists including Pupa Curly and Bella Caríb, a number of books including copies of this guide, and an intriguing selection of craft items. Zericote woodcarvings are sold at **Brodies Dept. Store.** At 39 Albert St. West, **Rachel's Art Gallery** offers paintings, novelties, and art supplies. The **Philatelic Bureau**, inside the General Post Office on the western side, sells stamps, which you can give to your stamp-collecting friends or relatives. At 93 North Front St., the **Budget Store** sells an extensive collection of tee-shirts, jewelry, and used books and clothes. **Go-Tees** on Regent St. has an assortment of tee-shirts and other souvenirs. Featuring photo processing and accessories and Belizean music, **Venus Photos and Records** is at the corner of Albert and Bishop Streets. Other photo supplies are available at **Brodie's** on Regent St. and at **Rosales Ampli-Foto**, 42 Albert St. Practical items such as Coleman fuel and machetes can be purchased at **Habet & Habet** at the corner of West and Basra Streets. **Hofius Hardware** is at 19 Albert St. Out of town at the Belize Biltmore Plaza, **El Papagayo Gift Shop** has a fine selection of crafts and other items.

BOOKSTORES: The nation's largest selection of books and magazines is to be found at the **Book Center** on Regent St. West. Another place with a fine selection is the **Book Center**, 114 North Front St., just up form the Swing Bridge. **Mom's** sells current magazines and newspapers, and the **Budget Store**, 93 North Front St., has used books. Books can also be found in the gift shop of the **Audubon Society** on Fort St., **National Handicraft Center**, and at **El Papagayo Gift Shop** at the Belize Biltmore Plaza.

VICINITY OF BELIZE CITY: The city can be used as a base for exploring many nearby areas, including Altun Ha, Bermudian Landing, the Zoo, and the Baboon Sanctuary. (For information on tours see above). Other cayes can be visited for day trips or for longer stays (see the next chapter). Located 16 miles from Belize

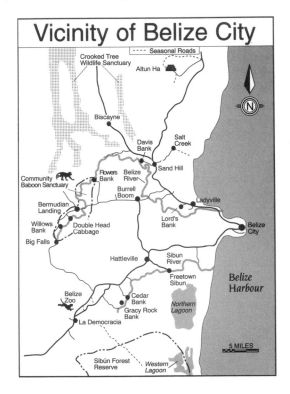

Vicinity of Belize City

City on the road to Cayo and housing 2-3,000, **Hattieville** was originally a temporary shelter for hurricane victims. While today most of the buildings are ramshackle, they appear permanent enough. The highest of all the limestone outcrops. **Gracie Rock** near the Sibún River still has the ruins of the set for the movie, *Mosquito Coast.*

FROM BELIZE CITY: Belize City is the transportation hub, and you'll likely pass through here one or more times if you're traveling around the nation by bus. Terminals of the four main bus lines are located in Mesopotamia, a slum area around the Collet Canal and Magazine Rd. The oldest and largest company is Batty which serves the north and west.

   to the north: The main bus route runs from Belize City to Orange Walk (two hrs.) to Corozal (one hr.) to Chetumal (one hr.). Batty buses (☎ 02-74924) depart hourly from 4 to 11, leaving from 54 E. Collet Canal. Their buses to Chetumal depart at 4, 5 and 6 (express) and at 7, 8, 9, 10, 11. Both the express and the regular bus are the same price. From Magazine Rd., Venus (☎ 02-3354/7390) buses leave hourly at 11:45, 1, 1:30, 2, 2:30, 3, 3:30, 4, 4:30, 5, 5:30, 6, and 7. Buses to Sarteneja leave on North Front St. at the gas station, near the boats for Caye Caulker; one generally leaves at

Local Airlines in Belize

Name	Phone	Destinations
Tropic Air	026-2012 02-45671 800-422-3435 in US	Corozal, San Pedro, Caye Caulker, Caye Chapel, Placencia, Punta Gorda, Flores
Maya Airways	02-72312 800-552-3419 in US	San Pedro, Caye Caulker, Caye Chapel, Placencia, Dangriga, Punta Gorda
Island Air	026-2435/2945 02-31140/31707 fax 02-44502 800-521-1247 in US	San Pedro, Caye Caulker, Caye Chapel, Corozal
Skybird	02-32596/33744	Caye Caulker
Caribee Air Service	02-44253 fax 02-31031	Charter only
Su-Bec Air Service	02-44027	Charter only
Javier's Flying Service	02-45332 fax 02-32731	Charter only

around noon. For information about buses to other destinations, see the specific destination involved.

heading south: James buses leave from the Pound Yard Bridge in front of the Esso Service Station on Mon., Wed., and Fri. at 7 AM and on Sat. and Sun. at 9. The late departures allow passengers arriving from Guatemala to make connections. All stop in Belmopan, Dangriga, and Mango Creek. Z-Line buses (☎ 02-702201/73937) depart from Magazine Rd. daily at 10, 12, 2, and 4; an additional bus departs Mon. at 6 PM. A new bus line offering a direct bus to Placencia (which would depart on Mon., Wed., and Fri. at noon) may also be running. Ask around.

heading west: From 54 E. Collet Canal, Batty buses leave Mon. through Sat. at 6:30, 8, 9, and 10, as well as on Sun. at 6:30, 7:30, 8:30, 9:30, and 10:30 AM. From 19 W. Collet Canal, Novelo's (☎ 02-71160/71161) buses depart at 11, noon, 1, 2, 3, 4, 5, 5:30, and 6, Mon. to Sat., and at noon, 2, 3, and 4 on Sun.

by boat: Boats (BZ$15, going; BZ$12 return) leave for Caye Caulker until 4 PM from A&R's Shell Station on North Front St. near the Swing Bridge. The *Andrea* (BZ$20) for San Pedro on Ambergris Caye departs Mon. through Fri. at 4 PM and on Sat. at 1 PM from the dock of the Bellevue Hotel, 5 Southern Foreshore.

departing by air: It's a BZ$30 taxi ride to the International Airport or you can take the shuttle. If you're leaving the country, be sure to save the BZ$22.50 you'll need to pay the departure tax. If you want to change money back, you'll need to fill out a form; expect to lose a few percentage points. In the departure lounge – which functions both for international and domestic flights – you'll find the duty-free shops, as well as a cafeteria. If going to the Municipal Airport, you can take a cab or face a long, hot walk. Planes leave for all over the country (Corozal, San Pedro/Ambergris, Caye Caulker, Caye Chapel, Dangriga, Placencia, and Punta Gorda) from both terminals. For individual listings, see "getting there" under the specific destination.

The Reef and the Cayes

 You can travel the world over and not find anything like the cayes. Australia has its barrier reef but no islands; the Caribbean and Indonesia have islands galore but no comparable reefs. Stretching south of Chetumal Peninsula, these offshore islands are without a doubt the most striking feature on the Caribbean coast of the Yucatán Peninsula. Although locals maintain there are as many of these islands as there are days in the year, they actually number around 450. Over 150 miles of barrier reef form the edge of the coastal shelf block, with cayes strewn along this block as well as the deep sea banks just offshore. Most are uninhabited; the major settlements are on Ambergris Caye and Caye Caulker. Traditionally, these villages have subsisted through fishing and cocals (coconut plantations), but they are becoming increasingly dependent upon tourism for their livelihood. Underwater visibility is seldom less than 50 feet, and during March, April, and May, you may be able to see as far as 100-200 feet. The clearest area is around Lighthouse Reef Atoll.

GEOGRAPHICAL FEATURES: With a combined area of some 212 square miles, the cayes run the length of the country and lie 10-40 miles offshore. There are three types. Densely covered with mangroves, the wet cayes are partially or fully submerged at times and resemble bizarre floating forests sailing on the Caribbean. Barren coral outcrops comprise the second category. Finally, sand cayes are like miniature South Pacific islands, with coconut palms and white sand beaches. The three atolls are Turneffe Reef, Glovers, and Lighthouse. Although the area (including coastline, reef, and islands) has been proposed as a World Heritage Site under UNESCO protection, Belize is not a signatory to the World Heritage Convention. Only about 20 of the 450 cayes have been developed at all for tourism.

LAYOUT: Two tiers of atolls lie outside the Barrier Reef area. The Turneffe Island group is the first one to the east; the two groups further out are Lighthouse Reef and Glovers Reef. Their northeast-to-southwest tilt is due to a block-fault system which shapes the shelf and the Bahía de Chetumal. They are set apart from the Barrier Reef and from one another by sharply-sloped submarine trenches. The first cayes you reach travelling from Belize City are The Drowned Cayes, a chain of wet cayes.

FORMATION: For the most part temporary, a caye is formed when a mangrove seedling takes root at a shallow point on the coral rock of a continental shelf. As the red mangroves grow, silt and debris accumulate, soil forms, and the caye grows. Always tenuous, it may be wiped off the map by a tropical storm or hurricane, or even by a change in the currents. Islands split apart by hurricanes include St. George's Caye and Caye Caulker. Atolls are circular or horseshoe-shaped coral reefs with slender, sandy islets formed by wind, storms, and surf.

HUMAN HISTORY: The first people to reach the cayes were Maya, who settled on a number of the islands. Probably the most important settlement was on Ambergris, but ancient middens (shell heaps) are found on a number of cayes. The area was first charted by Spaniards arriving between 1528 and 1532. After the battle of St. George's Caye in 1798, English names were permanently applied to the territory. Today, except on the islands developed for tourism, the standard of living remains extremely basic. Of the three main traditional livelihoods (fishing, coconut farming, and sponge cultivation), only fishing remains prominent, and lobsters and conch are becoming increasingly scarce. There's generally no electricity, and rainwater remains the only water source. Chickens and pigs supplement the inhabitants' diet, but everything else must be brought in by boat.

ENVIRONMENTAL PROBLEMS: Although from the air the cayes may appear to be bits of paradise, domestic sewage frequently washes back onto the windward side of the inhabited islands, and tar may be a problem on some beaches. The islands and the reef are part of a complex and highly fragile ecosystem, one which fishermen and tourists alike have affected with devastating consequences. On Ambergris the construction of so many hotels has drawn down the water table to the point where, until the recent completion of a new water system, locals have had to drink sewage-laced salty water. Overfishing has threatened the fish population, and lobsters may become extinct in the area if the illegal harvesting of pre-reproductive ones continues. Out-of-season fishing, meanwhile, threatens the fish population.

Another problem has come from land developers who have transformed protective mangrove reef habitats into beachfront lots as on the south end of Ambergris Caye. This reduces fish and wildlife habitats, cutting down the amount of organic material released into the surrounding water, and exposing the coastline to erosion. These same developers are creating a series of canals and lots in an area of dwarf basin mangroves downwind of the San Pedro airport, using material suctioned from seagrass beds. This area is apparently not high enough or stable enough to support homes. If homes are built, they will have a negative effect on the surrounding seagrass beds. In tourist areas, the presence of nutrient-rich effluent from overloaded septic tanks and garbage dumps is fostering algae growth, posing a mortal threat to reefs and seagrass communities. Another threat comes from spills of fertilizer, oil, and other materials by ships coming in and out of Belize City.

Cayes Near Belize City

Moho Caye

A half-mile offshore from St. John's College on Princess Margaret Drive, this island once quarantined victims of smallpox and other contagious diseases. A cemetery contains some of their remains. It's the home of **Maya Landings** (☎ 02-45798, fax 02-30263), a yacht rental operation which also features diving; excursions are offered to the Río Dulce and to the Blue Hole. To get here either hire a boat or pull a Chairman Mao and swim.

Gallows Point

Set seven miles east, this is the nearest point to the town where you can snorkel. Moderately-priced, the **Wave** (☎ 02-73054) offers fishing, scuba, and glass bottom boats; airport transportation and meals are included in the rates. For information write 9 Regent St., Belize City. **Weir Dow Marina** is also on the island. Set just to the south of Gallow's Point Reef, **English Caye** has a lighthouse which marks the entrance to English Caye Channel. Feel free to drop in and visit; it may be possible to stay overnight if you're camping.

Spanish Lookout Caye

The very expensive **Spanish Bay Resort** (☎ 02-77288/72725, fax 02-72797, ☎/fax 02-31960; Box 35, Belize City) offers a restaurant/bar and an attractive ambience. This diving resort's 10 rooms are in five cottages on stilts; they have fans. It's about a 20-minute

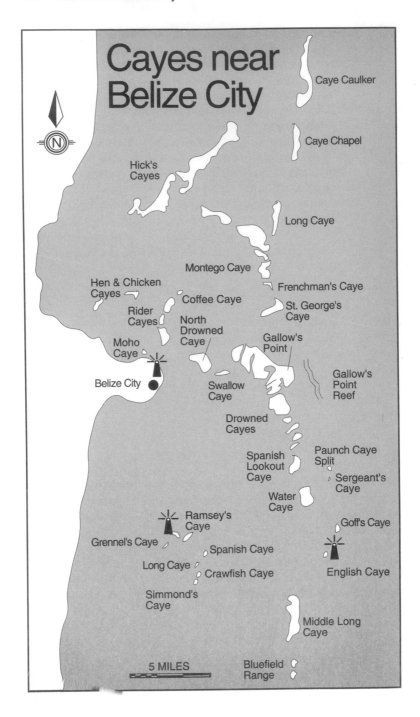

Cayes near Belize City

boat ride and some two miles from the barrier reef. Offices in Belize City are at 71 North Front St., and dive packages are available from US$500 all-inclusive for three nights. In the US, ☎ 800-359-0747.

The Bluefield Range

Set some 21 miles southeast from Belize City, this small set of three mangrove cayes hosts five-unit, moderate/expensive **Ricardo's Fishing Huts** (☎ 02-44970 or VHF Chan. 68). There are no baths. You may be able to accompany Ricardo on his fishing rounds. Tent sites (around BZ$6 pp, pd) are also available. Write PO Box 55 or contact Anna Lara at the Mira Río Hotel (Box 55, 59 North Front St., Belize City).

Middle Long Caye

Located near the Bluefields Range inside the barrier reef, southeast of Crayfish Caye and southwest of English Caye, this mangrove island hosts the two-room budget **Moonlight Shadows Lodge** (☎ 08-22587). Write 5 Mahogany St., Belmopan for more information.

Ambergris Caye and San Pedro

One of the most famous of the cayes, Ambergris is the nation's major tourist destination. Over half of visitors to Belize come here only, and the majority are divers.

Although it's the largest caye (about the same size as Barbados), most of the island is composed of mangrove swamp, and most of the residents live in the attractive seaside village of San Pedro at its southern tip. Some are descendants of British and French buccaneers, but most are of Yucatec Maya-Spanish (*mestizo*) descent and are remarkably bilingual. Once this was a fishing village. Now the sandy streets abound with locals and tourists driving golf carts. If you're a middle class North American or European, you'll feel right at home in San Pedro. But if you're a backpacker or low-budget traveler who likes lots of local flavor, you may find San Pedro to be a bit sanitized for your tastes.

NATURAL FEATURES: Flanked by a long beach, the island's windward side is straight in comparison with the leeward. The largest of the 12 lagoons is the Laguna de San Pedro to the west of the village. About 2½ miles long, it's fed by 15 creeks. Navigable

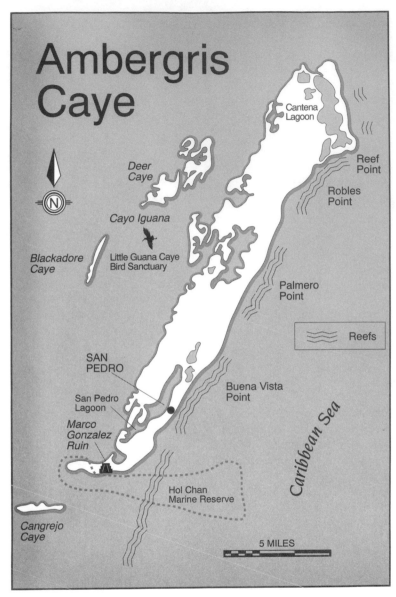

Ambergris Caye

Cantena Lagoon

Deer Caye

Reef Point

Robles Point

Cayo Iguana

Blackadore Caye

Little Guana Caye Bird Sanctuary

Palmero Point

Reefs

SAN PEDRO

San Pedro Lagoon

Buena Vista Point

Marco Gonzalez Ruin

Caribbean Sea

Hol Chan Marine Reserve

Cangrejo Caye

5 MILES

channels at the island's south end traverse mangrove swamps and a number of the lagoons. Except at Rocky Point, the beach parallels the reef. The Boca Bacalar Chico – a six-foot-wide, 2.5-foot-deep tidal channel said to have been dug by the Maya so that they could bring their canoes through – separates this caye from Mexico. It was enlarged and deepened by the Mexicans in 1899. Approximately 20 miles long, it is now two to four miles wide. The passage between Ambergris and the mainland has served whalers, pirates, and smugglers through the ages. Many of them wrecked. The most famous is the British frigate the *Water Witch*, which went down off of the island's southern tip along with a cargo of gold and silver bullion, some of which is still believed to lie below. The nation's richest fishing waters are found around the caye, and the Barrier Reef is approximately 500 ft. offshore; channels or breaks in the coral permit the local fishermen to pass through safely.

ENVIRONMENTAL PROBLEMS: Marring the island's placid atmosphere, there is a degree of hostility to expatriates and developers, whom the locals hate "because they always talk in six figures." One current conflict is whether or not to build the North-South Road. Advocates claim that it will relieve the population pressures on the southern six miles, allowing expansion to the north 20 miles. Opposition comes from landowners, who wish to keep their property secluded, and from environmentalists, who charge that the road will devastate the delicate environment.

GETTING THERE: Most travelers arrive by air. Reliable San Pedro-based Tropic Air (☎ 02-45671 in Belize City) flies direct from Belize City, Belize International, and Corozal. Maya Airways and Island Air also fly. Expect to pay around BZ$70 each way from Belize International and BZ$40 each way from Belize Municipal. The *Andrea* (BZ$20 OW) departs from the Belle Vue Hotel's dock (5 Southern Foreshore) at 4 PM Mon. to Fri. and at 1 PM Sat., returning at 7. A number of skiffs also depart from the Swing Bridge area. Ask around. The *Triple J* generally departs at 9. It may also be possible to catch a ride with one of the cargo boats departing from the Custom Wharf near the Fort George Lighthouse.

FLORA AND FAUNA: On the main part of the island, which is still separated from San Pedro by a waterway, a great deal of wildlife survives. You might see frigatebirds, herons, flamingos, or egrets. Ocelots have been sighted in the mangrove forests, and sea turtles still come ashore to nest. Nearby Bird Caye hosts the nesting grounds of some 30 species, including the cormorant, spoonbill, various ducks, avocets, and both the greater and the reddish egret.

HISTORY: The island was formed from the accumulation of coral fragments. First, a shoal patch appeared. Such patches tend to build up in long lines paralleling the mainland. It is believed that their orientation may correspond with submarine geological strata, rather than being solely the product of sea current flows. Little is known about the first Maya residents, except that they routed the Spanish in 1508. Presumably Ambergris was a stopover point for Maya traders. Pirates settled here during the 17th C. Artifacts and even skeletons, which have been unearthed all over town during the course of construction projects, attest to San Pedro's long historical roots. Although it is believed to have been named after the sperm whale secretions washed ashore on its beaches during the 19th C., the exact origin of the island's name is unknown.

During Yucatán's War of the Castes (1848-49), an initial four families migrated here from Bacalar in Quintana Roo. Mexico tried to annex the territory in 1851, but the locals protested, and the matter was amicably settled by an 1893 treaty. In 1874 James Blake purchased the entire island (save for one parcel controlled by the Catholic Church) and began collecting rents. Nearly a century later the Belizean government stepped in and made a "forced purchase" of the island, selling parcels and lots to the islanders. Over the years, the local economy has shifted focus from logwood to chicle to coconuts to lobster. The last became a valuable export item beginning in the 1920s. After a protracted struggle, the islanders established fishing cooperatives, which effectively protected them from exploitation. As a result, income levels rose.

The island was devastated by Hurricane Hattie in 1961, but the population recovered in succeeding years. The earliest tourists arrived in the 1920s, and the first real hotel, Celi McCorkle's San Pedro Holiday Hotel, was established in 1965. It charged US$10 for a room, three meals, and laundry service. Tropic Air began flying to the island in 1979. In 1990, the government announced its intention to purchase the 22,000-acre Pinkerton Estate, which embraces more than the upper two-thirds of the island, excluding the beach frontage. Tentative plans call for two new town sites in the area, with plots to be offered to Belizeans at reduced rates. These days, San Pedro is in the midst of a tourism boom, with correspondingly high property prices. One sign on a vacant beachside plot near town reads, "Price went down from $200,000 to $140,000 US. Terms available."

SIGHTS: Given San Pedro's reputation as a "resort," one might expect a wide, wonderful beach. Instead, what you have is a narrow ribbon of sand that has – owing, perhaps, to dredging of sand that has damaged the reef – receded dramatically over the past decade. Nevertheless, the beach does run along the island's length. If you want, you can wade (or take the ferry: BZ$1) across the river and follow the beach all the way to Mexico. Barking dogs will keep you company much of the way.

Downtown San Pedro

SECONDARY SCHOOL

TO OUTLYING RESORTS

CARIBBEAN SEA

LAGUNA ST.

WATER TOWER

BOCA DEL RIO DRIVE

SANDPIPER ST.

26

N

25 PARADISE HOTEL

24

23

CEMETERY

22

CARIBENA FISHING CO-OPERATIVE

CARIBENA ST.

21
20
19
18

ANGEL CORAL ST.

PELICAN ST.

17

16

15

13

AMBERGRIS ST.

14

BUCANEER ST.

PESCADOR DR.

BARRIER REEF DRIVE

PLAZA/PARK

12

LAGUNA DE SAN PEDRO

10

11

7

9

8

BLACK CORAL ST.

5

6

2

TARPON ST.

TO RAMON'S HIDEAWAY, MATA ROCKS AND OTHERS

COCONUT

PRIMARY SCHOOL

4

AIRSTRIP ENTRANCE

3

TO BARRIER REEF

1

NOT TO SCALE

1. Sun Breeze Motel
2. Leny's Restaurant
3. Park
4. Rubie's Hotel
5. Holiday Hotel, Celi's
6. Tackle Box
7. Coral Beach Dive Shop
8. Coral Beach Hotel
9. Rock's Shopping Center
10. Belize Bank
11. Spindrift Hotel, Atlantic Bank
12. Police Station
13. Big Daddy's Disco
14. Elvi's Restaurant
15. Barrier Reef Hotel
16. Library
17. Island Plaza (drugstores, businesses)
18. Sea Breeze Hotel
19. Ambergris Lodge
20. Lily's
21. San Pedrano, Tomas Hotel
22. Conch Shell Hotel
23. Milo's
24. Sandal's Pub
25. Paradise Villas
26. Rock's Inn

One program sponsored by the US government in Central America (besides invasions, bullets, and bombs) is the Conch Hatchery. This engaging facility is northwest of town, about a 10-minute walk from the Paradise. The hatchery secures an egg mass and hatches it out. The baby conchs swimming around in the aquarium are truly adorable. Lest you think that San Pedro is nothing but cleanliness and affluence, you can continue on past the conch hatchery to the slum areas, where people live amidst wrecks of automobiles, rusting cans, and smashed plastic containers. In addition to the ferry, a barge will take you across to the other side, where you'll note the extensive mangroves. You'll also see signs along the shore with such messages as, "Don't mess with the baby conchs" and "Our mangroves forever."

Back in town a sand and concrete park sports tacky statues and signs. "Please do not litter the fountain" is posted on the side of the fountain. "Notice to Adults: Kindly do not use children's games" is on the slide. There's also a huge tire capped with a bell-shaped stone and a windblown pine tree encased by a grey painted wooden slat fence. Along this stretch, wind that would chill your buns off if you were climbing a mountain, provides welcome relief from the heat. On the other side of town, heading out past the airport, is what might be the world's only esthetically-designed gas station. Spanish in style, its carved wooden door features a shell as well as an elaborate Maya design – the profile of a warrior.

MARCO GONZALEZ RUINS: Named after the island boy who discovered them, the compact Mayan ruins of Marco Gonzalez sit on the southern tip of the island. They were excavated by Canadian archaeologists Elizabeth Graham and David M. Pendergast from 1986 to the present. Once located on the beachfront, the site is now a swamp. You have to get there by boat, unless it's dry. Dating from 200 BC to 1500 AD or later the city came under the cultural influence of Lamanai. It appears to have blossomed between 1150 and 1300, after which it faded. All of the site's structures contain shells, and the three large 13th C. structures are built largely of conch shells. The site is thought to have been one of the major coastal trading centers of the Maya world (others in Belize included Moho Caye and Cerros).

DIVE SITES: The most famous of these is Hol Chan at the island's southern end, which features the Hol Chan Cut. Other dive sites include The Pillars, Tackle Box Canyons, Pescador Tunnels, Mexico

Rocks, Rocky Point Canyons, Victoria Canyons, and Mata Canyons. Trips are often made to the Blue Hole and the Turneffes.

EXPENSIVE ACCOMMODATIONS: The **Mayan Princess Resort Hotel** (☎ 026-2778, fax 026-2784; Box 1, San Pedro) has 23 suites with kitchen and living room. All are beachfront, with a/c, queen bed and day bed. High season prices are BZ$220 s and BZ$250 d plus tax. The island's oldest, the 16-room **San Pedro Holiday Hotel** (☎ 026-2014/2103, fax 026-2014; PO Box 1140, Belize City) features a salt water pool, a restaurant (Celi's) and a deli, as well as water sports and diving. Rates are around BZ$150 for rooms with fan and BZ$170 for a/c rooms. More expensive apartments are also available (16% tax and service charge are added). In Belize City ☎ 02-44632.

to the north of town: The 41-unit **Paradise Resort Hotel** (☎ 026-2083, fax 026-2232; PO Box 25, San Pedro) lies at the end of Front St. The wood-and-thatch structures are old, yet attractively funished. Other rooms are more traditional but well appointed, with kitchenettes. The hotel has a distinctive sand, thatch, and wood ambience, and – with sand spread about everywhere on the grounds – is about the only resort in town where you really feel you're on the beach. Prices run from around BZ$100 s and BZ$140 d on up; 11% tax and service are added. For more information ☎ 800-537-1431 or 713-850-1664, fax 713-850-1664; or write PO Box 42809, Dept. 400, Houston, TX 77242. The 24-unit a/c **Paradise Villas** (☎ 026-2331, fax 26-2214; PO Box 1922, Belize City) are a set of recently-constructed condos which rent for about BZ$250. Offering horseback riding, partial a/c, and a pool, popular 14-unit **Rock's Inn Apartments** (☎ 026-2326/2717, fax 026-2358; PO Box 50, San Pedro) is designed for those who plan to do cooking. It's to the north of town along the beach. In the US ☎ 800-331-2458.

south from the airport: The 34-room a/c Spanish-style **Sun Breeze Resort** (☎ 026-2347/2191/2345, fax 26-2346; PO Box 14, San Pedro) is near the airport. It has a beachfront bar & grill and a restaurant, the Coco Palms. Also on the premises are a dive shop and boats, windsurfers, volleyball, and electric carts. Rooms rent from around BZ$180 s and BZ$300 d in-season, with tax and 5% service added. Set about 10 minutes walk from the airstrip, the **Hotel Playador** (☎ 026-2870/2872, fax 026-2871; Box 11, San Pedro) offers 10 cabañas with fan and one a/c cabaña, as well as nine a/c rooms. Rates run from BZ$190 s or d to BZ$250; 16% tax and service is added. The 52-unit, expensive **Belize Yacht Club** (☎ 026-2777, fax 026-2768; Box 1, San Pedro) is a group of modern Spanish-style condos that are being rented out. The resort offers diving, and a health club. It has a pool and the grounds are manicured. Each unit has choice of a/c or fan, queen bed, day bed, kitchen, and living room. Rates are from BZ$250 off-season (BZ$300 in season), not including tax. In the US ☎ 800-44-UTELL. One of the nation's most attractive small hotels, **Changes in Latitude** (☎/fax 026-2986) is run by Sue and Lori, two extremely friendly Canadian women. Their logo – a melting igloo amidst palm trees – exemplifies the climate change they came here for. Room rates are BZ$160 d for rooms with fans, and BZ$190 d for a/c rooms. Tax is added, and breakfast is complimentary. It's set next to the Belize Yacht Club, a half-mile south of the airstrip. Call for complimentary pickup. On the beach at the town's southern edge, **Ramon's Village Resort** has 60 thatched-roof cabañas, salt water pool, and complete services, including diving and fishing. From a distance, the resort has an authentic Maya look to it. Expect to pay from BZ$230 (plus tax) on up. Call 026-2067/2074, fax 026-2214, 544-443-2100, 601-649-1990; 800-443-8876 or 601-649-1990 in the US. Set 1½ miles to the south of town, **Caribbean Villas** (☎ 26-2715, fax 26-2885; Box 71, San Pedro) are a group of attractive apartment suites constructed in 1991. Their a/c suites have fully-equipped kitchens with electric stoves. There are two Jacuzzis, complimentary bike rental, and a "people perch" for birdwatching. Winter rates run from BZ$170 plus tax. In the US, ☎ 913-468-3608. At Woody's Wharf, the **Corona del Mar Apartments/Hotel** (☎ 026-2055, fax 026-2461; Box 3758, San Pedro) have suites with kitchen, bedroom with two double beds, sofa-bed in living room, plus a/c and fans. Rates range from BZ$150 d off-season to B$250 d during Christmas and New Years; 16% tax and service is added. Diving (with instruction), fishing, windsurfing, and glass bottom boat tours are available. Excursions can be arranged. In the US ☎ 800-426-0226. Also set to the south of San Pedro, **Mata Rocks Resort** (☎ 026-2336, fax 026-2349; PO Box 47, San Pedro) offers expensive accommodation ranging from BZ$150 s, BZ$170 d, BZ$200 t, and BZ$260 quad on up; 16% tax and service are added. The nine hardwood, stucco, and tiled suites, which vary in price, have kitchenettes, ceiling fans or a/c (some units), and sun decks. An outdoor bar is on the beach. For reservations contact Accent on Travel, 800-288-8646 or 503-645-7323, or fax 503-690-9308. On a secluded beach about two miles south of San Pedro, **Victoria House** (026-2067/2240/2304, fax 026-2429) offers rooms (some with a/c) and stucco-and-thatch cabañas with tile floors, as well as diving and fishing. In the US, ☎ 713-662-8000, 800-247-5159, fax 713-661-4025; or write PO Box 20785, Houston, TX 77225. Rates start from around US$85 s and US$95 d, not including 16% tax and service. A variety of packages (diving, fishing, and "lovers") are available. They also operate Fantasea Watersports (☎ 026-2576).

others: The five-room, expensive **Casa Tortuga Villa** (☎ 026-2386; 16 Mosquito Coast) has a/c or fan-cooled rooms. For further information, ☎ 303-925-3268 in the US. The seven-unit, expensive **Mosquito Coast Villas** (☎ 026-2531; fax 026-2331) feature fans and offer diving. The four-room, moderate-to-expensive **Tres Cocos** (☎ 026-2531; fax 026-2331) has fan-cooled rooms and also offers diving. Two-room, expensive **Xanadu Apartments** have fans. Located in town, the expensive, six-room **Alijua** (☎ 026-2113/2791, fax 026-2362) features fans or a/c cottage-style accommodation, with kitchens and cable TV. Rates are around BZ$100 s or d on up, with weekly and monthly discounts. The a/c three-unit **Palma Sola Chalet** (☎ 026-2130, fax 026-2834) is on Coconut Drive. For more information, ☎ 800-468-0123 or 305-473-1956 or fax 305-473-6011. Others include the two-room **Coconut Cottages** (☎ 026-2100; PO Box 19, San Pedro), the 10-room **Seven Seas Hotel** (☎ 026-2382/2137), the 10-room **Conch Shell Inn** (☎ 026-2062; around BZ$70 s, BZ$90 d), and the six-unit **Del Mar Garden Cottages** (☎ 026-2170, fax 026-2214; PO Box 89, San Pedro).

MODERATE ACCOMMODATIONS: With a pool, **Hideaway Sports Lodge** (☎ 026-2141, fax 026-2269; PO Box 43, San Pedro) is the least-expensive hotel with a pool. Unpretentious, it has a laid-back character, which reminds you that you are on the Caribbean coast of Central America and not in Miami. The recently remodeled rooms are simple yet comfortable; most have fans but a few have a/c. There is a good restaurant. Rates (which include breakfast, but not tax) run from BZ$80 d up to BZ$180 for a suite which holds six. Children under eight are free. The small **Hotel Casablanca** (☎ 026-2327, fax 026-2992) has a/c or fans and rooms from BZ$100 with breakfast. Its attractive rooms have bold decor, including bright red sheets – perfect for libidinously inclined couples. Also centrally located, the 20-room, unpretentious **Coral Beach Hotel and Dive Club** (☎ 026-2001/2013, fax 026-2864; Box 16, San Pedro) charges from BZ$60 s and BZ$90 d, plus 16% tax and service. It operates a restaurant and the Tackle Box Bar. Set in an elegant three-storey building, the **Barrier Reef Hotel** (☎ 026-2075/2049, fax 026-2719) offers 14 a/c rooms and is across from the plaza. It has a restaurant and charges BZ$100 s and BZ$130 d, with substantial off-season discounts available. The 24-room **Spindrift Hotel** (☎ 026-2174, fax 26-2551, 800-327-1939) is a reinforced concrete structure, with rooms starting from BZ$100, plus 11% tax and service.

BUDGET ACCOMMODATIONS: If you're on a budget, don't expect much here in the way of luxuries. One of the best bargains is the 16-room **Martha's Hotel** (☎ 026-2053, fax 026-2589; PO Box 27, San Pedro), which charges from BZ$30 s and BZ$55 d in the off season, or BZ$46 s and BZ$69 d in the winter months. Triples and quads are also available. Rates include taxes. Nine-room **Milo's** (☎ 026-2033) – which charges BZ$20 s, BZ$25 d, and BZ$35 t – is the least expensive. Naturally, the rooms are a bit dark, and baths are shared. **Rubie's Hotel** (☎ 026-2063/2434, fax 26-2434; Box 56, San Pedro) charges from BZ$25 for simple rooms with wooden floors and shared baths. More expensive rooms are around BZ$50. Some rooms overlook the ocean. The a/c **San Pedrano Hotel** (☎ 026-2054, fax 026-2093; 4 Barrier Drive) charges BZ$50 s, BZ$60 d, BZ$75 t, and BZ$85 quad, plus tax and service charge for its wooden-floored rooms; off-season is less expensive. Meals are served upon request. They also have an apartment. Ten-room **Lily's Hotel** (☎ 026-2059;) is on the waterfront. Rooms are large and wood-paneled, with flourescent lighting and fans; some have an ocean view. Charges are from BZ$80 in season. Out past the airport, the six-room **Pirate's Lantern Guest House** at the South End (☎ 026-2146, fax 026-2796) features private baths and fans for BZ$25 s, BZ$35 d. The attractive eight-room **Tomas Hotel** (☎ 026-2061) charges from around BZ$60 s or d. Other budget hostelries include the 10-room **Cruz Apartments** (☎ 026-2091); the four-room **Islander Hotel** (☎ 026-2065); four-unit **Laidy's Apartments** (☎ 026-2118); eight-room **Lourdes Hotel** (☎ 026-2066) on Middle St.; and four-unit **Palm's Condominiums** (PO Box 26, San Pedro). Finally, if staying for an extended period, houses are available for rent.

NORTHERN AMBERGRIS ACCOMMODATION: All of these are relatively expensive and can only be reached by boat. The closest of the resorts on the island's north end, at three miles, the colonial-style 22-room **El Pescador** (☎/fax 026-2398, 800-628-1447; PO Box 793, Belize City) offers "a special fishing experience" for the devoted fisherman. Fish in the area include sailfish, wahoo, snook, lady fish, tarpon, bone fish, and jack crevalle. If you don't fish, there's nada to do here! A number of all-inclusive packages are available; they range in price from US$1,400 pp, double accommodation. **Captain Morgan's Retreat** (☎ 026-2567, fax 026-2768; Box 38, San Pedro) is three miles north of the river. It has 21 thatched-roof, wooden cabañas with fans and bath; there's a pool with a wooden deck and restaurant. Rates start from BZ$190 s and BZ$240 off-season and rise to BZ$260 s and BZ$340 d during the winter. Service charge of 5%, plus 6% hotel tax, are additional.

Fishing, diving, and snorkeling are available. In the US ☎ 800-447-2931 or 218-847-3012; fax 218-847-0334. On the beach at the north end, **Journey's End Caribbean Club** (☎ 026-2173; PO Box 12, San Pedro), a self-contained resort, features a combination of cabañas and villas, with French cuisine, tennis courts, TV, sailboards, and sailboats. If you're looking for a truly Belizean atmosphere, this isn't the place: you could be anywhere in the tropical world when you're here. In the US ☎ 800-447-0474 or 305-899-9486. Set some six miles north of San Pedro, the six-room moderately-priced **Green Parrot Resort** (01-49163, fax 026-2331; Box 36, San Pedro) has secluded beachfront cabañas with fans, plus boating and fishing. It is the project of Stuart Corns, a retired engineer from California. Leave a message at 026-2147 or fax 026-2245. Also to the north, **The Belizean** is currently closed but may have reopened under new management by the time of your visit.

FOOD: San Pedro is an expensive place, where you will spend BZ$20 or more to eat well. As often holds true in Belize, for some strange reason seafood is more expensive than meat or poultry here. **Lenny's Place**, in front of the airstrip, is reasonably priced. One very popular spot is **Elvi's Kitchen** on Pescador Drive (Middle St.). It has good seafood and reasonable prices. In the Spindrift, **Mary Ellen's Little Italy Restaurant** (☎ 026-2866) offers Belizean and Italian dishes. Located in Fido's Courtyard, **La Parilla** serves inexpensive Mexican food. **The Hideaway** is reasonable and has good food. Its fried chicken, shrimp creole, and conch dishes are popular; breakfast here is good value. **The Royal Palm Inn** features authentic Indian curries on its menu. **The Emerald** is a reasonably priced Chinese restaurant; it has cheap rice and bean dishes as well. Often packed and very attractive, the **Jade Garden** has an inexpensive vegetable fried rice; it's open daily from 7:30 AM to 10 PM. **The Grill Restaurant** is cool and breezy, but pricey. **Celi's Restaurant**, attached to the Holiday Hotel, is one of the most famous bistros. It serves three meals, and dinner includes lobster, shrimp, and fish. Set south of the airstrip, **Duke's Place** serves moderately-priced Belizean, Caribbean, and Mexican food in a romantic atmosphere. **The Paradise** offers an "all you can eat" Sunday brunch for BZ$15, and a beach BBQ from 7:30 that evening for BZ$30. The a/c **Coco Palms Restaurant** at the Sea Breeze serves elegant seafood and hearty Mexican dishes. Also try the **Pirate's Tavern**. **Mickey's Place** at the Hotel Playador is open daily and serves huge burritos for lunch on Wed. The classy **Lagoon Restaurant** is in the Hotel Casablanca on Pescador Drive. **Coral Gardens**, Front St., serves chicken and fries for BZ$6, and Chinese dishes for BZ$10-15. **Vic-**

toria House (☎ 092-2067) has buffet service and a special "Queen Victoria Brunch" on Sun. from 8-1; free transportation is provided. **Big Daddy's** has a nightly beach BBQ. **The Holiday Hotel** and **Mata Rocks** also have beach BBQs. Informal and excellent value, **The Reef** on Middle St. has seafood and daily specials, as well as *salbutes* and *tacos*. Food is served in an informal atmosphere to a reggae beat.

snacks: Several shops have baked goods and pastries. **The Pizza Place** sells slices for BZ$2.75. **HL Burgers** is on Middle St. **Manelly's**, on Barrier Reef Drive across from the Lion's Den, has ice cream. **Celi's Deli** in the Holiday Hotel offers take-out items from 6-6 daily. **The Casa de Café** serves expensive coffee (BZ$2), muffins, and slices of cake (BZ$2.50). **The Barrier Reef** has sandwiches for lunch. **Luigi's** serves Mexican food. **The Vitaminas Juice Bar** is in the Alijua Building. It also serves sandwiches and ice cream. In the park at night a lady sells rice and beans, chicken, and salad for BZ$5; a hotdog vendor stands right by her.

ENTERTAINMENT: At night the city is quiet, save for the sounds of Spanish language TV pouring into the streets. But there are a few places to go and the action starts late. Frequently featuring live bands, **Big Daddy's Disco** is the mainstay. Located next to the park and marked by an unforgettable sign, it has a sand floor bar with a thatch peaked roof, booths, dartboard, maps, and a disco papered with checkerboard-style painted egg cartons which glow under the blacklight. Free snacks are dispensed during happy hour, which runs from 7 to 9 daily. Its "two for one" cocktails are largely fruit juice. A newer venue, **Tarzan's** is set across the road. It's an impressive disco, complete with tropical backdrop. Set at the end of the pier by the Coral Beach, the **Tacklebox Bar** offers live bands during tourist season. Thankfully, the sea creatures once imprisoned in the back have been freed. The **Purple Parrot Too Bar** at Fido's Courtyard offers live music from Thurs. to Sunday. With a giant sandal hanging outside, the **Sandal** has a collection of sandals hanging on the walls, along with dartboards, plus Grace Jones and Bob Marley posters. The **Casablanca** has a romantic rooftop bar. Distastefully furnished with stretched zebra skins acquired by a previous owner, the bar at the **Paradise** features the Paradise Freeze, a blend of amaretto, angelica, vodka, orange juice, and coca creme. Also try **Barrier Reef**, **Fido's Bar**, and the outlying resort called **Journey's End** (accessible only by boat), which has bands-on weekends. Finally, visit the **Pier Lounge** in the Spindrift for the Mon. crab races and the Wed. evening Chicken Drop, at which locals bet which number a chicken will defecate on first. Numbers from one to 100 are marked on a large board. It's a winner-take-all jackpot.

FOOD SHOPPING: Stores are packed with overpriced imported US processed food. The prices reflect high import duties, as well as added shipping costs. The largest store is **Rock's Supermarket** just down from the Coral Beach Hotel. The large food store below **Milo's Hotel** has space invader machines, which add audio ambience. Sample prices here: cinammon bread, BZ$3.25/loaf; 100 g. of custard creams from Britain for BZ$2.25; Mott's Apple Juice, 64 oz./BZ$11.50; can of coconut milk, BZ$7.35; Ivory Snow detergent, 32 oz./BZ$12.20; Mexican-manufactured Kellogg's Corn Flakes, 200g/BZ$2.40; Hunt's Tomato Paste, 6 oz./BZ$1.70; and Campbell's Cream of Mushroom Soup, BZ$2.30. Another store with similar prices is run by the same people who bring you **Martha's Hotel** above. **Super Jenny's** has cabbages (BZ$3.35), packages of two bell peppers (BZ$2.24), two tomatoes (BZ$3.15), and other items.

EVENTS: The **San Pedro Carnival** is held from the Sun. to Tues. preceding Ash Wednesday. Processions are held at Christmas and Easter. The **Fiesta of St. Peter**, the town's patron saint, takes place on June 29 and, as an added treat, the fleet is blessed the same day. The anniversary of the town's 1985 incorporation is celebrated on Nov. 27. Another huge event (and the most recent in conception) is the **Sea and Air Festival**. Generally held in mid-August, it includes volleyball, windsurfing, waterskiing, a beauty pageant, mountain biking, kiting, greasy pole climbing, cardboard bat racing, tug-of-war, catch & release fishing, a grand parade, and other events. Each night is customarily dedicated to a Central American nation. Because of the recent influx of Garifuna, Settlement Day is also celebrated here on Nov. 19.

SERVICES AND INFORMATION: The small **library** is open Mon.-Fri. from 5 to 8 and on Sat. from 1 to 4. Amazingly in this day and age, the library operates on the honor system: just leave your name and the name of the book at the counter. **Belize Bank**, a **PO** (open Mon. to Fri. 8-noon, 1-4:30), and a **pharmacy** are in the same building as the Spindrift Hotel. A branch of the Atlantic Bank is next door on Barrier Reef Drive. The Belize Bank and the Atlantic Bank are the only ones that will change Canadian dollars. **Hol Chan Marine Reserve Office** (☎ 092-2420), Caribena St., is chock full of information. An informative window into expat existence on the island, *The San Pedro Sun* is the informative weekly newspaper.

⌐'s Laundromat (092-2373), Pescador Drive, is open daily. **Rosalita's Massage & Beauty Center** (☎ 026-2242), Barrier Reef Drive near the Holiday Hotel, offers shiatsu and Swedish-style massages as well as hair care. Also try **Andor's Massage** (026-3079) near Ramon's.

rentals: Bicycles can be rented for around BZ$15 pd. Golf cart rentals are also available. With one office in Fido's and another next to the Catholic Church, **Joe Miller Photography** (☎ 026-2577/2556, fax 026-2568; Box 74, San Pedro) has underwater cameras for rent and other services.

TOUR COMPANIES: Formerly Universal Travel & Tours, **Travel & Tour Belize** (☎ 026-2031/2137, fax 026-2185) has three offices – by the airport, in the Alijua Building, and on Barrier Reef Drive in the Spindrift Hotel lobby. They offer a wide variety of tours, diving, and excursions as far afield as Caracol, Tikal, and to Mexico's Kohunlich. Also offered is bird watching, river and deep sea fishing, sailing, and snorkeling. Located on Barrier Reef Drive (Front St.), **Amigo Travel** (☎ 026-2180/2435) has moped and bike rentals, glass bottom boat and snorkeling trips, horseback riding, and tours to the cayes and other localities. Offering snorkeling, river trips, and other excursions, **Belize Visitor & Tours** (☎ 026-2728, fax 026-2402; Box 74, San Pedro) is on Pescador Drive (Middle St.). Located in Fido's Courtyard, **Island Rentals** (☎ 026-2697 and 026-2488 eve., fax 26-2597) has a variety of water sports, water taxi service, beach cookouts, night snorkeling, excursions and tours to many localities, including Altun Ha. They also rent all types of equipment, from golf carts to underwater cameras, kayaks to bicycles. **Excalibur Tours** (☎ 026-2051/2604) offers fishing, snorkeling, diving, waterskiing, and other activities. Run by dive master Changa Paz, the **Amigos Del Mar** (☎ 026-2706 and 026-2261 eve., fax 026-2648; Box 53, San Pedro) has diving, instruction, rentals, and excursions, including trips to the Turneffes, the Blue Hole, and a night dive at Hol Chan. **Ramon's Reef Resort** (☎ 026-2439) operates the *Sailing Fantasy* catamaran. **The Hideaway Sports Lodge** (☎ 026-2141, fax 026-2269) offers a variety of snorkeling, fishing, and diving packages. **Fido Badillo** (☎ 026-2286) operates day trips to Altun Ha, fishing trips, and beach BBQs. **Heritage Navigation** (☎ 026-2394) runs its 66-foot *Winnie Estelle* on day trips to Caye Caulker for around BZ$90 pp. They depart from the Paradise Hotel dock at 9 AM. *The Nicola* (☎ 026-2255) runs river trips to Altun Ha, Caye Caulker excursions, fishing, diving, and other trips. Also try **Hustler's Tours** (☎ 026-2279/2538/2075). Finally,

Bill Henkes will take you out on his yacht *The Yanira* for BZ$50 pp, pd. Write him c/o General Delivery, San Pedro.

dive boats: Several of the nation's live-aboard dive boats are based in San Pedro, although they generally must be booked well in advance. The *Manta IV* (☎ 026-2371) has a shark cage, caging you not the shark, which will make *Jaws* come to life bloodlessly. **Bottom Time Dive Shop Out** (☎ 026-2348) offers day trips to the Turneffes. With offices on Front St., **Out Island Divers** (☎ 026-2151; PO Box 7, San Pedro) provides one- to three-day trips to Lighthouse Reef and The Blue Hole, as well as specialty charters to Glovers Reef and the Turneffes. They have a tent camp at Long Caye on Lighthouse Reef; their *Reef Roamer II* is stationed here as well, as is the *Tooth Fairy*, a private yacht. In the US, ☎ 800-BLUE-HOLE or 303-586-6020, fax 303-586-6134, or write Box 3443, Estes Park, CO 80517. Running a wide variety of day trips, the **San Pedro Dive & Snorkel Center** (☎ 092-2982) operates the *Merriweather*, a yacht based on Lighthouse Reef. **Fantasea Watersports** (☎ 026-2576) runs out of Victoria House and offers scuba instruction, fishing, and a variety of excursions and rentals. Note: Dive trips are frequently cancelled at short or no notice when the requisite minimum number of divers doesn't show up. On all trips, you pay an insurance fee and this entitles you to free use of the recompression chamber near the airport should you need it.

SHOPPING: Prices are generally high. Postcards sell for 75¢ instead of the usual 50¢, and other prices are set accordingly. One of the more memorable shops here is **Iguana Jack's Island Art**, which has painting, sculpture, and ceramic iguanas. Probably the best place to shop here is the **National Handicraft Centre** on Barrier Reef Drive.

FROM SAN PEDRO: The *Andrea* (☎ 026-2578, 02-74988) departs Mon. to Fri. at 7 for Belize City and on Sat. at 8 from the Texaco wharf near Lily's Hotel. The *Triple J* (☎ 02-44375) generally departs at 3 (BZ$20 OW); it stops at Caye Chapel and Caye Caulker. Leaving from the Lagoon Side Marina (a white house near the soccer field), the *Thunderbolt Express* (☎ 026-2217) travels from San Pedro Mon.-Sat. to Caye Caulker, Caye Chapel, and Belize City. It departs at 7 and 2, returning at 11 and 4. You may also be able to hitch a ride with a yacht. Be sure to reconfirm departure times with any of these three as they may be subject to change. Any boat with "C.C." prefacing the serial number on its side is from Caye Caulker. They arrive in early afternoon, docking beside the Tackle Box. If they take you, expect to pay around BZ$20. One expensive trip

(BZ$240-300) is a charter for the 26-mile run to Xcalak, Mexico. Unfortunately, there isn't much to do there save stock up on groceries or, perhaps, stay in the one budget-priced hotel.

Hol Chan Marine Reserve

 Set along the northern section of the barrier reef approximately four miles southeast of San Pedro, this reserve's central feature is its namesake – a natural break or cut (Hol Chan means "Little Channel" in Maya), which has produced striking coral formations. Established in 1987, its five sq. miles feature mangroves, a sinkhole and underlying cave in the seabed – a smaller version of the Blue Hole found in Lighthouse Reef – as well as a portion of the barrier reef. Some 40% of the diving that goes on in Belize takes place here, and significant damage has been done to the reef through snorkelers and divers either standing on coral or hanging onto outcroppings. Except for the gripes of a few disgruntled fishermen, the reserve has been well received by conservationists and hotel owners alike. Ironically, the developer responsible for the devastation of fringing mangroves at the south end of Ambergris Caye presently promotes the reserve in his brochure.

GETTING THERE: When planning a trip, be sure to stop by the Visitor's Center in San Pedro. Many companies offer excursions to the reef for around BZ$25. It's a 2.5-hour trip. Either bring your own gear or you can rent it. Night dives are also an ideal way to see the reserve, and you may find the waters bathed in bioluminescence.

ORIENTATION: At either side of the reserve near the reef crest, signs inform divers that they are entering a protected area. The reserve is divided into three management zones, each of which has separate regulations.

Zone A, The Reef (Cut) is just for snorkeling, and no fishing or collecting is permitted. Boats should moor at the buoys. All visitors must obtain an entry ticket before entering the zone and all boats operating here must register with the administrator. Both sides of the cut are lined with long, narrow banded forests of elkhorn, finger, and leaf corals. Out in the open, ghostlike tilefish guard the entrances to their burrows which are piled high with broken pieces of staghorn coral. A large cave hosts green moray eels and anenomes, and purple-headed and bright orange-bodied fairy basslets hover beneath rocky overhangs and outcrops.

Zone B, The Seagrass Beds (Lagoon), covers a three-square-mile area and is for both snorkeling and diving. A license is needed to fish, and no netting or spearing of fish is permitted within the Boca Ciega Blue Hole. No trawling is permitted, and all fishing boats operating here must register with the administrator. Consisting chiefly of sand and seagrass, the zone hosts a wide variety of marine life – from sponges to small coral formations to surgeon fish, parrotfish, manatees, turtles, lobsters, and conch. The area is excellent for a warm-up dive and for practicing underwater photography techniques.

Zone C, The Mangroves, covers one square mile and is also for both snorkeling and diving. It is composed of seven mangrove cayes separated from Ambergris by the Boca Chica Cut. Red, white and black mangroves can be found here. Be careful not to disturb the sediment at the bottom of their channels or the plants and wildlife on the surface. Fish found here include French and grey angelfish; blue striped, French, and white grunts; four eye and banded butterflyfish, schoolmasters, and grey snappers.

other rules and regulations: Tickets for diving and fishing in Zones B and C are required. Feeding or touching of fish is prohibited, as is touching or standing on live coral heads. Inexperienced snorkelers must wear a life jacket. A maximum of eight divers/snorkelers per guide is the limit, and the guide must join the group in the water. While Zones B and C are open 24 hours, Zone A is open only from 6 AM to 9 PM.

safety precautions: Only cerified SCUBA divers can dive in the reserve. Never dive alone, and avoid sea urchins and fire coral. Wear a tee shirt to prevent sunburn. Be cautious of the channel's strong current. Obtain prior clearance from the reserve manager before entering the cave in the Boca Ciega blue hole.

Caye Caulker

Also known as Caye Corker, the island's Spanish name is Cayo Hicaco, after the coco plum, now found only on the southern part of the island. Surrounded by a shallow placid blue-green sea, this island contains a peaceful fishing village. Once a backpacker's heaven, Caye Caulker's prices have risen dramatically. But it still remains relatively affordable for the low-budget traveler. Once synonymous with the island, the spiny lobster has been severely depleted.

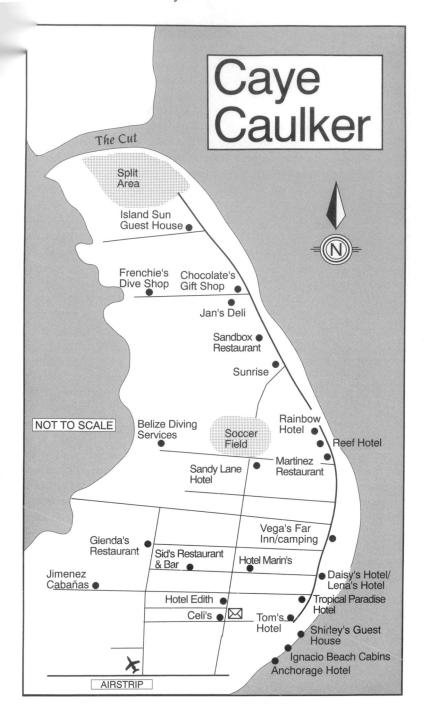

Caye Caulker

The Cut

Split Area

Island Sun Guest House

Frenchie's Dive Shop

Chocolate's Gift Shop

Jan's Deli

Sandbox Restaurant

Sunrise

NOT TO SCALE

Belize Diving Services

Soccer Field

Rainbow Hotel

Reef Hotel

Martinez Restaurant

Sandy Lane Hotel

Vega's Far Inn/camping

Glenda's Restaurant

Sid's Restaurant & Bar

Hotel Marin's

Jimenez Cabañas

Daisy's Hotel/ Lena's Hotel

Hotel Edith

Celi's

Tom's Hotel

Tropical Paradise Hotel

Shirley's Guest House

Ignacio Beach Cabins

Anchorage Hotel

AIRSTRIP

N

Paralleling their decline has been the expansion of the tourist "industry," along with the concomitant rise in prices. Satellite dishes are in evidence, as are new homes that clash with the traditional architecture. On the positive side, however, has been a growing spirit of ecological awareness and cooperation spurred on by the problems which have become evident to all. Establishment of a tour guide association is underway, reef mooring buoys have been installed, and an offshore reef reserve is planned. Other island features are the sand flies and mosquitoes, which zero in for attack on calm days and make life a misery. Although golf carts have grown in number on this once vehicle-free island (more than 70 at last count) and development is increasing, today's slow-paced lifestyle still resembles San Pedro a decade ago. The island is perhaps typified by the guy sitting in front of a "Go Slow" road sign offering to sell ganja to all passersby.

HISTORY: Visited by pirates and Mexican fishermen, the island was uninhabited as late as the 1830s. The first permanent residents were refugees from the Caste War in the Yucatán, and most of today's Jicacquenos can trace their ancestry directly back to Mexico. The initial industry was cocal, growing coconut palms and harvesting their nuts for oil. Lobster fishing became important from the 1920s and, after a struggle, a cooperative was formed in 1960 to assure reasonable prices. In a good year they can catch 1,000 lbs. of lobster tails, with an average of 50-70 lbs. per day during the height of the season. Today, the 600-member Northern Fisherman's Cooperative supplies nearly 10% of all the lobsters sold in the Red Lobster chain's 650 restaurants. Unlike other lobsters – which must be kept alive until they are cooked, lest a strong chemical reaction turn the meat into a putrid jelly – the rock lobster can be frozen. However, it lacks sizeable claws, so the meat is all in the tail.

Nearly every home standing on "Main Street" was demolished by 1961's Hurricane Hattie; the new version of town was constructed further inland using more hurricane-proof building techniques. The "hippies" discovered Caye Caulker during the 1960s. Over the years it has metamorphized and these days appears to be following in the footsteps of Ambergris. With overfishing and catching of undersized specimens rampant, lobster fishing appears doomed and tourism may soon become the island's sole source of income. As each lobster takes four to five years to mature, it is not practical to farm them. Unfortunately, the quiet charm and pristine environment that has given the island its touristic appeal over the decades is in danger as well.

EVENTS: Commemorating the introduction in the mid-1800s of the vitally important coconut palm, a three-day coconut festival is held in May. A Catholic mass inaugurates the festivities, followed by activities such as a food fair, processing tour, crowning of a Coconut King and Queen, and various coconut competitions, such as husking, tree climbing, grating, tossing, and chipping.

GETTING THERE: The preferable way to visit the island is still by boat. Boats (BZ$15 going, BZ$10 return) depart beginning around 10 AM Mon. to Sat. from the A&R Shell station, North Front St., on the north side of Haulover Creek near the Swing Bridge. About a dozen boats in total now make the run. A water taxi cooperative assures everyone of passage, and you'll be asked to take the boat which is next in line. (There's also a competing association composed of boats based in Belize City.) After less than an hour's journey, you're deposited at one of the piers – normally at the "front bridge" pier, although boats will drop you off at any pier you request, thus saving you a walk. Pay only upon arrival. There also may be a 5 PM boat from Belize City; check at the departure point.

by air: An airstrip was completed in 1991, wreaking ecological devastation on the southern part of the island and starting a decline in the island's serenity. Tropic Air (☎ 02-45671 in Belize City) will stop here on request on its flights to Ambergris Caye and from both Belize International and the domestic airport. Skybird (☎ 02-32596, 025-2535), Island Air and Maya Air also fly. Prices are around BZ$40 from Belize Municipal, BZ$70 from Belize International, and BZ$40 from San Pedro. From the airport a taxi service is available for BZ$5 pp. You can use the phone to call one.

from San Pedro: The *Andrea* departs at 7 AM from San Pedro and stops here before heading to Belize City. Some tour operators run day trips, and it's also possible to fly with Tropic Air and other carriers.

tours: The only group tour currently visiting the island is the one offered by the American Littoral Society (Highlands, NJ 07732; ☎ 908-291-0055). It is co-sponsored by the Siwa-Ban foundation. Of the tour's eight days, five are spent on Caye Caulker. The cost is around US$1,400, not including airfare, and the tour generally takes place at the end of April or early May.

ORIENTATION: With only a few streets and numerous but short sidestreets, it's nearly impossible to get lost on the island. To the north, the village ends at The Cut, a swimming hole created by 1961's Hurricane Hattie. The swift current can make it dangerous for children and poor swimmers. Separated from the rest of the

island by this barrier, the island's north doesn't have much, s&
swamps, mangroves, and a lot of coconuts gone wild. A nice pa.
leads along the southern shore, dividing the hotels from the piers
Along the way, you might see a hummingbird or an iguana basking
in the sun or descending from a palm. You'll also note the lobster
traps piled atop one another. Each year, they are beached for longer
and longer periods. From Shirley's near the airstrip, a seaside path
wends its way past iguanas, small anoles, and seabirds, until it
terminates in mud, muck, and mosquitoes. Near here, the toxic
village dump has bred a population of crocodiles. Island residents
are working on the declaration of an offshore marine reserve,
separate from the Siwa-Ban Nature Preserve and larger than the
one at Hol Chan.

SIWA-BAN NATURE PRESERVE: On the northern end of the
island, this proposed reserve, to be modeled after Hol Chan Preserve, will preserve the flora and fauna of the littoral forest, mangroves, seagrass, and barrier reef. The littoral (seaside) forest will
protect coco plums, seagrapes, and areas of red mangrove. The
seagrass habitat will extend from the littoral forest and mangrove
zone into part of the barrier reef. The preserve's name comes from
the black catbird (siwa-ban in Yucatec Maya), which is a relative of
the tropical mockingbird. Also present in the area are over 125
species of birds and the endangered American crocodile. For more
information or to make a donation, contact Ellen MacCrae at
Galerie Hicaco or send a tax deductible donation to The Siwa-ban
Foundation, 143 Anderson, San Francisco, CA 94110-5602.

SWIMMING: The water's too shallow to swim from shore. You
must go to The Cut -- a deep channel at the village's north end
created by Hurricane Hattie in 1961, when it sliced Cay Caulker in
half. You can see the erosive damage done here from cutting down
mangroves. Note that saltwater crocodiles are sometimes seen in
this area. Beware of fire corals. There's also a new area for swimming created by the new dock opposite The Reef.

DIVE SITES: It's about a mile to the Barrier Reef. Hol Chan is
another popular destination. The Sponge Avenue, North Cut, and
Swash are snorkeling and diving locations off the east coast. Mack-
erel Hole and George's Cut are near the South Cut. A difficult and
potentially dangerous cave system is located off the island's west
coast. Diving services are listed below under "shopping, services,
and tours."

COMMODATIONS: There are still a lot of relatively cheap gs around, although prices are rising and newer, more upscale ccommodations are being built. The most deluxe is the 12-unit **Tropical Paradise Hotel** (☎ 022-2124; PO Box 1573, Belize City), which charges from around BZ$45 s to BZ$130 for a triple suite. It has ceiling fans. Don't smoke pot in your room: busts have occured here. Popular with budget travelers, **Tom's Hotel** (☎ 022-2102) overlooks the water, and one room even has an ocean view. Tom charges around BZ$20 for a room and BZ$50 for a cabin. One of the best budget hotels is the small **Hide-A-Way** (☎ 022-2103), which features five comfortable rooms with fans. Located behind the evangelical church and on the same street as the Health Center, the hotel is around the corner from Deisy's Hotel. Near the center, inexpensive to moderately-priced, nine-room **Vega's Far Inn** (☎ 022-2142; PO Box 701, Belize City) also offers the island's only camping (about BZ$15 pp). They have rooms for BZ$22 s, BZ$35 and BZ$42 d; suites for BZ$100 are also available.

near The Cut: One of the cheapest hotels, noisy, eight-room **Rivas Guest House** (☎ 022-22127) is above the Aberdeen restaurant. The **Mira Mar Hotel** (☎ 022-44307) is next door and the **Sandy Lane Hotel** is behind it. Formerly the Hotel Martinez, 16-room **The Reef** (☎ 022-2196) is next. The unspectacular **Rainbow Hotel** (☎ 022-2123) follows, charging around BZ$50 s and BZ$55 d. It has been accused of environmental violations. **Chocolate's** (☎ 022-2151; PO Box 332, Belize City) has one room for BZ$100, with a great view and a small refrigerator. Cheaper rooms (some of which may still be under construction) are BZ$35. Attractive **Island Sun Guest House** charges BZ$50 for a simple room with a bath. They rent bicycles and snorkel equipment. Note: Theft is more likely if staying in the north end. Watch your possessions.

towards the airport: The **Anchorage** (☎ 02-45937) has four white cabins with thatched roofs from around BZ$30 and up. **Ignacio's Cabins** (☎ 022-2212; PO Box 1169, Belize City) are cute and have private bath. Charges are BZ$30 d; triples are also available. Run by expatriate Shirley Young, the attractive **Shirley's Guest House** (☎ 022-2145) charges BZ$32 s and BZ$41 d. The **Caye Caulker Guest House** (☎ 02-2249) charges BZ$35 d.

others: Other hotels include eight-room **Edith's Hotel** (☎ 022-2150); nine-room **Hotel Marin** (☎ 022-44307); six-room, moderately-priced **Sea Breeze** (☎ 022-2176); **Daisy's Hotel** (☎ 022-2150; PO Box 196, Belize City); the three **Jiminez Huts** (☎ 022-2175); the moderately-priced **Seebeez** (☎ 02-22176) next to Tom's; the 15-room **Lena's Hotel** (☎ 022-2106); **Morgan's Inn** (☎ 02-22178);

Johnny's Rooms (☎ 022-2149); the **Caribe Hotel** (☎ 022-2159); and the **Trend Hotel** (☎ 022-2321).

Northern Long Caye: This small island has the budget-priced, basic, eight-room **Castaways** (Box 1706, Belize City).

rentals: Ask around if staying a long time. Houses may be rented from around BZ$800 per month. Camping on the beach is prohibited. Contact **Heredia's Apartment & House Rentals** (☎ 022-2132); or the four-unit **M & N Apartments** (☎ 022-2111). For information, write Box 1018, Belize City or ☎ 22-2132.

FOOD: The bad news first: the lobster that Caye Caulker is so famous for are being overfished out of existence. You'll notice that the lobster you receive is undersized. The reason for this is that lobsters of nonreproductive size are being caught en masse and sold to local restaurants throughout Belize. A legal lobster tail must weigh at least four oz. and should measure no less than 3½ inches from eye to carapace. It's up to you whether to eat them or not, but the islanders are undoubtedly killing the goose that laid the golden egg. Someday there will be no lobsters at all.

Food prices here are climbing, with many restaurants charging BZ$1.50 just for a cup of coffee. **Glenda's** is famous for large bottles of fresh-squeezed orange juice priced at BZ$4 for breakfast, along with fresh baked cinnamon rolls. For lunch there are burritos and *ganaches*. Another excellent place is **Syd's Bar** nearby which, unfortunately, is legendary for the long wait to be served in the evening. Either go here for lunch or bring a thick novel. **Marin's** has a nice atmosphere and accompanying fairly high prices. Just up from the soccer field, **Mrs. Paquita** sells cake and fresh brewed coffee inside her blue-green wooden house. **Pinx Diner** is an informal restaurant. Also near The Split, the **Sandbox** is another fine and quite affordable restaurant. It's run by the affable Mary Jo Prost, a former manager of the Seaside Guest House in Belize City. Naturally enough, it has a sandy floor. Dishes include snapper almondine, *ceviche*, and both vegetarian and meat lasagna. **Jan's Deli** is next to the Sandbox and the **Mini Super-Market** is nearby. On the main drag by the sea and just up from Dolphin Bay Travel, **Claudette's Fast Food** has inexpensive, handmade burritos: fish, chicken, or vegetable. It's strictly take-out, but you can sit at the tables in the back of the house and watch as the fishermen clean off their catch by the pier and the pelicans fight for the cast-off remains. **Sobre Las Olas** has vegetarian and other dishes, including breakfast with fried jacks and omelettes. Upstairs, **Home Cooking** also has breakfast.

Located near the soccer field, **J&L's** has ice cream and coffee. Also try the **Martinez Restaurant**, and the **Tropical Paradise**, famed for its seafood. Located in a blue house on the second street inland from the ocean at the island's western end, **Emma** sells lobster pies for BZ$1; they're ready at noon and gone by two. Also try her chocolate coconut. Across the street from Marin's, **Mrs. Rodriguez** serves meals at 5 PM; she also has limited accommodation. **Koko Riko** has seafood, as well as pizza specials on the menu. There's also a pastry shop which serves good coffee and rents snorkel gear. But you'll have to find it on your own, as the owner threatened to "sue the author's ass" if he were included.

MARKET SHOPPING: There are a number of small stores, including **Chan's Mini Mart** – which has a variety of goods including pasta and bread. Sample prices in stores: onions, BZ$1/lb.; carrots BZ$1.40/lb.; Campbell's Vegetable Soup, BZ$2.15/can; Del Monte Peach Halves, 16 oz./BZ$3.95; Joy dishwashing detergent, 22 oz./BZ$6.50; and Head & Shoulders shampoo, 7 oz./BZ$8.75.

ENTERTAINMENT: Down near The Cut, the **Reef** is the popular hangout, a favorite of Rastaphonians. The **I&I** is also popular. You'll also note the ubiquitous television sets. In this village of 600 there are two cable companies: one controlled by the UDP, the other by the PNP. Sadly, whereas entire families of Jicacquenos once sat out on the pier at night, enjoying the night air and shooting the breeze, today they stay glued to the tube.

SHOPPING, SERVICES, AND TOURS: A tourist information center is planned. Be sure to shop around before taking a tour or going snorkeling: a wide range of trips is available. You don't even need to ask. They'll ask you – 16 times a day. A "private" **pay phone** is held hostage by the Sea Shell Gift Shop. The only other phone is in the telephone office on Main St. near Vega's. Celi's doubles as the **post office** and sells copies of *Amandala*. One of the best places to visit – both for information and for shopping – is marine biologist Ellen MacCrae's **Galerie Hicaco** (☎ 022-2178). Ellen has a good collection of photos for sale, as well as Maya handicrafts from all over the nation. She also offers reef tours (BZ$29) and bird walks (BZ$12). Her husband rents out windsurfers. You can view her "Life Strategies in Barrier Reef Environments" slide show upon arrangement. Unfortunately, she is often off-island leading International Expeditions tours, but you may be lucky and catch her at home. **Toucan Gift Shop** has a variety of goods. Friendly **Cindy Novelo** runs a boutique. Her husband Jim (☎ 022-2195, fax 022-

2239) runs trips on his boat, the *Sunrise*. Trips include excursions Hol Chan, Goff's Caye, Half Moon Caye, Glovers Reef, the Turne fes, and other destinations. A long-standing favorite is the day-long excursion to the Turneffes, Half Moon Caye, and the Blue Hole. He can take you to see manatees or dolphins. Charters are also available. Stop by the shop and chat. Also visit **Chocolate's Gift Shop**. The semi-mythical Capt. Chocolate takes visitors to Goff's Caye (BZ$50 pp including snorkel gear), on which you see manatees. Other excursions include a river trip (BZ$60 pp). Inquire at his shop. Another operator is Charlie, whose **Turtle Tours** is based on Main St.

Island Sun offers snorkeling rentals as well as bikes. **Daisy's Hotel** (☎ 022-2150) rents kayaks. **Frenchie's Dive Shop** (☎ 022-2234) leads dives to all of the major sites. **Belize Diving Services** (☎ 022-2143) is near the soccer field. Also formerly located here, **Sea-ing is Belizing** (☎ 022-2189) has been forced to relocate and will have found a new location by the time of your arrival The owners charge BZ$4 for their slide shows of the jaguar preserve and coral reef ecology. The building contains a gift shop. photo gallery, and a bookstore. **Caye Caulker's School of Scuba** (☎ 022-2292, fax 022-2239), the island's dive school, is next to Edith's. The **Martinez Restaurant** also has a glass bottom boat. **Emma Gill** charters her outrigger sailboats. *The Gamusa* (☎ 022-2196) is owned by the Reef Hotel. **Jan's Deli** rents golf carts. Also try contacting **Ricardo's Adventure Tours** (☎ 022-2138), **Allen Nuñez, Harrison, Indio, Ras Creek**, and others about snorkeling and other trips. Popularly known as "Karate," artist and writer **Philip Lewis** paints tee shirts and designs island maps. He's seldom on-island these days, but you may see his work around.

CONDUCT: The island has been plagued by Rastaphonians. Coming from as far away as Roatan, most of these dreadlocks-with-attitude are thoroughly obnoxious and their presence is resented by locals. Many of the men supplement their income by playing gigolo to naive visiting foreign women and selling drugs, including crack. Don't let this ragamuffin posse spoil your visit. The Jicacquenos are still friendly and hospitable in the extreme, and you can really have a fine time talking to them.

FROM CAYE CAULKER: Most boats swing by the "front bridge" in search of passengers from around 6:30-7 AM. You can reach the international airport from the Belize City dock by 8:30 if you take a taxi. Boats also depart about the same time for San Pedro (BZ$20

:ss); ask around. In addition to the morning run, there's also
ierally a 3 PM trip. Tropic Air, Island Air, and Maya Air also fly.

Caye Chapel

 Only 2½ miles long, this is one of the nation's most
beautiful islands – one which has always been protected from hurricane damage by a solid portion of the
Barrier Reef. Its sloping two-mile beach faces east. Situated 16 miles away from Belize City, Caye Chapel is set on one of
the higher reefs – rising five to 10 ft. above sea level. The numerous
coconut palms are reminders of the first planned venture on the
caye, a coconut plantation. Some of the dead from the Spanish fleet
battle of St. George's Caye in 1798 were buried here.

getting there: Tropic Air (☎ 02-45671 in Belize City) will stop
here on request, as will Maya Airways. Expect to pay around
BZ$40 OW from Belize Municipal and the same from Ambergris.
Another option is to charter a boat.

PRACTICALITIES: Expensive **Pyramid Island Resort** has 32 a/c
beachfront rooms and beach houses. They also have a private
airstrip, yacht marina, and restaurant. There are tennis, badminton,
basketball, and volleyball courts, as well as a golf driving range,
and water sports – include sailing, snorkeling, diving, and fishing.
It has the best beach in Belize and a great Sunday barbecue.
Daytrips run here from Caye Caulker and Ambergris Caye. Call
02-44409/31802 or write PO Box 192, Belize City. In the US, write
PO Box 1545, Ashland, KY 41105-1545. **Note:** The resort hasn't
always had the best reputation in the world, so you should check
around to see how it's currently operating.

St. George's Caye

 Set nine miles northeast of Belize City, this caye was
first inhabited by buccaneers, who used it as a base for
smoking and drying manatee and turtle meat for sale
to fellow pirates and logwood traders. For this reason
the Spanish early on had named it Cayo Cosina
(Kitchen Cay). According to the first known map of the caye, issued
in 1764, it had over 70 houses, next to which stood pens for storing
turtles awaiting slaughter. In 1796 a group of fishermen and loggers, with the help of one British man-of-war, repelled an attack by

32 Spanish ships. This battle was the last attempt by the Spanish to forcibly expel the English from the area. Partly washed away by hurricanes and storms during the recent decades, an old colonial-era graveyard stands on the southern tip. Until Hurricane Hattie hit in 1961, St. George's Caye, along with nearby Sergeant's Caye, had summer homes for Belizeans and, in the case of Sergeant's Caye, for New Yorkers. Hattie turned Sergeant's Caye into a sandbar and divided St. George into four sections. Only two houses remained standing.

PRACTICALITIES: The best known lodging here is expensive 16-room **St. George's Lodge** (☎ 02-44190 or PO Box 625, Belize City). Among its features are windmill-generated electricity and a solar-powered hot tub. Two dives per day and meals are included in the rates. There are no phones, no TV, and no nightlife – making it the perfect getaway. Rates are around BZ$480 pp, pd and up including tax. In the US ☎ 800-678-6871. The six-unit **Island Cottages** are under the same management. Owned and managed by the Bellevue Hotel, the expensive 15-unit **Cottage Colony** (☎ 02-77051; PO Box 428, Belize City) offers attractive colonial-style units lined up in a row, with fan or a/c, plus a restaurant and diving. It's run by the Bellevue Hotel, 5 Southern Foreshore.

diving: Among the nearby sites are a large cave that you can swim through, the Ice Cream Cone (which features humongous gorgonians), the Aladdins (spur-and-groove topography with immense variety), Bruce's Column (a large pillar with sponges and grouper), Little Finger (grouper concentrations), and Eel Gardens (lots of eels). You can also dive off of Gallows Point Reef, Rendezvous Wall, or other southern Turneffe dive sites. And you can dive or snorkel off nearby Goff's Caye.

The Turneffe Islands

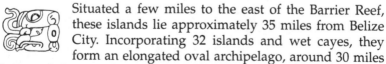

Situated a few miles to the east of the Barrier Reef, these islands lie approximately 35 miles from Belize City. Incorporating 32 islands and wet cayes, they form an elongated oval archipelago, around 30 miles long and four to 10 miles across. At their center is a placid blue lagoon. The nation's largest atoll, its area is some 205 square miles. The mangroves are so closely grouped that, when viewed from a distance, they give the appearance of being one continous flat island. Openings known as bogues lead into large interior lagoons that are four to eight feet deep and that are filled with turtles and

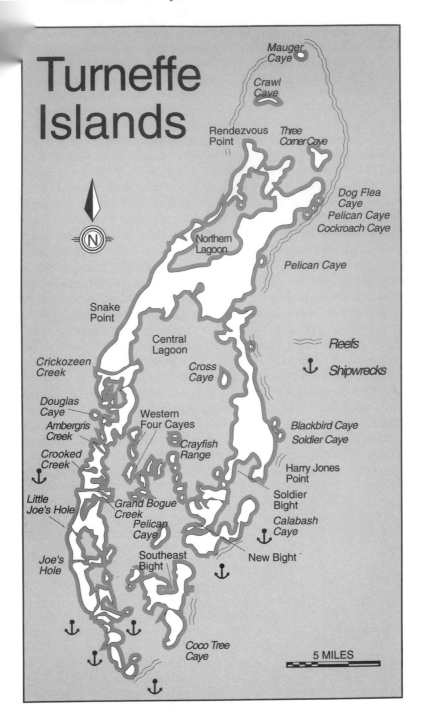

Turneffe Islands

Mauger
Caye

Crawl
Cave

Rendezvous   Three
Point   Corner Caye

Dog Flea
Caye
Pelican Caye
Cockroach Caye

Northern
Lagoon

Pelican Caye

Snake
Point

Central
Lagoon

Reefs

Crickozeen
Creek

Cross
Caye

Shipwrecks

Douglas
Caye

Western
Four Cayes

Ambergris
Creek

Crayfish
Range

Blackbird Caye
Soldier Caye

Crooked
Creek

Harry Jones
Point

Little
Joe's Hole

Grand Bogue
Creek
Pelican
Caye

Soldier
Bight

Calabash
Caye

Joe's
Hole

Southeast
Bight

New Bight

Coco Tree
Caye

5 MILES

N

fish. There is also a large population of American crocodiles, they are difficult to spot.

cayes: Sparsely sheltered Calabash Caye is the center of the r cal coconut trade. There are three mangrove cayes in the northern end of the atoll: Three Corner Caye, Crawl Caye, and Mauger Caye. Mauger Caye's name derives from the Creole word for "meager," denoting a time when crops fail and everything falls into stagnation. Southern Lagoon and Northern or Vincent's Lagoon are the two interior lagoons. Captured females were brought to the atoll by pirates after the sack of Bacalar during the 17th C. These islands were famous around the beginning of the 20th C. for their sponges, which were destroyed by a fungus in 1939.

fishing: The waters surrounding this atoll swarm with fish, including the smaller bonefish and permit and the larger sailfish, grouper, marlin, and blackfin tuna. Bonefish (averaging three to five lbs.) can be fished from the wadeable flats. While they peak at around mid-June, tarpon can be fished in mangrove creeks from mid-May through December. Billfish are around from January to April.

diving: One of the best places to dive in Belize, the area offers challenges for every level of diver. It has 23 cuts punctuating its reef, and some of these offer superb snorkeling and diving. Unfortunately, the reef is still recovering from the effects of 1961's Hurricane Hattie; otherwise, there would be even more sites. Accordingly, the major dive sites are on the "Elbow," the atoll's southern tip and off the atoll's north end. Diving here is not for beginners. Dives along the atoll's eastern side are wall dives. The more gradually-sloping reefs on the west have large coral heads. Many boats from Ambergris also dive here off the north end. Triple Anchors is graced by three 18th C. Spanish anchors; one is to the northwest of the mooring buoy. Other sites include Black Beauty, whose highlight is an enormous black coral, the deteriotated condition of which makes the case for not purchasing black coral jewelry; the *Sayonara*, which features a deliberately-sunk (in 1985) wooden skiff; Cabbage Patch, with concentrations of lettuce and other coral; Cockroach Wall, with garden eels residing in a sandy expanse, as well as large tube sponges; Permit Paradise with a concentration of permit; Dory's Channel, which features large gorgonians and tube and barrel sponges; and Myra's Turtles (or Myrtle's Turtle), at which a hawksbill makes a perennial appearance. This last is one of the nation's best places to dive. Still others are the Dark Forest, Calabash Wall, Lefty's Ledge, Majestic Point, Vincente Wall, Rendezvous Wall, Gailes Point, and Black Rock Mountain.

PRACTICALITIES: The Turneffe Island Lodge (Box 480, Belize) on 12-acre Caye Bokel (meaning "Elbow" in Dutch) claims to the longest continually-operated island resort in the country. It's reached by a two-hour boat ride. Accommodation is in 12 twin-bedded bungalows with screened porches, private baths, and ceiling fans. There is 24-hour electricity. Dive trips may be available to the Blue Hole and Glover's Reef in their 42-foot dive boat, *The Bodacious*. On-island facilities include volleyball and horsehoes. Rates are around US$1,700 pw for boat and guide, and US$1,300 for dive packages. Three- and four-night packages and fish/dive combos are also available. Expect to dive about 20 times in the course of a week. Non-fishermen pay US$900 pw, and special rates are available from June 11 to November 19. For more information, ☎ 800-338-8149 or 904-641-4468; or write 11904 Hidden Hills Dr., Jacksonville, FL 32225. Very expensive **Turneffe Flats** (☎ 02-30116, fax 02-78808), a fishing and diving lodge, has six bungalow units with fans. It's set on Northern Bogue at the atoll's northeastern side. In the US, ☎ 605-578-1304, fax 605-578-7540; or write PO Box 36, Deadwood, SD 57732. A self-styled "ecotourism paradise," the expensive five-unit **Blackbird Caye Village** opened in 1991. Its thatched cottages are on stilts. "The Dolphin Embassy," a marine research center partially funded by Francis Ford Coppola, is here, as well as Blue Planet Divers. For more information, write 81 W. Canal St., Belize City or ☎ 02-77670. In the US, ☎ 713-658-1142, fax 713-658-0739; or write Betty Taylor, 1415 Louisiana #3100, Houston, TX 77002.

Lighthouse Reef Lagoon

The outermost of the outlying banks, Lighthouse Reef was designated as "Eastern Reef" on old charts. Its lighthouse gave it the current name. With its northern end about 50 miles due east from Belize City, the 78.5-square-mile, irregularly-shaped atoll is about 28 miles long, varying in width from two to six miles. Almost totally bounded by a barrier reef, which is solid on the eastern side, the reef's southern edge forms a half-moon curve five miles in diameter. Scattered into two groups at the northern and southern ends of the bank, its six cayes are all widely separated. Being set at the northern tip of this near-perfect semi-circle gives Half Moon Caye its name.

DIVE SITES: There are some 40 dive sites in Lighthouse Reef. One of the nation's best dive sites is the Long Caye Wall (or Long Caye

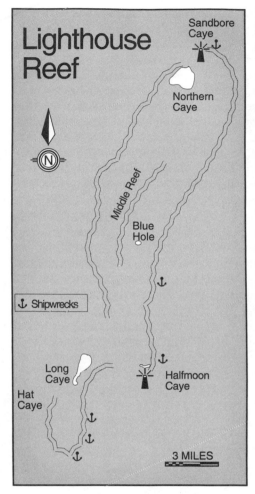

Ridge) at Long Cay here. It is named after its spur and groove formations. Gorgonians, sponges, and various corals are found here in abundance. Getting its name from the schools of silver sides no longer found here, the Silver Caves give you a chance to view nocturnal sea creatures on a day dive. You might see basket starfish or the rare sclerosponges. Once considered extinct, they have been rediscovered only within the past few decades. Set off of Long Caye's northwest corner, The Aquarium is named for its wide variety of colorful fish and other marine life. Sharks are frequently sighted at nearby Nurse Shark Lodge; it also has a number of spur and groove formations with loads of sea life. Similarly, eagle rays reside at Eagle Ray Wall. Others include, Blue Hole, Half Moon Wall, The Abyss, Tres Cabañas, and Woody's Favorite Bight.

Half Moon Caye Natural Monument

Across the atoll from Long Caye, this island is widely reputed to be the most spectacularly beautiful in Belize. The island is so remote that German subs were able to use it undetected as a WWII refueling station. The island has long been the haunt of the nearly extinct booby bird, as well as conch and lobster poachers. Half a mile wide and 1½ miles long, Half Moon has white sand beaches with a drop-off on

. north and a shallow lagoon on the southern end. It was first
designated a "Crown Reserve" in 1928. The National Park System
Act of 1981 precluded further clearing of the island – protecting
both the caye and Belize's only nesting colony of red-footed boobies (about 4,000-strong). Unfortunately, the "National Monument"
designation protects only the caye and portions of the lagoon and
barrier wall. The 45-acre reserve contains two separate ecosystems:
the eastern half has coconut palms while the west, fertilized by
seabird guano, is covered with lush vegetation. Nearly all of the
birds are white: in most other colonies red-footed boobies have dull
brown plumage. Half of the island is their sea rookery – one shared
with their chief adversary, the magnificent frigatebird. There are
also over 220 species of reef fish in the vicinity. Belize's largest land
crabs share the southern sandy beaches with loggerhead and
hawksbill turtles that come ashore to lay their eggs in season. The
98 other bird species present include ospreys, frigate birds, white-
crowned pidgeons, and mangrove warblers. Other reptiles include
the "bamboo chicken," a red iguana with black stripes on its back,
and the smaller (up to four feet) "wish willy," which is yellow with
black bars on its back.

SIGHTS: Set in the middle of the nesting area, a bird-viewing
platform is accessible by a trail that begins on the island's northern
side. Manned 24 hours a day by the National Customs Department, the solar-powered lighthouse offers a stupendous view; it's
on the eastern tip. Along with the one on Sandbore Caye to the
north, it gives the reef its name. Originally constructed in 1820 (the
current version dates from 1931), it has not always served its
purpose – as several wrecks attest. Over the years, many have
arrived in search of the Spanish galleon, *Juan Baptista*. It sunk about
a mile off the reef in 1822 with a cargo of gold and silver bullion.
Also included in the park, Half Moon Wall is a dive site which
offers a number of varied coral formations. Garden eels are numerous here. Numerous snorkel sites also lie offshore. In particular,
check out the buttressed coral formations to the southwest.

   practicalities: Camping is no longer permitted owing to ecological concerns – the island is simply getting too much attention
from *homo sapiens*. Day trips sometimes stop here. Caye Caulker's
James Novelo is one operator who does so.

Great Blue Hole

Proceeding eight miles north from Half Moon C. traveling through the lagoon in the center of Lighthou Reef, you come to this great cylindrical hole in the se bottom, popularized by a Jacques Cousteau television special. Appearing from the air as an indigo blue circle in the midst of a larger azure blue one, this is the nation's most famous dive site. From surrounding ocean depths of five to 15 feet, this "hole" plunges to 412 feet and is 450 feet across. A giant cavern is reached at 140 feet, with enormous stalactites up to 10 feet in diameter hanging 20-60 feet down from the cavern roof. Formed some 12,000 years ago, the hole is a geological phenomenon akin to a limestone sink, and its caves undercut the entire reef. A "monster" was sighted in its depths in 1970, but you're not likely to see much more than sponges or worms.

diving it: This is a decompression dive and should be attempted by experienced divers only. The nearest recompression chamber is in Miami! Operators on Caye Caulker and dive resorts such as Lighthouse Reef Resort will make the dive. **dive boats:** Out Island Divers (☎ 026-2151; PO Box 7, San Pedro) have a tent camp on Long Caye, and their *Reef Roamer II* is stationed here as well, as is the *Tooth Fairy*, a private yacht. In the US, ☎ 800-BLUE-HOLE or 303-586-6020, fax 303-586-6134; or write Box 3443, Estes Park, CO 80517. **snorkeling:** Shallow coral reefs surrounding the perimeter make for fine snorkeling. *did this w/Toby others done!*

Northern Two Caye

The **Lighthouse Reef Resort** (PO Box 26, Belize City) features five private a/c cabañas, bar, restaurant, and private airstrip. The resort offers fishing, diving, volleyball, snorkeling, and windsurfing. Packages run around US$1,050 for the resort package, US$1,200 for the diving package, and US$1,400 for the fishing/diving package. Flights usually run on Wednesday and Saturday. For more information, contact Blue Lagoon, Inc., PO Box 40915, Houston, TX 77240-0915; or ☎ 800-423-3114 or 713-937-4045. Worldwide you can call 1-813-439-1486.

ɟlovers Reef Marine Reserve

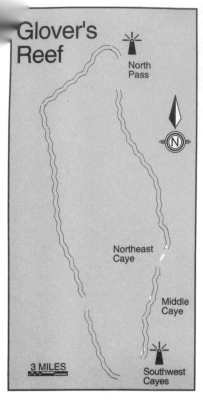

Set south of the Turneffes about 20 miles off the coast and 70 miles southeast of Belize City, this circular chain of bare coral outcrops, about 20 miles long and seven miles wide, surrounds a crystal clear lagoon that shelters more than 700 patch reefs in its 80 square miles. It was once the abode of pirate John Glover. Uninhabited now, it is occasionally visited by fishermen. Of its six small islands, Middle Caye was purchased by Wildlife Conservation International in 1990, thus protecting it from becoming a tourist lodge. It will eventually house a ranger station. In an attempt to preserve the atoll for sustainable fishing and to protect recreational use, Glovers Reef was decared Belize's second underwater marine reserve in May 1993. Approximately 75% of the atoll is zoned for general use, but five of the six cayes have been designated as conservation areas. Middle Caye is also zoned as a wilderness area. Northeast Caye is not included, and the atoll's southeastern portion has been zoned for seasonal closure to allow its recovery from out-of-season fishing.

PRACTICALITIES: The Lomont family operates **Glover's Reef Atoll Resort**. Not a "resort" in the usual sense of the word, but rather a very basic set of accommodations, their establishment is on Long Caye. You must bring your own food, and there's well water, but no electricity. Be as prepared as you might be if you were camping. A stove is supplied, but a backpacking stove would prove superior. Washing is done using a bucket from a well, and outhouses serve as sanitary facilities. They charge around BZ$200 pp, pw for a cabin or tent and RT passage, and US$70 pw for transport and camping. It takes six or more hours to get out to the

atoll. The boat departs on Sunday and returns the next Saturd
but departure or arrival may be delayed by bad weather. Othe
wise, you'll have to charter. Canoes, rowboats, motorboats, snor
keling and diving gear are available for rent. The Lomonts will sell
you conch, lobster, and fish. They have a small store and will accept
orders for goods from town for a 20% markup. Meals are BZ$8-10.
If you arrive ahead of time, you can overnight in their Glover's
Atoll Guest House for BZ$10.50. That gets you a bunk berth.
Camping is BZ$4 pp. Group rates are also available. The Lomonts
lease Northeast Caye out to kayaking groups. Belize's Wall Divers
(Box 448, Belize City) also operates out of here and offers courses,
including reef ecology, snorkeling instruction, and sports fishing.
For more information, write PO Box 563, Belize City or call Belize
Communications at 08-22149, 092-3310, 08-23180, fax 08-23505.

Set to the southwest and specializing in fishing and diving,
expensive **Manta Resort** (☎ 02-31895/45606 or VHF Chan. 70) offers cabañas, as well as a two-bedroom house, set on 12 acres.
They have nine fan-equipped rooms. A spacious, thatched-roof
restaurant and bar are built over the water. Activities include snorkeling, diving, fishing, volleyball, canoeing, and windsurfing.
Eight-day, seven-night packages run from US$1,050 to US$1,595
pp based on double occupancy. Write PO Box 215 or 3 Eyre St., Belize City; ☎ 800-342-0053 or 305-226-2029 in the US.

DIVE SITES: Glovers remains one of the least explored sites for
diving in Belize. Offering both a shallow reef area and an exhilarat-
ing drop-off, Long Caye Wall has a stand of coral which can be
reached from shore on calm days. Near Southwest Caye and Manta
Resort, Southwest Caye Wall offers excellent wall diving down a
steep drop-off. On the atoll's western side, Emerald Forest Reef has
excellent diving as well as snorkeling. You can see large stands of
elkhorn coral here. Also on the same side are Split Reefs, which has
both shallow and deep areas, as well as Baking Swash Reef, a
narrow, coral-lined channel, also with shallow as well as deep
reefs. Named after the diminutive palm- and mangrove-covered
island to its rear, Middle Caye Reefs has a wide variety of marine
life contained within a small area. Be sure to explore the turtle grass
beds, which house a number of creatures. Sea life is most diverse
near the dropoff. Named for its abundance of groupers, Grouper
Flats, set along the northeast side, has both shallow and deep reefs.
Shark Point is known for its sharks and is not for the timid soul.

The North

 Largely a plain, once covered by the sea, the nation's north still retains traces of its past existence underwater in the form of shallow valleys and low ridges – ripples in a seabed eons ago. As it does along most of the country's eastern perimeter, the coastal land is largely swamp, suitable only for seabirds. The north is the main agricultural center, producing most of the sugar, corn, and beans. But vast areas have remained untilled since Maya civilization lapsed over a thousand years ago.

EXPLORING: In addition to three natural reserves, the north has a number of Maya ruins, including Lamanai, an archaeological reserve. The area serves as a gateway to the wonders of Mexico. A two-lane highway runs north, serving the main towns of Orange Walk and Corozal, enroute to the Mexican border town of Chetumal. Public transportation heading off the main road is scarce, but distances to most attractions are not substantial.

The Bermudian Landing Community Baboon Sanctuary

Established in 1985 by zoologist Dr. Rob Horwich and a group of local farmers (with assistance from the World Wide Fund for Nature), this reserve, comprised of privately-owned land, protects over 1,800-1,900 "baboons" (black howler monkeys). These are an endangered sub-species of the howler that lives only in Belize, Guatemala, and Mexico. Combining tourism, conservation, and education, the project coordinates more than 150 landowners and eight villages. Its lowland forest parallels the Belize River and is bordered by cohune palm forests to the east and pine forest and savanna to the west. The reserve also provides a home for some 250 species of birds (which makes it a paradise for birders), deer, coatis, anteaters, peccaries, and iguanas.

HISTORY: An old logging camp, Bermudian Landing dates back to the beginning of the 17th C. Once called Butchers Landing, it is thought the name change in the late 18th C. was either because of

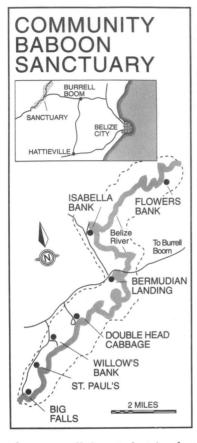

COMMUNITY
BABOON
SANCTUARY

BURRELL
BOOM

SANCTUARY

BELIZE
CITY

HATTIEVILLE

ISABELLA
BANK   FLOWERS
              BANK

Belize
River   To Burrell
             Boom

BERMUDIAN
LANDING

DOUBLE HEAD
CABBAGE

WILLOW'S
BANK

ST. PAUL'S

                  2 MILES
BIG
FALLS

Bermudian settlers or because Bermuda grass was grown for cattle. The large number of Scotsmen settling in the area is reflected by the name of the settlement, Scotland Half Moon, across the river. The area remained an unvisited backwater until recently, when zoologist Robert Horwich was conducting a survey of howler monkey habitats in Mexico, Guatemala, and Belize. He came upon a stable and healthy population only here and recognized the need for action to preserve howler habitats. Realizing that without community participation such a reserve would be doomed to failure, he sought to mobilize local support. Along with botanist Jon Lyon, Horwich laid the ground work for the reserve, surveying each villager's land and establishing ownership. Villagers were asked to avoid cutting 66 feet on each side of a waterway to spare figs, roseapples, sapodillas, trumpet trees, and hogplums, which the monkeys feed on, and to leave small forested strips between pathways as aerial avenues. The reserve was officially established on Feb. 23, 1985, and it currently receives some 5,000 visitors per year.

GETTING THERE: Buses leave Belize City for the sanctuary at noon-12:30 PM daily except Sunday. Mr. Oswald McFadzean's bus or truck leaves from the corner of Orange and Mussel Streets, and both Mr. Sydney Russell's and Mr. Valentine Young's buses depart from the intersection of Euphrates and Cemetery Streets. The bus returns from Bermudian Landing at 5:30-6 AM. Fridays and Saturdays are busy, so arrive early to be sure you get a seat. Check with the driver well in advance to confirm the departure time; times and days may be subject to change.

by car: From Belize City proceed 13½ miles along the Northern Highway. Go left at the Burrell Boom cutoff, traveling 14 miles past Burrell Boom and Mussel Creek until you reach the Belize

Altun Ha *(opposite)*

Xunantunich (_above_)   saw this
Lamanai Head (_opposite_)
Placencia Fishing Boat (_below_)

Raft, Ambergris Caye *(above)*
At Maya Center *(opposite)*
Climbing Temple II, Tikal *(below)*

Pelicans, Caye Caulker *(above)*
Caracol *(opposite)*
Lamanai *(below)*

Dangriga *(above)*
Hidden Valley Falls, Mountain Pine Ridge Reserve *(opposite)*
Caracol *(below)*

Cahal Pech *(above)*
Garifuna Girl, Seine Bight *(opposite)*
Market, San Ignacio *(below)*

River again. Take the right fork to cross the new bridge into Bermudian Landing. On the way, you pass over railway trestle bridges and slow-moving Black Water Creek (its color is due to tannin). The large building on the right after Burrell Boom was intended to be a sewing factory. The Chinese investors pulled their support after the Belizean government recognized Taiwan. It remains closed. The homes you pass on the way have neither electricity nor running water. They do have television, however: the sets run on car batteries. At another bridge constructed by USAID, where you cross over the Belize River again, there's a sign marking the entrance. You'll soon see a rope bridge stretched over the road from the famous fig tree that starred in the documentary, *El Amate*. At first, Dr. Horwich had only a single rope across the road. One monkey was crossing when the rope started to spin. After that the monkeys preferred the road. It took some time for the troop to trust the bridge again. One troop still resides in this area; another is near the school. **donations:** Send these to Howlers Forever, c/o Dr. Robert Horwich, RD 1, Box 96, Gays Mills, WI 54631.

TOURING: The best preparation for your visit is the excellent field guide, which sells for around BZ$30; it's available at the Audubon Society bookstore on Fort St. in Belize City. You'll want to have your mosquito repellent with you, as well as a camera flash for the trails. Begin your visit at the Visitors' Center, which has a number of very informative displays. You can view a sample planned agreement for the reserve, a map showing how the sanctuary has grown, the throat bone that gives the howler its howl, a grison skeleton, a mummified baby armadillo, gibnut and tapir skulls, a mummified marine toad in a box, various pickled snakes, turtle shells, and a display about crocodiles. After you visit the sanctuary, a guide can take you around on a trail. He might point out the sensitive plant, which closes at noon, show you cohune palms and nuts and describe their uses, and tell you about trees and their medicinal or other uses. An example is the ringworm tree, which can cure ringworm. One highlight is a gigantic "wee wee" ant nest, guaranteed to put you more in awe of nature than you were before. Your visit can be as short as half an hour or as long as 90 minutes. Canoe trips on the Belize River, fishing, and horseback riding can also be arranged.

PRACTICALITIES: The public phone is 021-2001 in Bermudian Landing and 021-2004 in Double Head Cabbage. Camping at the Visitor's Center costs BZ$3/tent; rooms are BZ$20 d, and meals are BZ$4 for breakfast, BZ$5 for lunch, and BZ$4 for dinner. Basic food

Mask of Chac, Great Plaza, Tikal *(opposite)*

and supplies are available from local stores. Vegetarians can be catered to. Guides cost BZ$5/hr., BZ$20/half-day, and BZ$40/day. Suggested admission to the reserve is BZ$10 and this includes the services of a guide. Guides for canoeing the Belize River may be available for the same price. For more information and reservations call Sanctuary Manager Fallet Young at 02-4405. State the number in your party, when you will arrive, whether coming by car or bus, if overnight meals are needed, if you have a tent, and if you wish to dine with a local family (at the prices above). Another alternative is the **Jungle Drift Lodge** (☎ 02-32842, fax 02-78160; PO Box 1442, Belize City). It has cabins (BZ$30 s, BZ$40 d, BZ$60 t) overlooking the Belize River. Each holds up to three and has a fan; the bathroom is detached. Discounts are offered to students and for extended stays. They run a number of tours and provide transport to the lodge. Another alternative is to stay at the moderate two-room **Little Eden Guest House** on Burrel Boom Road (currently for sale but it may have reopened by the time of your visit). Canoes or kayaks can be rented at **Baboon River Canoe Rentals** (☎ 028-2101) in Burrell Boom. If you are looking for something to eat, rice and beans are generally served next to the gas station at Burrell Boom.

Crooked Tree Wildlife Sanctuary

Set approximately halfway between Belize City and Orange Walk, just off the Northern Highway, this 3,000-acre reserve, consists of lagoons surrounded by marshes and logwood swamps. It is administered by the Belize Audubon Society and only the reserve's western portion is open. The fishing and farming village of Crooked Tree, across a causeway two miles from the main road, is in its center. This six-by-three-mile island is connected by a 3/4-mile causeway to the mainland. There are three neighborhoods (Crooked Tree, Pine Ridge, and Stain) in the village. The total population is 650. In addition to a fishery, there are a number of small farms. A strong relationship exists between the locals and the Baymen: many have blond hair and blue eyes. A close community, many residents are related to each other; it's rather like one extended family. Locals plant corn, cassava, cacao, and rice. Logging, fishing, hunting, cashew cultivation, and charcoal making are traditional activities. Note the mango and cashew trees in the area, some of which are believed to be several hundred years old.

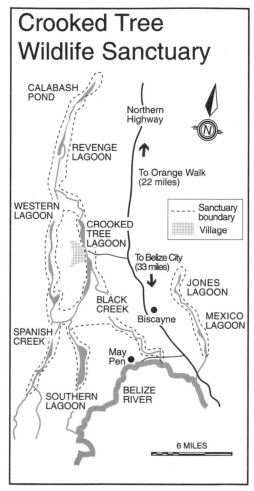

Crooked Tree
Wildlife Sanctuary

CALABASH
POND

Northern
Highway

REVENGE
LAGOON

To Orange Walk
(22 miles)

WESTERN
LAGOON

CROOKED
TREE
LAGOON

Sanctuary
boundary

Village

To Belize City
(33 miles)

JONES
LAGOON

BLACK
CREEK

Biscayne

MEXICO
LAGOON

SPANISH
CREEK

May
Pen

SOUTHERN
LAGOON

BELIZE
RIVER

6 MILES

Of the thousands of birds wintering here, the most prominent transient resident is the jabiru stork. It nests and rests in these lowlands from November to April or thereabouts. This is the largest nesting population of these magnificent birds in all of Central America (see description under "birds" in the "Introduction"). Its relative, the wood stork, is a smaller version with black on its wings and tail and a grey head. Other frequent flyers include black-collared hawks, tiger herons, snowy egrets, ospreys, and snail kites. Also present are howler monkeys, turtles, coatis, iguanas, and crocodiles. Back on land, you may see spider monkeys. Although they prefer higher trees, they do come to feed on the breadfruit trees. The best times to see wildlife are in April and May. The nearby community of Spanish Creek, located in the reserve's southwestern corner, has turtles and crocodiles.

festivals and events: An Agricultural Show is held in mid-March, and a Cashew Festival was held for the first time in May of 1993.

GETTING THERE: Until recent times, Crooked Tree was accessible only by boat. Today, at Mile 33 of the Northern Highway, a dirt road leads off to a causeway which, traversing the Northern Lagoon, ends four miles later at the village of Crooked Tree. Some residents rent their boats out, but in April and May the water level may be too low to launch a boat. Two daily buses run on unpredictable schedules; inquire about times at Orange Walk or at Batty's in Belize City. Or ask Mr. Johnny Jex near Mike's Bar when he's leaving that morning. You can also hitch or walk from the junction to the village, where you can rent a boat. But be sure to leave yourself enough time. Many tour companies will also arrange excursions.

SIGHTS: Birds, birds, and other wildlife. There are a number of trails through the village, and it may be possible to see jabiru storks nearby. The best are the *Jacana Loop Trail* and the *Trogon Trail*. The *Limpkin Trail* is good in April and May. The Muscovy duck and the black-bellied whistling duck nest in trees by the side of the lagoon. Aside from walking around the village or on the paths near Chau Hiix Lodge, the best place to see birds is on the lagoon itself. Charter a boat or rent a canoe. Enroute, you may see local cows in the river munching on water lilies. Aside from the birds and other wildlife, the only notable attraction in the area is **Chau Hiix**, an archaeological site to the west of the village in a cohune palm forest known as Blackburn Ridge. Originally named Indian Hill, it has been known to the community and protected for more than 150 years. It was renamed Chau Hiix (meaning "jaguarundi" in Kekchi Maya) by American archaeologist, Dr. Anne Pyburn. A professor at Indiana University, she had seen one of these elegant cats on an initial visit to the site. Dr. Pyburn was approached by the village council, who wanted to excavate, preserve, and increase visitation at the site. Thought to have been a stop on the trading routes, Chau Hiix is the only known source for a type of black-colored chert. Chalcedony and jasper found in the area are also thought to have been likely barter items. Along with her students, Dr. Pyburn began test excavations in 1992 and major excavation work began in May 1973. To date, most excavation has been in the form of test trenches to determine the dates of each structure and check on its preservation. Although some of the stone tools found along the shores of Crooked Tree Lagoon date back to 500 AD, the earliest structures here are believed to date from the Early Preclassic (1100 BC). The most recent buildings probably date from 800-900 AD, but the site is believed to have been occupied right up through the Postclassic period (1000-1500 AD). English loggers, working in the area during the 1700s may have driven away the last remaining Maya residents. Chau Hiix could be the only Maya site of this size in Belize that has remained free from looters. The site's center is dominated by the "Kinich-ku," an enormous 80-foot-high pyramid. Constructed of stone blocks, it was once covered with a layer of

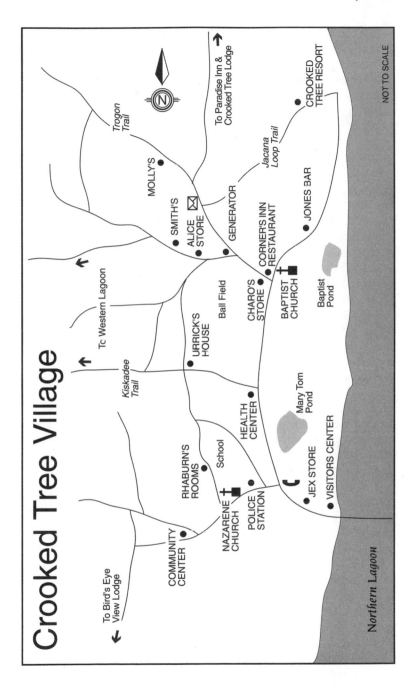

blood-red painted plaster. It overlooks the Great Plaza, which covered a 180-by-300-foot area. The entire plaza was raised 15 feet above the ground with a layer of earth, stone, and plaster. Two tiny square platforms, constructed from blocks and rubble, are thought to have been used for sacrifices as well as burial services for their leaders. A number of other structures are grouped around the plaza.

touring: You can hire a boat in the village to bring you here. You will spend around BZ$140 RT for up to seven passengers. If you come by canoe, expect to spend three to four hours each way. After arrival, the caretaker will give you a brief tour, after which you'll be free to explore on your own. The area is a superb birding site and has many animals. One good place to observe them is in the central main open-space area during the early morning hours. You may see a coati come to forage or any one of a number of birds – including trogons, toucans, and red bellied woodpeckers. Some birders enjoy this site so much that they have trouble tearing themselves away. The site largely consists of ruined mounds in the midst of forest composed of cohune palms and pocono boys. Strangler figs are also found. Orange strips tied to stakes delineate the corners of buildings. The holes you see on the ground are left by fallen cohune palms. Keep your eyes to the ground to spot armadas of leaf-cutting ants struggling with their burdens down the trees and across the paths. Palm leaves rustle eerily in the wind, and shadows play on the vegetation in the subdued light. Back near the dock, be sure to observe the wild papaya tree with its miniature fruit and the snail egg colonies attached to the trees; the pink ones still have snails inside. **note:** If you see an artifact here, please leave it *in situ*. And take care not to dislodge stones.

PRACTICALITIES: The modest **Visitor's Center** is on the right side of the causeway at the end; they have information, including a brochure about accommodation and other facilities. Make sure that you don't just get the flier for Molly's! The village now has 24-hour electricity. There are three larger shops, as well as three smaller ones. The village community telephone is 02-44333. Dolls are made to order by the **Crooked Tree Women's Group** for around BZ$20 each. To order, see Violet Wade. A gift shop is planned and may be there when you visit. In the area, one of the best known guides is Sam Tillett.

Featuring four rooms and a dorm, **Bird's Eye View Lodge** (☎ 02-44101; Box 1976, Belize City) looks inauspicious, but is hospitable. Dorm beds are BZ$20 and rooms are around BZ$110 d for bed and breakfast. In the US contact Dino Jones at 718-845-0749. Pickups from the airport and Belize City are available. **The Paradise Inn** (☎ 025-2535, fax 025-2534) has cabañas for BZ$70 s and BZ$90 d plus tax. Inexpensive meals are offered in the restaurant, and fishing, birding, horseback riding, and boat trips are offered. In the US, ☎/fax 718-498-2221 or write Box 153, Vanderveer Station, Brooklyn, NY 11210. Offering seven cabañas and a restaurant/bar, eight-room **Crooked Tree Resort** overlooks Crooked Tree Lagoon, about 30 miles northeast of Belize City. Write PO Box 1453, Belize City or ☎ 02-77745. Horseback riding is available here. Adventurous and hardy travelers can stay with a family and experience local life directly. **Molly's Rooms** (☎ 02-44101/44333) is run by the warden's mother and offers private rooms for BZ$20 s and BZ$30 d. Baths are shared, and meals are BZ$6 each. Horseback riding, guided nature walks, birding, and airport pickup (BZ$80) are also available. Another homestay, four-room **Rhaburn's Rooms**, is operated by Pastor Owen and Miss Maggie Raeburn. Others include those run by Mr. Richard, Alma Smith, Ruby Crawford and Miss Kelly. A small restaurant has been opened, and other accommodation is planned. Contact the smaller hotels through the community phone: 02-44101 or 02-44333.

outlying accommodation: For a very different and quite special experience visit **Chau Hiix Lodge** (☎ 02-73787, fax 02-77891). A former fishing lodge now geared towards birdwatchers, Chau Hiix is off by itself – a 40-minute boat trip along the lagoon. It is generally accessible by road only during April and May. Surrounded by trails and facing the lagoon, the lodge has one of the best locations for birdwatching in all of Central America. While quite comfortable, the rooms are nothing spectacular. They are wood-paneled, with two beds and a bathroom. But the *outdoors* is why you're here. You can see an amazing amount of birdlife on the trails, and you might see jaguar or ocelot tracks, and even spot a wild peccary. Jabiru stork nest upriver. Nearby, you can see an airstrip where two small planes were torched by drug smugglers in 1989 and 1991. Having been loaded, they were too heavy for takeoff. A rusting British Army vehicle, shot full of holes from target practice, stands nearby. A generator runs at night, and there's a comfortable living/dining area to relax in. Because the lodge can only hold eight to 12 occupants, you're guaranteed intimate service. The home cooking is hearty, and vegetarians can be catered to. A trained guide is always at the lodge, and some packages include your choice of a trip to the Community Baboon Sanctuary or to Lamanai. Packages start from US$525 pp, double-occupancy, for three nights and four days. Prices range up to a high of US$1,175 pp, single-occupancy, for seven nights and eight days. The package includes RT transportation from Belize International, room and three meals, drinks, snacks, tours, and guiding. Airport departure tax, alcohol, and tips are not included. For more information contact their US representative, Best of Belize (☎ 800-735-9520, 415-884-2325, fax 800-405-BEST, 415-884-2339; 31F Commercial Blvd., Novato, CA 94949).

Lamanai Archaeological Reserve

 One of the nation's most impressive Maya sites, as well as one of the longest continually occupied, Lamanai's ruins are set along the New River Lagoon within the 950-acre Archaeological Reserve. Its name (originally "Lamanyan," meaning "Submerged Crocodile") is one of the few original Maya city names known. It accords well with the large number of crocodile carvings found here and the crocodile bones found in burial sites. It still remains a great "lost city." Over the square mile area, not even 5% of its 718 structures have been excavated.

HISTORY: One very notable feature of Lamanai is the site's longevity: it was occupied by the Maya from 1500 BC until the 19th C. – some 200 years longer than most of the other sites in Belize. Lamanai is believed to have been on the main trade route from the Yucatán to the central Maya areas. The Spanish arrived here in the 17th C. and the English in the 20th C. via the New River. It is believed that at one time 60-70,000 Maya lived here. The earliest mention of Lamanai is on Nicholas Jannson's map of the Yucatán peninsula. It shows "Lamanay," but incorrectly labels it as being on the shore. Lamanai was excavated by Canadian archaeologist David Pendergast during the 1970s and 1980s.

FLORA AND FAUNA: In addition to the wildlife passed on the New River Lagoon enroute (see below), the reserve is rich in howler monkeys and various bird species. You might spot black oropendolas roosting around the Temple of the Mask and the High Temple. Black vultures may be spotted soaring off in the distance from the top of the High Temple. The double tapping sounds of the Guatemalan ivorybill make its presence evident. A variety of toucans may be found at structure N10-9 and, at the High Temple, the collared aracari cries out shrilly through the forest. Generally found near the area of Stela 9, pairs of rufous-tailed jacamars are slender and medium-sized birds whose iridescent coloring and

Lamanai Self-Guiding Nature Trail Key

1. Santa María (*Calophyllum Brassiliense*). Its anise-flavored leaves can be used to cook and wrap fish.
2. Cohune Palm (*Orbignya Cohune*). Its leaves are used for roof thatching and for walls.
3. Trumpet Tree (*Cecropia Peltata*). A food source for the howlers, the hollow trunks are said to have been made into Maya trumpets.
4. Tubroos (*Enterolobium Cyclocarpum*) The trunks are used to make dugouts.
5. Cotton Tree (*Ceiba Pentandra*). Considered sacred by the Maya, who gave it a place at the center of the cosmos, with its roots in the ground and its leaves in the sky.
6. Allspice (*Pimenta Dioica*). A popular dish for howler monkeys.
7. Red Gumbolimbo (*Bursera Simaruba*). Its leaves and bark are used as a tonic.
8. Pimenta Palm (*Acoelorraphe Wrightii*). This tree can be recognized by its stout and prickly trunk.
9. Bucut (*Cassia Grandis*). This tree is notable for its large black seed pods, which may grow up to three feet.
10. Cedar (*Cedrela Mexicana*). The scent of its bark repels insects.
11. Rubber Tree. Cuts in the tree show where rubber has been extracted.
12. Breadnut Tree (*Brosimun Aicastrum*). This tree was used as a food source by the Maya.
13. Copal Tree. Its sap was used for incense by the Maya.
14. Cordonica. Its roots can be used to treat snake bites.

needle-like beaks cause them to resemble overgrown hummingbirds. Spotted around the lagoon's edge, the northern jacana has pale green legs, yellow-paneled wings, and a brown body. Seen near the ground, the citreoline trogon has a bright yellow chest, a black-and-white tail, and a blue-and-green back. Less common are agoutis, spider monkeys, tarantulas, peccaries, nine-banded armadillos, and jaguarundis.

GETTING THERE: The bus runs to Indian Church but, as there's no daily run, it's not practical. Despite what you may have read elsewhere, it can be difficult to find a boat to rent and boats are not commonly available in either Guinea Grass or Shipyard! If you have a four-wheel-drive, you may approach from San Felipe during the dry season.

tours: Unlike other sites, which can easily be visited on your own, this is probably best seen as part of a tour. One of the best tour operators is **Herminio Novelo's Jungle River Trips** based in Orange Walk (☎ 03-22293; 20 Lover's Lane or PO Box 95, Orange Walk Town). An active promoter of ecotourism in Belize, Mr. Novelo is a lively and enthusiastic guide who knows his subject. His usual pickup site is from Orange Walk's toll bridge, where he meets passengers arriving from Belize City. *Maruba* (☎ 03-22199) and *Lamanai Lady* (☎ 02-31063, fax 02-30263) leave from Jim's Cool Pool. **Lamanai Mayatours** (☎ 03-23839) also operates out of Orange Walk. From the departure point, you travel along the river, with the jungle on both sides, passing the Mennonite settlement of Shipyard to the right. You could be in Pennsylvania (watch for Mennonites fishing). Eventually, you reach the wide New River Lagoon. On the way you might spot black oropendolas, collared aracaris, citreoline trogons, immature blue herons, rufous-tailed jacamars, northern jacanas, fishing bats, herons, purple gallinules, and turkey vultures, as well as the ubiquitous crocodiles sliding into the water on your approach. You'll also pass immense termite mounds on tree branches. The entrance to the park is a series of huts on the right.

TOURING THE RUINS: A small but excellent museum is up from the pier. It contains primarily ceramic artifacts. Dating from the 6th C., pyramidial N9-56, the Mask Temple, has a 12-ft.-high mask carved on its side, the largest such carving discovered so far in the entire Mundo Maya. Note his crocodile headdress and classic Olmec features – thick lips and broad nose. The deteriorated stela of a Maya ruler stands in front under a corrugated zinc shed. The temple was constructed from the early to late Classic Maya eras. To the rear of the temple, there's a grove of *ramon* (breadnut) trees and a view of the lagoon. The closed-off tunnel here enters an excavation which disclosed another large mask 15 feet inside. Back on the path there's a throne with a symbol vaguely resembling either a yin and yang sign or a bow tie (depending upon your inclination) and an excavated tomb. There's a well preserved small temple dating from 100 BC at its base. The well preserved Stela 9 shows the ruler Smoking Shell, along with heiroglyphs portraying his title and reign. Done up in the Late Preclassic style and the largest of its kind in the entire area, the massive N10-43, The High Temple, faces a small ball court and provides a breathtaking 360° view of the surrounding wilderness from its 100-foot summit. Excavations here have uncovered thousands of blades, a dish dating from 700 AD, which contains the skeleton of a bird, a giant bowl, and numerous Preclassic vessels, as well as other finds. It is the largest securely dated Maya structure. Back on the road, note the woodpecker holes in the surrounding cohune palms. When the gigantic marker disc was raised at the the small ball court in 1980, lidded vessels containing miniature vessels were uncovered, as well as a number of shells and small jade objects found floating on top of a pool of mercury. Little is known about the rules governing the game played on this court, but it is certain that they held great ritual and cultural significance. Dating from around 500 AD, with modifications in the 700s and 1200s, Temple N10-9 has yielded numerous finds, including jade earrings, a jade mask, a bowl with an animal motif, and a large black-on-red bowl.

Nearby at Indian Church are the remains of two 16th C. churches. Incorporating Maya temple blocks, the older one has only its lower walls remaining intact. Next to it stands a Maya stela, possibly erected by Maya who had destroyed the church as an affirmation of their age-old beliefs. Ruins of the second church, destroyed for the same reason, are in the vicinity. A bit more of it remains intact. To the west are the ruins of a sugar mill – with flywheel and a sunken brick-laid reservoir – built by Confederate refugees. Part of the British Honduras Estate Company which had several sugar operations around Belize, the mill's machinery was imported from the Leeds Foundry in New Orleans and installed in 1869. The bricks used for its construction had been brought in as ship's ballast. Its laborers are thought to have been Maya as well as Chinese (because of the Chinese coins found at the site). After the owner died of yellow fever, the mill was abandoned in 1875 and now a strangler fig has overtaken the flywheel.

PRACTICALITIES: There's no water on the trail, so be sure to bring it along. Binoculars may come in handy. Near the dock are thatched structures, where you can eat. There are tee shirts available for sale as well as some wood carvings.

The only place to stay is at **Lamanai Outpost** (☎/fax 02-33578), a 13-cabaña facility with 24-hour electricity and fans. Two-night packages (US$340 pp, double-occupancy and up) are available. The four-night package (US$640 pp, double-occupancy) includes a day trip to La Milpa ruins as well as Blue Creek and the Programme for Belize. Accommodation only is BZ$140 s and BZ$180 d. Children under 12 are free; children 12-16 are BZ$20. Extra persons (four max. in rooms) are BZ$40, not including 6% tax and BZ$5 pp, pn service charge. The lodge offers wind surfing, canoeing, massages (BZ$16 per hour), and night river trips, where they shine a light on the crocs.

Altun Ha

 Set 30 miles to the north of Belize City and just a few miles from the coast, Altun Ha is a rare example of a Maya coastal center. Built on limestone rising just above sea level, the site is separated from the Caribbean by a swamp. Its name derives from the Maya words for the nearby village, Rockstone Pond. That, in turn, takes its name from the large freshwater pond, a reservoir lined on the bottom with yellow clay. At its peak, Altun Ha occupied almost 4½ square miles, and as many as 8-10,000 may have lived here, with some 3,000 residing at its center. There are about 500 mounds or structures in total. Many inhabitants collected shells and worked them into beads and pendants. The presence of jade, obsidian, and shells suggest that it was an important trading as well as agricultural center. It is thought that there may have been a settlement as early as 1000 BC and that a culture existed here by the end of the first century. The first major structures date from that time. They appear to have been occupied until the 10th C. – possibly until the 14th-15th C. Although it was once supposed that this was on the fringe of Maya influence during the later periods, excavation has proved that Maya inhabited the area from ancient times onward. It was thought that, as the area's soil is largely inappropriate for agriculture, the excellent water supply must have been what lured the Maya. The current theory holds that the Maya fed themselves through a system of raised fields and canals built in swampy areas. While tombs at other sites were constructed in the form of vaulted and plastered crypts, Altun Ha's were built simply, using walls of boulders and flint slab ceilings. Each crypt held spectacular jade objects.

LAYOUT: Altun Ha is similar in design to other sites. Five pyramids and a palace surround Plaza A, the northernmost of the two central plazas. The solid pyramids were once topped by altars or chambered structures made of masonry or wood and thatch. Plaza A contains Pyramid A-1, the Temple of the Green Tomb, which yielded over 300 jade pieces. Badly damaged Temple A-6 , to the right as you come in, has two parallel 157-foot-long rooms, each with 13 exterior doorways. Plaza B was added around 550 AD, rising 59 feet. The most spectacular find was the carved jade head of the sun god (Kinich Ahau) found in the seventh tomb at the summit of the Temple of Masonry Altars. Also known as the Sun God Temple because of the images of the Sun God carved on either

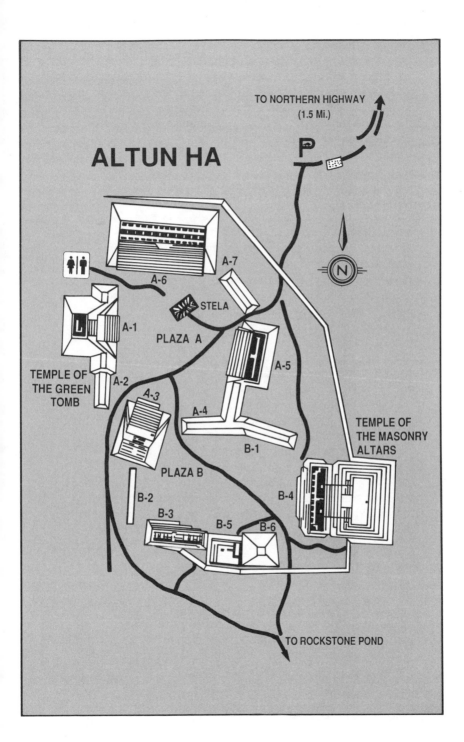

side of its bottom set of steps, as well as the carved jade head, this is the site's tallest building. This temple's circular stone altars date from around 600-700 AD. Remains of incense and blackened jade beads and pendants were found around the base. Fed by rain runoff and springs, and dammed by the ancient Maya, Rockstone Pond is 1,500 feet south of Plaza B. The medium-sized temple (200 AD) standing next to it was used to receive offerings from Teotihuacán in the Valley of Mexico.

GETTING THERE: Unfortunately, the road here is the former Northern Highway, and there is now not much in the way of bus service. But you may be able to take a bus from Belize City to Maskall; Altun Ha is a few miles further. Tour and taxi are the easier ways to visit. Many visitors fly in to Corozal or Belize City and make day trips here from San Pedro. If you are a low-budget traveler and can't afford a tour, there are a number of ruins which equal or surpass Altun Ha in interest (notably Xunantunich) and which are more readily accessible.

visiting: Entering, you register and pay. A guard will show you around. First, you pass Plaza A; a strangler fig is to your left and a large mound is to the right. Straight ahead is a large structure, A-3, which has a representation of Chac, the Rain God. To its right are cohune palms. From the top, you can see the Temple of the Masonry Altars. The stairs of the latter are slippery and steep, so watch your step on the way up. This is the temple where the jade head (see above) was discovered, and the views are well worth the somewhat strenuous ascent. From the base, a slippery trail leads back through cohune ridge terrain to Rockstone Pond. This is where the mosquitoes move in for the kill. On this trail, you'll see trees such as pocono boy, hog plum, sea grape, and trumpet. When you arrive at the pond, you might be able to spot a croc or two in the water. In 1993, one nine-footer took a dog that was swimming in the water! It's common to see Salvadorians fishing here. Birdwatching is good during early morning or late afternoon hours. You might see wildlife such as brocket deer.

PRACTICALITIES: It is open from 9 to 5. Entrance fee is BZ$3. Fruit wines are on sale at **Maralyn and Albert's** place along the Old Northern Highway to the north; watch for the sign on your right as you head north. There are a few souvenir stands as well.

outlying accommodation: The well-run **Maruba Resort** (☎ 23-22199) is a health spa located at Mile 40½ on the Old Northern Highway near Maskall. It's run by youthful Nicky Nicholson and his older sister Franzisca, who designed the resort. The uniquely decorated rooms are adorned with hibiscus flowers. Specially prepared vials of body oils, insect repellent, and anti-itch cream are provided. Well-suited for those who want something more adventurous than Cancún but aren't prepared to rough it, Maruba has grounds adorned with bromeliads, blooming heliconias, and coconut palms. The majority of guests are women seeking a spa experience. A small zoo has a kinkajou and a peccary. A comfortable and atmospheric thatched-roof restaurant and bar has eclectic local art, including wood carvings and masks, and a wide variety of world music plays in the background. There's a large outdoor hot tub, a pool with a fountain, and a variety of services, from pedicures to facials. Massages and wraps are given with New Age music soothing the atmosphere. While two types of massage oil are provided, there's little apparent difference between the two except the price. A variety of tours and excursions are available, including a trip to nearby Altun Ha and a visit to Lamanai aboard the resort's private boat. A resort exclusive is a hike through the bush led by a local, who explains the area's natural history. A visit to a looted Maya mound may be included. You'll learn about the pocono boy palm, the trumpet tree, the mountain cow rib, and the water tea time vine. Rates are around BZ$170 s, and BZ$215 d, plus 16% tax and service. In the US write Box 300703, Houston, TX 77230; ☎ 800-627-8227 or fax 713-799-2031. Near the village of Maskall, low-budget accommodation is provided by **Maralyn and Albert** at Mile 31½. Watch for the "local wine for sale" sign.

Colha: Although not an attraction for visitors, this ancient archaeological site, set along the highway north of Maskall, shows evidence of Maya habitation dating back 4,500 years.

Orange Walk Town

 Situated on the left bank of the New River, Orange Walk Town (pop. 11,000) is 66 miles north of Belize City and 30 miles south of Corozal Town. From its center, roads branch off in four directions – linking the 20-odd outlying villages. Orange Walk isn't a particularly attractive place to stay. It is a major sugarcane and ganja center. Sugarcane trucks rumble through the town continually during the harvest season, spilling pieces of cane here and there. Cane-laden trucks line up at the sugar mill to the south of town.

The town is best used as a base to visit the Cuello and Lamanai ruins. There are a large number of low-life bars here – seemingly more per capita than anywhere else in Belize. At night you may be offered a piece of rock – and they don't mean Gibraltar. In direct contrast, Mennonites, visiting from the outlying settlement of Blue Creek, abound and almost 20% of the stores are owned by East Indians.

SIGHTS: The ruins of Ft. Cairns (now the new town hall) and Ft. Mundy (near the police station; now the government rest house) serve as reminders of the days the town warded off Maya attacks. In 1872, an outnumbered detachment of the West India Regiment fended off an attack by the Icaiche Maya; an obelisk by the taxi stand commemorates the encounter. Just past the police station is a park and children's playground. Here, you will find the statue of a soldier, though no one seems to know who he is or why the statue was erected. In the area you're likely to hear the sound of barges blowing their horns on the river.

HISTORY: One of the nation's first settlements, it began as a timber camp. *Mestizos* arrived en masse in 1849. The local Icaiche Maya attacked the town in 1872 but were defeated. Today their descendants reside in the village of Botes, near the Río Hondo on the Guatemala border. Once this was mainly a center for chicle tapping and maize growing, but the sugarcane industry has grown substantially in recent years and has come to dominate the local economy.

ACCOMMODATION: The best place to stay is undoubtedly 31-room **D'Victoria Hotel** (☎ 03-2518/2364). The BZ$45 s or BZ$50 d you pay here entitles you to use the swimming pool and enter the disco. The comfortable rooms are equipped with private shower and fans; more expensive (around BZ$85) double rooms come with a/c. The management and staff are friendly and helpful. There's a cable TV in the lobby, along with complimentary coffee. The two low-end places, **Jane's Hotels** (03-22473), on 2 Bakers Street and on Market Lane, charge around BZ$15 for spartan rooms. The latter is in a bad location – near the sleazy, hustler-ridden Club America, a bar-brothel nicknamed "Vietnam." Next up in price and above the restaurant of the same name, **Tai San's Hotel** (☎ 03-22752) is at 30 Queen Victoria Ave. and charges BZ$20 s and BZ$30 d. All other hotels are higher priced but still in the budget range. Next to a gas station on the northern side of town, **Chula Vista Motel** (☎ 03-2365) has seven rooms from about BZ$40 d. Also try the 11-room **Nueva Mi Amor Hotel** (☎ 03-2031) at 19 Belize/Corozal Rd. or the nine-room **La Nueva Ola Hotel** (☎ 03-22104), 73 Otro Benque Rd. Set near the center of the town, but on the water, **Lamanai Maya-**

tours (☎ 03-23839; Box 90, Orange Walk) has bungalows renting for around BZ$110 d. Outside of town, **Circle K Lodge** (☎ 03-22600), at Mile 48½ along the Old Northern Highway, is not particularly recommended.

FOOD: One of the few places serving fish is the attractive lounge next to the Hotel Baron. Log-cabin-style **Eddie's Cabin**, 46 San Antonio Rd., features gibnut. Also try the **Lover's Lane Restaurant**, right by the park, run by the friendly Novelos. **Julie's**, near the police station, features good inexpensive creole cooking. Others to try include **La Favorita**, 15 Lover's Lane, the **Golden Gate Restaurant**, 10 Main St., and **El Beliceño**. The classiest place is "**The Diner**," which is behind the hospital on Clark St., a good walk (or short taxi ride) from the north of town. For bread, **Panaderia La Popular**, Beckie's Lane, sells onion bread and sweet "Chop Suey Bread."

CHINESE FOOD: Orange Walk has a large number of Chinese Restaurants. Cool and spacious **Lee's, New Light, Kingfa**, and **Golden Gate** are all nearly in a straight line on Yo Creek Rd. **Jane's Chinese Food Corner**, 21 Main St., also has burgers and "lobster thermidor." Next to the park, **Happy Day's Ice Cream Parlor and Restaurant** has the monthly pages from a calendar of Chinese movie stars pinned up on the wall. **San Martin Bar and Restaurant**, 4 Park St., and the **New Chinese Restaurant**, 1 Park St., offer good value. Just around the corner, **Happy Valley Chinese Restaurant**, allegedly "in air conditioned and romantic atmosphere," has similar prices. Still another choice is **Tai San** on Belize Rd.

SERVICES: There are three banks. Schnookles Travel Services and Postal Agency is on the southern outskirts, along the Belize-Corozal Rd.

    tours: Herminio Novelo's **Jungle River Trips** is based in Orange Walk (☎ 03-22293; 20 Lover's Lane or PO Box 95, Orange Walk Town). They offer good tours of Lamanai. Also try the **Godoy family** (☎ 03-22969) at No. 4 Trial Farm to the north of town on the right. They can take you on a tour of their orchid farm.

FROM ORANGE WALK: Buses run hourly toward Corozal and Chetumal and half-hourly toward Belize City. Since the town is a way station, there's no telling the exact time a bus will pass. Just wait at the gas station up from Baron's in the center of town.

Vicinity of Orange Walk Town

El Posito

This is about four miles west of Guinea Grass. It was once partially excavated and, although it has been largely reclaimed by the jungle, you can see a wide range of Maya ruins.

Shipyard

Visible along the river if you travel from Orange Walk to Lamanai by boat, this Mennonite community makes furniture. Locals here are a mixture of progressive and traditional.

Cuello

This is a later site than Lamanai and not developed for visitors. There's not much to see here, except for a small pyramid and a few mounds. Archaeological indications are that it was founded by 2500 BC and continuously occupied for the next 3,000 years. It is believed that many of the pyramid-plaza architectural techniques originated here. Excavations at this site have demonstrated that, by the end of the Early Preclassic (1000 BC), the pyramid-plaza ceremonial architecture, house design, a social structure, staple foods, and ceramics were well established, laying the path for further development. The site also contains the earliest known Maya masonry building, a rectangular plaster-covered limestone structure in the central courtyard dating from 650 BC. Typically glazed a monochrome red-orange, Swazey ceramics, the earliest ceramics found in Belize, have been found here. Not all of the discoveries here indicate an easy existence. Over 20 skeletons showing evidence of torture and sacrifice have been found in a mass burial site dating from 400 BC. Containing five individuals believed to have been part of the same family, the oldest known human burial plot (dating from 3,000 years ago) was excavated here in 1993. A total of 180 graves have been unearthed. As with nearly all Maya sites, the original name is unknown and the site's current name comes from the property owners.

practicalities: To get here, follow Bakers St. west from the center of town for about an hour. A taxi will charge around BZ$10 RT. To the left as you enter through the pasture, there are a set of completely unexcavated ruins amidst a thick grove of ramon trees. The site is open Monday to Saturday, and is closed on Sunday. As the site is on private property, ask permission inside the first building you come to (a soap factory) and pass through the gate to the left of the rum factory. Turkey buzzards scatter as you approach down the road. It's pleasant enough just to sit atop the pyramid and watch the cows munching grass

Nohmul

 This major ceremonial center, whose name means "Great Mound," rises atop a limestone ridge extending from the west of the Orange Walk/Corozal boundary to the west of San Pablo village. Spread widely apart, there are two "twin" ceremonial groups, surrounded by several plazas and connected by a raised causeway or "sacbe." The main building is an Acropolis-like structure on which a pyramid has been mounted, the tallest building in the Orange Walk/Corozal area. Abandoned during the Classic Period (350 BC-250 AD), it was reoccupied during the Early Postclassic (600 AD-900 AD). Unfortunately it has been extensively plundered, and one structure was even used for road fill!

getting there and touring: The site is situated among sugarcane fields a mile to the west of San Pablo village, 7½ miles north of Orange Walk on the Northern Highway. All Orange Walk-Corozal buses from Belize City or from Orange Walk pass by. Ask the driver to let you off at the entrance to Nohmul in San Pablo, which is at the Keystone Bar. Before visiting you might try contacting Estevan Itzab in the house across from the village water tower. From the road, keep walking straight in. A bit up to the right from the first road intersecting at right angles, you come to a wood-fired bakery and then a school. Keep straight on the road, passing sugar cane fields and corn until the road bends sharply to the left. At this point, take the road to the right, heading off into the trees and then the smaller road off to the right again. You'll see a hill covered with vegetation. To the right, you'll see an excavated grotto and to its left, there's a path. Climbing up, you'll come to a stone platform. Descending and then heading up the other, vegetation-covered hill, you can see where artifacts have been looted. The top – surrounded by cecropia trees – affords great views of the lush area. Everything is still save for the sounds of clattering martins. From the top, you can continue down the other side, see more trenches, and take a path to the right which leads back to your starting point.

Blue Creek

There are Mennonite settlements around the progressive community of Blue Creek Village, about 30 miles from Orange Walk. As you approach, sugar cane fields give way to fields of sorghum and corn. The small hydroelectric dam and plant here is an example of the ingenuity of this remarkable people. Having dammed the Rio Bravo and cut the channel to provide water for the plant's operation, they still lacked hydraulic equipment to control the water's flow. After a Constellation cargo plane crashed at the international airport, the Mennonites purchased the wreck. They converted its fuselage to a barn and its hydraulic gear was used to control the flow of water! There are also furniture-making operations in the village. Half of the community here belongs to the Evangelical Mennonite Mission Church (EMMC), while the remainder have joined the slightly more conservative Kleine Gemeinde. The Old Colony church, which monopolized the village's religious industry until 1966, has disbanded, with its remaining members moving elsewhere in Belize or even as far afield as Bolivia.

Corozal Town

 Set on the edge of attractive Corozal Bay, this small town (pop. 8,000) abounds with flowering flamboyants and coconut palms, as well as a number of old buildings. Lying 96 miles north of Belize City, it is nine miles from the Río Hondo, which delineates the Belize-Mexico border. Safer than Orange Walk, this attractive community is also just 20 minutes from Chetumal, Mexico. As with other towns, it's not so much a destination in itself as a base from which to visit the surrounding area. If you're looking for an attractive town to visit, Corozal is an apt candidate. Its only drawbacks are that the bay is too polluted for swimming and that a number of indolent locals think all *gringos* are Daddy Warbucks and will try to get a handout. Politely refuse; don't encourage dependency.

HISTORY: Originally a private estate named after the cohune palms found in the area, the town was settled largely by *mestizo* refugees from the massacre at Bacalar, Mexico during the Caste Wars (La Guerra de las Castas, 1848-1880). In this war the Maya struggled to drive *mestizos* and Spanish Creoles from the Yucatán. The town was largely rebuilt after 1955's Hurricane Janet wreaked devastation, destroying its Mexican-style adobe walls. It has been

Corozal Town

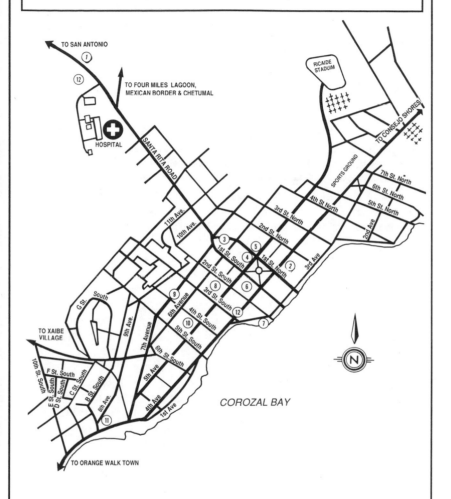

TO SAN ANTONIO

TO FOUR MILES LAGOON,
MEXICAN BORDER & CHETUMAL

RICAIDE STADUIM

HOSPITAL

SANTA RITA ROAD

TO CONSEJO SHORES

SPORTS GROUND

7th St. North
6th St. North
5th St. North
4th St. North
3rd St. North
2nd St. North

11th Ave.
10th Ave.

1st St. South
2nd St. South
3rd St. South

1st St. North

2nd Ave
3rd Ave

4th St. South
5th St. South
6th St. South

C St. South

9th Ave.
8th Avenue
7th Avenue
6th Avenue

TO XAIBE
VILLAGE

10th St. South
11th St. South
F St. South
E St. South
D St. South
C St. South
B St. South
8th Ave.
7th Ave.
5th Ave
4th Ave
1st Ave

COROZAL BAY

N

TO ORANGE WALK TOWN

1. To Santa Rita Ruins
2. Batty Bus Terminal
3. Venus Bus Terminal
4. Post Office, pay phone
5. Belize Bank
6. Town Hall
7. Market
8. Bookstore
9. Nestor's Hotel
10. The Capri
11. Taxi Stand

largely rebuilt and now has parks and modern streets. The old fort harks back to the era when there were frequent Maya attacks from across the border. In typical Latin style, the Catholic and Protestant churches, the library, the town hall, and other governmental buildings surround the main square. Santa Rita, one of the most important Post-Classic Maya ruins, is just east of town, and Cerro Maya or Cerros, another archaeological site, is at the head of the bay across from town. The surrounding area depends upon the sugar industry. Other major products include rum, corn, citrus, and coconuts. Among the holidays celebrated here are Carnival, Columbus Day, and many other fiestas.

ARRIVING BY AIR: If flying in from Ambergris with Tropic Air (☎ 02-45671, 026-2012; BZ$60 OW) or with Island Air, you sweep over the ocean and across a vast expanse of jungle, swamp, and more swamp. There's no habitation as far as you can see. As you approach the landing strip, you fly over *milpas* (cornfields) hacked from the jungle. At the strip, taxis (BZ$5 pp) await to speed you the two miles to town. Or you can take the short walk out to the road and flag down a passing bus. It will take you either to Chetumal or to town, letting you off at the small bustling market.

SIGHTS: Interlaced with diagonal foot paths, the park has a broken fountain as its centerpiece. Nearby, a **mural** by Manuel Villamor Reyes in the town hall depicts the area's history. Villamor originally painted the vibrant mural in 1953 and, when asked to restore it in 1986, he decided to redo it entirely. Among other things, it portrays an owner whipping his slaves, snobbish nobility, deforestation, a Maya temple, a great hurricane, chicle tapping, and sugarcane processing. If the town hall is closed, you may view the rear wall mural through the side windows. Constructed to ward off Maya attacks, the ruins of a small fort stand in the corner of the plaza. Located on private land, the **Aventura Sugar Mill** is seven miles from town on the Northern Highway just past the village of the same name. The chimney is the most prominent feature remaining. Sugar processing began here during the 1800s. The ruins of a 16th C. church are also found here.

Santa Rita ruins: Completely ringing Corozal are the ruins of Santa Rita Corozal. It's not nearly as impressive as other sites, with only one partially-restored structure still standing. Located about a mile to the northeast, the Maya Santa Rita ruins were first explored by British medical practitioner, Thomas Gann, at the beginning of the century. Originally the mighty Maya city known as Chetumal, it was still thriving in 1531 when conquistador Alfonso

Davila was booted out. While it is linked by pottery styles to the Yucatán, some of its murals resemble those found at Tulum. The site was extensively excavated by the Chases of the University of Southern Florida from 1979 through 1985. Most of the exciting finds have been removed to Belmopan's Archaeological Vault. To get to the largest Classic Period construction at the site, take the road heading north and then continue left on a smaller road as the highway veers to the right. The site's largest remaining pyramid is set across from the Coca-Cola factory. The site's Structure No. 7 dates from 350 AD. The purpose of the temple's construction was ceremonial, to provide both living quarters and, later, a tomb for the chief. Six murals from No. 1 were destroyed by superstitious Indians in 1900, before Gann could copy them The site is open from 8 to 5 daily; BZ$2 admission. To get here, turn left at Hilltop Bar and follow the road. Pedro, the one-armed guard, will show you around and give you a wonderful description. It's worth the trip alone just to meet him.

Cerro Maya ruins: Cerro Maya or Cerros ruins were excavated by David Freidel of Southern Texas Methodist University. They are now partially underwater. Admission is BZ$2. One temple is 64 feet high. Its masks have been covered with plaster to stave off erosion. The center blossomed in the Late Preclassic. Abandoned around AD 100 – probably because the growth of inland Maya centers had made it economically untenable – it was not remodeled like other sites. A canal 4,000 feet long, 20 feet wide, and six feet deep – part of the raised terrace agricultural system – surrounded the site, enclosing some 90 acres. Two ball courts and a pyramid-plaza group were in the center. Its pyramids displayed stuccoed and painted masks. Structure 5C has four masks: two representing the sun and Venus, with two others not positively identified. It was acquired during the 1970s by Texas-based Metroplex Properties, Inc. The Cerro Maya Foundation was formed to excavate the site, reconstruct it as a tourist attraction with a museum, and to build a hotel with a swimming pool. This all came to naught when the foundation went bankrupt. It can now be reached by boat from Corozal or by a roundabout dry-season-only land route though Chunox, Progresso, and Copper Bank. Taking the shore route on foot, it is necessary to find an accommodating boatman to ferry you across the New River's mouth.

Four Miles Lagoon is set by the road to the Mexican border, about seven miles from Corozal; it's possible to camp here if you contact the owners. There's good swimming.

FESTIVALS AND EVENTS: The liveliest times of the year are when the Mexican-style fiestas punctuate the day-to-day monotony. The three major events are Carnival, Columbus Day, and Christmas. The latter features colorful *posadas* in which the nativity is re-enacted.

ACCOMMODATIONS: Located in the town, the cheapest hotel (BZ$11 s) is the 30-room **Capri** (☎ 04-2042) at 14 4th Ave. (cor. 5th). It's ideal only if you're truly on a low budget; a blaring TV is located by the bar downstairs, bugs are plentiful, and weekend dances can keep you up late. Conveniently located **Nestor's** (☎ 04-22354), 123 5th Ave., is also low-budget and very popular. Rooms, which are being refurbished, have private baths with hot water. It's not a yuppie spot but neither is it a dive: value by Belizean standards is reasonable for what you get. Room rates are BZ$20 s, BZ$25 d, BZ$29 d with twin beds, and BZ$35 with double twin beds. There's a BZ$5 key deposit, and tax is added. It also has a restaurant. Just past the southern entrance to town, the 17-room **Hotel Maya** (☎ 04-22082, PO Box 112) is pricier, at around BZ$33 s and BZ$58 d. Located at the South End, on the main road to the south of town, the **Caribbean Village** (☎ 04-22045; PO Box 55) charges BZ$10 for a campsite and rents seven cabins for BZ$30. Set on the sea a bit over half a mile to the south of town, attractive 26-room **Tony's Inn and Resort** (☎ 04-22055, fax 04-22829; PO Box 12, Belize City) charges in high season from around BZ$70 s and BZ$90 d for its cheapest rooms on up to BZ$160 for a "deluxe" quad; 16% for tax and service are added. Popular with tour groups, it is the most upscale place to stay and has a good restaurant. Rooms have both a/c and fan and the "deluxe" rooms have a/c, cable TV, and fan. Budget-priced eight-room **Hotel Posada Mama** (☎ 04-22107) is on G St. in southern Corozal and is partially a/c. Some 3½ miles from the Mexican border, the **Camino Real Hotel** offers a restaurant and four rooms in the inexpensive price range. You can also camp along the shore of Four Mile Lagoon near the border. The Adventure Inn closed its doors forever in April 1994.

FOOD: Nestor's has reasonably priced food, real coffee and expresso, two TVs, and a decor which includes mannequins and posters of bikes, Randy Travis, and a young Elvis crooning. **Club Campesino** on 4th Ave. has fried chicken in the evenings from 7 to midnight. Try **Donna's Cafe** near the Texaco station for breakfast and local food. The market has plenty of good food (rice and beans with beverage for BZ$4.50) and ambience aplenty. It is set right on the dock, and both fresh and dried fish are sold here. **Dubie's** is exceptionately good value for rice and beans and for fish dishes. **Splendique** is at the northern edge of town. The **Chula Vista** is another alternative. For pastries try the **Flamingo** at the northeast edge of the park.

out of the center: Set at the northern end of town on the sea front, **Crises** features good local food. In the opposite direction from the plaza, you can try the **Hotel Maya** for Spanish cuisine. For hamburger and steak, try inexpensive **Miss Joe's Caribbean Restaurant** in the middle of the Caribbean Village. It closes during the afternoon. **Tony's** has the nicest ambience (and some of the highest prices) of any local restaurant.

Chinese food: As in Orange Walk, there's no lack of choice here. **Bumper** Chinese restaurant is on the main road opposite the Capri. You can also try the **Mayflower** on 4th Ave., **King of Kings** on 3rd Ave., **Hong Kong** on 4th Ave., and the **Rexo** at 9th and 6th St. North.

ENTERTAINMENT: Located by the cemetery to the north of town, next to the Adventure Inn sign, **Gonz Z Roses** is a popular bar. On 1st Ave by the waterfront, the **Cascada Maya** has dances on weekends, as does the **Capri** to the south of town. Also visit the **Sky Top** and the **Blue Dahlia** in town.

SERVICES: The town's banks (open Mon. to Fri. 9-1, plus 3-6 on Fri.) are the Belize Bank across from the park, the Bank of Nova Scotia, and Barclays. Travel agents are **Menzies Travel and Tours** (☎ 04-22725/23415, fax 04-23414, VHF 148-600; Ranchito Village or PO Box 210) and Manuel Hoare's **Ma-Ian's Tours** (☎ 04-2274/22055) at No. 13 6th St., southern Corozal Town. Also contact **Leslie's Travel Service** (☎ 04-22377; 57 7th Av.), which offers charters and other services. For plane tickets contact **Jal's Travel Agency** (☎ 04-22163) on Fourth Avenue. **Johnnie's Auto Repair** is at 23 8th Ave. S.

FROM COROZAL: Buses for Belize City and Chetumal, Mexico pass through the town approximately once an hour. While the Venus bus station (☎ 04-22132) is near the northern edge of town across from the Shell station, Batty buses (☎ 04-23034) stop at their own station by the road just around the corner from the park. For Chetumal, Batty runs at 7, 8, 8:15, 9, 10, 11, noon, 1, and 2; Venus runs at 2:45, 4, 4:30, 5, 5:30, 6, 6:30, 7, 7:30, 8, 8:30, 9, and 10. For Orange Walk and Belize City, Venus departs at 6:15, 6:45, 7:15, 7:45, 8:15, 8:45, 9:15, 9:45, 10:15, 11:15, 11: 45, and at 12:15; Batty leaves at

12:15, 1:15, 2:15, 3:15, 3:30, 4:15, 5:15, and at 6:15. Maya and Tropic Air both fly to Belize City.

Chetumal, Mexico

 Founded in 1898, this modern city today is the capital of Quintana Roo and the gateway from Belize to Mexico. Once a somnolent tropical port, its designation as a duty-free port (6% duty as opposed to the usual 15%) has brought development galore, and this is a major shopping spot. The waterfront is a 10-minute walk from the marketplace, and most of the hotels are centrally located. While the city doesn't have much of a traditional Mexican air about it, it does serve as a good introduction to the country and as a base to get acclimated before moving on. There's really nothing to do in town, but the surrounding countryside has a good deal to offer. It makes a much more interesting day trip than, say, visiting Melchor from Benque Viejo.

ARRIVING: If you're going farther, it would be a good idea to get a Mexican visa stamp and visitor's card (free for US citizens) at the embassy in Belize City. In any case, when you cross the border, pass beyond the two desks at the front (where Belizeans wait) and go straight ahead to the desks at the back, where you'll be stamped in. The bus will be waiting for you on the road. If you have your own car, you'll have to pay to have it fumigated for medflies when entering Mexico. Moneychangers at the border give a lower rate than you'll get at the bank. However, if you need Belizean dollars and have cash, you can get BZ$2.03 per US dollar when you return. Buses arrive at and leave from the large, ultramodern terminal on the outskirts of town; either take a taxi or walk half an hour. If you haven't changed money at the border, you can change at Banamex (open 9-1:30) at the corner of Juárez and Obregón.

by air: Aerovias flies between Belize City and Chetumal for around US$30 OW.

SIGHTS: The best area to explore is the back streets, but the main sight is the **Zoo** (Zoológico Payo Obispo) along Ave. de los Insurgentes on the north side. Take a taxi or the ISSTE bus from the rear of the market on Ave. Héroes. There is a wide variety of wildlife indigenous to the area on display, from a manatee to spider and howler monkeys to ocelots and jaguarundis. **Calderitas**, five miles north of the city, is a great spot for a picnic. There are also RV hookups and camping. Public beaches are nearby. Isla Tamalcas, about a mile offshore from Calderitas, is home to the capybara, the world's largest rodent. With its partially webbed toes and coarse hair, it can weigh up to 110 lbs. Renowned for their swimming ability, capybaras are referred to locally as water pigs.

EXPENSIVE ACCOMMODATION: A 15% tax applies to all meals and accommodation. Equipped with swimming pool and a/c rooms, the **Hotel Los Cocos** (☎ 20544; Ave. Héroes at Chapultepec) is the city's best hotel. Less expensive is the **Hotel Continental Caribe** (☎ 20441; Ave. Héroes 171), also with a pool. Less expensive still (approximately US$30 d) are the **Hotel Real Azteca** (Ave. Belice 186), the **Caribe Princess** (☎ 20900; Ave. Obregón 168;), and the **Hotel Príncipe** (☎ 25167, 24799) at Prolongación Ave. Héroes 326.

BUDGET ACCOMMODATION: Expect to spend about US$10 pp. Alternatives include the **Posada Pantoja**, Lucio Blanco 95, set a half-mile northeast of the market; **Hotel Quintana Roo**, Obregón 193; **Hotel Baroudi** (☎ 20902), Obregón 39; the **Hotel Ucum** (☎ 20711), M. Gandhi 167; the **Hotel Jacaranda** (☎ 21455), on Obregón; **The Colonial** (☎ 21520), Benjamin Hill 135; **Tabasco** (☎ 22045), Ave. Zargoza 206; the **Hotel María Dolores** (☎ 20508), Obregón 206; and the **America**, Orthon P. Blanco 11. The **CREA Youth Hostel** is at the corner of Calz. Veracruz and Obregón (☎ 205255).

FOOD: For pizza try **Sergio's** at Obregón 182. The hotels also have good restaurants. The **Restaurant Pantoja**, at M. Gandhi and 16 de Septiembre, serves inexpensive meals, as does the nearby restaurant in the **Hotel Ucum**, M. Gandhi 167. There are a large number of cheaper restaurants, and the market is good value for dining.

food shopping: If you're driving your own car, you may wish to load up on food before returning to Belize. **Conasuper** supermarkets are at Independencia (two blocks west of the main drag) and on Zaragoza. Set at the corner of Ave. Héroes and Zaragoza and open 24 hours, the **Supermercado y Restaurante Arcadas** serves light food and sells groceries. If leaving by bus, you can stop in at the enormous **Blanco** department store-supermarket next to the bus station.

ENTERTAINMENT: Discos here include the **Focus** at the Hotel Continental, Ave. Heroes 171; the **Sarawak** at the Del Prado, Ave. Héroes and Chapultepec; and the **Huanos Astoria**, Ave. Reforma 27. There are also a number of cinemas; check the newspapers.

EVENTS: An international road race takes place annually in Dec.

SHOPPING: Shops are open 8-1 and 6-10. The market is well worth a visit. Located on the town's outskirts, the prison has a gift shop selling jewelry, hammocks, and other handmade wares.

SERVICES: The Correos (post office) is at Plutarco Elisa on C. 2A. The Telégrafos Nacionales (telegraph office) is at Ave. 5 de Mayo s/n. The Biblioteca Central (central library) is at the corner of Ave. Primo de Verdad and Ave. Hidalgo.

VICNITY OF CHETUMAL: The **Lagunas de Siete Colores** ("Lagoon of Seven Colors") lies 23 miles north at Bacalar, which also features a 17th C. fort with a small museum. Moderate **Hotel Las Lagunas** is here, as is **Laguna Milagros Trailer Park**, where camping is permitted. Set on the lake, **Rancho Encantado** offers eight casitas which hold a total of 29 guests; they also have a villa for rent. Breakfasts and dinners are included in the rates. Call 800-748-1756 or write Box 1644, Taos, NM 87571. On Hwy. 307, 20 miles north of Chetumal, **Cenote Axul** is a beautiful deep-blue watering hole. On Hwy. 186, 45 miles west of Chetumal, the Maya site of **Kohunlich** (open daily 8-5) was built between AD 100 and 900. Its main attractions are the two six-foot masks in the Temple of the Masks. There were eight originally, but six have been destroyed by looters.

FROM CHETUMAL: Long-distance buses run to Tulum (four hours), Merida (five hours), and Mexico City (22 hours). For Belize, Batty buses depart daily at 5, 6, 6:30, 8:30, 10, noon, 1, 1:30, 3, and 5. The noon bus is an express, stopping only in Orange Walk. Also an express, the 1:30 bus stops only at Orange Walk and Corozal Town. There's an additional bus on Monday at 2. Venus buses depart at 4:30, 8, 9, 11, 2, 4, and 6 daily. If you want to proceed directly to Guatemala and Tikal, Batty buses leave at 2:30 and 4 AM for the Guatemalan border. Don't try to bring cigarettes and alcohol bought in Mexico into Belize; it's officially forbidden – although Belizean customs seldom searches you.

by air: Aerovias flies directly to Belize City. Note: West German and Japanese nationals require a visa for Belize, which can be obtained at the consulate in Chetumal.

Shipstern Wildlife Reserve

Established in 1981, this reserve protects 31 square miles and 22,000 acres of tropical moist forest, an area devastated by Hurricane Janet in 1955. There are also vast areas of savannah and the Shipstern Lagoon, which is sprinkled with mangrove-covered islands. Taking its name from the abandoned village of Shipstern in the reserve's south, this is the nation's only protected area which contains both the more seasonal northern hardwood forests as well as saline lagoon systems and mangrove shorelines. Wide belts of savannah – containing saline mudflats, limestone hillocks crowned with palms and hardwoods – separate the forest from the lagoon. Tracks between the hillocks show the variety and quantity of animal traffic. Shallow and barely navigable, the Shipstern Lagoon provides an important habitat for many birds, including migrants during the winter months.

FAUNA: The area is a naturalist's nirvana with over 200 species of birds. Warblers, keel-billed toucans, fly-catchers, collared aracari, and at least five species of parrots reside in the forest. Lesser scaup, American coot, 13 species of egret, Yucatán jay, black catbird, and blue winged teal fly over the lagoon. Other dwellers include manatees, coatis, jaguars, ocelots, tapirs, deer, peccaries, pumas, raccoons, 60 species of reptiles and amphibians including the Morelet's crocodile, plus innumerable butterflies and other insects.

butterflies: The butterfly breeding center at the reserve's headquarters exported pupae to Britain until 1991when the operation was suspended because of time constraints. Because butterflies become quiescent on overcast or rainy days, it's best to visit on a sunny day.

GETTING THERE: A bus departs from Belize City around noon (from the Shell station on North Front St. by the Caye Caulker dock). The trip to Sarteneja Village is three hours (including a stop in Orange Walk), and the bus returns at 3, 4, and 6 PM. A direct bus from Orange Walk generally leaves at 6 PM, but you should ask.

by car: From Orange Walk, it's a one-hour drive. Pass through San Estevan and take the turn to the Mennonite community of Little Belize just before Progresso. From there proceed to Chunox. The reserve is three miles before Sarteneja.

HIKING: The *Chiclero Botanical Trail*, a self-guiding nature trail, leaves from the visitor's center. It displays three different types of northern hardwood forest, along with 100 or so species of trees. You'll see sapodillas, ceibas, and strangler figs. **tours:** Prices are BZ$12.50 for one to four, and an additional BZ$2.50 for each extra person. Belizeans receive a 50% discount.

Sarteneja

Founded in 1849 by settlers from Valladolid, Mexico who were later joined by groups from Tulum, the Maya name (tza-ten-a-ha) literally translates as a request for water, and this small fishing village (pop. 1,000) is built over an archaeological site. Situated on the largely uninhabited northeast peninsula of the same name, it once could be reached only by boat. The town was leveled by Hurricane Janet in 1955. Once this was the nation's boat building capital, but only two boat building operations survive today. The ruins of a 19th C. sugar mill stand a mile to the south of town. A bat-filled cave is next to the airstrip. The airstrip was closed in the mid-1980s after suspicions arose that it was being used for cocaine transshipment. Even today, it is alleged that boats transport drugs offshore for seaplane pickup. Locals can take you horseback riding and canoeing down the river. **where to stay:** Inexpensive 11-room **Diani's Hotel (☎ 04-22154)** is in Sarteneja Village; other – very basic – rooms are also available.

Blue Heron Cove

Set at Catfish Bight, this getaway lodge is run by Anne K. Lowe, and she provides the best description: "This place is my retirement home. My family now consists of five dogs, five cats (good snake detectors), and a bilingual parrot. [It] is very quiet and not suited to those who like the night sounds of a town or city. The night sounds here are a Pigmy Owl, the cries of other night birds, and my five dogs chasing animals out of my vegetable garden. What I have here is 317 acres of forested land with about five acres cut. There is a lawn of sorts and flower beds with tropical shrubs. There is a house, three small cottages, and two large cottages, plus one that I use when the archaeology students who are working at Cerros come in the summer. Last summer there were 30 students and teachers. There is a trail of more than two miles behind my house to the ruins. Right now we do not have a proper water system so you will have to haul water buckets to flush your john and bathe, unless you want to jump in the bay. Although there is mud, white and sticky on the bottom, it is possible to swim. If you need to arrange transportation, Miro Tzul, who works for me part-time, has the village community phone in his house in Copperbank: 04-22950, best after 6." The five-room lodge is moderately priced; rates are around BZ$20 for dorm, BZ$50 s, BZ$60 d.

The Rio Bravo Conservation Area

 Managed by the Programme for Belize, this 250,000-acre tract has been preserved for research and sustained-yield forestry. The plan is for it to become part of the proposed tri-national Maya Peace Park, which would also encompass the Maya Biosphere Reserve in Guatemala and Mexico's Calakmul Biosphere Reserve.

FLORA AND FAUNA: Subtropical broadleaf forest predominates, covering some two-thirds of the area. It has been a source of mahogany, cedar, and a dozen other hardwoods, so most of the old growth has been harvested at some time. Mammals include 80 species of bats, all five species of cats, tapirs, tayras, monkeys, peccaries, Mexican porcupines, anteaters, and grey foxes. Up to 367 bird species live here although only 200 have been noted so far. The best time to see wildlife is in June.

HISTORY: In 1989, the Programme for Belize purchased 110,000 acres in the area, and it is currently managed as a large, regional resource management and conservation area. An additional 42,000 acres has been donated by Coca Cola Foods. Nearby landowners have cooperated, so the total land under management is nearly 300,000 acres.

MAYA RUINS: Over 40 ruins have been discovered in the area between Gallon Jug and Blue Creek. The largest is La Milpa (see below). **getting there:** Drive here in the dry season from the village of Orange Walk near Belmopan (not the other Orange Walk). Ask for Iguana Crick bridge. There's a private airport at Gallon Jug. For more information contact the Programme for Belize (☎ 02-75616/7; fax 02-75635; PO Box 749, 168 North Front St., Belize City). Or write Mr. William F. Burley, Director for Planning, Programme for Belize, PO Box 1219, McLean, VA 22101; ☎ 703-506-0175. **accommodation:** Stay at the inexpensive six-room Research Station, which offers cabañas and dorm-style digs. Package tours are also available. For information contact the Programme for Belize.

Chan Chich Lodge

Still a part of the reserve owned by founder Barry Bowen, expensive Chan Chich Lodge (☎ 02-75634; PO Box 37, Belize City) sits on the plaza of an ancient Maya temple. Opened in 1988, its dozen thatched cabañas have ceiling fans and are surrounded by rainforest and some three miles of trails. Other than guided walks, activities include horseback riding and canoeing. In the US, ☎ 800-343-8009 or write PO Box 1088, Vineyard Haven, MA 02568. **getting there:** You can charter a plane or drive four hours from Belize City.

La Milpa

 The area's largest archaeological site, La Milpa has some 84 structures, which means that the site ranks below only Caracol and Lamanai in size. It is set midway between the sites of Lamanai and Río Azul, both of which were occupied from the Late Middle Preclassic (600-400 BC), and it is believed to demarcate the northeastern limit of the Petén's cultural influence. Much of the site is thought to have been built during the Late Preclassic period. Its center stands some 600 feet above sea level atop a limestone ridge. In addition to two reservoirs to the south of the Great Plaza, a 300-foot-wide waterhole has been found beyond the southwestern edge of the ridge. **getting there:** The site is a three-mile hike from Chan Chich.

ARCHAEOLOGICAL HISTORY: La Milpa was first noted, and named, by Sir J. Eric Thompson in 1935. He speculated that it might well be the largest site in what was then British Honduras. Archaeologists David M. Pendergast and H. Stanley Loten visited in the 1970s, and archaeology officials inspected the site in 1979, following reports of looting, and again in 1985. During this period, looting (which mainly served to destabilize the ruins) went hand in hand with ganja growing. Other surveys of the site took place in the late 1980s, and Norman Hammond identified Stela 1 as dating from the Early Classic period. Mapping of La Milpa, under the La Milpa Boston University-National Geographic Project (LaMap) began in Feb. 1992. Its intention is to map the area and construct a picture of the ancient Maya community through examination of the available plants and mineral resources. The site's relationship to its landscape will be studied, and excavations will be conducted. As the site is located in a biosphere reserve, an effort will be made

during the course of the tour. One of the most memorable sights is a passage that goes directly back into the rock: an excavation by looters. Because the thieves knew precisely where to dig, they were thought to have been supervised by someone who had been the right-hand man of an archaeologist. Fortunately, they didn't find anything. The Caracol team extended the tunnel farther in and found the undisturbed tomb. As the site is not officially open, there's no admission charge. You can give your guide a donation at the end if you wish. There's no refrigeration on site, so your guide would likely appreciate a cold soft drink or beer should you have one on hand.

Chiquibul Forest Reserve/ Chiquibul National Park

Split in November 1991, the Chiquibul Forest Reserve covered 714 square miles (456,000 acres). In order to protect the endangered species found here (forest reserves may be logged), 265,894 acres were re-designated as Chiquibul National Park. Both the rare keel-billed motmot and the scarlet macaw are found here. Said to be the largest such network in the Americas and one of the five largest in the entire world, the Chiquibul cave system is nine miles to the south and is part of the park, as is Caracol National Monument (described above).

From San Ignacio to Benque Viejo
Cahal Pech

Situated west of the Macal River and commanding a panoramic view of San Ignacio and the Belize River valley, medium-sized Cahal Pech has 34 structures covering just over two acres. Given its natural setting, which offers such a contrast to the bustling town spread out below it, Cahal Pech is a real find for visitors. Discovered in the 1950s, the site was vandalized from 1970 to 1985, and was finally surveyed in 1988. Its name (meaning "Place of the Ticks" in Mopan Maya) arose during the 1950s when it was used for pasture. This ancient Maya settlement has undergone excavation by a team from Canada's Trent University. While nothing spectacular, the ruins are a good place to escape and perhaps spend some quiet time reading.

touring the ruins: To get here, continue straight up the hill past the Hotel San Ignacio and continue on ahead where the main road turns to the right. The surrounding area is devoted to pasture. Entrance is BZ$3. You'll see a Visitor's Center (often closed) as you approach. The ruins have been "restored," which means that layers of concrete have been put on them so that they resemble recent constructions. Along the peaceful sidepaths you can see butterflies and birds. It's a good place to escape from Cayo. Most of the buildings are grouped around seven plazas. Structure A-1 is the tallest, at 77 feet. Although Plaza A is the site's center, Plaza B is the largest. Six plain stelae, two ball courts, and an altar have been unearthed. Climb on top of Structure 9, which has been topped off with concrete. Cahal Pech differs from many other sites in that you can see the remains of residences. You'll find these in the relatively more spacious Plazas B, C, and F.

Windy Hill Cottages

Set at Graceland Ranch, expensive Windy Hill Cottages (☎ 092-2017) are at Mile 1½ Benque Viejo Rd. and are one of the more popular lodges. Facilities here include table tennis, a pool table, TV, and hammocks.

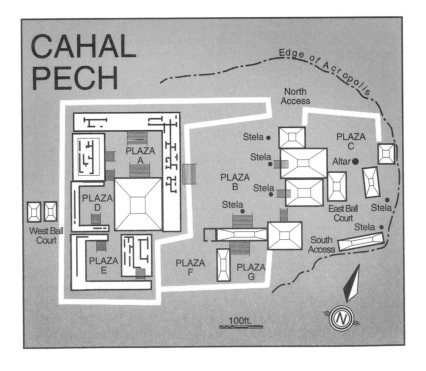

Chaa Creek

Located on the shores of the Macal River west of San Ignacio, Chaa Creek Cottages (☎ 092-2037, fax 092-2501; PO Box 53, San Ignacio, Cayo) feature elegant accommodation. The resort's adobe and wood-walled, palm-thatched cottages are decorated with Maya weavings. Field trails are marked near the lodge and some pass by Maya ruins. The Panti Trail borders the lodge. They have three programs: Belize Explorer, Belize Adventure, and Inland Expeditions. In addition to river canoeing, trips run everywhere from Xunantunich to Caracol and the Chiquibul area, where they have a remote camp. Rates run from around BZ$160 s and BZ$210 d. BZ$10 pp service charge and tax are added.

Panti Trail

Named after the Mayan healer Eligio Panti, the trail (☎ 08-231280, fax 08-23235) is located at Ix Chel, a farm owned by American expatriate and Panti follower Dr. Rosita Arvigo and her husband, Dr. Greg Shropshire. It is right next to Chaa Creek cottages and can be reached by boat or by taxi from San Ignacio. The trail's most remarkable feature is that all the plants and trees along it were found *in situ*, that is none of them were planted by Rosita. This in itself best illustrates the natural biological diversity found in the rainforests. Along the path are jackass bitters, cohune palm, hogplum, basket tie tie bay, cockspur (acacia), bullet tree, Spanish elder, bay cedar, and chico loro vine (used as a purgative). Brought back to Europe by returning sailors, the bark of the negrito, or "dysentery bark," was sold for its weight in gold in European apothecaries for over two centuries. Various trees have products displayed to illustrate their uses. In reference to its Spanish name of *escoba*, the "give and take" has a broom (made by Dr. Panti himself using leaves from the tree) next to it. It is so named because, while it will wound you with its spikes, the fibers from the base of its leaves will staunch the flow. There is copal, with some varnish, the allspice (once used as embalming fluid), wild pineapple, wild grapevine, which serves as a water source, bullhoof, used in birth control, fiddlewood, used by Maya for making musical instruments (its name comes from the Latin *fidele*, indicating toughness). The white *ramon* or breadnut was a staple for the ancient Maya.

Controversial to say the least is Rosita's "Doctrine of Signatures," which maintains that a plant has been marked by some supernatural power to indicate how mankind might use it. Examples of this, she claims, are the *cocol meca*, whose heart-shaped root vines branch out as if they were arteries, and which can be used to cleanse your blood. Another example is poison-wood, whose black oozing resin warns of its toxicity. Also on the premises is a reconstruction of a typical healer's hut with all of the necessary utensils. The gift shop offers a variety of herbs, tinc-tures, and other souvenirs.

Terra Nova: Dr. Arvigo's Belize Association of Traditional Healers (fax 092-2057) supervises the 6,000-acre Terra Nova Me-dicinal Plant Reserve in the Yalbac Hills. The intention is to trans-plant medicinal plant seedlings which are endangered in other areas. Medicinal healers will cull the reserve in a sustainable fash-ion, and field trips will be conducted. **about the owners:** Drs. Rosita Arvigo and Greg Shropshire are narapaths, graduates of the Chicago National College of Narapathy, a Czechoslovakian com-bination of folk medicine and modern chiropractic. Rosita appren-ticed for 10 years with Dr. Panti, an elderly Maya *curandero* (healer) in San Antonio, who introduced her to the local herbs. Rosita and her husband are currently studying local remedies in collaboration with the New York Botanical Garden and accumu-lating medicinal plants for the National Cancer Insititute's pro-gram, which is searching for AIDS and cancer cures. They also offer a number of seminars every summer. For more information, write Rosita Arvigo, General Delivery, San Ignacio, Cayo or ☎ 092-3870. **getting there:** If you're staying at Chaa Creek, it's a short walk. If you have your own vehicle, it's an easy drive. Otherwise you have three choices: 1) rent a canoe and come on your own, 2) take public transportation to Chaa Creek and make the long walk in or hitch, or 3) go on a tour – in which case you'll go upriver in a canoe, motorized or not as you prefer. The river trip is one of the most beautiful in Belize and is highly recommended. Maya Moun-tain (☎ 092-2164) and many others arrange tours.

Black Rock

Owned by Caesar Sherard who also operates Caesar's Place, this is one of the few formal Cayo-area facilities geared for the more truely adventurous traveler. The solar-powered resort has cottage accommodation (BZ$84 d), along with an open-air dining pavilion. Rooms in the more expensive Slate Lodge are BZ$120 d. Activities offered include hiking, horseback riding, canoeing, and excursions. Camping (BZ$10 pp) is also available, as are RV hookups. To get here, turn off at the Chaa Creek junction and follow the signs until you reach the one which says "Park here and follow the river."

From here, it's a 20-minute hike to the property. For more information ☎ 092-2341, fax 092-3449, or write Box 48, San Ignacio.

Ek' Tun

A relative newcomer to the Cayo scene is this 200-acre project. Access is available only by river, horseback, and on foot. Run by Ken and Phyllis Dart, this wilderness resort is set in an area rife with Maya ruins. Over 150 species of birds are found here (including the rare spectacled owl), and there is a waterfall on the premises. At present there is only one large thatched cottage here. Meals are cooked with fresh vegetables gathered from the garden. The cabin holds up to six. Rates are BZ$220 s, BZ$320 d, BZ$340 t, and BZ$400 quad, plus tax. Meals are BZ$64 pp, pd. A variety of tours and excursions are offered. For reservations and further information, ☎ 303-442-6150 in the US; write PO Box 18748, Boulder, CO 80308-8748; or write c/o General Delivery, Benque Viejo, Cayo, or ☎ 93-2536.

du Plooy's

A quiet, exclusive 12-room resort, du Plooys (☎/fax 092-3301) is at Big Eddy on the river's edge. Since opening in 1989, they have launched a reforestation project – planting over 2,500 trees in the their original 20 acres. A botanical garden and tropical fruit orchard is planned for an additional 40 acres. All rooms have generator-powered fans; kerosene lamps are provided for use after the generator shuts off at 10 PM. They have a variety of rooms. The least expensive rooms are in "The Pink House," a six-bedroom and two-bath guest house. They rent for BZ $70 s, BZ$80 d, and BZ $110 t, plus tax. The entire house is also available for rent. "The Jungle Lodge" is luxury-priced and three luxury bungalows – designed to resemble deluxe vacation villas – are also available. Horses and canoes are for rent, and custom-planned tours can be arranged. Call 800-359-0747 in the US.

Nabitunich Lodge

Within reach of budget travelers off-season, this set of eight thatched-roof cabañas with either stone or white stucco walls is an easy walk from the road. A 400-acre cattle farm, Nabitunich is run by a British-Belizean couple. The lodge originally was built to house doctors coming from the US to do volunteer work. Horseback riding is available, there's good birdwatching, and you can cool off in the river. Rates start at BZ$50 s and BZ$70 d, not including 16% tax and service. Call or fax 093-2096 or write Central Post Office, San Lorenzo Farm, Cayo.

Clarissa Falls

Set near the falls of the same name and run by a local woman, the simple and inexpensive three-cottage **Clarissa Falls Cabins** (☎ 093-2424; Box 44, San Ignacio) are off of Mile 5½, Benque Viejo Rd. Meals are served under a thatched-roof pavilion.

Vaca Falls

This is about nine miles south of San Ignacio on the east branch of the Belize River, surrounded by karst hills. Difficult, but worth it. Take the Negroman Farms road from Chial, turning off the road before San José Succotz. It's a two-hour walk to the falls. A second approach is via Chechem Ha (see below).

Xunantunich

The famous Mayan ruins of Xunantunich mean "Maiden of the Rock." The site was named after the Maya maiden seen, according to legend, by one of the temple's earliest visitors after its discovery. Following a pattern established in 16th C. Spanish, the Maya "X" is pronounced "sh." Thus, the site is pronounced "Shoo NAN-too-NEECH." Stress is on the last syllable, as in all Maya words. To reach the ruins, you cross the Mopan River using the hand-pulled cable ferry about 10 minutes walk from the village of Succotz. The ferry (free of charge) operates daily from 8 to 5, with a break from noon to 1. If you're coming from Benque Viejo, it's a peaceful and pleasant walk along the river, past women washing clothes, marred only by the occasional pile of garbage and a vine-covered overturned car – a reminder of the perils of the road. From the ferry stop it's a 20-minute walk uphill along a thickly-forested paved road to the top. From the entrance, there's one large site you can climb. Then you pass by a couple of stelae, so worn and weathered as to be indecipherable. In Plaza A-1 there's a pavilion sheltering three well-worn horizontal stelae with barely decipherable carvings of warriors. From here you can climb El Castillo, following a trail that winds back and forth along its face. There are stairs to the front, steps to the huge, ornate glyphs, representing jaguars, on the side. One set of stairs leads up to the top. From here, the towers

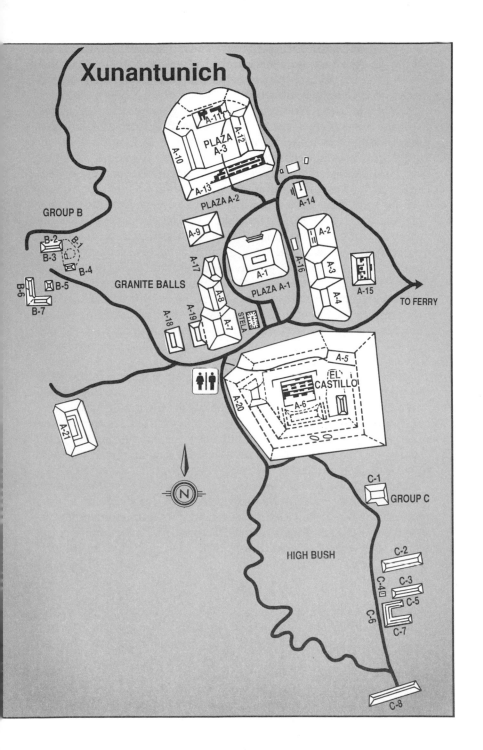

that give El Castillo its name resemble coke chimneys. Back down at the base, you can walk to the right, down to the remains of a ball field and farther on to the residential area excavated by Jes Thompson in 1938.

history: It was first explored in the 1890s by British medical officer Thomas Gann. The Peabody Museum's Teobalt Maler photographed El Castillo in 1904. Returning in 1924, Gann unearthed large numbers of buried items and made off with the carved glyphs of Altar 1, which have since disappeared. It was excavated again in 1938 by archaeologist Jes Thompson. Although a Cambridge University team exploring the site in 1959-60 made the discovery that a 900 AD earthquake apparently precipitated its abandonment, discoveries in 1993 show that it survived and apparently prospered until around AD 1100. The fact that (as with Lamanai) it was on a river may have helped it to survive longer than other such sites. Recent excavations have cleared the preserved sections on the western side of the building which match the famous one found on the east side. Dangerous cracks have also been uncovered, and steps are being taken to strengthen the structure. The southern group has now been opened up, and three stelae are now housed in the Visitor's Center.

layout: Three adjacent plazas run from north to south along its center. Rising at the southern end, is 130-foot-high El Castillo, an enormous pyramid which even today is the tallest building in all Belize, save for the Sky Palace at Caracol to the south. Most of the friezes have been destroyed by natural elements. A 9th C. one which shows through from a previous layer, uncovered by archaeologists but intentionally covered by the Maya, has carvings representing astronomical symbols including the Sun, Moon and Venus. All of these can be seen in the east during the morning hours. The mask with the "big ears" and the ornaments represents the Sun God. The sign for the moon is next, and the border's signs stand for Venus and the different days.

San José Succotz

The Mopan Maya in the village of San José Succotz have preserved much of their culture, and Maya is their native tongue. The big fiestas here are St. Joseph (March 19) and the Holy Cross (May 3). The local dances ("hog head, " "mañanitas," "quinceaños," and "el baile de los mestizos") are all performed to the accompaniment of marimba music. An annual fair is held in April. Because its inhabitants sided with the British, the Icaiche, a rival indigenous group, burned the settlement to the ground in 1867. The 12-room, moderately-priced **Xunantunich Hotel** (☎ 093-2264) is located in this village.

Chechem Ha Cave and Resort

One of Belize's most accessible true remaining adventures, this one-of-a-kind site features a cave containing Maya pottery galore in a beautiful setting. It's also a starting point for a visit to Vaca Falls. Although not for arachnophobes, claustrophobes, nor those who have a fear of ladders, Chechem Ha is well worth a visit. It's one of the only sites in Belize (and one of the few in Central America) that is under the control of locals who are profiting directly from it. The Morales family discovered the cave after they found their dogs were periodically disappearing for 15 or 20 minutes at a time. Following the canines, they discovered the cave. Although the cave is on their property, as an ancient site it is the property of the Belizean government. The cave has been investigated by archaeologists who have dated the pottery and carted the better pieces off to storage. Judging by the remains of corn and other items found within the urns here, it was used for storage, although it is likely that one area was also a ceremonial site. For the Maya, who knew nothing of geology, the cave must have seemed a frightening and bizarre place – an entrance to the underworld. While visiting, try to imagine the cave as they might have seen it.

getting there: From San Ignacio, take the Benque bypass and then the road past a basketball court and the Chinese-built hydroelectric dam. If asking directions, ask for the road to Bob Dole's place. On the way, you must drive along a dirt road and pass by beautiful secondary forest. Following the sign to the right, follow the rough road (a four-wheel-drive is preferable) down to the Morales farm. Unfortunately, no public transportation is available, but it may be possible to hitch a ride. Lodges such as Chaa Creek and Maya Mountain Lodge will arrange transport. If you want to take a taxi, it should cost BZ$35. Be sure to bring a flashlight; otherwise, you'll need to rent one.

visiting the site: This is no sound-and-light experience but a real adventure. Youthful and knowledgeable William Morales is likely to be your guide for the tour. He leads the way, pointing out flora and fauna enroute. The entrance to the cave is secured from trespassers by a locked steel grating. Once inside the cave, you can climb up ladders to get a closer view of the pottery. In certain areas you must duck down pretty low to get through. The oldest pots date back 2,000 years; others were made 1,500 years ago. Most are unadorned. Although you're unlikely to encounter the nesting gibnuts, you might meet the three fruit bats. Pancho is the one who hangs from the ladder. There are some large stalactite formations. To reach the ceremonial chamber, you need to hold onto a rope and climb down a brief but narrow passage, which ends in a short drop-off. It's not as difficult as it might first appear.

practicalities: If you're looking for a simpler and less expensive experience that is genuinely Belizean, Chechem Ha is an ideal place to stay. Facilities at the resort are very basic, but it possesses a great deal of charm for exactly that reason. Individuals who would not feel ill at ease staying in a log cabin in the mountains or camping will feel at home here. Those who want a/c and constant attention won't. The hospitable Morales family are your hosts, and they make a real effort to please. Prices are a reasonable BZ$44 pp for accommodation in cabañas and all meals. Otherwise, breakfast is BZ$10, lunch is BZ$12, and dinner is BZ$20. Meals consist of local dishes, including rice and beans, panades, fried plantains, fish, and the like. A household specialty are handmade, piping-hot tortillas. The round, thatched-roof cabins have two single beds and kerosene lighting; the bath is detached. There's no generator. A path leads down to the river where you can relax. Vaca Falls are nearby; visitors must pay to visit. The tour to the Pottery Cave is BZ$50 for up to four. While this is not inexpensive (especially if you are alone), you are given a lot of personal attention. The more distant Bat Cave (four hours RT) is BZ$200 for up to six. Similarly distant, though less rough, the Ghost Crab Cave costs BZ$100 for up to three. The smaller Gibnut Cave is BZ$50 for up to six. For more information call Luis Morales at 093-2109; contact him on radio frequency 147.625, or write Antonio Morales, Elizabeth St., Benque Viejo del Carmen, Cayo.

Benque Viejo del Carmen

 Set on the east bank of the Mopan tributary of the Belize River, Benque Viejo (pop. 3,500) lies at the nation's western frontier – 81 miles from Belize City and right next to the El Petén frontier of Guatemala. Its name probably derives from the Spanish translation of "old bank," with "bank" denoting a riverside logging camp. Its orderly layout makes it the best-planned town in Belize. This *mestizo* settlement has all the trappings of Guatemalan culture – marimbas, fiestas, spicy Hispanic food, and archetypal Catholic religious events. But its public services, including a firehouse, police barracks, and running water, make it abundantly clear that it *is* in Belize. Catholicism predominates and Spanish is the tongue of daily life, but the streets have names like George, Churchill, and Baron Bliss. There's nothing in particular to interest the visitor here, but it's a pleasant enough place to stroll around in. **events:** Held in July, "Las Alboradas" is the local celebration featuring Linda Beliceña, the local marimba band. Indigenous dances are performed. **getting there:** Most buses heading from Belize City to San Ignacio also stop here; they board in the center of town.

ACCOMMODATIONS: Possibly the cheapest hotel in the country at BZ$5 pp, **Hospedaje Roxie** is across from the cemetery and near the police station at 70 St. Joseph St. Others include the **Okis Hotel** (☎ 093-2006, BZ$10), 47 George St. and **The Maya Hotel** (☎ 093-2116, BZ $10 s, BZ$18, shared bath), 11 George St. More expensive rooms with private bath are also available at the latter. Run by the Hong Kong Chinese native who started Maxim's in San Ignacio, **Maxim's** (41 Churchill St., ☎ 093-2360, fax 093-2259) offers attractive rooms and good food. Room rates start at BZ$65 s and BZ$85 d plus tax. It opened in 1994. The moderate 12-unit **Woodlands Resort** (☎ 093-2264) offers horseback riding, fans, restaurant, and camping facilities. The **Ahl Bahzil Hotel Cabinas** (☎ 02-31276 or 093-2346, fax 02-30412 or 093-2501), on the road to Benque, are slated for opening in 1995. Behind them on the same hill, the **Vista del Carmen Resort** will probably open in 1995. At present, you can dine at its restaurant. An alternative, which is well out of town near the soccer field on the way to San José Succotz, is moderate-expensively priced **Rancho Los Amigos** (☎ 093-2261); it's run by Edward and Virginia Jenkins. The lodge is for the more adventurous: it has pit toilets and outdoor showers. The four cottages are thatched and attractively decorated. Trails and caves are nearby.

FOOD: Very inexpensive, the **Hawaii Restaurant** on Main St. features large commando pictures by the posted menu. Just above is a placard reading, "Enjoy yourself, it's later than you think." Also try the **Riverside Restaurant** on the water nearby, the cafeteria-style **Okis** up the street, and **Restaurant Los Angeles** on Church St. You'll sometimes find vendors around the square.

FROM BENQUE VIEJO: For Belize City, Novelo's buses depart from 119 George St., Monday to Saturday at 4, 4:30, 5, 5:30, 6, 6:30, 6:45, 7, 9, and 10, and on Sunday at 6, 7, 9, and 10. Batty's buses leave at 6, 7:30, and 9. Shared taxis or (less frequent) buses will take you to the Guatemalan border. Otherwise, it's a 20-minute walk.

The Petén, Guatemala

 Occupying about a third of the nation but with less than two percent of the population, the Petén is Guatemala's last frontier – an area rich in Maya ruins and wildlife, combining tropical rainforests, lowland swamps, and dry savannahs. Part of an untamed and nearly-virgin wilderness stretching from the Lacondon forest of southern Mexico across the Maya Mountains into Belize, the Petén is almost a country unto itself. It is a jungle environment ruled no longer by the jaguar but by the repressive Guatemalan military. Everywhere you go you will see outposts, manned by olive green uniformed youth brandishing automatic weapons, and signs featuring, among other things, a fanged military hunk posing with a submachine gun. As you travel on, the wooden structures on stilts of Belize are supplanted by thatched huts and miserable poverty.

flora and fauna: This is a major reason to visit. More than 250 species of birds have been sighted in the Tikal area alone, and mammals include jaguars, monkeys, coatis, deer, tapirs, and ocelots. There are also crocodiles, as well as innumerable species of insects.

history: Maya civilization spread to the area some 2,500 years ago. Of the total of 102 Maya sites reported in the Petén, many still remain buried beneath the jungle floor. The Maya civilization reached its architectural, artistic, and scientific zenith in this area during the Classic Period (300-900 AD). The area was abandoned at the end of the 12th C., and the Maya apparently moved north to the Yucatán. When the Spanish first arrived, the Petén had been partially colonized by the Itzá, a Toltec-Maya tribe from the Yucatán, who now lived in the Lake Peten Itzá area. The whole of the area was not subdued until 1697, more than 150 years after the rest of the nation had been brought under the conquistador's heel. Resisting attempts to Christianize them, the Itzá were finally conquered, marking the submission of the last independent tribe. Under the Spanish, the area remained a backwater in which chicle collecting was the major economic activity. In recent years, it has become a shelter for the FAR (Rebel Armed Forces) and other guerrilla groups. Today it is under attack from loggers and recent emigrants and the region is rapidly becoming deforested.

exploring: The Petén has been accessible by car only since 1970. Today there is a mere skeletal framework of roads – many of which are impassible during the rainy season. The chief attraction,

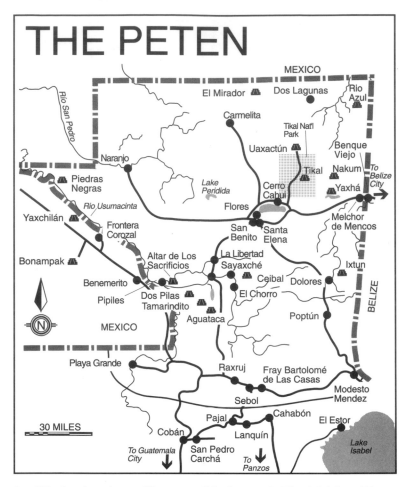

THE PETEN

the Tikal ruins, is readily accessible by road. The Melchor-Flores highway is in bad shape until the Tikal turnoff. Buses run from Melchor to Flores and from Flores to Tikal, Guatemala City, Poptun, and other locales.

organizations: If you've been moved by the situation in Guatemala and wish to do something to help it, **Casa CAMI** is an organization founded by Rodolfo Robles, former secretary general of the union which led the historic strike against Coca Cola. It works with displaced refugees, runs cultural programs and projects to preserve traditional culture, and operates a sewing cooperative. Send tax deductible donations (made payable to "IF, A Nonprofit Corporation") to Friends of Casa Cami, 3105 Freedom Blvd., Lake Freedom, Watsonville, CA 95076 or ☎ 408-724-5526. In Guatemala, their offices (☎ 2-515021, fax 83075) are at 2A, Av. 6-40, Zona 2, Guatemala City.

books: Tom Barry's *Inside Guatemala* (IBSN 0-911213-40-6), published by the Inter-Hemispheric Resource Center, is good for background information. A number of guidebooks provide good information for travel in the nation. Travel & Trade's *Mexico & Central America Handbook* is one example.

Melchor, Guatemala

If you are coming in from Flores, this small town's paved streets will be a refreshing relief. Just across the river from Benque, Melchor is equally placid, yet worlds apart. If you don't have the time to venture into Guatemala, a short trip here will at least give you some perspective on the national ambience.

GETTING THERE: Closed on Saturday and Sunday, the bank at the border offers a significantly better rate than the moneychangers, and no commission is collected. Immigration will give US citizens a tourist card valid for a month for a US$5 cash payment. If you're only going to Flores/Tikal, the visitor's card may not be necessary but you'll still pay the same. From the border, it's an easy walk into town. The bus to Flores (three hours or more) generally waits at the border and then travels into the market area of town, where it waits some more before departing; make sure you get a seat. Minibuses for charter (bargain hard!) generally wait just past the Immigration.

PRACTICALITIES: Many of the hotels here are for low-budget travelers and are around US$1-2. Try the **Maya, Zacaleu**, or the **Mayab**. More deluxe (but still reasonable at around US$12 s and US$14 d) is the **Hotel Palace**, a set of attractive bungalows and a café which serves pizza, seasonal fruits, juices, and other items. Camping (Q10 pp) is also offered. It's next to the Banco Café. You can change money here (which involves two forms being laboriously typed) or with the moneychangers at the border. There are a number of small restaurants around but, despite the proximity of the river, fish is in short supply. In addition to the souvenir stands near Immigration, there are several long rows of street stalls in the market where you can pick up basic items, as well as "Tikal" and other tee shirts for around US$3; it's generally easy to knock a dollar off the price by bargaining. There are many restaurants, including a Mexican one by the river. Not much nightlife exists here, save some bars with red lights over the doors. But during the daytime you can always take a dip in the river to cool off.

returning to Belize: Heading through Immigration, US citizens pay Q5 to exit. From the border, there's a Novelo bus leaving at intervals for Melchor, San Ignacio, Belmopan, and Belize City. You can also take a shared taxi to Melchor (BZ$2) or charter one to San Ignacio.

Flores, Guatemala

 Officially still the region's capital, Flores today is a small, poor colonial-style town on an island connected by a clay causeway to the mainland. There are a few nice streets on the island but nothing much to see. Across the causeway a dusty road leads to the contiguous towns of Santa Elena and San Benito; the latter has a cinema and some sleazy bars.

ARRIVING BY AIR: From Belize International, it's a beautiful 40-minute flight with Tropic Air. Along the way, you fly over stretches of virgin rainforest which contrast vividly with checker-board-square Spanish Lookout, a Mennonite settlement, with its tin-roofed structures precisely lined as though on a monopoly board. The effects of slash-and-burn are clearly in evidence, and it is striking just how little primary forest is left. Dipping down into Flores, you pass over Laguna Petén Itzá before passing the island of Flores and descending to the airport. US citizens will be required to fill out a Visitor's Card form and pay US$5. While Europeans may not need a visa, they may be asked to show a return ticket. Curiously, there is no customs check at the airport because Flores is not considered to be a frontier. You can change money with the moneychangers, who offer a slightly lower rate (US$=Q5.50) than the bank on Flores island. The departure section of the airport has a cafeteria and a number of overpriced souvenir shops. They do have some valuable books here – such as the Guatemalan edition of *Birds of Tikal*. If you're on a tour or headed for one of the hotels at or near Tikal, you will find a representative waiting for you at the airport. If not, you have three choices: a) bargain with a taxi driver for a ride (around Q10), b) take the cheap local bus from the main road, or c) walk to town – about 20 minutes.

sights: There isn't much to do in Flores itself. But the place is attractive to wander in, and its main plaza hosts some badly-weathered Maya stelae. One thing you may do is take one of the local ferries – in a large, traditional-style canoe – from San Benito across to one of the lakeside villages. It will cost you a *quetzal*.

Service is irregular. Boatmen also offer trips for tourists at touristic prices. Don't find them; they'll find you! While walking around the lake, note how many of the structures are now underwater, thanks to rising water levels. One interesting sidetrip is to the **Cueva de la Serpiente**, also known as the Grutas Actun-Can, a cave that features stalactite formations. To get here take the causeway road from Flores along through Santa Elena, then turn left when it forks in front of a small hill, then turn right. Admission is charged.

ACCOMMODATION: The best place to stay for low-budget travelers is probably functional and reasonably clean **Hotel Jade** by the causeway in Santa Elena. They charge US$2 s or d. It's attached to the neighboring **Hotel Leo Fu Lo**, which has an atmospheric Chinese restaurant. Both leave much to be desired in terms of sanitary facilities. The **Hotel Sac Nicté**, which offers rooms with private bath, is one block over. The 60-room **Hotel San Juan** (☎ 081-1562) is priced around US$10 d; more expensive rooms have a/c. Expect to be awakened early in the morning by buses; use earplugs. The best hotel on the Santa Elena side is modern, Spanish-style **Hotel Del Patio-Tikal** (☎ 081-1229), which has 21 rooms and a restaurant. Rooms have color TV and fan. There is an attractive garden and a restaurant which will prepare a box lunch for you to take to Tikal. Rooms run upward from US$60 s or d. Call 800-327-3573 in the US. Under the same management as the identically-named establishment in Tikal, the **Jaguar Inn** (☎ 081-002), Calzada Rodríguez Macal 879, has attractive rooms for US$30 d. Near the bus station and also on Calzada Rodríguez Macal , the 17-room **Costa Del Sol** (☎ 081-1336) has a pool; some rooms have a/c and refrigerators. Set on the lake, the 20-room **Hotel Maya Internacional** (☎/fax 081-1276) is a set of thatched bungalows priced from US$32 s and US$38 d. Others include **Hotel El Diplomático** and **Hotel Don Quijote**. Set between the town and the airport, the 36-room **Hotel Tziquinaha** (☎ 081-359) has a pool, tennis court, and restaurant; it's popular with tour groups. It has rooms with color TV and a/c. Rates run from US$55 s, US$65 d, and US$70 t. Set five miles east of town at Lake Petenchel, the **Hotel Villa Maya** (☎ 081-086) charges US$100 s or d for attractive rooms; write 3 Calle 10-58, Zona 10, Guatemala City for further information.

across the causeway: Flores itself tends to be more expensive, and most of the hotels also have restaurants. The 21-room **Hotel Petén** (☎ 081-1692, fax 081-1662) is one of the best upmarket bets. Rooms go for US$25 d. Opened in 1990, the **Posada El Tucán**, facing the water, has five rooms with shared baths for around US$5 s,

US$10 d, and US$12 t. The 42-room **Hotel Yum Kax** (☎ 081-1686) has rooms from US$11 s and US$15 d; more expensive rooms are a/c. Popular with group tours, the 23-room a/c four-story **Hotel Savanna** (☎ 081-1248) is set far from the causeway. Rooms at the rear overlook the water, and there's a small island offshore which is connected to the hotel. Rates are US$22 s, US$30 d, and US$40 t.

FOOD: There are any number of restaurants, with more opening all the time. Restaurants across the causeway tend to be more expensive. Try **Cafe Maya** in San Benito, **Cafe Lago Azul** in Santa Elena, or **Café Doña Amantes**, which serves lasagna as well as pie slices. One place guaranteed to infuriate animal rights advocates, the **Restaurant Gran Jaguar** serves game.

services: The only tourist information is at the airport. Representatives of the major hotels congregate nearby during flight arrival times. Guarded by rifle-equipped military, the Bank of Guatemala is in Flores. It's open Monday to Thursday from 8:30 to 2:30 and on Friday from 8:30 to 3:30. You can change at a lower rate at the Hotel San Juan in Santa Elena. The post office in Flores doesn't have stamps; you must buy them at the stationery store nearby. Another Correos y Telegrafos is situated just west of Santa Elena's Hotel Patio. Be sure to carry a flashlight at night because there are frequent blackouts.

LANGUAGE STUDY: Guatemala has long been a mecca for language study, and an innovative program has been established here in the Petén. Set in the village of San Andres, on the northwest shore of Lake Petén-Itza, the **Eco-Escuela de Español** combines language study with rainforest ecology. Costs are around US$100 per week, including accommodation, food, and lessons. For more information, ☎ 202-429-5660, fax 202-887-5188, or write Conservation International Eco-Escuela, 1015 18th St. NW, Washington, DC 20036.

FROM FLORES: Aeroquetzal, Aerovias, and Tapsa fly to Guatemala City. Although, as a foreigner, you pay much more than Guatemalans, flying is better than an excruciating 14-hour bus ride on bad roads. If you must take a bus be sure to take a *servicio especial*, which may whittle the trip down to 10 hours or so. Buses also run to Sayaxché. Check at the Hotel San Juan in Santa Elena for times. **for Mexico:** If you wish you can skip Belize and go straight through to Chetumal the same day by catching the 5 AM bus. It costs around US$30. You will save more than half of this by taking local buses.

The Tikal Ruins

 The most spectacular of the 102 Maya sites found in the Petén, and one of the oldest Maya sites, Tikal ("Place of the Voices") rises from the Petén jungles. Set some 40 miles from Flores and surrounded by 230-square-mile Tikal National Park, the ruins are dominated by five steep-sided granite pyramids that rise 120 feet from the ground. So astounding are the ruins to the eye that Director George Lucas used Tikal to represent the hidden rebel base on the fourth moon of the Planet Yavin in the classic film, *Star Wars*. Originally, the city was stuccoed, and plastered red-painted temples with blue trim rose from the white plazas. Today, as there is little ornamentation and the stelae have been almost completely eroded, the imposing size and quantity of the structures is what impresses. Amazing as it may seem to the sore-footed visitor, only a small part of Tikal can be visited: over 3,000 structures and 200 monuments still lie under the forest. Still, stripped of their gaudy grandeur of yore, the temples have little of the ornate carving that makes Quiriguá and Copán so awesome. For some, the best part may be hunting for howler monkeys in the jungle or watching the parrots, toucans, or other birds. Crenellated turkeys stroll the lawn in front of the café near the museum.

GETTING THERE: The Tikal bus leaves at 7 from the front of the Hotel San Juan in Flores. Unfortunately, the bus company consistently overcharges foreigners – about US$2 instead of US$1. Pay only the correct fare, which will be reluctantly accepted if you insist. Slightly faster minibuses are available for about US$3.50 each way. Taxis may also be chartered from the town or the airport. A paved, fairly smooth road from El Cruce, the crossroads, leads up past Laguna Petén Itza to the park entrance, where you are ordered out of the bus with the gruff pronouncement that foreigners must pay 30 *quetzales* (around US$6) to enter. Guatemalans pay US$2, but they generally remain on the bus. A final way to reach Tikal is to charter a minibus from the border (bargain hard!). You can also take the Flores bus and get off at El Cruce, but you risk getting stuck. Realistically, if you have the time, Tikal should be more than a day trip, and you should be prepared.

tours: Many of the lodges in the Cayo District and elsewhere offer package tours. **by air:** While there is no airport at Tikal itself, many visitors first fly to Flores and then travel from there. Tropic Air (☎ 02-45671, 026-2012, 800-422-3425) runs an excellent day

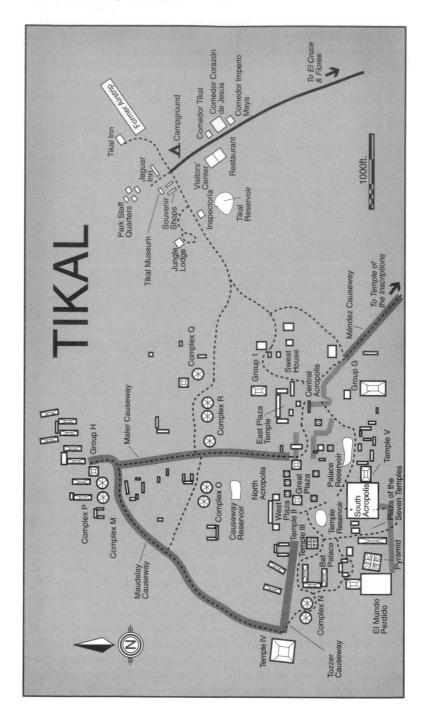

tour for US$200; this rate includes ground transport, guided tour, and lunch, but does not include departure taxes (add around US$20). The flight alone costs US$58 OW and US$116 RT.

preparations: Be sure to wear good shoes, be prepared for rain, and take something along to eat and drink. As there is no water on site (only expensive soft drinks) and the lodges are reluctant to give you water (even with your lunch!), it's better to bring along a good supply. Bottled water is pricey but available from hotels. Bring a good supply of *quetzales*. You may have difficulty in changing a traveller's check here unless it's being used in payment for a hotel room.

HISTORY: Tikal's historical roots are fuzzy, to say the least. Its beginnings have been placed at 750 BC, during the middle Preclassic Era (ca. 1000-300 BC). Although inscriptions and burial paraphernalia provide information only after 300 AD, it is believed that Tikal's rulers migrated from the area of Kaminaljuyú some 2,000 years ago. The names of a number of rulers (including Curl Nose, Stormy Sky, and Ah Cacaw, and Chitam) have been identified with certainty. Others are more speculative, and there are undoubtedly a number who have not been identified. In any case, the names of the rulers are based on the shapes of their glyphs, as their actual names are not known. For example, Curl Nose has a curly nose, and Chitam is named after the Maya word for peccary because that animal appears on his glyph. These rulers were believed to be living gods, and their forefathers were venerated as gods in turn. It is believed that this essentially feudalistic society operated from the Central Acropolis – specifically from Group G, and the Palace of the Windows. Jaguar Paw, the first ruler, was followed by Curl Nose and then Stormy Sky. From the period between the death of Stormy Sky in AD 457 to the accession of Ah Cacaw in AD 682, little is certain. Ah Cacaw ushered in the Golden Age of Tikal which was continued by his son, Ruler B (Half-darkened sun), and grandson, Chitam. During this period most of the great pyramids were constructed. It is believed that the city of Tikal declined around 900 AD. After that, all goes dark until Tikal was rediscovered in 1848 by a government expedition under Modesto Mendez and Ambrosio Tut. Later in the 19th century, an expedition led by Gustave Bernoulli removed some of the lintels from Temples I and IV to Basel. Visiting in 1881 and 1882, Alfred Amudslay was the first to photograph the site. Work continued by Teobert Maler in 1885 and 1904 on behalf of Harvard University's Peabody Museum. Next to visit were Sylvanus Morley, who studied the heiroglyphic texts, and then Edwin Shook of the Carnegie Institution, who discovered

Group H and the Maler and Maudslay Causeways. In 1951, the Guatemalan military cleared an airstrip, making the area truly accessible for the first time. The Tikal Project, initiated by the University of Pennsylvania's University Museum in 1956, has been continued since 1970 under the auspices of the Guatemalan government.

ORIENTATION: Entering the area, you will pass the hotels and the museum on the way to the entrance. There are a number of places to eat, and there's a large market behind the museum. The museum has a lot of weathered stelae with descriptions of them on the wall. It also displays photographs and has a number of rubbings on rice paper, metates (grinding stones for corn), jewelry, and stone tools. It's easy to spot a crenellated turkey strolling the grounds.

The ruins begin at the end of a path that cuts to the left of the Jungle Lodge. At the entrance to the ruins, you present your admission ticket (good for that day only) and enter the grounds. Be sure to note the large ceiba tree on the right, just before the guardhouse. Enclosed on the east by Temple I (The Temple of the Giant Jaguar) and on the west by Temple II (The Temple of the Masks), the Great Plaza is the center of the present-day site. To its west is Temple III (The Temple of the Jaguar Priest) and still further west is enormous Temple IV; the unexcavated Temple V lies to the south of the Great Plaza, and to the southeast – all by itself – is Temple VI (The Temple of the Inscriptions). From the top of the stairway flanking the plaza's southern side, the stelae and Northern Acropolis are in front, Temple I is to the east, and Temple II is to the west. Most of these restored structures date from the late Classic Period (AD 700-800).

EXPLORING THE RUINS: While in Tikal try to imagine the city as it was a thousand years ago. See it in the morning before 10, when the fog sometimes makes the landscape resemble an East Asian painting, or savor the damp, faintly tart odor of the forest after an afternoon rainfall. Be sure to bring food with you and plenty to drink; vendors do sell pricey soft drinks at scattered intervals, but they don't bring them to the top of pyramids. Its worth bringing a compass, as the routes are largely unmarked. Keep an eye out for wildlife (best seen early in the morning and in late afternoon), as well as for the lowly leafcutter ants.

routes: The best way to enter is to pass by Complex Q and R, and then either take the Maler Causeway around past Group H and down to Temple IV, or cut straight across and down to Temple

IV. From Temple IV you can visit the Plaza of the Lost World, Temple III, the South Acropolis, the Great Plaza, the North Acropolis, and the Central Acropolis. From the Central Acropolis, it's a pleasant walk southeast to the Temple of Inscriptions. Visitors with less time may want to visit the Great Plaza first and then visit other locations as time permits.

TWIN-PYRAMID COMPLEXES Q AND R: The first major structures you come to heading in to the park are these, which were built to mark the beginning of a *katun*, a two-year period. These two complexes, part of a total of nine found at Tikal so far, were probably used in conjunction with large public functions relating to cosmic order and the passage of historical time.

TEMPLE IV: Measuring some 212 feet to the top of its roof comb, this magnificent structure incorporated some 250,000 cubic yards of rubble in its construction. Built by the order of Ruler B, the temple is thought to have been finished somewhere around AD 740. Its six lintels have now become naturalized Swiss citizens and reside in Basel. Climbing to the top of this temple is a true adventure: you grab hold of a couple of branches and head up wooden ladders. From the first level – which affords an amazing view – you must head around the corner and climb a steel ladder up to the uppermost platform.

LOST WORLD PYRAMID: To get here follow a path leading south from Temple IV on the west side of the Palace of the Windows. Built before AD 300 and stripped and stabilized in the 1980s, this Late Preclassic 100-foot-high truncated pyramid once had four stairways flanked by masks. Unlike many other temples, it was not created as an ancestor memorial but functioned as part of a calendar ceremony complex. Just north of the Lost World Pyramid, the unfortunate Temple 5C-49 or Lost World Pyramid Plaza was being stripped of trees and readied for reconstruction in 1979-80, when it collapsed after a series of heavy rainstorms.

TEMPLE III: Unrestored, this temple is known as the Temple of the Jaguar Priest after the lintel which depicts an unknown personage thought to be either a pregnant woman, the leader Chitam, or his brother. It may have been the last temple built. Right in front of the temple, Stela 24 and Altar 7 are also believed to be some of the last of their kind built. The altar depicts a woven mat (a symbol of authority) flanking each side of a deity head, depicting the God of the Eccentric Flint, which rests in a bowl. Extending out from the bowl are strips of paper used in the bloodletting ceremony. Entering the temple, you will see a passage going off to the side. Using a flashlight, you can follow the passage to see the Preclassic area inside.

THE GREAT PLAZA: Although today this is the most impressive part of restored Tikal, it was *not* the city's center. That lies to the east in the unexcavated E Plaza at the intersection of the Mendez and Maler Causeways. Instead, it appears to have been an elite ceremonial area erected on behalf of the ruling nobility. In its center are Temples I and II with the North Acropolis in the center background. To the south, the Central Acropolis, a huge palace complex, housed the elite and held their offices. Temple I (The Temple of the Giant Jaguar) was built around AD 700 by Ah Cacaw, as was Temple II which it faces. Temple I displays Ah Cacaw at its top; he was once painted a vividly contrasting red and cream.

The best known silhouette of any Pre-Columbian monument, the Jaguar Temple is a symbol of the Guatemalan nation. Its nine terraces have horizontal grooves on their lower portions, along with inset or recessed corners – architectural techniques used to create a shadowy chiaroscuro effect extending vertically and horizontally, thus enhancing the visual impact of the 145-foot pyramid. The steep climb up is well worth it. From its top, the Northern Acropolis is to the right, Temple II is across the plaza to the west, the Central Acropolis is visible to the left, and the Great Plaza's 70 stelae and altars, spread out across an area the size of two football fields, lie below. Underneath the pyramid, a vaulted grave chamber (now reconstructed in the site's museum) held Ah Cacaw's remains, along with assorted jewelry, ceramics, and bone artifacts. Once adorned with a roof comb featuring a massive face with earplugs on each side, Temple II (The Temple of the Masks) takes its name from the two enormous masks set on each side of the third terrace's stairway. They flank a platform thought to have been used as a reviewing stand.

Lying between Temple I and the Central Acropolis Palace, the Great Plaza's Ball Court was built during the Late Classic era. Only partially excavated and stabilized, it is similar to others found in the Petén. Originally comprising some 42 structures, extending 700 feet east to west, and covering some four acres, the Central Acropolis or Palace Group, was built over a 500-year period. While the buildings facing the Great Plaza appear to have been used for administrative functions, the layout and construction of the rest make the term "palace" appropriate, and the most palace-like structure of all is the Great Eastern Court Palace or

Court 6, 5D-46. Dating from 200 AD, the Northern Acropolis is a group of funerary structures built to honor the ancestors of the elite. They have been rebuilt time and time again. In total it contains as many as 100 structures and Jaguar Paw, Curl Nose, and Stormy Sky were buried here. Once partially painted a garish red, it was as impressive as any other monumental structure anywhere before 700 AD.

THE EAST PLAZA: Just to the north of the Central Acropolis and to the rear of Temple I lies the East Plaza, which features a large rectangular conglomeration of buildings (Structures 5E-32 to 5E-36). This plaza functioned as a central market area. It's well worth your time to explore this area. At the entrance to the "Maler Palace," as the building facing the plaza is known, you can distinguish three masks – one over each entrance. Maya graffiti (a carved sketch of a head) can be seen inside, and archaeologist Maler's signature can be seen on the side of a doorway. Structure 33 here provides the chance to view a wide variety of different layers and see how the structures have been built on top of one another. Note the false arch you can see here. The pigeon holes here serve unknown purposes. Just to the west is a ball court. You can view the remains of the reservoir – now lined with lush vegetation – to the rear.

TEMPLE VI (THE TEMPLE OF THE INSCRIPTIONS): Thought to have been completed around 736 AD and later renovated, this temple is at the end of a path heading off to the right from the path leading from the Great Plaza back towards the entrance. The temple's glyphs, found on the east side of the roof comb, record a series of dynastic successions which began in Olmec times. Many of the rulers are probably mythic. Stela 21 here is believed to represent Ruler B; the drops falling from his hand are thought to depict blood flowing from his incised penis. As the stela is not colored, it is impossible to ascertain if the blood is blue or not.

ACCOMMODATION: Because of the strong demand, it can be difficult to find a room here, and you may not find good value for what you get. **The Jaguar Inn** is the least expensive, but it only has a few rooms, so you need to reserve well in advance by writing them at Tikal; accommodation in tents is around US$20 d; rooms are US$40 d, including two meals. An interpretive trail runs past the property. The renovated **Jungle Lodge** (☎ 501519) is now priced at around US$35 s and US$50 d and is the largest hotel. The **Hotel Tikal Inn** charges from US$35 s and US$65 d. With a pool, it is perhaps the best of the lot.

low budget: If you're on a tight budget, Tikal is bad news: it's one of the priciest places to stay in Central America. Cheapest is the once-free camping area, which now charges US$6 per person, per night for the privilege of hanging a hammock or pitching a tent. There are no facilities, not even water, but you can rent a hammock at a similarly inflated price.

outlying: Set along the road outside of Tikal, the luxurious, 128-room **Hotel Camino Real-Tikal** (☎ 800-228-3000 in the US), a Westin Resort, has a restaurant, cafeteria, bar, pool, and conference rooms.

FOOD: There are a number of rather pricey restaurants, but several *comedores* are affordable, including an inexpensive and very popular one next to the campsite. Water is difficult to obtain from the restaurants; some will try to sell you bottled water with your meals. You should bring a good supply, along with snacks to munch on while atop the ruins.

ENTERTAINMENT: There's nothing to do at night save listen to animal sounds. However, if there's a full moon you might apply for permission to enter the ruins at night from the Inspectoria, climb a pyramid, and sit in the moonlight – perhaps you could bay at the moon.

TOURS: Tour guides can be shared at US$30 for a four-hour tour. An alternative is to pick up a copy of *Tikal, A Handbook to the Ancient Maya Ruins* by Michael Coe (possibly available in one of the shops) and do it yourself. The ideal itinerary would be to spend one day just wandering around on your own and the second in the company of a guide.

SERVICES: There's a post office, along with a couple of stores.

Vicinity of Tikal

 While there's not a lot in the Petén, there are a number of other Maya ruins. To visit them requires time, flexibility, and stamina. One possible way to visit is with **Yaxha-Petén Tours**. They run Campamento El Sombrero at Laguna Yaxha to the southeast of Tikal. There is a selection of four tours, which visit Nakum, Yaxha, Naranjo, Kinal, Río Azul, Topoxte, and other locales. Trips are by jeep or on horseback and they generally involve camping. For more information contact

Agencia Tivoli (☎ 0811-285/329) at 4 C. 0-43 in Santa Elena or Circus SA (☎ 314051) in Guatemala City at Ave. Hincapié 3-81 Z.13.

Uaxactún

Located 15 miles north of Tikal, these ruins and accompanying village line an abandoned airstrip. Beneath one of its temples, the oldest building ever found in the Petén, dating back to 2000 BC, has been excavated. The ruins have been stabilized – to prevent further deterioration – by plastering cracks with white mortar. Group E and Group H are 15 minutes to the right from the airstrip; Group A and Group B are to the runway's left, about a 20-minute walk. You'll notice the damage done to Group A. It was done by early archaeologists, who simply dug into the temples, looking for graves but nearly wrecking the temples themselves. **getting there:** It's a six-hour walk here from Tikal. The path begins between the museum and the Jungle Inn. Although beans and *tortillas* will be available, plan on camping or pitching a hammock. If you have a four-wheel-drive vehicle, you can also drive here.

El Mirador

Rediscovered in 1926, this site predates Tikal. There are a series of massive pyramid structures which, in turn, support three smaller pyramids. The Dante Complex, the largest set, rises to 216 feet, the highest Maya building known. The Tigre Pyramid to the west is 132 feet high. In order to get here you must make a difficult two-day jungle trek from the chicle-gathering village of Carmelita, 40 miles north of Flores. Carmelita can be reached by road from the village of San Andrés on the northern side of Lake Peten Itzá. The trek takes 5-7 days RT and should not be attempted during the rainy season.

Río Azul

Much smaller than El Mirador, this site is 104 miles from Flores to the northeast and was rediscovered in 1962. Covering some 750 acres, it has been extensively looted. It takes three days RT by jeep to get here along a barely passable road.

Lake Yaxjá

The Flores-Melchor bus passes five miles from the lake; which is located halfway to the border. You'll have to walk two hours. Rediscovered in 1904, the extensive, unrestored Yaxjá ruins are to the left. The ruins of Nakum are 12 miles to the north. There are two main groups of structures. You will also find some miniature ruins on the lake's island of Topoxte.

Sayaxché

Set 38 miles southwest of Flores along the Río de la Pasión, this town has a number of sites nearby, but you'll need to hire a boat or a horse to get at them. To the north is El Ceibal (600 AD-900AD) with stelae and a circular temple. To the south are the ruins of Don Pilas, Aguateca, and Tarmarindito on the shore of Lake Petexbatún. Down the river is the Altar de los Sacrificios and the difficult-to-reach sites of Yaxchilán and Piedras Negras along the Mexican border. It takes two to three hours to get here by bus, and the best place to stay is the **Guayacan**. Talk to Julian at La Montana restaurant about arrranging trips to the ruins. El Ciebal is upriver and is the most accessible.

Biotopo Cerro Cahuí

Set up to preserve the crenellated turkey, the Cerro Cahuí wildlife reserve on the east side of the lake covers an area of old growth rainforest. To get here take the Tikal bus to El Remate and walk or take the minivan to Jobompiche. Stay either at the reserve or at the basic but attractive and hospitable **Gringo Perdido** (☎ 370674), a "Parador Ecologico," which has a restaurant. Rates, although not cheap for Guatemala, are reasonable, and you may camp here. You can swim in the lake or hike the trails. The **Hotel Camino Real Tikal** is also nearby. Another alternative in the area is **La Mansión del Pájaro Serpiente**, a resort composed of thatched-roof cottages on stone foundations, which is near El Remate. Pickup at the airport is available. Call/fax 501514 in Santa Elena.

Onward in Guatemala

Many visitors to Belize will also want to visit Guatemala. What follows is a brief description, giving you an idea about some of the places you may want to visit. A good route would be to fly from Flores to Guatemala City (US$50), proceed immediately to Xela (Quetzaltenango) by express bus (four hours, $3), spend a week in that area, continue on to Atitlán, Antigua, and environs before returning to southern Belize via Guatemala City, Copán (Honduras), Quiriguá, Livingston, and Puerto Barrios. **note:** Livingston, Puerto Barrios, and Quirigua are described under the "Punta Gorda" section of the following chapter.

tours: One major company operating in Guatemala is **Maya Expeditions** (☎/fax 37466; 15 C. 1-91 Zona 10, Edificio Tauro Local 10, Guatemala City, Guatemala). They offer trips to Tikal, Quirigua and other ruins, turtle watching, birding, rafting, bungee jumping, volcano and jungle trekking, and other activities. They are dedicated to serving individuals willing to leave civilization's excess baggage behind to seek out unique adventures. These are true expenditions providing "unforgettable experiences of discovery." In the US, write Section 66, Box 527270, Miami, FL 33152.

Guatemala City

The nation's capital, it is also one of the Americas' least inviting capital cities. The main reason to stay here is to visit the museums, and/or make travel connections. If you should have time to kill, it's a fascinating experience to hop aboard any city bus and explore this vast and monstrous urban sprawl. Don't worry about getting lost. The bus will eventually come back to where you got on. But allow an hour or two because the routes can be quite extensive.

Antigua

This is the nation's tourist capital: every time you turn the corner you'll likely encounter another foreigner or someone who wants to sell you something, or both. It is a beautiful city, a restored ex-colonial capital with many churches and it is surrounded by volcanoes. It also has the largest concentration of good restaurants and cafés.

Chichicastenango

This town is famous for its Thursday and Sunday markets, which have made it into a tourist mecca. Another reason for interest is the potent mixture of animism and Catholicism prevalent among the Maya people in the area.

Lake Atitlán

A preeminent tourist attraction, this lake's chief resort town is Panajachel. Ferries traverse the lake, stopping at each village. The nicest village to stay at is San Pedro de la Laguna at the southern end.

Quetzaltenango

The second largest city (pop. 100,000), Quetzaltenango is popularly known as Xela (pronounced"Shey-la"). This small, pleasant, and sometimes chilly town is an excellent base for a highlands tour. Nearby places to visit include markets (including an extraordinary one on Friday at San Francisco El Alto), the hot baths at Almolonga and the vapor baths in the hills close to town, Laguna San Cristobal near the village of San Martin, the wool center of Momostenango, and many other small villages and attractions. Xela also has a few English schools and is a better place to study than tourist-ridden Antigua. One good school to contact is **Ulew Tinimit**, 14 Ave. "A," 8-38 Zona 3. Apdo. 346, Quetzaltenango. Call 502-061-4886.

The South

 Comprising tropical rain forest as well as coastal swamps, the long-neglected but treasure-filled South rewards nature lovers and amateur social anthropologists alike. The nation's highest point at 3,800 feet, Victoria Peak rises amidst the verdant and vibrant Cockscomb Jaguar Reserve. While the main Garinagu (Garifuna) settlements are around Dangriga and Punta Gorda along the coast, the Kekchi and Mopan Maya indigenous peoples reside in the interior, still retaining many customs.

exploring: This long economically neglected area is rough but beautiful. A bad road – difficult and sometimes impossible to negotiate during the wet season and horrifically dusty during the dry – leads to Punta Gorda in the south. The reddish color of the rainforest soil is from the high iron and clay content. As the trees have been cut on both sides of the road, the soil has been free to blow about everywhere. (If you're headed towards Cockscomb directly, a rough road leads off from the Western Highway in the Sibún area.) Along the way are nature reserves, and a separate branch road leads to Placencia Peninsula. Its fishing village is fast becoming the nation's major tourist destination after San Pedro on Ambergris Caye. In the Toledo area around Punta Gorda, it's preferable to have your own vehicle, but you can get around by bus and hitchiking if you have patience. The area's temples are unique in that they, virtually alone among Maya structures, were built without mortar. Last but not the least of the area's charms, the few spectacular cayes off the coast are worth a visit, if you're willing to travel the distance and pay the cost. The most unusual is Wee Wee Caye, which has been transformed into a biological field station and welcomes guests.

Dangriga (Stann Creek Town)

With its clapboard houses on stilts and relaxed lifestyle, this small Garifuna settlement (pop. 7,700) resembles something straight out of a Somerset Maugham novel. A smaller but more placid version of Belize City, relaxing Dangriga is fun to visit for a day or two. In this town everyone checks you out upon arrival, and everyone knows just what you're doing.

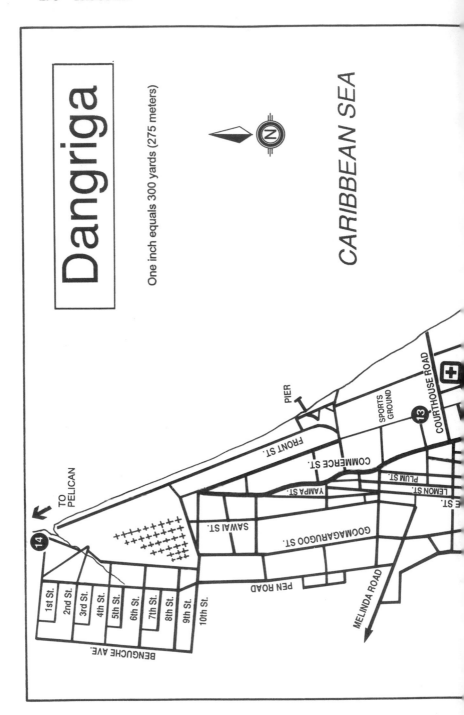

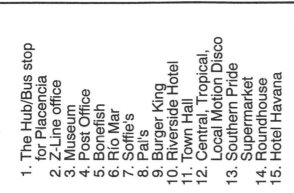

1. The Hub/Bus stop for Placencia
2. Z-Line office
3. Museum
4. Post Office
5. Bonefish
6. Río Mar
7. Soffie's
8. Pal's
9. Burger King
10. Riverside Hotel
11. Town Hall
12. Central, Tropical, Local Motion Disco
13. Southern Pride Supermarket
14. Roundhouse
15. Hotel Havana

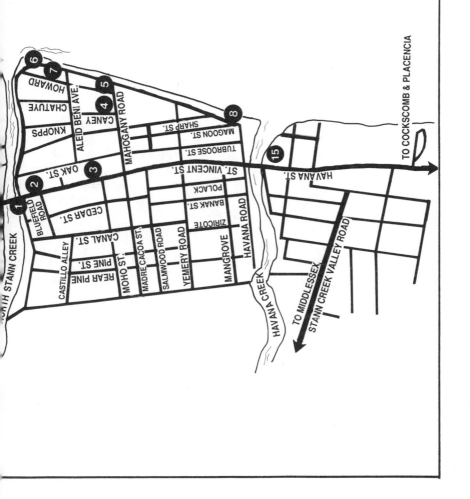

ORIENTATION: To the north of town is the Pelican and the airstrip. North Stann Creek divides the town in half, with a ribbon of wooden houses lining its banks. Nearly all of the hotels are within a 10-minute walk of the footbridge.

HISTORY: Around 1640 a group of English Puritans from the ill-fated island settlement of Providence in the Bay of Honduras moved to the mainland to trade with the Mosquito Coast native Americans for silk-grass, a thick-leaved bromeliad used to make rope. A Captain Elfrith dealt with pumpkins, potatoes, and other crops brought from the island at two trading *stanns* located at Upper and Lower Stanns Creek. The town gradually developed into Belize's second largest city. Most of the town's inhabitants are Black Caribs descended from those that arrived in 1823. St. Vincent, the main street, is named after their ancestral abode, and Dangriga – its new name dating from the 1980s – means "standing water" or "clear water" in Garifuna. These were leader Elijo Beni's first words upon his arrival. The town was almost completely destroyed by Hurricane Hattie in 1961.

GETTING THERE: This is one of the most beautiful bus rides in Belize, despite the dusty, pot-holed road. Enroute from Belmopan you pass rising hills, cohune palms, citrus groves, and fruit-laden trucks. Along the way you pass villages with names such as Middlesex and Steadfast, cross rust-red bridges, and pass through some very green territory. After Middlesex, the Hummingbird Highway continues as Stann Creek Valley Rd. Approximately seven miles before town, the Dangriga turnoff is marked by a decrepit bus stand, and an asphalt road leads on into town, where the bus makes one stop before the terminal near the bridge in the town's center. If you're planning on driving from Belize City, it's best to take a four-wheel-drive vehicle; remember to fill up your gas tank before departing. Taking the New Road will save you about an hour. The Z-Bus departs from Belize City's Pound Yard Bridge at 10, noon, 2, and 4 (BZ$10). James Bus leaves Monday and Saturday at 9, Tuesday, Wednesday, and Friday at 6. Upon arriving, you're likely to be accosted by a group of jobless touts who'll perform tricks such as opening cab doors for you and attempting to lead you to a hotel. Be cordial but otherwise ignore them, and don't be concerned if they curse you out. Don't, under any circumstances, give them money. You won't have any problem finding a hotel on your own. There are too many hotels in Dangriga given the number of visitors the town attracts and more are on the way.

SIGHTS: Inaugurated in 1991 by owner and founder Janice Lambert, **Melda's Historical Museum**, at 21 St. Vincent St. across from Belize Bank, is the only place where you can get an overview of Garinagu culture. Inside, you'll find a collection of cultural items ranging from *egei* and *matate* grinders to mahogany bowls and plates to *makaras* (rattles). It's open daily except Thursday and Sunday; admission is charged. You might wonder about the ostentatious house just down the river from the Riverside Hotel. It's the residence of a Zabaneh; his mother owns the Riverside, and his brother owns the Blue Marlin Lodge. The most peculiar sight is the "outhouses by the sea" complex – a dock with a shack at the end. The huge dock at the southern end of town is where the citrus concentrate is loaded. Williams Beach is two miles south of town. To reach it, stay on the coastal road and keep an eye out for the big pier. A BZ$1 admission charge allows you to use the facilities including a changing room and artificial sand beach. Giant pigs wander about on the grass nearby. The water is a bit muddy. It's possible to camp here, but the sand flies are really bad. Cassava bread is manufactured at Sabal's Estate at Four Miles. Making *ruguma*, the bread, is a two-day process. After processing and grinding the cassava root, it is baked on huge griddles.

ARTISTS AND CRAFTSPEOPLE: One place to stop by is the studio of internationally-famed Garifuna artist **Benjamin Nicholas** (☎ 05-22785) at 25 Howard St. His oil paintings depict events in Garifuna history as well as lifestyle and culture. In Benjamin's words, he paints to preserve Garifuna culture for posterity. Very friendly and sagacious Benjamin is never at a loss for words. A sign in his studio reads: "HAVE YOUR CULTURE. RECOVER IT WHERE LOST. ENRICH IT WHERE POSSIBLE. ACQUIRE AS MUCH FOREIGN TECHNOLOGY AS YOU CAN WITHOUT IDENTIFYING WITH THE CULTURE FROM WHICH IT STEMS. THE REDISCOVERED TRUTH: LIFE IS A LIFE LONG LEARNING PROCESS." Drum maker **Austin Rodriguez** makes drums from cedar, mayflower, and mahogany. Curing deer and cow hides in the sun with lime and salt, he then uses "tagithe" vine to attach the skin. Drums may be made to order, and his most popular drums are African rather than Garifuna in design. Austin also builds dories, makes round boards for kneading bread, and carves *matas*, vessels for pounding plantains into *hudut* (plantain mash). Women often bake cassava bread in the backyard. His house is at 32 Tubroose St. If possible, stop by and make an appointment first, because he may not be able to stop work to meet you. **Marcie Sabral** makes handcrafted cotton Garinagu dolls, as well as innovative patchwork quilts. She initially learned these in a class and has perfected the technique on her own. Her cute dolls carry cassava graters and other accessories and are dressed in local style. People come from all over the world to visit her, and her dolls are also sold at the Pelican and other places. Marcie's dreadlocked husband can tell you all about his hunting and farming activities. She's at 55 Citron St. (05-22651); head up the staircase on the right side of the house that has a second-story door with no stairway.

THE TEMPLE: Garifuna religion, the *dugu*, is an important cultural complement to Catholicism. As the Garinagu are a bit secretive about their religion, it's best to visit this religious edifice with a local. To get here turn right by the Housewive's Market. Inside this unprepossessing structure – a concrete, wood, and corrugated iron-roofed building with sand-covered floor – you might see kerchiefed local women chanting *abaímahani* (songs of remembrance) as part of the *dugu*. A black-and-yellow flag with "Dangriga" cut in black cloth letters is on a pole next to a portrait of Jesus, flanked by pictures of healing ceremonies. Multicolored nylon net hammocks hang on either side.

EXPENSIVE ACCOMMODATION: On the sea front with a dock, 20-room **Pelican Beach Resort** (☎ 05-22044, fax 05-22570; PO Box 14, Dangriga) is close to the airstrip and about a half-hour walk from the main part of town. One of the few hotels in the nation to have bathtubs in its rooms, the Pelican's comfortable rooms feature hot water, a desk, and a fan. Brown, wooden slat-style arm chairs face the ocean and benefit from the cool breeze. In addition, there's the town's classiest restaurant, a gift shop, and a display of early paintings by Garifuna artist Benjamin Nicholas. They also offer boat trips to Gales Point and the Manatee Hole and bird sanctuary. Rooms start from around BZ$90 s and BZ$120 d (plus tax) with discounts off-season; children under 12 are free. A number of packages, some combining stays on the reef with a night in the hotel, are also available. You can also stay at their complex on remote South Water Caye, which has simple facilities and similar rates (see below). A new luxury hotel built by another Zabaneh is under construction to the south of town and should be open in 1995.

MODERATE ACCOMMODATION: Run by the same owners as the Manta Reef, the recently refurbished 10-room **Bonefish Hotel** (☎ 05-22165, fax 05-22296; PO Box 21, Dangriga), 15 Mahogany St., provides comfortable rooms with private bath and hot water, a/c, cable TV, and carpeting. Any of a number of tours can be arranged. If you want to stay in the heart of town and have the bucks to burn, this is the place to stay. Rates are BZ$90 s, BZ$120 d for "deluxe" rooms, and BZ$70 s, BZ$90 d for "semi-deluxe" rooms. A good restaurant is on the premises. On Ecumenical Drive in Dangriga, the eight-unit **Jungle Huts Motel** (☎ 05-23166/22142, fax 05-23038; PO Box 10, Dangriga) has inexpensive to moderately-priced (around BZ$90-100) corrugated tin and thatched-roof cabins with a/c and fans.

BUDGET ACCOMMODATION: Conveniently located right beside the bridge, the 16-room **Riverside Hotel** (05-2168/2163; PO Box 21, Dangriga) is at 5 Commerce St. Rooms are priced at BZ$21 s and BZ$22 d. It's very clean and good value; baths are shared, and there's a central sitting room. In the US, ☎ 800-256-REEF. On the other side and slightly superior is the **Hub Guest House** (☎ 05-22397; PO Box 56), 573 South Riverside. Just down the main street a bit to the north, the **Tropical Hotel** (☎ 05-22002), 115 Commerce St., and the **Chameleon**, 119 Commerce St., are less expensive, running about BZ$12. The **Catalina** (☎ 05-22390), 37 Cedar St., charges only BZ$7.50 s. Located at 977 Waight St. (Southern Foreshore), the nine-room **Rio Mar Hotel** (☎ 05-22201, PO Box 2, Dangriga) has rooms for BZ$35 s and BZ$45 d and on up; rooms have TV. Featuring a balcony with views, nearby 10-room **Soffie's**, 970 Chatuye St., is run by the ebullient returnee from the States of the same name; she charges BZ$50 s or d with TV. Nine-room **Pal's Guest House** (☎ 05-22095) is at 868 Magoon St; take a left before the bridge. Rooms rent for BZ$40 s and BZ$60 d. Less expensive rooms with shared bath are also available. Built in 1994, the **Havana Hotel** (☎ 05-22665/22375) is at 490 Havana St. Run by a friendly schoolteacher, its attractive rooms come with radio and are priced at BZ$33 s and BZ$40 d plus tax. If you're staying in town for a while, furnished houses are available for rent inexpensively. **note:** In the cheapest hotels, be wary of theft.

FOOD: Just next to the Riverside on Commerce St., **Burger King Restaurant** isn't what you think it might be, but an ordinary Belizean diner offering standard fare, including daily specials. The inexpensive **Ship Mates Restaurant** is just around the corner from the bus terminal and facing the river. On Commerce St. near the police station, **Ritchies** is a popular local breakfast and dining spot; breakfasts here feature local dishes such as fry jacks and johnnycakes. Computer printout posters extolling God are on the wall, and a 3-D red and gold sign on the cash register reads, "My boss is a Jewish carpenter." Another popular local restaurant is the **Sea Flame**, 42 Commerce St. Also try **Sophie's**, 970 Chatuye St., and **The Hub** near the bridge and bus terminal. The **Bonefish Hotel**, 15 Mahogany Rd., offers the town's most elegant dining. Also try unmarked **Marlene's** on Ramos Rd. The **Starlight** and the **Sunrise** are two of the town's Chinese restaurants. There's also a small fish market which is down by the bridge and along the coast near the Central Fishermen's Co-operative. A vegetable market operates here on Thursday and Friday. Hard to find unless you dine in a home, local dishes include cassava bread, *sere* (fish cooked with coconut milk) , *hudut* (mashed plantains), and *fu fu*. If you attend a ceremonial occasion you may find locals drinking *gafé*, a black, heavily sweetened coffee-like drink made with ground roasted corn or rice.

ENTERTAINMENT: The happening place is the **Local Motion Disco**. **The Road House** and **The Road House**, both up the beach near the Pelican, have live music on weekends. They share the same name because the original moved and built its own structure; the owner of the first decided that he owned the name, and thus the confusion. One of the two is also known as The Blue Horizon. Otherwise, at night all is quiet save for the whir of bicycle wheels, and the thud of reggae. The cool night breeze and the overhead canopy of stars shape the ambience.

SHOPPING: PJ's Gift Shop, on St. Vincent St. across from Belize Bank, has a variety of local souvenirs including cassettes. **Omar Souvenir and Gift Shop** is at 28 St. Vincent St. **Wong's Store** below the Local Motion Disco sells cassettes. The Pelican also has a small gift shop which should be stocking this book.

    the drums: Both in the stores and on the streets you'll inevitably see two-headed Garifuna drums. They are made of hardwoods such as mahogany or mayflower and with a head made from peccary, deer, or sheepskin; the thin metal wires or strings strung across the heads serve as snares. Always played by hand, they measure up to three feet across. They're accompanied by *sisira* (gourd shakers).

SERVICES: A BTIA tourist infomation office operates inside PJ's Gifts on St. Vincent St. across from Belize Bank. Inside the store there are tapes of Garifuna music along with local handicrafts. The PO is on Caney St. The Z-Line office is inside the Tropic Zone Club.

TOURS: The **Pelican** offers trips to Gales Point and the Citrus Factory, and Cockscomb and Hopkins; they can also arrange transport to the islands. **Rosado's Tours** (☎ 05-22119; 22020, 35 Lemon St.), arranges boat charters, car and van tours, fishing, snorkeling and scuba trips. **Tino's Taxi** (☎ 05-22438), 127 Commerce St., provides taxi service, as does Rodney (☎ 05-22294), near the airstrip, **Neal** (☎ 05-23309), and **Nash** (☎ 05-23283). A tour guide who provides boat charters for fishing and scuba, **Lester Eiley** (☎ 05-22113) is at 25 Oak St. For fishing and charters to offshore cayes, contact Captain Buck or Nolan Jackson Jr. at **Ship Mates** (☎ 05-22171). Passage to Tobacco Caye is BZ$30 pp, OW. **note:** If going through a third party, be sure to clarify prices with the boat captain *before departure* in order to avoid misunderstandings.

FESTIVALS AND EVENTS: Dangriga is one of the best places to experience Garifuna culture, but you must plan on staying around for a while. The town is particularly noted for the Waribaggabagga dancers, who sometimes perform at the Pelican, and the Turtle Shell Band, who use turtle shells, guitar, and keyboards. Andy Palacio is the most famous of the town's punta artists. Island Expeditions stages Garifuna Culture nights at the Eden Rose Bar every Saturday night during peak season and sometimes on Monday as well. Attendance is free to all comers. The town's major event (and one of the nation's) is **Garifuna Settlement Day** (Nov. 19), when the arrival from Roatan is reenacted. A week before the date, drums pound late into the night, and Garinagu from all over the world descend on Dangriga. At 5 AM there's a reenactment of the landing at the river, followed by a large parade later with a semi-trailer flatbed truck carrying a reggae band. There's also a mass held in Garifuna to celebrate. *Yankunu* (John Canoe) dancers revel in the streets around Christmas, being traditionally greeted with money, candy, or rum. Conch shells are sounded on Christmas eve at midnight. Held on the ninth night after someone dies, a Nine Night is an all-night revel; if you think you know how to party, you'll be surprised. One ceremony rarely witnessed by outsiders is the *dugu*, a week-long healing ritual in which a female shaman goes into a trance and talks to the dead. Drumming, dancing, and sacrifice of pigs accompany the ritual (see "Religion" in the Introduction).

FROM DANGRIGA: Z-Line (☎ 05-22160) departs for Belize City at 5, 6, 9, and 10 AM and at 3:30 PM. The fare is BZ$6 to Belmopan and BZ$10 to Belize City; it takes four hours. To the south, buses run to Punta Gorda at noon and 7 and to Independence (BZ$9) at noon, 2:30, and 7. You should note that pilferage has been a problem along the PG route; keep an eye on your baggage. Promised Land Bus Service (☎ 06-23152, BZ$8) runs at around 2:30 PM daily except Sunday. (Check on these times as this service is new and may change). All buses to the south stop at the entrance roads to Hopkins and to Sittee River, in Independence, and in the main part of Maya Center.

by air: Maya Airways (☎ 02-72312) has flights to Belize City, Placencia, and Punta Gorda. Buy tickets from the shop on the main street with the Maya Airways sign or at Pelican Beach Hotel.

Vicinity of Dangriga

 Often neglected by visitors, the area from Dangriga to the south has much to offer. If you have a vehicle (or go on a tour), you can visit Cockscomb Wildlife Sanctuary (p. 292), Hopkins (p. 291), and other attractions. Tours of **Melinda's Farm** (☎ 08-22370) can also be arranged; they make the famous Marie Sharp's Hot Sauce as well as other jams and chutneys.

Some of the least appreciated attractions of this area are its offshore cayes. Here you can still find pelicans, herons, egrets, warblers, and other birds everywhere, as well as opossums, deers and armadillos on the larger islands. Fishermen live on both Ranguana Caye (see "Vicinity of Placencia") and Laughing Bird Cay (which has now been declared a National Park). Desolate Slasher Sand Bore is bordered by dead coral, which drops off to a lagoon filled with barracuda and other fish.

Gales Point Manatee

Originally founded by logwood cutters, this fishing village of 300 is 15 miles north of Dangriga. The Belizean government designated some 115,000 acres as the Manatee Special Development Area – which includes the Northern and Southern Lagoons, pine ridge, mangroves, as well as 22 miles of beachfront. In addition to including the nation's primary nesting beach for the hawksbill turtle, the area is the home of Central America's largest population of Caribbean manatees. Formed in 1992, the Gales Point Progressive Cooperative (GPPC) is working for small-scale development. The GPPC has formed the Manatee Farmer's Association (a group of cooperating small farmers), the Manatee Tour Operators Association (boat operators and tour guides), and the Gales Point Bed & Break-

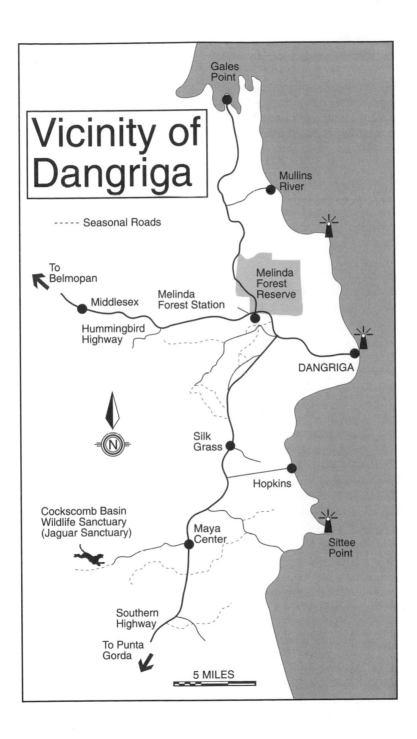

Vicinity of Dangriga

- - - - Seasonal Roads

Gales
Point

Mullins
River

To
Belmopan

Melinda
Forest
Reserve

Middlesex

Melinda
Forest Station

Hummingbird
Highway

DANGRIGA

N

Silk
Grass

Hopkins

Cockscomb Basin
Wildlife Sanctuary
(Jaguar Sanctuary)

Maya
Center

Sittee
Point

Southern
Highway

To Punta
Gorda

5 MILES

fast Association. Products produced locally include wines and jams as well as cohune fly brushes and "tie tie" baskets.

GETTING THERE: Dories (BZ$20) leave at Wenesday. and Saturday at 10 AM from the Bolton Bridge in Belize City. They may depart on other days as well. Expect to pay BZ$250 for a charter. If you're coming by car, you can either approach via Dangriga or turn down Manatee Road (New Road) at La Democracia (Mile 31) on the Western Highway – a distance of 25 miles in all. It may be possible to hitch a ride.

ACCOMMODATION: Lodging is provided through the Gales Point Bed & Breakfast Association. There are currently eight B & Bs (accommodating a total of 20 guests) and a seven-room, two-story hotel on the waterfront is under construction. Five percent of total revenues from the B & Bs is remitted to the GPPC, and profits from the hotel will be used to support the management of protected areas. None of the B & Bs have indoor plumbing. Rates are BZ$10 s, BZ$15 d, BZ$20 per cabaña, and BZ$5 per tent for camping. Weekly rates are available, as are long-term rates for researchers and volunteers. Interested parties should contact Hortence Welch upon arrival. No reservations are required, but you can make them through Seaside Guest House in Belize City (☎ 02-78339) or the Gales Point Community Phone (☎ 05-22087: ask for Alice or Josephine).

Set on the peninsula's tip, the eight-room expensive **Manatee Lodge** (☎ 08-23320, fax 08-23334; PO Box 170, Belmopan) is now styled as an ecotourism lodge. Rates (around BZ$160 s and BZ$210 d plus 16% tax and service) include the use of a canoe, and a number of excursions are possible. The management also runs Hidden Valley Inn in the Mountain Pine Ridge. In the US ☎ 800-334-7942 or 904-222-2333, fax 904-222-1992, or write 1220 E Park Ave., Ste. 12, Tallahassee, FL 32301.

FOOD: Meals are provided by villagers and are priced at BZ$5 for breakfast, BZ$8 for lunch, and BZ$14 for dinner. Manatee Lodge also serves meals. There's only one small general store in the village, so you should bring everything you might need.

EXCURSIONS: If you have your own vehicle, you can use the town as a base to visit a number of places. Bird Caye offshore hosts nesting herons, egrets, wood ibis, and roseate spoonbills. The mangrove-lined Northern and Southern Lagoons are rich in birds and other wildlife, including manatees. Hear the roar of bulls during mating season. For information on trips contact Kevin Andrewin. Dories hold six to eight people. Trips include the Manatee Watch (BZ$60/dory), Seashore (BZ$60/dory), Cornhouse Creek (BZ$75/dory), Ben Loman (Lomond) Cave (BZ$100/dory), Bird Caye (BZ$150/dory), and a Night Trip (BZ$100/dory). A walking excursion to Darby Pot Cave costs BZ$40 per guide.

FROM GALES POINT: Dories (BZ$20) leave on Wed. and Sat. at 4 AM from the operators' piers. A charter to Belize City is BZ$250/dory. A 15-mile dirt road leads to the Hummingbird Highway, but there's no regular transportation. A charter could meet you from Dangriga by arrangement, but it would be quite expensive. If heading to Belize City, take Manatee Road 25 miles to La Democracia (Mile 31) on the Western Highway.

Possum Point Biological Station and Sittee River

Near the small village of Sittee River about six miles before Maya Center, this ecological field center is operated by Paul and Mary Shave. Located in a lowland tropical forest, the attractive facility caters to biology students and natural history groups. Courses in tropical field ecology are offered here and the marine lab on Wee Wee Caye, nine miles east offshore, teaches coral reef biology. The latter is a really remarkable place. Although you can tour the tiny island in five minutes, it's truly a living natural history museum – offering you a chance to live amidst a mangrove ecosytem. Understanding what's going on here takes time. Aside from the narrow gangplank leading to the toilet and the entrance dock, the mangroves remain as they always have. Although the island is named after the leaf cutter ants, more remarkable inhabitants are the *wowlas* (boa constrictors), which you can spot hanging in the trees – sometimes they don't change position for days on end. The island has been leased from the government, and everything has been built on a shoestring.

PRACTICALITIES: The Shaves offer reasonably-priced packages, which include stays at Possum Point and Wee Wee, and simple but hearty and delicious cuisine. They also offer transport to and from the reef for snorkeling and between the stations on their fleet of *wowla* boats, 25-foot fiberglass dories equipped with 55-hp outboards. You need to bring all equipment, including your own sheets. Accommodation is simple yet comfortable, and the dining room-study area features Mennonite furniture and hammocks for lounging about. The building on the island which appears to be a Shinto shrine is, in reality, a generator, and electricity is available during the dinner hours – after that, light is supplied by kerosene lamps. There are a few inconveniences that come with the territory. Sandflies can be absolutely ferocious. At night you must walk the gangplank – past mangroves blanching white as your lantern hits them – heading towards the loo, which has a hole so large it might bring back childhood fears of falling in! At night there's not much to do save sit out on the pier and watch the stars. Accommodation (up to 30 people) is similar at Possum Point; it's a paradise for ornithologists, herpetologists, entomologists, botanists and all-around nature lovers. Most of the 44-acre site has been left in its natural state and there's over a mile of trails. Excursions are available. Paul and Mary also run the Sittee River Scenic Park (Bocatura Bank) for tent campers; efficiency cottages are available for rental. Write Paul and Mary Shave, Sittee River S/C, Belize, Central America; community ☎ 05-22006, fax 05-22038.

OTHER ACCOMMODATION: At 19 High Sand in Sittee River, the six-room inexpensive-to-moderate **Sittee River Lodge** (☎ 05-22006) offers fan-cooled rooms and a restaurant. **Glover's Atoll Guest House** is a set of rundown houses on stilts which have dorm beds. Also here is the budget-priced four-unit **Sittee Fish Camp** (Box 1820, Belize City) and six-room **Prospect Guest House** (☎ 05-23389/22006).

OTHER PRACTICALITIES AND SIGHTS: There's a small general store in the village which has a limited selection of goods. The river is a great place to kayak or to canoe. It's a four-mile walk to Hopkins along a dirt road, and a bus may be running. Set to the southeast of Hopkins, mangrove-clad **Sittee Point** has a light tower and is at the mouth of the Sittee River. Set three miles from the junction with the Southern Highway, the **Sittee Sugar Mill** is the most interesting place to visit in the area. Operated by locomotive steam engines, the Regalia Estate and Serpon Estate mills were imported from England and Scotland. One engine has been identified as having been made in Richmond, VA and is the only known example. They were opened in 1863, and the Serpon Estate was operated by a Mr. Thomas Bowman, an ancestor of the Bowmans who today run the Pelican Beach. The engines were hauled in by mules. The mill was slated for bulldozing in 1989 and was saved

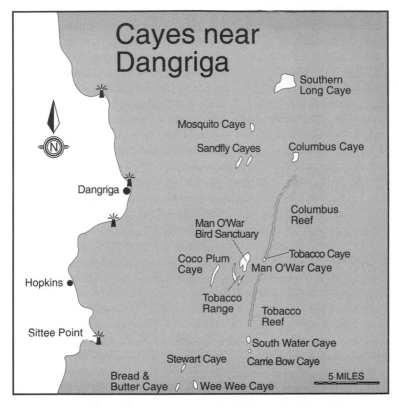

Cayes near Dangriga

only through an 11th hour appeal. Although the site has been cleared (through the efforts of a student team from Trent College in 1992), the mill still retains much of its foliage. Some parts even have trees growing through them. A Visitor's Center is planned. Bring water and plenty of mosquito repellent.

Tobacco Caye

First settled by English Puritans who introduced tobacco as a crop around 1640, this lies just north of South Water Caye and opposite Dangriga, from which you can reach it via a 12-mile, hour-long boat ride. One of the most attractive cayes, this five-acre island has a small population and a number of stately palms. Earthwatch volunteers have participated in studies here of nocturnal predators such as moray eels. **getting there:** It may be cheaper if you find a group of locals going. Otherwise, you'll need a charter. This would be an excellent place to base yourself if you're a kayaker doing day trips. There are no phones, little fresh water is available, electricity is generator-generated, and the culinary mainstays are rice and beans, coconuts, and seafood. The reef is 50 feet offshore.

WHERE TO STAY: Moderately-priced **Island Camps** (☎ 02-72109/05-222109; Box 174, Dangriga) has 10 units. Six-room **Reef End Lodge** (☎ 05-22171; PO Box 10, Dangriga) charges around BZ$80 s and BZ$130 d with meals; better rooms are BZ$150 d. Rates include use of snorkels, fins, and canoes. Offering attractive Caribbean-style cabañas on stilts, six-unit **Ocean's Edge Fishing Lodge** (☎ 05-22419) charges BZ$130 s and BZ$200 d plus tax, including three meals; fishing is BZ$250 for two and diving is BZ$70 pp, per dive. In the US, ☎ 800-967-8184 or 713-894-0548. The seven-room budget-priced **Fairweather & Noble Rose** (☎ 02-72866; PO Box 240, Belize City) offers meal plans with its lodging.

SNORKELING: According to Kirk Barrett, the best snorkeling here is found outside the reef wall. In *Belize by Kayak* he writes, "For incredible snorkeling, wade through the shallows to the reef wall behind the island (to the east). Walk north up the reef wall around 300 to 500 yards, then carefully dive in on the outer side of the wall. There are mountains and ravines of coral out here and plenty of fish life.... Be careful when going to the outer side of the reef wall. Only attempt this on a calm or low wind day. Tobacco Range, a group of mangrove islands with sandfleas and a few inhabitants, and Man-O-War Caye (Bird Caye), a nesting island for boobies and other birds, are nearby."

South Water Caye

This small, attractive island will form part of the proposed South Water Marine Reserve.

WHERE TO STAY: The **Pelican Beach Resort** (☎ 05-22044, fax 05-22570; PO Box 14, Dangriga) owns part of this island and has modest accommodations in stilt-style houses. Holding up to six, **The Osprey's Nest** and **The Frangipani House** rent for BZ$190 per day; meals (if desired) are BZ$60 pd. Sleeping up to 22 and designed for school groups, **The Pelican's University** charges BZ$110 pp, pd for room and board; the boat is BZ$230 each way. The 14-room **Blue Marlin Lodge** (☎ 05-22243, fax 05-22296; Box 21, Dangriga) is an expensive fishing and diving resort. Call 800-798-1558 or 218-847-4441. All-inclusive all-year diving packages are around US$1,195 pp, d, and fishing packages are around US$1,650 pp, d; both are for eight days and seven nights. Five-day, four-night and "vacation" packages are also available. Service charges, room tax, and bar tabs are extra. For information about the five **Leslie Cottages** (☎ 05-22004), in the US ☎ 800-548-5843 or 508-655-1461.

Carrie Bow Caye

The Smithsonian rents this small gem of an island from the Bowman family and operates a research station here. Researchers arrive here for brief periods, and the caye may be visited by appointment. The reef to the east of the island has good snorkeling.

Hopkins

 Twenty minutes by boat from Dangriga, this village, home to some 1,000 Garifuna fishermen, stretches two miles along a curving bay. Without much in the way of facilities, it's a perfect get-away spot – no yuppies here! The town was founded in the aftermath of a 1942 hurricane and is named for the late Roman Catholic bishop, Frederick Charles Hopkins. The village was leveled by Hurricane Hattie.

GETTING THERE: Head for Dangriga first and check there (not with the touts!) for current information. A shuttle bus leaves Dangriga at noon on Monday, Wednesday, Friday, and Saturday for Hopkins. By boat is preferable but more difficult; ask around at the dock. Final alternatives are to take the bus to the junction and walk in, take a taxi (expensive) from Dangriga, or walk from Stittee River.

WHERE TO STAY: Run by the only women's cooperative in Belize, six-room, thatched-roof **Sandy Beach Lodge** (community ☎ 05-22033) is at the southern end by the beach. The lodge consists of two attractive thatched-roof cabins. Charges are BZ$24 s and BZ$36 d. Meals are BZ$5 breakfast, BZ$7 lunch, and BZ$10 dinner. Popular with kayakers, "Jungle Jean" Barkman and her husband have a small lodge with cabañas for BZ$20-30 pp; there's an outhouse and outdoor shower. Retired 60-something midwife **Mama Nuñez** offers basic rooms in one of her huts or in her house; she'll also cook for you, and you may camp here for a fee. She's around 200 yards north of the Sandy Beach Lodge; ask a local. **Sybill**, a Swiss expatriate, runs a thatched-roof restaurant which sometimes has music at night. At the junction of the road leading to the Southern Highway, **Hopkins Paradise** is a collection of cabins. The hotels will help you arrange meals with local families. There is telephone service. As there's no sewage system, take care with the water.

FROM HOPKINS: You can walk to Sittee River (around four miles) via a dirt road in the dry season. Check locally for transport times back to Dangriga.

Cockscomb Basin Wildlife Preserve
(Cockscomb Jaguar Reserve)

 Located off the Southern Highway to the south of Dangriga, this is both the first and only jaguar reserve in the world. A tropical moist forest with 180 inches annual rainfall, the reserve covers 99,000 acres. A small Classic Period Maya ceremonial center, the ruins of Chucil Balam lie secreted in the forest. There are abandoned logging camps with such descriptive names as "Sale si se puede ("leave if you can") and "Go to Hell Camp."

FLORA AND FAUNA: Once considered to be just a moving object for hunters to shoot, some 50 of the nation's 500 jaguars are now protected here. Other cats include jaguarundis, pumas, ocelots, and margays. There are also tapirs, kinkajous, pacas, brocket deer, iguanas, *tommy-goffs* (fer-de-lances) and boas. The 290 bird species recorded include toucans, curassows, scarlet macaws, Agami herons, and king vultures. The red-eyed tree frog also dwells within the reserve. Many of the larger trees were felled by Hurricane Hattie, and the canopy height now ranges from 50 to 150 feet.

CLIMATE: A distinct dry season runs from February through May. Between 10 and 180 inches of rain falls during the wet season from June through January.

HISTORY: The surrounding forest reserve was set up in 1984; the wildlife sanctuary in its interior was established two years later. In 1984 the New York Zoological Society sponsored a two-year field study of jaguar ecology in the Cockscomb Basin. Conducting the study was Dr. Alan Rabinowitz, who lived among the Maya, radio tracking jaguars for over two years. Rabinowitz recommended that a sanctuary be established in the area, and he received backing

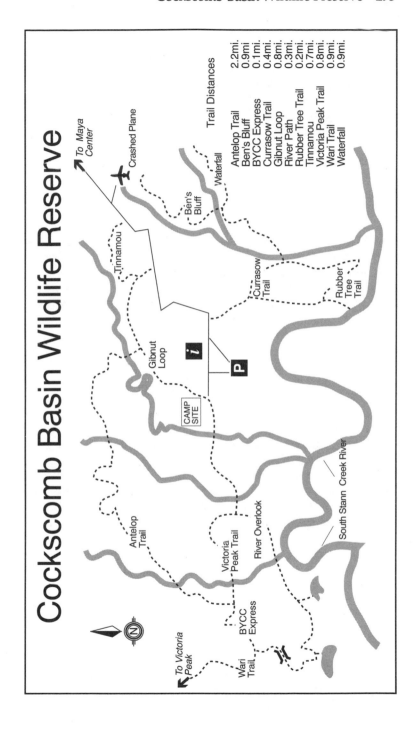

Cockscomb Basin Wildlife Reserve

To Maya Center

Crashed Plane

Ben's Bluff

Waterfall

Trail Distances

Antelop Trail	2.2mi.
Ben's Bluff	0.9mi.
BYCC Express	0.1mi.
Currasow Trail	0.4mi.
Gibnut Loop	0.8mi.
River Path	0.3mi.
Rubber Tree Trail	0.2mi.
Tinnamou	0.7mi.
Victoria Peak Trail	0.8mi.
Wari Trail	0.9mi.
Waterfall	0.9mi.

Tinnamou

Currasow Trail

Rubber Tree Trail

Gibnut Loop

i

P

CAMP SITE

South Stann Creek River

Antelop Trail

Victoria Peak Trail

River Overlook

BYCC Express

N

To Victoria Peak

Wari Trail

from the Belize Audubon Society. The World Wildlife Fund US also promised financial assistance. In 1986 the government declared 3,000 acres of the 108,000-acre forest to be a sanctuary. The community of Maya who lived within the reserve's confines were relocated in 1986 (without compensation) to the village of Maya Center five miles away, and newly-appointed sanctuary manager Ernesto Sacqui was sent to the US for training. In 1990, after assurance of further backing had been received from the World Wildlife Fund US, the reserve was expanded to 108,000 acres. A new chapter in the reserve's history came with the introduction of a troop of 14 howler monkeys translocated from the Community Baboon Sanctuary; further translocations are planned.

GETTING THERE AND PRACTICALITIES: Cockscomb is for people who don't mind roughing it a bit, and not for those who require every comfort supplied. This isn't a game park you can drive through; it requires both time and effort to see the wildlife here. A permit (obtainable from the site headquarters, the Belize Audubon Society in Belize City, or the Pelican Beach Resort in Dangriga) is required. If you don't have your own vehicle, you can take any Placencia or Punta Gorda bus and get off at Maya Center; the entrance to the reserve will be on your left just before the bridge at the beginning of the village. (Another alternative is to take a tour from Placencia or Dangriga.) Before entering the reserve, sign in at the craft center, a cooperative run by village women. The center features stone carving, beadwork, and basketry. You must walk or drive the six miles from Maya Center on the main Southern Highway. It's a stiff uphill hike, but it's worth it. On your way up, note the home with mahogany doors near the crafts center. Ostentatious by local standards, it's the home of the local Baptist preacher. Within the reserve, it costs BZ$15 to berth in a bunk or BZ$3 to camp. Berths can accommodate up to 20; gas stoves and all utensils are supplied. You should bring all food as the store at the base has only limited supplies. If you don't want to stay here, the nearest accommodation is in Sittee River (Possum Point and Glover's Atoll), but to really *see* anything you need to spend time around the reserve – especially at dawn and dusk. Be sure to visit the new Visitor's Center. Its displays are the work of Peace Corps volunteer, Bonnie Gestring.

hiking: Director Ernesto Sacqui will be happy to answer all of your questions. There are a continually expanding variety of trails. It's best to get an early start at dawn to maximize your chances of seeing wildlife. The *River Path Trail* and the *Currasow Trail* connect via the *Rubber Tree Trail*. You can swim in the river, but exercise caution. Watch for howler monkeys. The *Antelop Trail* connects with the *Gibnut Loop Trail*, which connects the *Victoria Peak Trail* and the *Tinamou Trail*. Named after a species of bird, this trail is beautiful, good for seeing wildlife owing to the propensity of wild fruit in the area, but it can be muddy and slippery. An airplane suspended in a tree is near the trail's east end. It's been there since 1983, when it missed the runway (now reclaimed by the jungle). *Ben's Bluff Trail* leads from the riverside and a swimming hole to a ridgetop, commanding a view of the entire Cockscomb Basin. Allow half a day for this venture and keep in mind that it's quite steep in places. Other trails lead as far afield as 3,543-foot Victoria Peak, a three-day hike. Guides can be hired at BZ$25 apiece but, as a minimum of two are required, it's better to go in a group to hold down costs. There are no shelters, but your guides will make a hut. A permit must be obtained in advance from the Forestry Dept. in Belmopan; you must state the number of persons in your party, as well as the exact dates of your visit. It's a rugged but spectacular trip. The Maya site of Maintzunun ("Small Hummingbird") lies about 10 miles north of Cockscomb.

Placencia Village

 Set approximately 100 miles south of Belize City, skinny 16-mile-long Placencia Peninsula points south from the mainland, edged by a white sandy beach stretching from Riversdale to Placencia Village. At its southern tip lies the relaxed, attractive fishing village of the same name. Placencia's main drag is an often-crowded sidewalk, and goods are transported around by wheelbarrow. The village's history dates back to the infamous Portuguese pirate Cabral, who settled the peninsula along with his buccaneer chums. Many of the residents are fair-skinned descendants of English and Portuguese settlers. There have been a number of Spanish galleons wrecked offshore, and Spanish "pieces of eight" are found on the beach from time to time. Up until recently, the only way to get to Placencia was by boat. The road continues to transform the area.

These days, Placencia is on its way to rivalling San Pedro (Ambergris Caye) as a major tourist destination, and resorts are springing up all along the beach past Seine Bight. Modern construction in the village is beginning to change its atmosphere. The new airstrip, which permits flights to land near the village, rather than across the water in Big Creek, also encourages more visitors.

More and more Europeans are coming here. Fortunately, there is still no Club Med or Holiday Inn, and there are none planned.

GETTING THERE: Tropic Air (☎ 02-45671) and Maya (☎ 02-72312) fly to Placencia from both the domestic airport (BZ$93) and from Belize International (BZ$110). With Tropic you can connect with flights from Corozal, or San Pedro, and they also fly from Punta Gorda for around BZ$30. From the airstrip, you can walk easily to Kitty's Place and other neighboring resorts, but it's about 1½ miles into town – a taxi ride of BZ$10. If walking be sure you take the right direction or you'll end up in Seine Bight (about a mile). Although flights still run to Big Creek, which is across the lagoon from Placencia, there is no reason not to fly directly to Placencia. Buses to Independence leave from Dangriga, and a direct bus runs at 2 or 2:30 from Dangriga daily (double-check this). The new Promised Land Bus Line may be running from Belize City, with daily service. If you arrive on the Independence side, you must cross by boat – BZ$20 to cross – so it's preferable to take the direct bus to Placencia. While the road trip is quite beautiful, it's also long, and the road is not in great shape, to say the least. If you're driving, watch carefully so that you don't miss the turnoff.

ORIENTATION: The village is small, but confusing if you arrive at night. The sidewalk – rather crowded at times – varies from a foot to three feet in width and it runs from the edge of town down to the dock area. From there a path leads off to the right, passing a few restaurants, including Brenda's. The dusty clay main road more or less parallels the sidewalk, but it leads up past the outlying resorts to Seine Bight and beyond. From the village, you'll come first to the Village Inn, then Turtle Inn, Kitty's Place, Rum Point Inn, Serendipity Resort, and finally Seine Bight.

INEXPENSIVE/MODERATE ACCOMMODATION: One of the nicer places is five-room **Ranguana Lodge** (☎/fax 06-23112), which has a sister operation on the caye of the same name. Each wood-paneled unit has a double and single bed, as well as a refrigerator. Expect to spend around BZ$150 total. The 12-room **Sonny's Resort** (☎ 06-23103/44975, fax 02-32819) charges BZ$66 s and BZ$88 d; its cabins are more expensive. Set right on the end of the peninsula, the eight-room **Paradise Vacation Resort** (☎ 06-23260, 23179) has simple rooms renting for BZ$26.50 with shared bath to BZ$37.50 and BZ$47.50 for rooms with private baths. **Tradewinds Cabanas** (☎ 06-23101/23109) offers rooms for BZ$100/night. The **D&L Resort** (☎ 23243) charges BZ$36.75 s and BZ$47.25 d; it has four

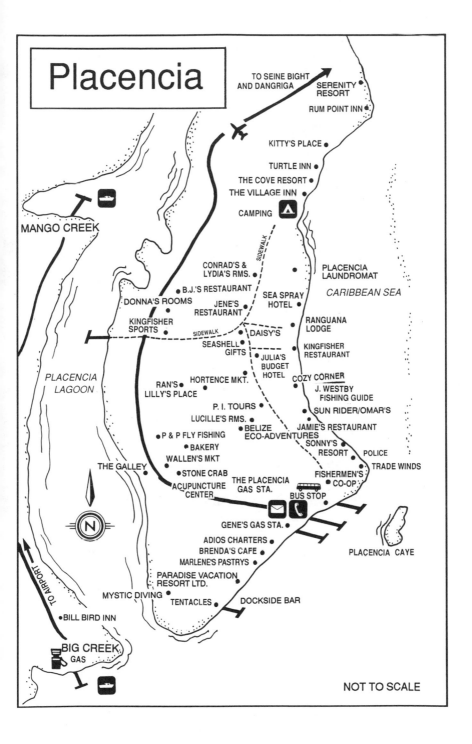

double rooms, with one shared bath and one apartment with two bedrooms, kitchen, and bath. Set on the peninsula's tip, **Harry's Cabanas** (☎ 06-23155) is another possibility.

RENTALS: **Ted's Rentals** (☎ 06-23172) near the bakery has short- or long-term house rentals; houses go for BZ$500 and BZ$650 a month. Near the ball field and off the main road towards the end of town, **Patty's Place** (☎ 06-23121) has a fully-furnished house for rent, as well as four rooms with shared bath; short- or long-term rentals are available. To rent a fully-equipped beach house with hot water call **Lydia** (☎ 06-23117) locally or **Lou** (☎ 02-45732) in Belize City.

BUDGET ACCOMMODATIONS: As it grows more and more popular, Placencia, like Caye Caulker, becomes increasingly expensive and low-priced rooms can be scarce. Count on a minimum of BZ$10 pp, but be prepared to pay twice that. Most of the hotels are run by relatives of either the Leslie or the Eiley families. Arriving here at night poses a problem: it's a bit bewildering to find your way around. Many of the cheapest places are not signed. It can be noisy here (clucking chickens and so on), so it's not a bad idea to bring along a pair of earplugs. **Julia's Budget Lodge** (around BZ$16 s and BZ$26 d) is one alternative. Jo Ann, the Canadian who runs the library, has a bungalow for rent for around BZ$20. At the top of the budget range in terms of price, six-room **Seaspray Hotel** (☎ 06-23148) is across from Jene's and by the water. It charges BZ$21.20 s and BZ$31.80 d. **Conrad's and Lydia's** (☎ 06-23117) is farther up the sidewalk to the left. **Paradise Vacation Hotel** is at the pier end of town: when you arrive at the end of the road turn right and follow the path for about 10 minutes. At the same location as Omar's, **Sun Rider Guest House** (☎ 06-23236) has three rooms for BZ$32 s and BZ$42 d. **Lucille's**, near Sun Rider, charges BZ$10 s and BZ$20 d. Featuring four rooms, low-budget **Jamie's Rooms** (☎ 06-23138) is off the main drag and near the library.

camping: At northern end, unmarked **Mr. Clive's** has inexpensive camping (BZ$2 pp) and is frequented by kayakers. He'll also watch your vehicle while you're out kayaking for a small fee. He doesn't like to be disturbed except from 7 AM to 5 PM. There's a toilet here but no shower. Don't leave valuables in your tent.

OUTLYING ACCOMMODATION: Once you get out of the village, prices climb and, short of a walk or drive, you're confined to eating at your hotel. All those listed have excursions (fishing, snorkeling, hiking, etc.) available for their guests. Run by a Cuban family, the **Village Inn** (06-23217, fax 06-23267) is inexpensively-priced. In the US, ☎ 305-887-6453. Simple but attractive rooms with shared bath rent for BZ$50, and a cabin trailer with kitchen rents for BZ$130. Food is served. Expensive **The Cove Resort** (☎ 06-23233, fax 06-23224; PO Box 007, Placencia) is a half-mile north of the village. It features six cabins with queen-sized beds, has a restaurant and bar, and is set on a long stretch of beach. Located a mile north of Placencia and run by US expatriates, **Turtle Inn** (☎ 06-22069) holds up to 20 in six thatched cottages. Numerous trips and excursions are offered – diving, jungle camping, and river voyages. It's popular with student groups, and group rates are available. An unusual feature of the lodge is that all electricity is solar-generated. Bed and breakfast is around BZ$105 s and BZ$170 d, plus tax. Call 303-444-2555 in the US or contact Dr. Lois Kruschwitz, 2190 Bluebell, Boulder, CO 80302. One of the area's oldest resorts, **Kitty's Place** (☎ 062-3227, fax 062-3226; PO Box 528, Belize City), 1½ miles north of the village, is an intimate and well-run resort which offers a variety of uniquely-designed hardwood rooms set in small, Caribbean-style houses. One house typically has a total of two to four rooms and is two storeys. Rooms have special amenities, such as bedside reading lamps, coffee makers, and hammocks. Each unit is airy and has an overhead fan. Kitty runs a full-service dive ship, rents bicycles, and offers sport fishing and snorkeling trips to the cayes, as well as other excursions. Her attractive restaurant, set upstairs from the office and extending onto a veranda, is well-run and popular. Breakfast is BZ$13.20 and dinner is BZ$33-44. Prices run from BZ$60 s and BZ$80 d for a room in The Belizean to BZ$180 s and BZ$210 d for a fully-furnished studio apartment, which sleeps three. Consisting of 24 closely-spaced but attractive and sunny cabañas with fans, **Serenity Resort** (☎ 06-23232/23231) is the brainchild of a amiable retired US policeman. He has one of Placencia's best restaurants, plus a 32-foot glass bottom boat, and can arrange fishing and various excursions. Call 800-331-3797 to receive a brochure. High season rates run around BZ$150 s, BZ$170 d, and BZ$220 t; 16% tax and service charge is added, and a BZ$50 surcharge is applied to each unit during Christmas and New Years. A more expensive duplex unit is available. Breakfast and lunch are BZ$15 and dinner is BZ$30. Farther on is **Rum Point Inn** (☎ 06-22339, fax 06-23240), which offers eight dome-shaped ferroconcrete cabañas with fans. Also on the property are a bar, library, restaurant, beach, and sunfish. It also has a dive shop and the *Auriga*, a 43-foot dive boat. Dive packages are available. The owners, the Beviers, are Mayaphiles, and their son Wade is well-informed about environmental concerns. In the US, ☎ 800-747-1381 or 504-465-0769 or fax 504-464-0325.

STILL FARTHER OUT: Set on the other side of Seine Bight village, **The Nautical Inn** (☎/fax 06-22310), is one of the newest resorts. The attractive and comfortable units were imported prefabricated from Arizona, which cut down on construction time. Facilities include restaurant, bar, volleyball, canoes, bicycles, beauty salon, gift shop, massage, and a Hobie Cat. Fishing, snorkeling, and scuba are available. Rates are BZ$160 s and BZ$190 d, plus tax; packages and tours are available. Consisting of two small cabañas on stilts set side by side on the beach, hospitable **Blue Crab Resort** is on the beach past Seine Bight. Rates are BZ$130 s, BZ$150 d; tax is included and food is BZ$50 pp, pd additional. One of the owners has lived in Taiwan so Chinese food is a specialty, and vegetarians can be catered to. Excursions can be arranged. In the US, ☎ 800-359-1254. The cabañas are not underpriced for what they are, but the exclusivity and isolation are pluses. At Maya Beach seven miles north of Placencia, the **Singing Sands Inn** (☎/fax 06-22243) has six attractive thatched cabañas set in a row. Renting for BZ$130 s and BZ$150 d (plus 15% tax and service), they each have hot water, fans and lights. There's a restaurant and bar, and bicycling, canoes, and windsurfers are available. Diving is one of the resort's specialties, and the full-service dive shop offers certification.

FOOD: Food prices here have gone up, and you can actually eat more cheaply at budget places on touristy San Pedro than in the village. One of the best places to eat, **Omar's Fast Food** serves vegetable, seafood, and meat burritos (made with handmade tortillas), juices, and other dishes; it's way above McDonald's in quality. Farther down and on the other side, **Jaime's**, set in a screened porch by the sea, is another fine place to eat local food. **The Driftwood Cafe** has moderate prices. **Shirleen's** is good for breakfast. **BJ's** has reasonably-priced meals, including breakfast. Serving snacks only, the **Stone Crab** is off the sidewalk and near the store. Run by the large, good-natured lady of the same name, **Brenda's** offers breakfasts (BZ$6-8), lunches, and set dinners (BZ$15 including drink and dessert). She's off the path to the right, heading straight on from the pier. **The Snack Attack** has snacks.

   more expensive: Back on the sidewalk and almost to the pier, pricey **Sonny's** is often packed. Attractive and atmospheric but expensive, **Tentacles** overlooks the water; it serves Belizean and Italian food. Located to the right as you head down the road towards the edge of town, **The Galley** has slow service and entrees for around BZ$14. It has an attractive atmosphere, and many locals in the tourist industry come here to drink. You may get an earful about Mutabaruka or any number of other subjects from one of the imbibing guides. Out of town near the airport, **Kitty's** also has a good and attractive restaurant; dinner is around BZ$30; a set breakfast is BZ$8. **Serenity** also has good food.

FOOD SHOPPING AND BAKED GOODS: Bread at the bakery sells for a very pricey BZ$3 per loaf. **Ms. Nora** nearby bakes delicious coco bread loafs (BZ$1), which are usually available in late afternoon. **Crissy's Pastries** nearby has cakes, pies, cookies, *panades*, *salbutes*, and *tostadas*. Off the sidewalk, **Daisy's** serves good cakes, ice cream, and other delights. **Wallen's Market** is near the Stone Crab on the Main Rd. It has a very limited (and quite expensive) selection of fresh produce, so try to buy what you may need before arrival. Food is costly, as everything has to be brought in. In front of Jaime's and near the beach, **Kay's** has homemade jams, yogurt, granola, and orange juice, as well as other items. The **fishing cooperative** next to the pier sells fish cheaply.

SOUVENIRS: There are a few shops around. Near Wallen's Market, the **Orange Peel Shop** sells gifts, tee shirts, and other artwork.

ENTERTAINMENT: Although the power situation has improved and there is electricity now right up to Seine Bight, occasional blackouts do occur, so carry a flashlight if going out at night. The liveliest place is **Cosy's Disco**, to the rear of the police station. It's so dark that you can't see your hand in front of your face. Nowadays it doesn't pick up until late, when cable TV is off the air. Another choice is the **Dockside Bar** at the end of the peninsula.

SERVICES: The person to see for information is Heidi, who runs the **Visitor Services**. A native speaker of German from Switzerland who has lived in Canada, Heidi Ribary is extremely helpful and friendly and she can make tour arrangements. She offers fax and other services. The market will change traveller's checks at US$1= 95¢ Belize. Hotels will also change money. To use a Visa card, you must take a boat over to Big Creek, where a **bank** opens on Fri. The mail service has improved. There's now a real **PO**, and it's much more likely that your letter will actually arrive instead of getting lost in the shuffle. There's also a BTL office (open weekdays from 8-noon and 1-4, Saturday from 8-noon) which has four **phones** inside. Both are just to the right of the fish cooperative at the end of the peninsula. Set below the rectory, the **library**, run by masseuse

Patricia, is open during part of the day on Monday, Wednesday, and Saturday. A BZ$3 deposit is required. Conveniently located near the airstrip, **Kitty's** will make reservations for Tropic and Maya; many other hotels will as well. Have your clothes washed at the **Placencia Laundromat** (☎ 06-23123). **Ted Berlin** (☎ 06-23172) is the village's acupuncturist. **Patricia** will give you a massage. See her at the library or book through Serenity (☎ 02-22305).

TOURS: Prices are not low for trips – especially for fishing. Conveniently located, **Visitor Services** (☎ 06-23153; see "Services" above) will make arrangements for you. Incorporated in Visitor Services, **Blue Runner Guiding** (☎ 06-23153) offers fishing, snorkeling, river trips, camping on the cayes, and sailing. Packages are available. **MacDougall's Travel** (☎ 06-23144, fax 06-23186) will make fishing and other tour arrangements; ☎ 916-741-8027 in the US. **PI Tours** (☎ 06-23156/23209) has a variety of excursions, including camping, flyfishing, snorkeling, and scuba. Contact **Whiprey Caye Guiding** (☎ 06-23130). Run by Ellis "Red Boy" Burgess, a student of Maya glyphs, **Placencia Tours** (☎ 06-23186) offers trips to Cockscomb, ruins, and other natural wonders. **Mystic Morning Guides** (☎ 06-23162) offers scuba, snorkeling, fishing, and camping. **Nature Guide** (☎ 06-23206) features scuba, sport fishing, snorkeling, camping, excursions. **Kevin's Guiding** (☎ 06-23178) offers scuba, fishing, snorkeling, kayaking, camping, and excursions. **Joy Tours** (☎ 06-23135) has sport fishing, snorkeling, and excursions. **Nite Moves Guiding** (☎ 06-23117) offers scuba, snorkeling, sport fishing, and excursions. **Conrad's Guide Service** uses the same phone number and provides similar services. **Ran Villanueva** (☎ 06-22027) has fly and other types of fishing and snorkeling. **Mystic Divers Diveshop** (☎ 06-23182) features scuba, snorkeling, fishing, and excursions. **Kingfisher Adventures** leads flyfishing and snorkeling trips to Laughing Bird Caye and to the barrier reef. In the US, ☎ 800-403-9955 or fax 919-848-3624. **Glen Eiley** (☎ 06-23182) conducts fishing and caye trips in a 25-foot skiff. **Adios Charters** (☎ 06-23154, Mike or Bonnie Cline) has a 36-foot trimaran. Also for fishing, try **Joel Westby** (☎ 06-23138). **Belize Ecoadventures** (☎/fax 6-23250) arranges tours and hotels. In the US, ☎ 604-984-8182 or fax 604-984-8727. **Placencia Tours** (☎/fax 06-23188) has a variety of trips. **Sea Horse Guides** (☎/fax 06-23166) leads fishing, snorkeling, and other trips. In the US, ☎ 510-452-1771. **Southern Tour** (☎ 06-23166) has fly and sport fishing, scuba, camping, snorkeling, and sailing. **Black Star Tours** (☎ 06-23123) arranges fishing, snorkeling, scuba, and tours. Most of the outlying

Placencia Tourist Guide Association Members

Name	Tel.	Specialties
Black Star Tours	06-23123	fishing, snorkeling, scuba, and tours
Blue Runner Guiding	06-23153	fishing, snorkeling, river trips, camping on the cayes, sailing
Conrad's Guide Service	06-23117	scuba, snorkeling, excursions
Joy Tours	06-23135	sport fishing, snorkeling, excursions
Kevin's Guiding	06-23178	scuba, fishing, snorkeling, kayaking, camping, excursions
Mystic Divers	06-23182	scuba, snorkeling, fishing, and excursions
Mystic Morning Guides	06-23162	scuba, snorkeling, fishing, camping
Nature Guide	06-23206	scuba, sport fishing, snorkeling, camping, excursions
Nite Moves Guiding	06-23117	scuba, snorkeling, sport fishing, excursions
Placencia Tours	06-23186	land excursions
Sea Horse Guides	06-23166 fax 06-23166 (510) 452-1771	fishing, snorkeling, water skiing, excursions
Southern Tour	06-23166	fly and sport fishing, scuba, camping, snorkeling, and sailing
Tracy Guiding	06-23134	sport fishing, snorkeling, excursions
Ran Villanueva	06-22027	fly fishing, snorkeling
Joel & David Westby	06-23138	fly fishing
Whiprey Caye Guiding	06-23130 214-617-2210	fly fishing, snorkeling, and scuba

resorts have excursions. **Kitty's Place** (☎ 062-3227, fax 062-3226; Box 528, Belize City) runs a full-service dive ship, rents bicycles, and offers sport fishing and snorkeling trips to the cayes (Silk and others) and the barrier reef.

DIVING: Placencia Dive Shop (☎ 06-23227, fax 06-23226) is at Kitty's Place. A two-tank dive is BZ$130 pp to the inner cayes and BZ$150 to the barrier reef. **Rum Point Inn** (☎ 06-23239) has a dive shop. **Seahorse Guides** (see above) also offers diving and certification. The **Paradise Vacation Hotel** (☎ 06-23179) has a 33-foot Bertram a/c twin diesel boat for fishing, diving, and caye excursion charters; it will hold up to six. In the US, ☎ 409-245-9203 or fax 409-245-1803.

FROM PLACENCIA: From Independence to Belize City, it costs BZ$19 with Z-Line. Promised Land Bus Service for Dangriga and Belize City (☎ 06-23152) runs at 6 AM from the gas station daily; check to make sure of this time and frequency. To get to Punta Gorda you must either return to Dangriga or get a dory (motorized canoe) to Mango Creek (Independence). **for Honduras:** Manuel Zabaneh, Jr. (☎ 06-22131) takes travelers to Honduras from Big Creek for BZ$70 when he makes trips on his boat. **for Guatemala:** for boats from Placencia to Livingston, Guatemala ☎ 06-23160 or inquire inside the BTL office.

Vicinity of Placencia

Although the village is a great place to relax, the surrounding area is rich in attractions. You may want to visit Cockscomb or take a trip up the Monkey River. Heading out to the cayes, you'll see beautiful islands off in the distance, may spot dolphins running with your craft, catch sight of a sting ray, or visit an island whose shores are piled high with conch shells.

Cayes Near Placencia

Lying a few hundred yards from the coast, **Placencia Caye** is an all-mangrove caye. On the island of the same name, the four-unit **Wippari Caye Lodge** (☎ 06-23130) offers moderate-to-expensive accommodation from about BZ$40. Inquire at Tentacles. **Laughing Bird Caye National Park** is one of the nation's most beautiful small

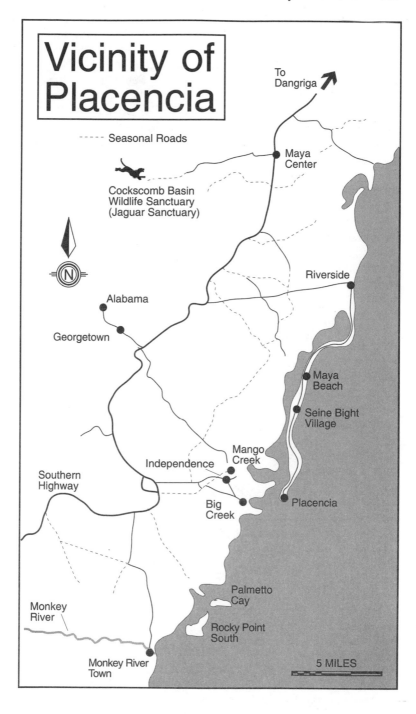

Vicinity of Placencia

- - - - Seasonal Roads

Cockscomb Basin
Wildlife Sanctuary
(Jaguar Sanctuary)

N

To
Dangriga

Maya
Center

Riverside

Alabama

Georgetown

Maya
Beach

Seine Bight
Village

Mango
Creek

Independence

Southern
Highway

Big
Creek

Placencia

Monkey
River

Palmetto
Cay

Rocky Point
South

Monkey River
Town

5 MILES

islands. It's a popular snorkeling and kayaking spot. The best snorkeling is on the east side of the island and off the southern end. It's named after the laughing gulls, though they no longer live here. The stream of visitors has driven them off. Set to the northeast of Placencia, **Rendezvous Caye** is rumored to be owned by a legendary British rock star. Well offshore near the barrier reef, the **Silk Cayes (Queen Cayes)**, three small islands with three palms, are some of the most beautiful spots for kayaking and snorkeling; outfitters usually camp on Middle Queen Caye, the largest of the three. To the west of the Queen Cayes, **Hatchet Caye** is the island where an American was caught dynamiting coral heads in order to allow access for a larger boat. Lying to the southwest of Hatchet Caye, **Little Water Cay** is a privately-owned island which operated the Little Water Caye Resort (☎ 02-31237, 06-22267, fax 02-31482; Box 1666, Belize City) as a nudist colony until the authorities found out about it.

Ranguana Caye

This small sand palm caye has the **Ranguana Lodge and Reef Resort**. Attractive cabins rent for around BZ$100 pd. Located here, **Reef-Link Kayaking** (☎ 515-279-6699; ask for Sonna Newton) is a kayak rental agency; guides are also available. The Ranguana-Laughing Bird-Silk Cayes-Round-Popion Caye- and Ranguana circuit is one kayaking route that might be done using Ranguana as a base. Write c/o S. Newton, 3806 Cottage Grove, Des Moines, IA 50311. Be sure to obtain a copy of *Belize By Kayak* (from the same source) in preparation for your trip. Bonefish and jack fishing is good, and the best snorkeling is found on the island side of the barrier reef a mile or so southeast of the caye.

Independence

This consists of a few houses on a bank opposite Placencia. Although it may be separately marked on maps, it is the same place as Mango Creek. A banana port is under construction here. The town experienced a brief boom in 1962 when the Hercules Powder Co. of Delaware installed a US$5 million plant to extract the remaining resin in pine stumps left after logging. Although there was believed to be enough raw material to last a decade, the plant closed down after only three years and was moved to Nicaragua, leaving 200 households without employment. Although the official reason given was that the price of resins in the US had fallen to the point where the plant was no longer profitable, in fact the

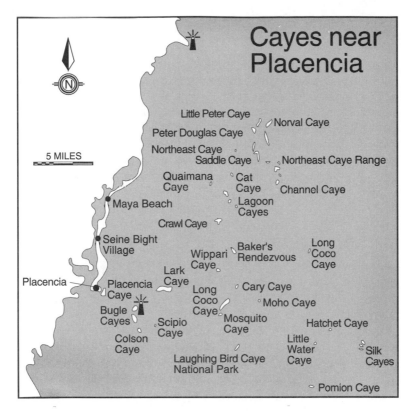

Cayes near Placencia

Little Peter Caye
Norval Caye
Peter Douglas Caye
Northeast Caye
Saddle Caye
Northeast Caye Range
5 MILES
Quaimana Caye
Cat Caye
Channel Caye
Maya Beach
Lagoon Cayes
Crawl Caye
Seine Bight Village
Baker's Rendezvous
Long Coco Caye
Wippari Caye
Lark Caye
Placencia
Placencia Caye
Long Coco Caye
Cary Caye
Moho Caye
Bugle Cayes
Scipio Caye
Mosquito Caye
Hatchet Caye
Colson Caye
Laughing Bird Caye National Park
Little Water Caye
Silk Cayes
Pomion Caye

number of stumps had been miscounted. The experience provided the internal government of the time with an example of the way in which foreign investment can be a two-edged sword, causing misery as well as creating opportunities.

PRACTICALITIES: A mail boat runs from Placencia here on Monday, Wednesday, and Friday. Stay at moderate 16-room **Hello Hotel** (☎ 06-2201) or at **Ursella's Guest House**, #227 Gran Rain St., which offers six inexpensive rooms. At the corner of Fadden and Seagull in Mango Creek Village (Independence), two-unit **La Quinta Cabanas** (☎ 06-22093) are inexpensive. Anther alternative in Independence is the budget-priced seven-room **Little Jungle Lodge** (☎ 06-22225). The best place to eat (BZ$5 a meal) is **Miss Ella Forman's house**, a cute little white home behind the restaurant with the Fanta sign. Stay at the hotel above **People's Restaurant**. Formerly the Toucan, the a/c 12-room **Bill Bird Lodge** (☎ 06-22084/22092, PO Box 1137, Belize City) and accompanying restaurant is in nearby **Big Creek**.

Seine Bight

Three miles north of Placencia, this somnolent but hospitable Garifuna village makes an interesting destination to bike, hitch, or walk to. It's a pleasant walk along the coast, but you bear witness to the debris of our Great Western Civilization, which washes up on the shore. Legend has it that Seine Bight was founded by pirates in 1629; its name was most likely given by immigrant French fishermen arriving after they were expelled from Canada when Britain took control.

PRACTICALITIES: Development has come here only very recently; electricity has only been available since April 1994. The bar, **Wesebahari** (Garinagu for "Feel Good"), has a giant lobster-shaped bamboo root. "Don't ask for Mr. Credit. He is dead" is chalked on the wall to the rear of the bar's counter. Run by Dewey Nuñez, the **Kulcha Shack** has rooms with shared baths for around BZ$30. He also serves food and provides live entertainment some evenings. In the village center, compact **Auntie Chigi's Place** (☎ 06-22015, 08-22491) charges BZ$80 for one or two people in each of two small, two-bedded rooms with a shared kitchen. It's good value relative to what you get elsewhere, and it's run by local Edna Martinez. **note:** The Nautical Inn is reviewed under Placencia "outlying accommodations" above.

Monkey River Town

This small Creole village (pop. 200) sits at the mouth of the Monkey River. **Ena's Hotel** is the town's only lodging, and there's a grocery shop run by Miss Merna. **upriver:** This is a pristine rainforest environment. As you cruise by, iguanas dive into the water, landing with a splash, troops of howler monkeys cavort through the trees, and birds flit from tree to tree. In his *Belize by Kayak*, Kirk Barrett tells of spotting a jaguar on a sandbank as he navigated a bend in this river. After 10-12 miles you come to a fork: Bladen Branch is to the left and the Swasey Branch is to the right; both eventually intersect with bridges along the Southern Hwy. Four new archaeological sites were discovered here in 1993; two had been looted prior to their discovery. The largest is on an island in the Monkey River; it is in the form of a C-shaped plaza surrounding a pyramid.

Bladen Branch Nature Reserve

This 97,000-acre reserve created in 1990 encompasses the Maya Mountains, as well as fringing limestone karst foothills pockmarked with caves and sinkholes. The slopes are covered with old-growth broadleaf forests and swiftly-flowing streams empty into the Bladen branch of the Monkey River. One Maya ruin, Quebra del Oro (Passageway of Gold), has been discovered, and there may be others. Over 300 animal species include the jaguar, the keel-billed toucan, the river otter, Baird's tapir, and Morelet's crocodile. Proponents of the reserve were the Belize Audubon Society, the World Parks Endowment, and Lighthawk, an organization of volunteer pilots who operate airplanes that assist environmental organizations. **getting there:** You must be a researcher to obtain permission from the Audubon Society, which will help you with transport.

Punta Gorda

 Almost 210 miles by road from Belize City, this town, popularly known as "PG" (pop. 3,234), is the last sizeable settlement in southern Belize. Despite its Spanish name, PG contains Garifuna, Creoles, Kekchi, Mopan Maya, Chinese, Lebanese, and East Indians. All of its five streets – Front, Main, Back, West, and Far West – parallel the shoreline. A fishing and farming community (beans, maize, and rice), it receives over 170 inches of rain annually. It was one of the places originally established for the Black Caribs after they fled Honduras in 1823. Today, it is the capital of the Toledo District. Schools line Front St., and youngsters are imported from surrounding villages on weekdays in season. Nearby are the ruins of Lubaantun as well as indigenous villages. Trips can be also made to the Sapodilla Cayes.

GETTING THERE: The most frequent service is offered by Z-Line (☎ 02-73937), which leaves Belize City at 8 and 3, arriving at 5:45 PM and 12:45 AM. Buses leave Dangriga at noon and 7. James also runs. Allow nine hours or more from Belize City. Leaving from Pound Yard, Belize City, Williams Bus Service is yet another line.

ARRIVING BY AIR: Tropic Air (☎ 02-45671) flies from Belize Municipal (BZ$120 OW, BZ$216 RT) and from Belize International

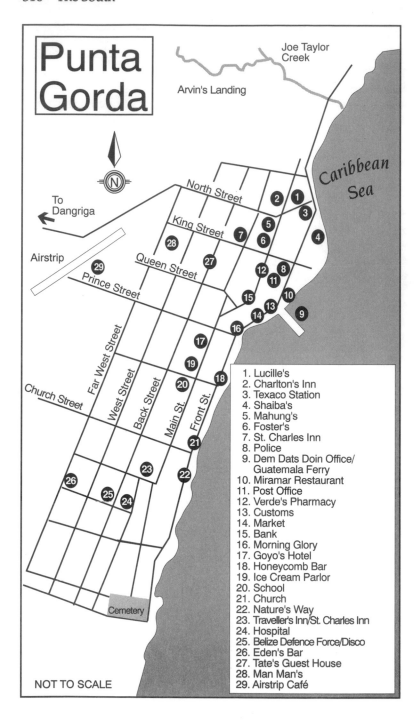

Punta Gorda

Caribbean Sea

Joe Taylor Creek

Arvin's Landing

To Dangriga

Airstrip

North Street

King Street

Queen Street

Prince Street

Far West Street

West Street

Back Street

Main St.

Front St.

Church Street

Cemetery

NOT TO SCALE

1. Lucille's
2. Charlton's Inn
3. Texaco Station
4. Shaiba's
5. Mahung's
6. Foster's
7. St. Charles Inn
8. Police
9. Dem Dats Doin Office/
   Guatemala Ferry
10. Miramar Restaurant
11. Post Office
12. Verde's Pharmacy
13. Customs
14. Market
15. Bank
16. Morning Glory
17. Goyo's Hotel
18. Honeycomb Bar
19. Ice Cream Parlor
20. School
21. Church
22. Nature's Way
23. Traveller's Inn/St. Charles Inn
24. Hospital
25. Belize Defence Force/Disco
26. Eden's Bar
27. Tate's Guest House
28. Man Man's
29. Airstrip Café

(BZ$140 OW, BZ$280 RT), as does Maya Airways (via Dangriga). If you take Tropic Air's flight, on the way to Punta Gorda you make a last sweep over Belize City and then over the sea before swinging back to the coast, passing marshes, jade green rivers, and pristine rainforest. You will see cohune palms protruding like giant upright featherdusters, small offshore cayes, and citrus farms of staggering proportions. Cut through it all is a road network; the clay color of the strips is clearly visible from the air. As you descend, you spot the former VOA antenna, rainforest-covered Seven Hills, and the former British army base.

ECOTOURISM TRAIL: First proposed in 1991, an ecotourism trail around the town is still in the development stages. The idealistic vision of Nature's Way's Chet Schmidt, the four-mile trail and greenbelt surrounding the town has several aims: to preserve land while providing a sustainable lifestyle for locals; to provide income through jobs in tourism; to build up a Homesite Farmer's Fund. This fund will be used for developing permaculture farming techniques to replace slash-and-burn and to serve as an ecological model for others. The trail will begin at the end of Main St. on the town's outskirts and will then head inland through mangrove swamps and along a creek to a Maya home. There, local customs and slash-and-burn will be discussed. Then the trail will lead on to a new permaculture site. Next will be a mini-zoo and then a stop at an East Indian farm where locals will discuss their history and lifestyle. At St. Vincent Block – a tract of land deeded by Garifuna forefathers for farming use – there will be a replica of a traditional Garifuna village (circa 1920), where such activities as cassava bread making will be demonstrated. Next will be a visit to Toledo Community College. The trail will culminate with a canoe trip down a quarter-mile strip of river to the coast. Campgrounds will be located at both ends of the trail and guest houses are to be constructed as St. Vincent Block, which will also be known at Habiabara Garinagu Cerro – meaning "Garinagu Village" in Garifuna. Entertainment, geared towards cruise ship passengers and individual travelers, will feature music, dance, food, and drink for BZ$40 pp. For information on the trail's current status, contact the Garinagu Village at Nature's Way Guest House (☎ 07-22119; Box 75, Punta Gorda).

ACCOMMODATION: Located on the seaside far past the town center, one of the best places to stay is low-budget **Nature's Way Guest House** (☎ 07-22119), which charges BZ$16 s and BZ$35 d. Equipped with bunk beds, many of its attractive rooms face the sea. A large selection of charters is offered. For more information write PO Box 75, Punta Gorda. One of the better places to stay smack dab in the middle of town is the 12-room **St. Charles Inn** (☎ 07-22197), 21 King St. The 10-room inexpensively-priced **Charlton's Inn** (☎ 07-22197) is at 9 Main St. **Tate's Guest House** (☎ 07-22196), run by postmaster William Tate, has rooms with a/c and cable TV for BZ$40 d. It's around the corner from the St. Charles. The **Punta Caliente Hotel & Restaurant** (☎ 07-22561), 108 José Nuñez St., is clean, very friendly, and has inexpensive rooms. Just one street over and run by a relative, the **Circle C** (☎ 07-22726), 117 West St., charges BZ$25 d for rooms with shared bath and BZ$35 and BZ$50 for rooms with private bath. The most expensive hotel is **The Travellers' Inn** (☎ 07-22568, fax 05-22814), which is next to the Punta Caliente. Its attractive a/c rooms have cable TV, and there's a restaurant. Rates are BZ$105 s, BZ$135 d, and BZ150 t, including tax. Three good values for low-budget travelers are **Mahung's Hotel**, 11 North St. cor. of Main (☎ 07-22044; PO Box 21); seven-room **Verdes Guest House** (☎ 07-22069), 22 Main St. at Middle; and the eight-room **Foster's Hotel** (☎ 07-22117), 19 Main St. For an unforgettable sojurn, **Man Man** rents out the beds and hammocks in the hut in back of his house. Other hotels include the **Wahima Hotel**, 11 Front St.; and the **Isabela Hotel**, also on Front St. You can also camp for a reasonable fee at **Arvin's Landing** just outside of town to the north.

FOOD: The best place to eat has the best atmosphere. A meal with **Man Man** is an unforgettable experience. Located at the corner of King and Far West Streets, it's marked by the "Five Star Restaurant. Recipes by Duncan Hines" sign by the entrance. Serving whatever he can get fresh from the market and his garden, Man Man and his wife, both Garinagus, dish out hearty and healthy portions. If you're vegetarian, they will cater to your tastes. If not, you may have the opportunity to sample such local delicacies as cow's foot soup. The second best place to eat is the screen-windowed un- marked restaurant next to Verde's Guest House. **Reina's** is a greasy spoon popular for breakfast. Open only in the evenings, **Bobby's Restaurant** sometimes has conch soup. Serving overpriced Chi- nese food, the **Mira Mar Restaurant** is at 95 Front St. Also try the **Kowloon. Goyo** is near the main plaza, as is the **Palma,** a store which features snacks such as *ganaches*. Near the gas station at the beginning of town, **Lucille's Kitchen** has reasonable prices. Lucille herself works on her sewing machine behind the bar when she's not serving. **Shaiba's** is classier but comparatively expensive. **Granny's Kitchen** across from Shaiba's serves breakfast as well as rice and bean dishes for BZ$7.50. You can also try the small food stall set right next to Palavi's Hotel, which sells Belizean food as well as flour tortillas every evening. The **Morning Glory Restaurant**, 59 Front St., also provides Belizean meals and opens for breakfast. For snacks try the **Wahima** and **Punta Gorda Bakery**. Just out of town near the soccer field, the **Roundhouse** is a popular bar and restaurant. A bakery is up the road from the Texaco station along the coast at the town's entrance. Just down from the Clock Tower, the **Ice Cream Parlor** serves ice cream and sandwiches.

ENTERTAINMENT: Set across from Traveller's Inn, the **Massive Rock Disco** is the most active place in town; video movies are shown in the early evening. **South Side Disco** is the second liveliest place in town. **Bobby's** sees a lot of action, as does the neighboring **Starlight**. The **Mira Mar** is also a popular spot for imbibing.

SERVICES: Dem Dats Doin operates a tourist information office (☎ 07-22470) in the town's center next to the ferry pier. Extremely helpful, they're open daily (except Thursday and Sunday) from 7:30 to 11:30. They also have cards and attractive and impressive boxed insects (butterflies and large beetles) on sale. Ask about "the indigenous experience," as well as their homestays. They also have a number of tours, as does **Nature's Way Guest House. Charter by Land/Sea** is at 12 Front St. (☎ 07-22070, PO Box 18). A newcomer on the scene is the **Toledo Explorer's Club**, 46 José María St. It is not so much a club as a tour agency which offers tours and camping trips; customized trips are available. Stop by for more information. **Jack and Janet Nightingale** (Box 11, Punta Gorda) offer sailing trips aboard the *Juanita*; inquire at Arvin's Landing. **Belize Hotel and Tourism Centre** (☎ 22834) can make travel arrangements.

SHOPPING: The travel agency sells travel guides at higher prices than elsewhere in the nation. A small branch of the **National Handicraft Centre** is at the corner of José María and Prince Streets.

FROM PUNTA GORDA: Z-Line buses (☎ 07-22165) depart daily at 5 and 11AM (arriving at around 2:30 and 9 PM); the fare to Belize City is BZ$22, Independence is BZ$9, and the fare to Belmopan is BZ$19. James buses leave at noon on Tues. and Fri. and at 6 AM on Thurs., Sat. and Sun. from the terminal opposite the police station. The late departures allow passengers arriving from Guatemala to make connections. All stop in Belmopan, Dangriga, and Mango Creek. They have more leg room than their competitors, and their conductors are trained as tour guides. The San Antonio bus departs on Mon., Wed., Fri., and Sat. at 12:30 for the 1 hr. 20 min. trip; the San José bus leaves at 12:30 on Wed. and Sat. The San Pedro Columbia bus departs at 1 PM on Mon., Wed., Fri., and Sat. There's also a schoolbus on school days as well as a freight and passenger truck which leaves the village at 6 AM on Wed. and returns around noon. Buses also run to Silver Creek and Indian Creek. Service to all these locations may have improved by the time you read this; times may have changed as well, so be sure to inquire. Hitchhiking is a viable if slow option. Wait at the bakery along the coast road on the way out of town to the north.

by air: Both Tropic and Maya fly. To reserve and purchase Tropic tickets contact Heston Wagner at his shop next to the St. Charles Inn at 23 King St. In addition, for both Maya and Tropic tickets contact Penell & Sons at 50 Main St. Also, both Maya and Tropic have offices at the airstrip.

by boat: The boat for Guatemala leaves on Tues. and Fri. at around 2, and it takes two hours. Fare is about BZ$13. It returns those same days in the morning, arriving around 10. The Tues. boat tends to be faster, as there is less demand. The ferry ticket agent (Indita Maya, ☎ 07-22065) is at 24 Middle St. and sales start at 9:30. Be sure to buy your ticket as soon as you arrive. If you need a Guatemalan visa, you're out of luck. The Immigration office is next to the PO and near the pier. Buy some *quetzales* from the female moneychanger or from passengers arriving from Guatemala. Bring food and water for the boat as none is available on board.

Vicinity of Punta Gorda

Although there isn't much to do in town at present, many places in the surrounding Toledo District have much to offer, and details are found in this section. Because of the paucity of public transport, getting around Toledo can be difficult unless you have your own vehicle. However, people will stop to give you a lift. Toledo continues to grow and diversify. When it is finally constructed, a newly-surfaced highway is likely to radically transform this area. Currently, dolomite is being mined in the district, and cacao is being exported by a British firm. Controversy ensued early in 1994 when it was disclosed that Malaysian businessman Ting Jack Heng had been granted a concession to log some 200,000 acres near the Guatemalan border. After protest spearheaded by

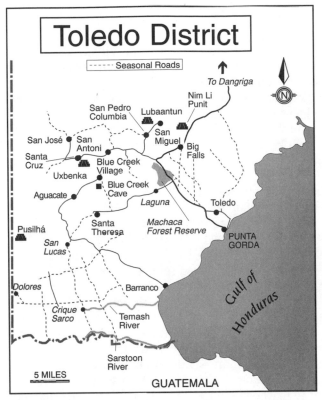

Toledo District

----- Seasonal Roads

To Dangriga

Nim Li Punit

San Pedro Columbia   Lubaantun

San José   San Antoni   San Miguel   Big Falls

Santa Cruz   Blue Creek Village

Uxbenka   Blue Creek Cave

Aguacate   Laguna   Toledo

Pusilhá   Santa Theresa   Machaca Forest Reserve   PUNTA GORDA

San Lucas

Dolores   Barranco   Gulf of Honduras

Crique Sarco   Temash River

Sarstoon River

5 MILES   GUATEMALA

the Belize Alliance of Conservation Non-Government Organizations (BACONGO), the concession was revoked.

nearby attractions: Operating until 1978, the nearly-intact **Saddle Back Sugar Mill** is 1½ miles from town past the airstrip. As it's on private land, permission should be obtained before entry. The remains of **Seven Hills Sugar Mill** can be reached by boat; contact Bobby Polonio at Bobbie's Restaurant for guided tours. The southern end of the barrier reef and the Sapodilla and Ranguana Cayes (see listing under Placencia) can be also reached by boat.

trekking: One challenging hike is from San Miguel, north of Punta Gorda, through a chicle gathering area to the Valley of Esperanza. It takes one or two days. Contact Alfredo Romero or his uncle in San Miguel for more information. It's also possible to hike from Santa Cruz to Blue Creek; check with the TEA for information.

Village Guesthouse Program

One way to explore the area is with the Village Guesthouse Program designed by the Toledo Ecotourism Association Village Guesthouse Ecotrail Program. Lodges have been built in Laguna, San Pedro Columbia, Santa Cruz, San José, and San Miguel. The basic lodges are generally thatched with cohune palm, and there are eight bunk beds in each; men and women are segregated, and the charge is BZ$16. Bathrooms are detached. Each meal – all with different Maya families – costs BZ$6. Tours of local attractions are BZ$5 ph. Musical performances are also available. Access to the villages is either by local transportation or by charter. Many visitors to Belize maintain that a stay in the village was the highlight of their trip. For information and reservations contact TEA, Box 75, Punta Gorda, or ☎ 07-22119. While in PG, stop by Nature's Way and chat with Chet. Be sure to give him (or mail him) the evaluation program so that the program may be monitored.

sights and attractions: Laguna offers a cave with pictographs and another with bats, a swamp with great birding, and hiking. Santa Cruz has a park (the Río Blanco), waterfalls and pools, as well as nearby Uxbenka ruins. At San Pedro Columbia, you can visit Lubaantun, ride in a canoe, and visit old cacao groves. San Miguel offers visits to caves, hikes to Lubaantun, and river canoeing. The most remote of the Maya villages participating, San José can only be reached by horse or on foot at times; it offers hiking.

The Indigenous Experience

This innovative project is the brainchild of the Villorias and is an attempt to facilitate contact and cultural exchange between locals and outsiders. For a BZ$10 fee they connect you with a Maya family homestay. You can stay with a family, share a lunch or dinner of pumpkin stew and corn tortillas or a breakfast of eggs and tortillas. As there are no special facilities or tourist amenities offered, nor is there any privacy, it's not for everyone. You'll bathe by moonlight in the cool river, stoop on the outhouse and use a corncob to clean yourself (if you wish), watch tortillas being shaped by hand, sleep in a hammock in the same room with the kids, and generally experience life as it's lived by millions all over the world. If you wish, you can have a "hands on experience," such as picking corn in the fields, harvesting coffee and cacao beans, threshing rice stalks, or chopping firewood – all of the innumerable activities that make up a sustainable subsistence lifestyle. But there's one typical "Third

World" experience you won't have – being kept awake all night fending off mosquitoes: there are none. Rates (all the money provides badly needed income for the family) are BZ$10 for a hammock and BZ$4 for each meal. For more information contact the Villorias at PO Box 73, Punta Gorda and enclose US$3 to help defray duplicating costs. If you're already in PG, visit their offices by the ferry pier (under "services" above). Again, remember to fill out the evaluation forms. If you have complaints and/or suggestions, be sure to let them know.

Forest Home

The remains of this settlement lie to the north of Punta Gorda. Founded in 1867 by defeated Confederate exiles, many of the original settlers at this site, discouraged by the extreme climatic differences and the rigors of existence, quickly returned. Missisippi Methodists bolstered their numbers, and the number of estates operating sugar mills had grown to 12 by 1870. Falling sugar prices sent production into a tailspin in 1890, and the Methodists refused to turn to producing moonshine, preferring to either dump the molasses or feed it to their cattle instead. The community finally faded in 1910, and only traces remain today.

Nim Li Pinit

Lying to the northeast of PG, this Maya site's name (meaning "Big Hat") comes from the carved figure wearing a large headress on the site's tallest stela. Only partially cleared, this two-plaza ceremonial center features at least 25 stelae, eight of which are carved; one, measuring 31 feet, is the longest found in Belize. Of the several groups of buildings, only the southernmost can be visited. While one structure is 36 feet high, another is only 9 feet high, but 215 feet long. The site's center consists of a ceremonial group and two civic and elite groups. Similar architecturally to Lubaantun, the site was discovered by oil workers in 1976. Although initially surveyed by Norman Hammond, in-depth excavation did not begin until Richard Leventhal worked here from 1983-1986. A half-mile walk from the Southern Highway, it's 25 minutes north of PG, at Mile 75. The only way to get here is by the bus running to Belize City. There are no facilities. The Maya village of Indian Creek is nearby, and you may see women washing their clothes in the stream flowing along the site's border. Whitney's store is just below the turnoff for the ruins. A sign on the highway points out the trail; if you're heading south, you'll know you've passed it if you see the Whitney Lumber mill on the east side of the highway. The beginning of the site is marked by a large ceiba tree. There's great birdwatching in the area, particularly from March to July when the fruit trees are producing.

Big Falls

Located just to the south of Nim Li Punit at the point where the Southern Highway crosses the Rio Grande. The nation's only readily-accessible warm medicinal mineral springs are on the Alaman Farm nearby. Ask Mr. Alaman at the General Store for permission to camp. There's also a small hotel here.

Dem Dats Doin

One of the most unusual places you'll visit anywhere in the world is right here, just 1.25 miles down the entrance road to San Pedro Columbia village – just look for the sign. In the course of the past 14 years, Alfredo and Yvonne Villoria have created their own appropriate technology farm which uses sustainable agricultural techniques. Both grew up in Hawaii but first met in LA; while Alfredo is of Filipino stock, Yvonne is German-Hawaiian. Dissatisfied with stifling, routine jobs, they traveled over much of the Caribbean and Mexico, searching for a place to settle. They finally selected Belize because its British-based legal system offered them security. Giving themselves five years to make a go of it, they're still here and doing quite well. With the biogas digester and the photovoltaics on the roof, they've reached 95% energy self-sufficiency. Conscious of the need to change agricultural practices among the Maya, they offer free tours to educators and children, exposing them to appropriate technology techniques.

the farm: For a BZ$10 donation, you'll get a personal tour of this inspirational place. During the course of the visit, Yvonne and Alfredo display flow charts and illustrations to help you understand what you're seeing. You begin in their house which, like everything else you'll see, they built by studying books. Supported by rosewood posts, its design is nearly as remarkable as the methane-cooled refrigerator from which they pull the lemonade served to guests. Nearby is a homemade ferroconcrete wash basin, a fuel-conserving Lorena stove, and the insect dryer in which captured bugs are processed for sale. The first stop on this demonstration of a "Self Sufficient Integrated Farm System" is the pig pen and methane vat. The giant pigs produce excrement which is fed into the biogas digester, which produces methane sent through a pipe to a "floating drum" storage container. Filtered, the gas is used for cooking, refrigeration, and lights; the sludge/fertilizer goes to the fruit trees and the garden. The pigs are either slaughtered when still relatively small or, when full-grown, are sold out of the area, so as to not compete with the local market. Nearby are the ferroconcrete reinforced fish ponds. The plan calls for raising tilapia in these to feed the pigs. Since these fish have not yet been granted immigrant visas owing to governmental restrictions, the ponds are filled with ordinary fish for the present. The more than 70 trees grown on the property include governor's plum, white custard apple, rambutan, acerola (Barbados cherry), macadamia, Ceylon gooseberry, Indian juju, three varieties of starfruit, soursop, Malay apple, anatto, passion fruit, guava, tropical almond, flying potatoes, and frangipani. Plants in the primarily ornamental garden include pineapple, bamboo, torch ginger, and sweet potatoes. The latter are grown in large tires; when it comes time to harvest them, they are flipped over. No chemicals or artificial fertilizers are used; jicama, a tuber which acts as a natural insecticide, is ground into a powder and sprinkled on the plants. There's also a small but attractive orchid grove, as well as a plant nursery from which cuttings are sold to locals. Rice hulls from a rice mill a couple of miles away are brought in to use as mulch. The whole tour takes 1.5-2 hours. To book, either take a chance and drop in, write them at PO Box 73 in Punta Gorda, or visit them in their office at the ferry pier in PG. The Villorias also run a small and inexpensive bed and breakfast operation, as well as supervising the "Indigenous Experience" (see above).

San Pedro Columbia

This small Kekchi and *mestizo* village is famous for its Kekchi embroidery. San Pedro must be close to God because there are seven different churches in this village of 150 families. **getting there:** From Punta Gorda, drive west for 1½ miles past the Shell station at the junction with the Southern Highway, then turn right down an unmarked road. San Pedro Columbia is two miles ahead. If you have no car, you must hitch or take a bus (San Antonio bus) along the Southern Highway and get off at the junction for San Pedro Columbia, which will be on your right. You'll know you're entering the village when you cross an iron grating in the road.

Lubaantun

Translating as "Place of the Fallen Stones" – which is the modern but not the original name – this is the foremost Maya archaeological site in the nation's south. A major Late Classic ceremonial center, the site sits poised on a tall ridge near San Pedro Columbia which the Maya built up to form a roughly rectangular shape, about 300 yards long by 160 yards wide. Square courts are surrounded by pyramids once topped by thatch buildings. Constructed upon a core of rocks, smaller stones, and layers of earth, the structures were faced with hard crystalline limestone blocks which resembled marble when viewed from a distance. What makes the site unusual is that there are no stone buildings set on platforms or pyramids, very little stone sculpture, and no stelae. It is thought that decoration was done in wood. From the highest structure you can just barely see the Caribbean more than 19 miles away.

layout: There are 11 major structures grouped around five plazas and three ball courts. Lubaantun differs from other Maya sites in a number of ways. For example, other than ball court markers, there are no stelae or sculpted monuments, and the entire site is essentially one temple complex. Unlike other Maya temples, no mortar is used. Rather than leveling off the site, the Maya systematically shaped and added fill to the slopes, and the tallest structure rises to 40 feet. The site is crumbling badly in the aftermath of too many visitors scampering to the top for a view. There isn't much to see here, but the serenity and ambience – augmented by the whir of cicadas, the crisp crackle of birds and the haunting rattle of a boring woodpecker – is wonderful. Keel-billed toucans and brocket deer frequently visit the ruins late in the afternoon.

getting here: Make the first right after the village church, then proceed down the clay and gravel road, turning left when you see the sign – about 20 minutes from the village in all.

HISTORY: Lubaantun apparently was occupied only briefly near the end of the Classic Period between 730 and 890 AD. It is believed that cacao was used to trade for the imported objects (jade, obsidian, and lava) found at the site – a thesis which the excavation of a ceramic musician wearing a cacao-pod pendant in 1970 supports. The site first came to attention when it was uncovered by members of the Toledo settlement in 1875, and it was first excavated by Thomas Gann in 1903. Harvard University's R. E. Merwin visited the site in 1915. Taking the first photos, he spirited away three carved ball court markers (each depicting two men playing the game) to Harvard's Peabody Museum. Another of the men who worked here was the famous archaeologist J. Eric S. Thompson in 1926-27 under the sponsorship of the British Museum. As Pusilha, 30 miles to the southwest, seemed to be more interesting, the British Museum expedition virtually abandoned this site during the late 1920s. In 1970 a group of Cambridge archaeologists and geologists under the leadership of Norman Hammond continued to excavate here, finding it to be larger than originally thought – surprising in light of the fact that it was used only from approximately AD 700 to 889, or possibly as short a time as AD 730-750. Although the stone was quarried locally, smaller objects such as blades and axes were imported. Some stone carvings have been found on ballcourt markers and on walls.

the crystal skull: The site's most controversial find is a crystal skull unearthed by Anna Mitchell-Hedges, daughter of expedition leader and Atlantis researcher, F.A. Mitchell-Hedges. Coincidentally or not, she found the skull on her 17th birthday. Its origins are uncertain, but all agree it is a remarkable piece of work. A similar skull is found in the Musée de l'Homme in Paris. Today the crystal skull abides with Anna in Ontario, Canada. For a rather zany view of the crystal skull, written by "New Age" folk in Marin County, CA , read *The Message of the Crystal Skull* (see "Booklist"). Note that it has Lubaantun situated incorrectly on its Belize map!

practicalities: The site is open 8-5. The caretaker may or may not be present to collect admission. In terms of ambience, the best times to visit are dawn and dusk. There's nowhere to stay, but it should be no problem to camp. You can stay in San Pedro as part of "the Indigenous Experience" or at the Village Guesthouse, which will afford you a bit more privacy (see above). You can ask the caretaker to ferry you back to San Pedro in a dory; tip him a couple of dollars.

Fallen Stones Butterfly Ranch

A roller coaster of a road leads up about a mile from the entrance to the Lubaantun ruins to Toledo's most remarkable lodge, one notable for its views, wildlife, and overall tasteful ambience. Falling Stones is all the product of one man's vision and imagination.

the butterfly farm: Outside visitors pay BZ$3 to visit the butterfly farm. Owner Ray Halberd has been intrigued by butterflies since he was eight, but his employment in tropical agriculture kept him busy over the decades and it has only been in recent years that his long-held dream of operating a butterfly farm has come to fruition. Ray operated a butterfly farm in the Philippines (on the island of Panai in Iloilo City) for 2½ years, until one day when seven gunmen showed up with the intention of kidnapping him for ransom. Luckily, he was not on the farm that day. "After that, I wasn't very keen to go back and stay there. The kidnappers were eventually apprehended. One was shot dead while resisting arrest, and the others are languishing in jail."

There are two rooms filled with eight different species of butterflies. As the butterflies have a tiled roof over their heads while Ray himself lives under a thatched roof, his workers consider him to be a bit deranged. The farm's highlight is its blue morphos. They live only about 12 days but spend their brief time filling the world with color. There will be some 4-5,000 blue morpho caterpillars in total when the farm is fully operational. The eggs resemble little drops of water. As it's difficult to tell the eggs from real dew drops in the morning, this is probably a technique used for camouflage purposes. Every butterfly has different colored pupae; some are jade green. You might see a newly-hatched one hanging from its pupa. You'll note that the resting blue morphos resemble owl butterflies except that the eye is not so large. Expertly camouflaged at rest, in flight they turn frighteningly bright. Each of the passion flowers found inside the enclosures caters to a different species. Another enclosure serves as a processing area where the pupae are fed.

When the farm is fully operating, 600 pupae of 35 species will be exported to Europe and the US every week, which should bring in BZ$3,000 gross. However, the process is extremely labor-intensive, and the pupae must be transported by courier, so this cuts down on the profitability. The lodge is intended to help support the butterfly ranch. Ray's intent is to turn the area around the lodge into a breeding ground for butterflies, clearing it for them and enriching the natural vegetation with food and nectar plant sources.

fauna: Right around the vicinity of the farm you can see magnificent blue morpho butterflies. Lesser-known, but nonetheless spectacular, white morphos can be found some four miles away. There are also three species of owl butterfly, as well as a number of heliconids. All three of Belize's toucan species are here, as are hummingbirds and other flying wonders. You might see an agouti come right up on the property to feast on coconut chunks, and jaguar tracks may be seen on nearby trails. There are also a couple of nests of the stingless Maya bees, which each produce about a pound of honey per year.

practicalities: The cabins are a combination of Kekchí and European design elements. You can sit on your porch and view the

Columbia and Maya Mountain reserves: only a vast expanse of jungle stands between you and San Ignacio. There are seven rooms in all; some can accommodate up to four. Solar power provides light and operates a fan, and shower water is warmed by individual heaters. Food is highly imaginative and surprisingly well prepared; vegetarians can be catered to. Meals are loosely based on Maya cooking, but an international dish (such as a West African peanut stew) is served for Sunday lunch, which attracts a wide variety of outside visitors as well. Repasts are served in the **Chiclero's Restaurant and Bar** as well as the open-air **Columbia View Restaurant** which commands a view of the village of the same name. Room rates are around BZ$130 s, BZ$155 d, BZ$180 t, and BZ$205 quad. Meals cost BZ$12 for breakfast, BZ$16 for lunch, and BZ$30 for dinner. BZ$100 OW is charged for transport to or from PG for one to three persons. For more information, write PO Box 23, Punta Gorda. In PG itself contact Alistair King (07-2126, 07-2104) in the Texaco Station at the northern edge of town.

Belize Agroforestry Research Center

 This remarkable farm is just a short walk from the ruins: take the path left to the river and then along a path and under a barbed wire fence. Pre- and post-Hispanic Maya agricultural techniques are practiced here. Crops grown include corn, bok choi, Chinese cabbage, cabbage, coffee, and cacao. Fruits include pineapple and carambola. In an attempt to revolutionize permaculture in the area, various techniques are under R&D. For example, lucena trees (a type of legume) are planted on slopes, girded, and allowed to die on top. Wingbean, jicima, and flying potato are planted and harvested; their leaves serve as mulch. Eventually, the tree is cut down, and the girdle is used for firewood or left in place as a natural terrace; meanwhile, new sprouts have started under the girdle. Also on the property are beehives and small Maya ruins on hilltops.

history: The brainchild of environmental activist/attorney Don Wirtshafter and horticulturalist Mark Cohen, this innovative project began in the 1980s. Appraising the area in 1980, Don brought back enthusiastic reports, which piqued Mark's enthusiasm. Seeing the potential for a tropical field station here, Cohen began to look for a site. The current property was originally leased from former Peace Corps volunteer Russell Turner who had lived on the parcel before returning to the States. He agreed to lease the land to them in 1988, along with an option to purchase for

US$10,000. The Tropical Conservation Foundation was created in order to fund the purchase, and the Belize Agroforestry Research Center was formed as a separate Belizean entity to supervise the property. After finally securing the needed funds in 1990, the Tropical Conservation Foundation became the official titleholder of 147 acres. Despite the name, there is no official government involvement in the project, and there is still little or no involvement on the part of Belizean farmers.

practicalities: Anyone with a serious interest in tropical agriculture is welcome to come for a visit or stay for a day or two. A BZ$20 donation per night is requested, along with an additional donation for food. If no one else is around, see Doles, the Belizean caretaker. For more information write the Tropical Conservation Foundation, 14 North Court St., Athens, OH 45701.

San Antonio

 There are a few shops and not much else here. You might see some women, members of an obscure Christian sect, wearing headshawls. An unusual feature of the town is the stone church and mission house. San Antonio's residents emigrated from San Luis Petén. When the original San Antonians arrived in 1886, they brought with them their patron saint San Luis, the church bells, and images of the saints from their original village. Locals from their original village arrived to reclaim their goods but were rebuffed. Shortly thereafter, the church was struck by lightning and burned to the ground; only the bells survived the fire. Both the school and church were built of hand-quarried stone. Its stained glass windows were a last-minute thought – procured when a member of the Order, walking down a street in St. Louis, Missouri, came upon a church being demolished. He persuaded the demolition company to donate them, collected donations for shipping, and they have been in place ever since.

One of the more amusing incidents in the history of Guatemala's claim to Belize took place in 1962 when Francisco Sagastume, a political opponent of President Ydígoras (who had staged a similarly unsuccessful "liberation mission" to Benque Viejo in 1958), arrived in town. Having already announced in the border village of Pueblo Viejo that liberation was at hand, and having burned photographs of Queen Elizabeth and the Duke of Edinburgh along with a Union Jack to dramatize the declaration, he encountered hostility from the locals, whose ancestors had fled from Guatemala three generations before. Proceeding to PG, the band was arrested at Stann Creek and sentenced to 10 years hard labor. This was the last Guatemalan attempt at "liberation."

practicalities: Stay at low-budget **Bol's Hilltop Hotel**, which has basic but clean rooms with fans. The village pay telephone is at the Bee Cooperative behind Bol's. There's no nightlife to speak of except for a bar or two. The village now has 24-hour electricity.

festivals and events: Sporting a brown masked face and smoking a pipe, a scarecrow-like Judas is hung in back of the church on Holy Thursday at around 10 AM and executed by a firing squad on Holy Saturday evening after mass. Costumed young men perform dances at fiestas, like the one which takes place around June 13. A recently revived deer dance takes place on September 25. The festival commences with an all-night vigil nine days before, during which the masks and costumes are wreathed in incense and offered food. The story of a hunter and deer told to the accompaniment of marimba music, the deer dance is high melodrama. As part of the celebrations, a pole is greased and a prize (usually money) is set atop it. Three men compete to climb it.

getting there: Chun's buses run from Punta Gorda's Civic Center daily at 4 PM and return at 5 AM. To get here from Lubaantun, drive to the road leading from Punta Gorda, turn west for about two miles, then turn right at the junction and go two miles.

Uxbenka

 A small ceremonial center "discovered" in 1984, Uxbenka is just nine miles east of the Guatemalan border in the foothills of the Toledo District, beyond San Antonio and near Santa Cruz. There are over 20 stelae here, one of which dates back to the Early Classic Period. As is typical in the area, the hills have been terraced and faced so that they resemble large buildings. Its name ("Ancient Place") was given to the site by residents of Santa Cruz. Onsite, you'll find two terraces with erosion-erased stelae sheltered underneath thatched pavilions. All in all, there's not much to see, but the refreshing breeze and views are great.

getting there: Although some trucks do pass on Saturday, the only assured way of getting here – unless you have your own vehicle or charter – is to make the long, hot four-mile hike along the rock-strewn dirt road. (Watch out for ticks if you sit down!) Turn to the right just before the village to find the entrance road to the site. The caretaker lives at the edge of Santa Cruz and may or may not be at the scene to dispense tickets.

Río Blanco Santa Elena Nature Reserve

Set three miles west of Santa Elena, this 500-acre expanse was declared a reserve in 1993. Santa Cruzeans know it as "Santa Elena Falls" after its waterfall. A proposal to increase the reserve's size to 25,000 acres is under consideration.

Blue Creek Caves

Infrequently visited, this cave and stream combination is out of the way but worth the trip. To get here, return to the junction (marked by Roy's Cool Spot Grocery), and then follow the sign to Aguacate. Blue Creek is five miles farther, past Blue Creek Village. Its entrance is marked by a narrow concrete bridge. Sign the register and follow the trail upstream to an open-sided structure, where there's a swimming spot. From there, take the path along the water. The path follows a creek, which dries up during the rainy season. The trail crosses the creek and then wends through an area with a lot of boulders. After 15 minutes, you must climb up to a canyon which leads to the Hokeb Ha cave entrance. An entrepreneur has leased the land from the government, built some cabañas, and declared the area to be the "Blue Creek Wildlife Sanctuary," a designation which has no legal status. He is requesting a BZ$2 donation, which is given to the village for trail maintenance. In 1994, the controversial "Jason Project" was based here and on South Water Caye. Using grants from the US Dept. of Education and large corporations (including at least one defense contractor) who wanted to clean up their image, the project brought a number of "argonauts," US schoolchildren, to Belize to participate in research. Radio reports were beamed to the US. Although the enterprise did help to put Belize on the map, there was little Belizean involvement, and it seemed at times as though Belize was a convenient exotic background with a catchy name instead of a real place with real people and real problems. One lasting legacy of the project is the canopy observation system, which is accessed via a 100-foot tower.

Pusilhá

About a mile east of the Guatemalan border, these low-lying ruins, built on a hilltop along the river, can only be reached by boat. There are over 20 carved monuments in the plaza. Some are zoomorphs similar to those found at Quiriguá. They date from the 6th to 8th C. AD. There's also a ball court, which is surrounded by walls.

Barranco

Belize's southernmost settlement, this small Garinagu village (☎ 07-22138) of around 200 can only be reached by boat (ask near the market) or by a bad road during the dry season. Its name ("Red Cliffs" in Garifuna) refers to the cliffs on which it sits. Founded in 1862, today the village has a decreasing population. There's no formal accommodation, but it's possible to stay with locals. Arrangements can either be made on your own or through the TEA. While here, be sure to meet Carlson Tuttle, who is working to revitalize Garinagu culture; he has an excellent library. Howler monkeys are found near the village, as are mangroves. The uninhabited Moho River is set between here and PG.

Sarstoon-Temash Nature Reserve

This 80,000-acre tract covers the area surrounding the mouth of the Temash River. It is a haven for waterfowl and can be reached by boat from PG. The Kekchí Maya village of Dolores can be reached by taking a boat upriver to Crique Sarco, then proceeding on foot.

Offshore Cayes

 Located near the mouth of the Deep River, **Wild Cane Caye** has mounds and artifacts belonging to the Mayas. Earthwatch has conducted research expeditions here under the direction of Dr. Heather McKillop of Louisiana State University. The **Sapodilla Cayes**, running down to Honduras, are great for snorkeling. **Nicholas Caye** has been developed for tourism. Its vegetation has been trimmed and cabañas constructed. It will become the Toucan Island Resort. Set to the southwest of Nicholas Caye, **Hunting Caye** is partly used as a base for the Belizean Defense Force. It has the remains of an old ship (as well as an enormous ancient anchor, overgrown by coral) in the depths off a nearby reef lying to the southeast. There is a lighthouse and a good harbor, as well as Crescent Moon, a lovely beach. If you visit here be cautious: it is a nesting ground for hawksbill turtles and too much activity could prove disruptive. **Lime Caye (Low Caye)** is another beautiful island. Tour groups from Livingston visit here. Also known as Sapodilla Caye and South Caye, **Ragged Caye** is the southernmost link in the chain. Although largely denuded by tropical storms, it is an excellent snorkeling spot. There is excellent diving around all of these cayes.

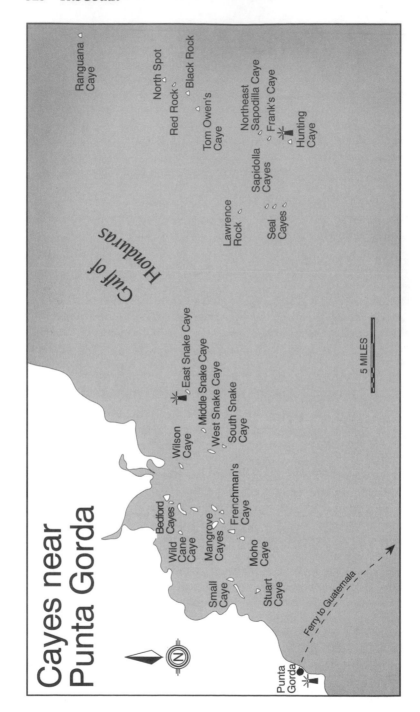

Cayes near
Punta Gorda

Gulf of
Honduras

5 MILES

Ranguana
Caye

North Spot

Red Rock
Black Rock

Tom Owen's
Caye

Northeast
Sapodilla Caye
Frank's Caye

Hunting
Caye

Sapidolla
Cayes

Lawrence
Rock

Seal
Cayes

East Snake Caye

Middle Snake Caye

West Snake Caye

South Snake
Caye

Wilson
Caye

Frenchman's
Caye

Bedford
Cayes

Wild
Cane
Caye

Mangrove
Cayes

Moho
Caye

Small
Caye

Stuart
Caye

Ferry to Guatemala

Punta
Gorda

N

Onward to Guatemala

Many travelers arriving in Punta Gorda will be headed toward Guatemala by boat. Two of the best Maya sites are within a few days of PG.

Puerto Barrios, Guatemala

This sleazy port town has little to recommend it, unless you're a sailor on shore leave. Its only attributes are a marvelously sagging cinema building, a lively market, and a fabulous Taj Mahal-style tomb – complete with trumpeting elephants – at the cemetery on the road out of town.

practicalities: Probably the best place to stay in terms of convenience is the **Caribeña** just up the road from the ferry to the left. The dining room of the **El Norte** has the best atmosphere and the hotel itself has a classic Caribbean atmosphere.

getting there: For information about the ferry see "from Punta Gorda" above. Upon arrival, an immigration official will grab your passports and stuff them into a leather bag. Then, after passing through customs and paying an "inspection fee," you must turn left at the corner and enter the Immigration Office. US citizens will generally be asked for US$6 or Q25 for a visitor's card and will be granted a month's stay. The nearest bank still open is the Banco del Café near the market. If you have cash US dollars, you can change them at the corner near the market. Belizean dollars bring a ridiculous rate so you should change these with the lady moneychanger near PG's pier; she'll also buy all your extra *quetzales* at a fair rate if you return that way. When returning from Guatemala City, hop on an express (five hours, US$6) and spend the night here. The ferry runs on Tues. and Fri. at around 8. Buy your ticket at the office up the street from the ferry and then proceed to Immigration, where you'll be soaked for an exit fee of Q10 for individuals and Q6 apiece for couples. This probably goes directly into the officer's pocket.

Livingston, Guatemala

This predominately Garinagu (Black Carib) village is set across the Bay of Honduras. The ferry no longer stops here so you must either charter a boat in PG or take the ferry from Puerto Barrios, then another (generally crowded) one from there. The waterfall, Las Siete Altares (The Seven Altars), is a few miles along the beach; visitors have been robbed here, so take nothing of value with you.

A popular excursion from here is a boat trip up the Río Dulce to the Biotopo (Reserve) Chocón-Machacas. The least expensive transport is with the mail launch, which departs on Tuesday and Friday.

accommodation and food: The classiest hotel here is **Tucán Dugú**, which has rooms for US$42 s and US$45 d. It offers standard, suite, and bungalow rooms; watersports; a pool, and two restaurants. Other places – all low-budget – include the **Casa Rosada**, the **Hotel Caribe** (☎ 048-1073), the classically Caribbean 13-room **Río Dulce** (☎ 481-059), the German-owned **African Place**, and the **Flamingo**. The **Restaurante El Malecón** is popular. Alternatives include the **Restaurante Margoth**, the **Restaurante Saby**, the **Restaurante Tiburongato**, and eating at some of the hotels.

Quiriguá, Guatemala

Containing the major Quiriguá Classic Maya ruins, Quiriguá National Park is a small expanse of old growth forest surrounded by banana plantations. Studied and excavated since the late 19th C., it has been lovingly restored and, from an artistic standpoint, rivals Copán as the Maya site with the most carvings and reliefs. The earliest structures at the site appear to date from the Late Preclassic (ca. 300 BC-200 AD), but the visible buildings and stelae date from 550-850 AD. Its site plan is similar to Copán. To the south an artificially-raised acropolis contains elite administrative and ceremonial structures. The large public plaza to the north holds the remains of public buildings, a ball court, and stelae. This plan contrasts with Tikal's radial format. The centerpiece of the ruins are its stelae, which are unmatched in Mayadom. Beginning with Stela H (751 AD), each successive stela – erected every five years – was larger and more imposing, until the grandaddy of them all, 35-foot-tall Stela E was erected in 771 AD. The tallest stela known, it weighs some 35 tons. Even more unusual and striking than the stelae, the zoomorphs are scattered over the plaza. The Great Turtle, Zoomorph P, is the most famous monument. This enormous boulder has been intricately and delicately carved with stone tools. The massive acropolis at the site is also impressive.

getting there: Even though it's a hassle to get here, the trip is worth it! Any bus running between Puerto Barrios and Guatemala City will pass. Just get out at the junction and transfer to the smaller local bus for a ride through the banana fields a few miles to the entrance.

practicalities: A minimal admission is collected at the entrance where postcards and other souvenirs are sold. As all but one of the stelae and all of the zoomorphs have been placed in open-faced thatch huts for protection, a flash and/or high ASA film is appropriate for photography. Bring water as well because no facilites are available on-site. The nearest place to stay is in the budget priced **Hotel Royal** near the village of Quiriguá. **Hotel y Restaurante Santa Monica** stands next to the Texaco station in Los Amates, and **Hotel Doña Maria** is at Km 181 near Puente Doña María (Doña María Bridge). The first is the cheapest and the second is most comfortable, but still low-budget at under US$10 d.

Copán, Honduras

"It lay before us like a shattered bark in the midst of the ocean, her masts gone, her name effaced, her crew perished, and none to tell whence she came, to whom she belonged, how long on her voyage, or what caused her destruction."

– John Lloyd Stephens writing about the discovery of Copán in *Incidents of Travel in Central America, Chiapas and Yucatan* (1841).

With excavated ruins covering some 40 acres and containing an acropolis and five plazas, the ancient Maya city of Copán is located in the southeast Maya lowland zone, on the Río Copán just inside Honduras and near the Guatemala border. The restored structures date from 600-800 AD, the Late Classic. Evidence unearthed so far suggests that Copán was occupied from Preclassic times on. Although its images are shared by other Maya sites, the presentation is Copán's own, and the site is without a doubt the greatest repository of Maya art. In addition to a large number of extraordinary stelae, there's also the Great Turtle, an enormous and magnificent carved two-headed stone turtle with clawed feet resembling those of a jaguar. Comprising as many as 2,500 glyphs, the Hieroglyphic Stairway is the site's top attraction. Another hallmark is the "Old Man of Copán," a representation of God N depicted at the northeast corner of Temple 11 (The Temple of the Inscriptions).

HISTORY: The area surrounding the site is believed to have been inhabited as early as 1000 BC. Although details are sketchy, Copán is thought to have flourished between 250 and 900 AD. The Heiroglyphic Stairway and a number of other imposing structures were completed during the reign of Yax Pac (763-820 AD), and the area is believed to have started its decline thereafter. The last carved date found is 822 AD. By 1200 AD the site had been reclaimed by

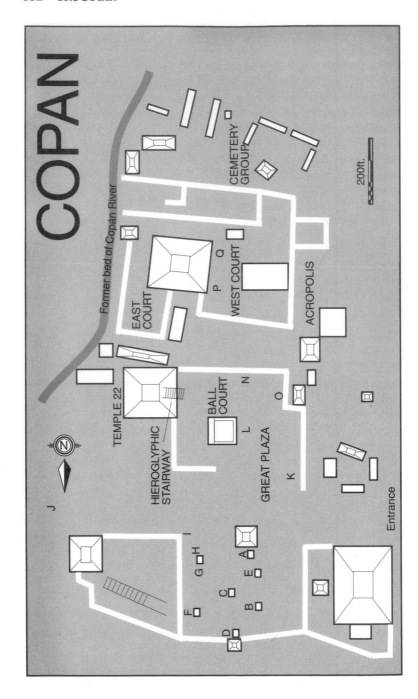

the forest. The name comes from the indigenous chief of the region, Copán Calel, who used the area as a base against the Spanish aggressors. The ruins remained neglected until explorers John L. Stephens and Frederick Catherwood arrived in 1841. They employed indigenous workers to hack away at the forest and expose the ruins. Stephens purchased the ruins from their owner for US$50 and for a time actually planned to have them disassembled and shipped to New York. British archaeologist Alfred P. Maudslay arrived to excavate the site in 1885 and successive work has been carried on by Harvard's Peabody Museum, the Carnegie Institution of Washington, DC, and by the Instituto Hondureño de Antropología y Historia. The latest project is to protect the sculptures at the site from destructive humidity and rainfall by moving them to a controlled indoor environment, an expensive proposition.

GETTING THERE: Entry to Honduras has become something of a cottage industry for both Guatemalan and Honduran customs officials. Buses to the border run from Chiquimula. The border at El Florido is usually open from 7 AM to 6 PM. Change Honduran *lempiras* with the moneychangers (US$1=around 7 *lempiras*). You must pay five *quetzales* to leave Guatemala and a few dollars worth of *lempiras* to enter Honduras. Let the immigration official know that you will only be visiting Copán (Las Ruinas) and ask for a temporary exit permit. When you return to Guatemala, you should be able to use the same tourist card. Food and drink is available on the Honduran side. From the border, you must take a minibus seven miles to the village of Copán Ruinas.

TOURING THE SITE: The entrance to the ruins is a pleasant half-mile walk from the village; your minibus may drop you at the entrance upon request. Don't make the mistake of visiting the site just once. If you're staying in the village, you can easily visit again during the late-afternoon hours when there are few visitors. Bring water with you. Food is available at cafeterias, but you might want to pack some snacks. If you take the detour along the way to the left, you'll pass two eroded stelae. As you enter the complex, you'll either need to pay or to show your ticket (which can also be purchased at the museum in the village and is good for all sites). Hondurans pay L5, Central Americans pay L15, and all others pay L30 (around US$4.25; good for two days). Once inside, there are a few books and tee shirts for sale at the Centro de Visitantes. Entering the grounds, turn to the left and walk through another gate, where your ticket is checked again. Three scarlet macaws with clipped wings sit on the fence. A variety of caged animals are inside to the left, including a despondent margay and hyper white-faced capuchin monkeys. Farther on, the grounds are essentially tranquil – the peaceful ambience ruffled only by tour guides and workmen doing excavations. The stelae are scheduled to be replaced on-site with replicas and the originals moved indoors for protection so you can count yourself lucky to be visiting now.

A short walk will bring you to the Principal Group and the **Great Plaza**. Here you'll find the most impressive and delicately-carved stelae in the Maya World. Originally all were thought to have been painted, but touches of paint survive only on Stela C. A number of them depict King 18 Rabbit (695-738 AD). In the **Central Plaza**, to the south of the Great Plaza, the ball court is Central America's second largest and one of the few which retains its paving; it dates from 775 AD. The bordering rooms were likely to have been used by observers. The magnificent 50-foot-wide, 63-step **Hieroglyphic Stairway** is now shielded from the elements by a tarp. Each block forms part of a sequence of glyphs which total 1,500-2,000, equalling the inscriptions found on 20 stelae combined. Partially because the stairway collapsed in the 19th C. and 30 of the risers are not in order, the inscription has still only been decoded in fragments. The Copán Mosaics Project is trying to restore the stairway on paper and decode its meaning. An enormous cache has been discovered below the stairway. The Temple of the Inscriptions nearby is also worth visiting. Set at its base, Stela N has both portraits and glyphs. The **East Plaza** and **West Plaza** are to its south. The latter's Altar Q has representations of what are thought to be 16 kings of Copán carved along its sides. One of the site's most imposing buildings, Structure 22 on the northern side of the East Plaza, has the most detailed reliefs at its top. Above one of its entrances, each head of the two-headed snake rests atop a figure which is supported by a skull. Carvings of Chaac, the Rain God are at each corner of the structure. Also notice the carved jaguar heads found at this plaza.

In the immediate surroundings, you might spot a white-faced monkey, a deer, and any one or more of a number of birds. The *sendero natural* (nature trail) may not have much in the way of wildlife, depending upon your luck. But you can head down straight and reach the river or turn right by some ruins and cross over to complete the circle and return.

About another half-mile down the road and off to the right is **Las Sepulturas**, a site in the process of restoration. The only other important concentration of ruins open to visitors besides those found at the Great Plaza, it was originally connected to the latter by a causeway. The structures here are thought to have housed the elite. It's believed that some 250 people resided here around 800 AD. The best time to visit is early in the morning when you'll have it all to yourself. Except for a few figures, missing their heads, there is little to see here, but the ambience is great.

Back in the village, there's a small museum which contains a significant number of artifacts.

PRACTICALITIES: Copán village is a nice and very friendly place to hang out for a few days. The **Hotel Marina** (around US$15 d) is the place to stay if you want comfort. Next down the list is the **Hotel Maya Copán.** The hotel prices here are a bit higher than elsewhere in Honduras for the bottom-rung accommodation. Try **Hotel y Restaurant Paty, Hotelino Brisas de Copán, Hotel Las Gemelos,** or **Hotel Honduras.** If staying at hotels close to the town entrance, expect to be awakened by the sound of early morning buses departing.

El Mundo Maya

One of the most intriguing aspects of Belize to the visitor is the abundant archaeological legacy of the Maya. Even today, some 1,700 years after it is believed to have reached its peak, Maya culture is a very rich and impressive lode. Although pieces are filling in, the puzzle of Maya civilization is far from complete, and much of what is known is mere conjecture based upon fragmentary evidence. As the guessing game continues, perceptions change and mistakes are rectified. The Maya World, its history and culture included, has been cemented together in perpetuity with the European conquerors and colonists whose initial disdain for the Maya turned to wonder as they discovered and explored the ruins. Eventually, they came to regret their initial haste to destroy and denigrate.

The People

GEOGRAPHY: The Maya inhabited some 125,000-225,000 square miles, encompassing the present day boundaries of El Salvador, W. Honduras, Belize, Guatemala, the Mexican states of Tabasco and Chiapas to the west, as well as the entire Yucatán Peninsula. While firm geographical boundaries exist to the north and east, boundaries are more difficult to fix in the southeast and southwest, where they correspond only to zones of cultural transition between Maya and non-Maya. The area has traditionally been subdivided into the lowlands in the north and the highlands in the south. With the exception of Copán, which is located in the eastern portion of the northern highlands, the most famous Maya sites are in the northern lowlands. Maya culture, in turn, is part of Mesoamerica, a larger cultural area extending from northern Mexico as far south as Costa Rica. The Maya both were influenced by and influenced neighboring cultures, such as the Olmec of the Gulf coastal plain, the Zapotec and Mixtec of Oaxaca (west of the Isthmus of Tehuantepec), as well as lesser known societies to the southeast. The borders of the cradle of Maya civilization are delineated by the presence of the sapodilla. This tropical evergreen, famous in the modern era through its sap, which has been used to produce chewing gum, was employed by the Maya for supporting beams and wooden panels. In addition, the sap was used to make the ball for traditional ball games. Mixed with a second regional resin, the tree's sap also supplied a highly prized licence used in Maya religious ceremonies.

HISTORY: Although it is not known what the people actually called themselves, the term "Maya" was applied to the entire civilization. Recent findings indicate that the Maya may have inhabited Belize from as early as 9000 BC, but it is thought that the civilization's influences extend back to the Olmec civilization which flourished on the nearby Gulf of Mexico from 1200-300 BC. The Olmecs were reknowned for their carving skill, as well as their calendar and system of hieroglyphics. Maya history is customarily divided into three periods: Preclassic or Formative (2500 BC-AD 250), Classic or "Golden Age" (AD 250-900), and Postclassic (AD 900-1540). The Preclassic is further subdivided into Early Preclassic (2500-1000 BC), Middle Preclassic (1000-300 BC), Late Preclassic (300 BC-AD 50) and Protoclassic (AD 50-250).

societal decline: No one knows what caused the Maya society to decline. One scenario is that of ecological collapse, brought on by population pressures which had caused over-exploitation of the environment. A series of theories hold that the society collapsed because of clashes and fissures within the social structure. Maya expert J. Eric Thompson reasoned that a combination of factors – such as natural disaster and agricultural problems – could have led to disillusionment with the elite, which was followed by a peasant revolt. Others believe that a civil war between population centers led to the civilization's demise, or that the Maya lowlands were invaded from abroad. Yet another theory holds that environmental pressures caused the civilization to splinter and decline. The rainforest may have been overexploited, there appear to have been water shortages, and the area may have been overpopulated. A final and perhaps the most intriguing theory is that the Maya prognosticated themselves out of existence. Prophecies may have foretold changes at the end of a *katun* (one of the cycles on their calendar), which the fatalistic Maya then brought to fruition, thus bringing about their own downfall. A further refinement of this theory is that the Mayan astronomer-priests may have ordained it. In the 10th C. it was announced that the fourth or present world was about to end, giving way to a fifth world without men. This may have brought on an artificial "judgment day," destroying the civilization in the process.

mingling: The story of the ancient Maya definitively concludes with the era of Spanish Conquest, when destruction and mayhem dealt a devastating blow to local culture. Columbus encountered a canoe full of Maya traders in 1502 while exploring the

Bay Islands off Honduras, and their decline began then and there. In addition to deaths by war and famine, introduced diseases such as malaria and smallpox took their toll. Ritual and belief were crushed by the repressive church, and the written script disappeared. Traditional crafts such as sculpture, featherwork, lapidary work, painting, and metallurgy were extirpated. The economic system was transformed as well. The best lands were taken over for plantation crops such as coffee and sugarcane, which soon replaced traditional staples, and iron and steel replaced flint and obsidian. Still, a certain amount of ideology and the spoken language survived the transition into this "new world order." For example, the Christian cross was already used by the Maya as their symbol for the "tree of life," the ceiba tree supporting the heavens. So the cross gained ready acceptance when the friars explained that it was the sign of God, who had died on the Tree of Good and Evil and now resides in Heaven. In addition, the Maya already practiced baptism in water, fasting, confirmation, as well as sexual abstinence before rituals, and they already were accustomed to dressing their idols and bathing them in incense.

THE MAYA TODAY: As the Chiapas revolt in Dec. 1993 made clear, today's Maya are second class citizens in an area they once controlled. Condescended to and persecuted, Maya live in Guatemala and Mexico. Human rights violations are numerous. Some 140,000 Guatemalans (largely indigenous) have been killed during the three decades of Guatemala's civil war, and government troops have been known to burn entire villages. In Mexico, eleven Maya were tortured following their arrest in a land dispute in 1990, and a few years ago some 100 Maya were beaten and locked up for 30 hours without medical attention or food. Today, in Chiapas, only around half the population can read (compared with literacy rates of 88% for all of Mexico), 70% lack access to potable water, and infant mortality is 500 for every 1,000 live births – 10 times the national average. For information on Maya in Belize, see the entry under the Introduction.

The Civilization

MAYA CULTURE AND TECHNOLOGY: One major cultural quality was an obsession with the passage of time. Although, the Maya did not measure time in smaller increments than European cultures, they invented a sun calendar more accurate than the Gregorian calendar used today, recorded the rotation of Venus, and

Maya Chronology	Maya Events	World Events
AD 1500 **Late Postclassic**	Cortez arrives (1519)	Renaissance in Europe (1400+) Ming Dynasty founded (1368) Majapahit Empire (Java) (1292-1398)
AD 1200 **Early Postclassic**	Marco Gonzalez flourishes (1150-1300)	Kublai Khan attempts invasion of Japan (1274) Crusades in Europe (1096-1271)

AD 900
Late Classic
	Lubantuun occupied
	(AD 752)
		Daibutsu (Nara, Japan) dedicated
		  (AD 700)
		Borobudor constructed (AD 800)
		Angkor Period, Cambodia
		  begins (AD 750)

AD 600 **Early Classic**	Caracol conquers Tikal (AD 562)	Mohammed born (approx AD 571) End of Roman Empire (AD 476)

AD 250
Late Preclassic
	Xunantunich occupied
	(AD 150)
		Yamato Period in
		  Japan (AD 100-600)
		Silkworm cultivation arrives
		  in China (AD 200)

400 BC **Middle Preclassic**		Alexandria, Egypt flourishes (300 BC-0 AD) Rice cultivation begins in Japan (300 BC) Mahabarata written (350-300 BC) Parthenon dedicated (438 BC) Gautama Buddha lives (583-463 BC)
800 BC **Early Preclassic**	Tikal first occupied (750 BC) Altun Ha first occupied (1000 BC)	
		Moses receives 10 commandments (1500 BC)
2500 BC		Stonehenge (2000-1500 BC) Sphinx constructed (3000-2500 BC) First year of Jewish Calendar (3760 BC)

predicted eclipses of the sun and moon. Conceiving the notion of zero, they were able to calculate numbers to over a million, and in their vigesimal (base 20) numeration system, a system of dots and bars represented numbers from zero to 19. Symbolized as a shell, the Maya zero didn't appear in Europe until the 12th C., and the bar-and-dot notation was superior for mathematical calculations, as compared with the more awkward system of Roman numerals employed in Europe at the same time. The Maya counted by twenties, four hundreds, and eight thousands, and their words for numbers reflect this system of enumeration. Indeed, they were so mathematically focused that little is known about Maya society itself, because most of the glyphs translated thus far relate to calculations of time and astronomical events. In some ways they were far ahead of their time. Modern astronomy has determined that the solar year has 365.2422 days. The Maya calendar has 365.2425 days! One of at least five calendars, the Haab has 18 20-day months (*uinals*) which make 360 days, leaving 5-5 1/2 *uayeb* or unlucky days left over. The other two calendars are a mysterious one of 260 days – which is interlinked with the other – and the "long count," an extension of the Haab, leading back to a mystical date of 3113 BC. The other two calendars were lunar and Venusian. Their society is believed to have been ruled by a hereditary theocracy. They knew how to build roads and make mortar. They also developed the corbel vault as an arch. Still, despite these advances, they used only the most primitive of agricultural methods, never discovered the wheel, and fashioned Neolithic style tools from polished stone.

WRITING: Maya writing is built on glyphs generally grouped into glyph groups, which are predominately squared or oval in shape. There are about 800 glyphs known, and they are usually referred to by their catalog numbers or by nicknames such as "upended frog." Maya centers each have their own emblem glyphs which are unique to the site concerned and only found at another when the inscription refers to contact with that center. The writing system is generally agreed to be logosyllabic – a combination of pictographic and ideographic scripts – and is thought to have become more and more phonetic over time.

AGRICULTURE: One of the oldest forms of cultivation was swidden agriculture (more popularly known as slash-and-burn), in which fields were burned and planted with crops ranging from beans, maize, chilis, and squash to manioc and sweet potatoes. After the land is cultivated for several years, it must lie fallow and new tracts have to be cleared. Fertilized by garbage, the household garden provided produce. As any visitor to a contemporary Maya community will soon realize, these practices are still in use today. Methods no longer or rarely found in use today include raised fields and agricultural terracing. Raised fields allowed high-yield use of poorly drained or swampy tracts. With crops raised on intersecting or parallel ridges of fertile, well-drained soil built up from the surrounding swamp, the low areas between fields provided rich soil as well as drainage. If underwater, fields may have been used to raise fish and other marine life. Many of the raised fields of northern Belize are thought to have been planted with both maize and cacao. Used for ceremonial or burial offerings, maize formed an important decorative and symbolic motif in Maya art and was regarded as the gods' greatest gift to mankind. It was (and still is) planted with a digging stick, which makes a hole into which a seed is dropped. The Maya venerated a maize god and the plant itself, considered an attribute of the earth god. Today's Maya continue to address the plant as "your grace." Another important crop was cacao which – when roasted, ground, and mixed with maize and water – formed the favorite drink. Prized as an article of trade, cacao also served as a currency.

SEASIDE SETTLEMENTS: Although thoughts of the Maya world bring to mind images of ruined temples in the jungles, settlements which were on the shore played an important role in the economic structure because of their access to the sea's wealth. In addition to marine life – such as shellfish, fish, manatees, seals, and birds – which provided food, shells were used in toolmaking and jewelry. Stingray spines and shark teeth had their own ritual uses. The coastal Maya began harvesting salt, an important export, some 2,300 years ago. In addition to its nutritional value, salt was used to preserve meat and fish, for barter, and in a number of ritual and medical procedures. Basalt, jade (jadeite), obsidian, and other resources from the interior were traded for salt, cacao, cotton, feathers, jaguar pelts, and spices. Maya would travel the coasts in large dugouts, which could hold 40-50 people. They settled Cozumel and Belize cayes such, as Wild Cane, at least 2,000 years ago and are thought to have ventured as far as the Turneffes, 18 miles from the coast. Important Belizean settlements include Cerros (near Sarteneja) and Marco Gonzales (on Ambergris Caye).

Religion

 COSMOLOGY: For the Maya, the supernatural permeated every aspect of society, regulating all aspects of daily life up to and including trade and competition. The threat of supernatural retribution kept people in line. Shamans evolved into a priestly class, transforming the society into a theocracy in which priests were rulers and rulers were priests. The world was governed by a cosmological order transcending the distinction between natural and supernatural realms. All objects, animate or inanimate, were infused with an invisible force. Such a power was formless where spirits occupied rocks, trees, or other objects. But in other cases the power was embodied in a zoomorphic or anthropomorphic deity. The universe was viewed as an ordered place in its natural state, and the sun, moon, planets, and stars – each thought to be animate – marked the passage of time. The *kin*, the basic unit of time, is the time it took the sun to rise from the underworld, pass across the sky, and be swallowed by the underworld at sunset.

RITUALS: During the Classic era, the elite practiced ritual bloodletting. Penis piercing and the passing of a cord through the tongue are shown on Maya painted vases, and the ceremonial blood-letting instrument used to cut the penis is also widely depicted. The two types of bloodletting were self-imposed bleeding, and the bloodletting or sacrifice of a captive. Blood was offered to express piety and call the gods. It is thought that intense pain brought on hallucinatory visions, which have been represented on stelae by a serpent monster rising out of a plate holding blood-soaked ritual tools. Such tools included a rope with thorns that was pulled through the tongue and pieces of paper used to catch blood from penile or ear incisions. It is well known that endorphins, chemicals related to opiates and produced by the brain in response to massive blood loss, can induce hallucinations. Adding to the effect was the use of *balche*, an alcoholic beverage made from fermented honey combined with the *balche* tree bark, and of wild tobacco leaves – much more potent than today's anemic varieties. When these were smoked in gigantic spliffs, they induced a trance-like stupor. Miniature stone figures of mushrooms have also been found, pointing to their ritual use as hallucinogens, and depictions of enemas appear on glazed pots. Bloodletting is considered to have been fundamental to the institution of rulership. The main occasions for bloodletting and sacrifice were ceremonial ones that dealt with the mythology of world order: marriage, the dedication of buildings, planting of crops, birth of children, and burials. Because of its ritual importance, the lancet itself was ordained as a sacred object. Many were ornately carved, but stingray spines were employed as well.

DEITIES AND MYTHS: Creator of the universe as well as god of harvest, sun, earth, and rain, Itzamná is the principal Maya deity. Ix Chel is the goddess of the moon, and Kinich Ahau is the lord of the sun. Gods of rain, the Chacs, enjoy continued popularity with today's Maya. The jaguar god of the underworld can be identified by his jaguar ear, a tau (shaped like the Greek letter T) tooth, a cruller (ring-shaped cake) in his forehead, and gathered hair. All told, there may have been thousands of other deities. Ritual acts and their details were governed by the calendar.

HUMAN SACRIFICE: One of several techniques, the most popular method, according to an account by Bishop Landa, was to pull out the victim's heart. Stripped, painted blue, and wearing a peaked headdress, the victim was grabbed by four *chacs* (priests), also painted blue. Then the *nacom* (executioner priest) plunged a flint knife into the victim's ribs just below the left breast. Pulling out the still-beating heart, he handed it to the *chilan* (officiating priest), who smeared its blood on the idol. If the victim had been executed atop a pyramid, the *chacs* threw the corpse down to the base, where low-ranking priests skinned it, putting the hands and feet aside. After removing his ceremonial zoot suit, the *chilan* donned the victim's skin and danced solemnly. If the unfortunate one had been a soldier, his body was sometimes eaten, and his hands and feet were reserved for the *chilan*. Another method of sacrifice was to shoot at the heart with a bow and arrow. Other methods included disembowelment (as portrayed at Tikal) and throwing victims into the Cenote of Sacrifice at Chichen Itza.

THE BALL PARK: One of the features you'll notice at many Maya sites is the ball park. A combination of modern volleyball, basketball, jai alai, and soccer, the game was played by two competing teams of two to 11 members. Weighing an average of about five lbs., the rubber ball could be hit with all body parts, save hands, feet, or calves, and it could be bounced against the court's side wall. Players scored by forcing the ball into the opposing team's end zone or by striking the side markers. Protective clothing fashioned from leather or wicker shielded them from impact.

The Temple Sites

 VISITING MAYA RUINS: Unlike Mexico and Guatemala – where manicured Maya ruins have been rebuilt as the archaeologists believe they may have once been rather than necessarily as they actually were – the Belizean ruins have been left intact much as they were found. If something's been broken or fallen over, it's left that way. This has its attractions: the ruins have an aura of authenticity, and the lack of gawking crowds makes it easier to lose yourself in the magic of these places.

ARCHAEOLOGICAL HISTORY: The presence of these ghost cities amidst the hot and humid and nearly impenetrable jungle has long baffled archaeologists. The first explorers deemed it preposterous that the impoverished peasantry residing near the ruins might have any connection with these sophisticated structures. Thus, they invented a mythic race of "Noble Maya," believed to have been descendants of the Lost Tribes of Israel, Greeks, Phoenicians, Vikings, Egyptians, or residents of Atlantis. Published in 1822 in London, the first book about the Maya, *Descriptions of the Ruins of an Ancient City,* was a 1787 report by a Spanish army officer, Captain Antonio del Río who, visiting the large site of Palenque, had taken down all of the partitions and cleared blocked windows and doors. He maintained that the Romans – or perhaps the Phoenicians or Greeks – had arrived and taught the Indians their construction techniques. American John Lloyd Stephens and his English companion, artist Frederick Catherwood, rediscovered Copán in 1839 and purchased the site from a local farmer for US$50. After visiting Palenque to the north a few months later, Stephens hypothesized that the two centers belonged to the same culture. Together they visited over 40 sites. Published in 1841, Stephen's *Incidents of Travel in Central America, Chiapas and Yucatán* caused quite a stir in its time.

In the 1860s an old manuscript, *Account of Things in the Yucatán* by one Father de Landa, was unearthed in the Royal Library of Madrid. As the first Catholic Bishop of Mérida, the Spanish capital in the Yucatán, Landa had torched irreplaceable sacred painted Maya texts. Ironically, his account – which contained drawings of glyphs used by 16th C. Maya – still stands as one of the basic informational sources relating to the early Maya. The manuscript was found by French Abbé Brasseur de Bourbourg who also discovered a portion of one of the extant pre-Conquest Maya codices.

Succumbing to the delusions of the day, Abbé Brasseur came to believe that the civilizations of the Old World and Egypt stemmed from the New World to which they had been brought by colonists from Atlantis. University research boomed during the last two decades of the 19th C. The foremost scholar of the time was Englishman Alfred Maudslay, who spent 13 years studying ruins, producing five volumes in the process. At the same time Austrian-born naturalized American Teobert Maler had arrived in Mexico in 1864 as an Austrian army officer serving with Emperor Maximilian. He carried out work for Harvard's Peabody Museum for two solitary but extremely productive decades. During the same time frame, P. T. Barnum presented to Queen Victoria's dwarf a pair of microcephalic dwarfs claimed to be the last degenerate descendants of a caste of high priests found in a lost Maya city. At the end of the 19th century a major breakthrough came with Dresden librarian Ernst Forstemann's deciphering of the Maya calendar, which permitted scholars to read the calendrical inscriptions. In this century, archaeological excavations have increased the amount of knowledge available, but many secrets remain under the cover of the jungle. During the 1950s, the most prominent archaeologists were Sylvanus Morley and J. Eric Thompson. Many of their suppositions are known to be incorrect today. For example, they maintained that the Maya were a peaceful people, that inscriptions never dealt with historical events, and that Maya city centers were used only for ceremony and never for residence. Undoubtedly, some of today's "truths" will be found to be fallacies as well. Today, there are a number of archaeologists operating in Belize, and new discoveries are constantly emerging. In addition to the looters and the rainy season, a lack of funding hinders archaeologists. Accordingly, many sites in Belize remain unexplored, and excavations are going forward at a slow pace.

LAYOUT: Most Maya settlements contain a main plaza surrounded by several lesser plazas, each surrounded by temples atop mounds or pyramids and neighboring lesser structures such as sweat baths, ball courts, and palaces. It is believed that the temples were inhabited by priests and nobles, while the plebes lived in surrounding huts. No doubt Maya priests spent many an evening atop a pyramid, conceived as a "link between the earth and the sky," charting the course of the sun, moon, and stars. Typically found in the vicinity of the temple and facing an altar, the stela is a sculptured stone monument, usually an upright monolith. Bearing glyphs and emblem-glyphs, it generally records the lives of a ruler. Stelae were erected at the end of every *katun*, a 20-year interval. At times Mayas demolished their monuments, building new structures on top of the old. According to Maya beliefs, every building has its life span. Once calculated to have reached its end, the building had to be partially destroyed and then rebuilt, a practice which has given many an archaeologist attempting to date a site any number of grey hairs. Offerings (obsidian chips; flint pieces shaped like tridents, half moons, and discs; sea shells; jade fragments; and pearls) were set out under the base of stelae, in temple foundations, and inside buildings under construction. Human remains have been found in the foundations of demolished buildings ready for reconstruction, leading to the supposition that the structures were destroyed upon their deaths. The *sacbe* ("white way") – remnants of long roads found at the sites – must have been used for ceremonial processions. Constructed on the base of large, roughly-shaped stones and topped with gravel or limestone chips, the roadways were pressed by large and heavy stone rollers. Another notable feature of the sites is that there are no defense systems – one of the reasons the Maya were initially supposed to have been a peaceful people.

CONSTRUCTION TECHNIQUES: Amazingly, these cities were constructed without the use of the wheel! Carried on the backs of humans, rubble was dumped and faced with limestone blocks joined together using lime mortar. The landscape was sculptured to suit the builders' needs: hilltops were leveled and, in areas lacking a steady water supply, plazas were cleverly sloped to secure runoff to their reservoirs. The most important structural element is the corbel arch. Also known as the false arch, the corbel is made by building up layers of stone on each side of the room: each layer protrudes further inward until they can be joined at the top with a single stone. Since these arches can support only a short wall, rooms are claustrophobic. The structure contained two or three narrow, dark chambers – each 60 square feet in area. As their function was to support the temple, Maya pyramids were always flat-topped. The temple was decorated with a "roof comb," a masonry backdrop for front-facing mosaic or stucco decorative elements. Most of these gables rise above the midline of a building, but others are supported by the front wall, lending a "flying facade" effect to the building. The best of these are found at Tikal.

Belize Glossary

atolls – Circular or horseshoe-shaped coral reefs with slender, sandy islets formed by wind, storms, and surf.

backra – A "raw back," indicating a white person.

baktuns – Maya unit of measurement comprising 144,000 days or 20 katuns.

bank – Place name indicating the former presence of a log-loading ramp.

boom – Place name indicating where a chain was draped across a river in order to catch falling logs.

bram – Drumming and dancing celebration.

broken ridge – A variety of trees including cohune palms.

bruckdown – Belizean calypso which combines music and words to tell a tale or make fun of a noted personage.

bush – Marijuana.

camioneta – Guatemalan word for bus, generally meaning a light van or truck elsewhere.

cayes – The offshore islands.

chicle – The sap of the sapodilla which was once used as the base for chewing gum.

chiclero – A gatherer of chicle.

chugú – Garinagu ceremony of feeding the dead which is rarely requested by a spirit less than 10 or more than 50 years after death.

cohune ridge – Mixed terrain comprised largely of cohune palms.

dugu – Garinagu feasting of the dead, a complicated and major ceremony. Also the name ascribed to the Garinagu religion in general.

glyph – Name often given to a Maya hieroglyph.

huipil – Maya woman's blouse, generally embroidered.

jumpup – Local dance.

katun – Maya unit of measurement denoting 7,200 days or 20 *tuns*.

kin – Unit of measurement for the Maya day.

landing – High place above flood waters where loggers could land to do their work.

line – Road.

lintel – Beam used to span an opening.

logwood – The first major export of the area, logwood was used to make dyes. The tree lost its attraction with the development of synthetic dyes extracted from coal tar.

Mesoamerica – Area from the Valley of Mexico to Honduras in which civilizations flourished.

milpa – A Maya agricultural plot, it is first burned over, then maize is planted by poking holes through the ashes with a stick. After a few seasons, the plot is abandoned.

palace – Maya temple structure which is more loosely constructed than a pyramid

pen – Place name indicating a cattle farm or enclosure.

pyramid – Pyramid-shaped Maya temple consisting of a large platform of stones faced with finished limestone blocks and capped by a temple.

range – The marshy islands that are mainly semi-submerged mangrove swamps.

roof comb – A Maya temple roof structure resembling the comb of a cock.

spur and groove – Reef topography in which coral ridges divide deep trenches which have sandy floors. Tunnels and overhangs are common, allowing a wide diversity of inhabitants in a small area.

stela – Sculptured stone monument, usually an upright monolith found at Maya temples. Bearing glyphs and emblem-glyphs, these generally record the lives of their rulers.

tea – A meal.

unial – Maya unit of measure denoting 20 days.

walk – Place name indicating a farm.

Booklist

Travel and Description

Association for Belize Archaeology. *Warlords and Maize Men: A Guide to the Maya Sites of Belize*. Belize: Cubola Productions, 1992, Second Edition.

Barrett, Kirk. *Belize by Kayak: A Guide for Sea Kayaking in Belize*. Des Moines, IA: Reef-Link, 1994. This is an outstanding guide for kayakers and well worth the investment. To order call 515-279-6699 (ask for Sonna Newton with Reef-Link) or write 3806 Cottage Grove, Des Moines, IA 50311.

Cubola. *Atlas of Belize*. Benque Viejo, Belize: Cubola Productions, 1991, 16th Revised Edition.

Godfrey, Glenn D. *Ambergris Caye: Paradise with a Past*. Benque Viejo, Belize: Cubola Productions, 1989.

Hunter, Bruce. *A Guide to Ancient Mayan Ruins*. University of Oklahoma Press, Includes descriptions of sites in Belize.

Stephens, John L. *Incidents of Travel in Central America. Chiapas, and Yucatán, Vols. 1 & 2*. NY: Dover Pub., Inc., 1969.

Straughan, Robert P. *Adventure in Belize*. New Jersey: A.S. Barnes, 1975. Written with a childlike simplicity, this book covers an extensive amount of territory.

Vermeer, Donald E. *The Cays of British Honduras*. Berkeley, CA: Department of Geography, University of California, 1959. The first comprehensive description of the area's small islands and reefs.

Flora and Fauna

Ames, Oakes and Donovan Stewart Correll. *Orchids of Guatemala and Belize*. New York: Dover Publications, Inc., 1985. This 779-page, highly technical tome, repackaged from the original, is for the orchid fanatic. A small section on orchids found only in Belize is included.

Anderson, Sydney. *Simon & Schuster's Guide to Mammals*. NY: Fireside, 1983.

Chaplin, C. C. G. *Fishwatcher's Guide to West Atlantic Coral Reefs*. Valley Forge, PA: Harrowood Books.

Emmons, Louse H. *Neotropical Rainforest Mammals*. Chicago, University of Chicago Press, 1990. This exceptional color-plate-illustrated field guide is the finest of its kind. A must for zoologists and serious laymen alike, it contains maps showing the range of species, detailed descriptions and natural histories of the animals concerned, and references to scientific literature.

Forsyth, Adrian. *Journey through a Tropical Jungle*. Toronto: Greey de Pencier Books, 1988.

Forsyth, Adrian and Kenneth Miyata. *Tropical Nature*. New York: Scribner's, 1987. This is a fascinating and fine introduction to the tropical rainforest and its complex ecosytems.

Forsyth, Adrian. *Portraits of the Rainforest*. NJ: Camden House, 1990.

Head, Suzanne and Robert Heinzman, eds. *Lessons of the Rainforest*. San Francisco: Sierra Club Books, 1990. This collection of essays covers everything from activism (by Randy Hayes, founder of Rainforest Action Network) to the canopy (by Donald R. Perry) to extinction (by Anne H. and Paul Ehrlich).

Jacobs, Marius. *The Tropical Rain Forest: A First Encounter*. New York: Berlin Heidelberg, 1988. Calculated to appeal both to laymen and scientists, this comprehensive and technical book was originally written in Dutch. It includes a chapter on Tropical America written by R. A. A. Oldeman.

Janzen, Daniel H., ed. *Costa Rica National History*. Chicago: University of Chicago Press, 1983. Although this superb volume is an excellent introduction to Costa Rican species, many are also found in Belize.

Kricher, John C. *A Neotropical Companion: An Introduction to the Animals, Plants, and Ecosystems of New World Tropics*. Principally researched in Central America. Princeton, NJ: Princeton U. Press.

Moser, Don. *Central American Jungles.* Amsterdam: Time-Life Books, 1975. Includes information about Belize, howler and spider monkeys, etc.

Peterson, Roger Tory and Edward L. Chalif. *Field Guide to the Birds of Mexico.* NY: Houghton-Mifflin, 1973.

Rabinowitz, Alan. *Jaguar.* NY: Morrow, 1986. Authored by one of the moving forces behind the establishment of the Jaguar Reserve.

Richards, P. W. *The Tropical Rain Forest: An Ecological Study.* Cambridge, England: University Press, 1981. First published in 1952, this is an in-depth technical account which is geared more towards biologists than laymen.

Ridgely, Robert S. *A Guide to the Birds of Panama.* NJ: Princeton University Press, 1989.

Rutzler, Klaus and Ian G. Macintyre. *The Atlantic Barrier Reef Ecosystem at Carrie Bow Bay, Belize.* Smithsonian Contributions to the Marine Sciences, No. 12. Washington, DC: Smithsonian Institution Press.

Sanderson, Ivan T. *Living Treasure.* New York: Viking Press, 1941. A handsomely illustrated account of the adventures of a naturalist couple.

Sheppard, Charles R. C. *A Natural History of the Coral Reef.* Poole, Dorset: Blandford Press, 1983. If your curiosity about the reefs has been piqued by your visit, this is a fine book to read.

Smithe, Frank B. *The Birds of Tikal.* Garden City, NY: Natural History Press, 1966. May be available in Guatemala.

Stanley, Paul C. and Samuel J. Record. *The Forests and Fauna of British Honduras.* Chicago: Field Museum of Natural History, 1936. A dry but thorough account.

Stephens, Katie. *Jungle Walk.* A self-published guide to the nation's wildlife. While far from comprehensive, it is well researched and well written.

Terborgh, John. *Diversity and the Tropical Rainforest.* NY: Scientific American Library, 1992

Tomlinson, PB. *The Botany of Mangroves*. NY: Cambridge University Press, 1985.

Wilson, Edward O. *The Diversity of Life*. Cambridge, MA: Belknap Press, 1992. A superb account of the history of extinction, the world's biodiversity and the imminent dangers to its species.

History

Dobson, Narda. *A History of Belize*. London: Longman, 1973.

Foster, Byron. *The Baymen's Legacy: A History of Belize City*. Benque Viejo, Belize: Cubola Productions, 1987.

Guderjan, Thomas H. *Ancient Maya Traders of Ambergris Caye*. Benque Viejo, Belize: Cubola Productions, 1993.

Hovey, Graham and Gene Brown, eds. *Central America and the Caribbean*. New York: Arno Press, 1980. This volume of clippings from *The New York Times*, one of a series in its Great Contemporary Issues books, graphically displays American activities and attitudes toward the area. A goldmine of information.

Koop, Gerhard S. *Pioneer Years in Belize*. Spanish Lookout: G. S. Koop, 1991. Tells the tales of the Spanish Lookout Mennonite Community.

Mannix, Daniel P. and Malcolm Cooley. *Black Cargoes*. New York: Viking Press, 1982. Details the saga of the slave trade.

Thompson, J. Eric. *The Maya of Belize: Historical Chapters since Columbus*. Benque Viejo, Belize: Cubola Productions, 1988.

Politics and Economics

Barry, Tom. *Belize: A Country Guide*. Albuquerque, New Mexico: The Inter-Hemispheric Resource Center, 1989. One in a series, this superb book surveys the political and economic situation, taking in the military, environmental and social issues, and foreign influences.

Barry, Tom. *Inside Belize*. Albuquerque, New Mexico: The Inter-Hemispheric Resource Center, 1989. This extremely well written book details topics ranging from foreign policy to conservation and the environment. Also included are chapters on human rights, the Belize Defense Force, feminism and women's status, agriculture, and foreign influences. A must for anyone wanting an in-depth knowledge of Belize.

Barry, Tom. *The Central America Fact Book.* New York: Grove Press, 1986. A guide to the economic and political situation in each of the region's nations together with a list of transnationals active in the region.

Bolland, O. Nigel. *Belize: A New Nation in Central America.* Boulder: Westview Press, 1986. A succinct and superb political, economic, and cultural overview.

Bolland, O. Nigel. *Colonialism and Resistance in Belize.* Benque Viejo, Belize: Cubola Productions, 1988. A collection of essays written over a 16-year period.

Bolland, O. Nigel. *The Formation of a Colonial Society: Belize, from Conquest to Crown Colony.* Baltimore: Johns Hopkins University Press, 1977. Details the social and economic conditions prevailing in the 18th and 19th C.

Carmack, Robert M., ed. *Harvest of Violence: The Maya Indians and the Guatemalan Crisis.* Norman, OK: U of OK Press, 1988. A superb and very frightening account of repression in Guatemala. Must reading for anyone visiting neighboring Guatemala who wishes to learn about the true situation.

Foster, Byron. *The Baymen's Legacy: A History of Belize City.* Benque Viejo, Belize: Cubola Productions, 1992.

Grant, C. H. *The Making of Modern Belize: Politics, Society, and British Colonialism in Central America.* Cambridge, Cambridge University Press, 1976. Focuses on the years 1950-1974.

Lewis, Gordon K. *The Growth of the Modern West Indies.* London: MacGibbon & Kee, 1968. Includes a chapter on Belize.

Shoman, Assad. *Party Politics in Belize.* Benque Viejo, Belize: Cubola Productions, 1989, Second Edition.

Thompson, Eric S. *The Maya of Belize – Historical Chapters Since Columbus.* Benque Viejo, Belize: Cubola Productions.

Sociology and Anthropology

Ashcraft, Norman. *Colonialism and Underdevelopment: Processes of Political and Economic Change in British Honduras*. New York: Teachers College Press, 1973. An anthropological study of small farming and urban markets researched between 1965-67.

Foster, Byron Heart Drum: *Spirit Possession in the Garifuna Community of Belize*. Benque Viejo, Belize: Cubola Productions, 1986.

Ivanoff, Pierre. *Monuments of Civilization, Maya*. London: Cassell, 1975. Although no information on Belizean sites is included in this book, there is an excellent section on Tikal.

Kerns, Virginia. *Women and the Ancestors: Black Carib Kinship and Ritual*. Urbana: University of Illinois Press, 1983. Studies the ancestral rituals and kinship among the Garifuna. A fascinating account.

Sutherland, Anne. *Caye Caulker: Economic Success in a Belizean Fishing Village*. Boulder, CO: Westview Press, 1986. An absorbing account of the island's socio-economic life.

Taylor, Douglas M. *The Black Carib of British Honduras*. New York: Wenner-Gren Foundation, 1951.

Art, Architecture, and Archaeology

Maya: Treasures of an Ancient Civilization. NY: Abrams, 1985.

Association for Belizean Archaeology. *Warlords and Maize Men: A Guide to the Maya Sites of Belize*. Benque Viejo, Belize: Cubola Productions, 1989.

Bryant, Alice and Phyllis Galde. *The Message of the Crystal Skull: From Atlantis to the New Age*. Marin County, CA: St. Paul Lwellyn. If you've heard about the crystal skull at Lubaantun and wondered about it, this book is a fountain of New Age-style misinformation – right down to the misplacement of the site on the map of Belize!

Buhler, Richard, ed. *Recent Archaeology in Belize*. Belize City: BISRA, 1976.

Coe, William R. *Tikal, A Handbook of the Ancient Maya Ruins*. Philadelphia: University of PA Museum, 1988.

Ferguson, William M. and John Q. Royce. *Maya Ruins in Central America in Color*. Albuquerque: University of New Mexico Press, 1984. Covering Tikal, Copán, and Quiriguá, this is a beautiful and informative book.

Hammond, Norman. *Lubaantun: A Classic Mayan Realm*. Cambridge, MA: Peabody Museum, 1975. A highly technical and extremely detailed account.

Morley, Sylvanus and George W. Brainerd. *The Ancient Maya*. Stanford, CA: Stanford U Press, 1983. Fourth Edition. Undoubtedly, the most thorough account, revised posthumously to keep it up to date.

Schele, Linda and Mary Anne Miller. *The Blood of Kings*. NY: Braziller, 1986.

Schele, Linda and David Freidel. *A Forest of Kings*. NY: William Morrow, 1990.

Sidrys, Raymond V. *Archaeological Excavations in Northern Belize, Central America*. Los Angeles: University of CA, Institute of Archaeology, 1983.

Thompson, J. Eric S. *Maya History and Religion*. Norman: University of OK Press, 1970.

Thompson, J. Eric S. *The Rise and Fall of Mayan Civilization*. Norman: University of OK Press, 1954.

Language and Literature

Edgell, Zee. *Beka Lamb*. London: Heinemann, 1982. This pioneering novel describes Belizean life – including the relationship between church and school – during the 1950s.

Edgell, Zee. *In Times Like These*. London: Heinemann, 1992. Edgell's latest.

Ellis, Zoila. *On Heroes, Lizards and Passion*. Benque Viejo, Belize: Cubola Productions, 1990, Second Edition. Seven short stories about Belizean life.

Godfrey, Glenn D. *The Sinner's Bossanova.* Spanning post-WWII Belize City life into the 1970s. Benque Viejo, Belize: Cubola Productions, 1987.

Hernandez, Felicia. *Those Ridiculous Years.* Belize: Cubola Productions. An account of childhood in Dangriga during the 1960s.

Musa, Yasser, Kiren Shoman, Simone Waight. *Shots from the Heart: Three Young Belizean Poets.* Benque Viejo, Belize: Cubola Productions, 1991.

Ramirez, Luke. *The Poems I Write.* Belize City: Belize Advert Productions, 1990. An impressive first volume from the nation's pre-eminent Garifuna poet.

Ruiz Puga, David. *Old Benque: Erasa una vez en Benque Viejo.* Benque Viejo, Belize: Cubola Productions, 1990. A collection of four short stories written in Spanish which deal with fictionalized accounts of supernatural events.

Warde, Shirley A., ed. *"We jus catch um."* Goshen: Pinchpenny Press, 1974. Transcriptions of eight folk tales.

Young, Colville. *Pataki Full.* Benque Viejo, Belize: Cubola Productions, 1991. Short stories commenting on Belizean morality.

Spanish Vocabulary

Days of the Week

domingo	Sunday
lunes	Monday
martes	Tuesday
miercoles	Wednesday
jueves	Thursday
viernes	Friday
sabado	Saturday

Months of the Year

enero	January
febrero	February
marzo	March
abil	April
mayo	May
junio	June
julio	July
agosto	August
septiembre	September
octubre	October
noviembre	November
diciembre	December

Numbers

uno	one
due	two
tres	three
cuatro	four
cinco	five
seis	six
siete	seven
ocho	eight
nueve	nine
diez	ten
once	eleven
doce	twelve
trece	thirteen
catorce	fourteen
quince	fifteen
dieciseis	sixteen
diecisiete	seventeen
dieciocho	eighteen
dieci nueve	nineteen
veinte	twenty
veintiuno	twenty-one
veintidos	twenty-two

treinta	thirty
cuarenta	forty
cincuenta	fifty
sesenta	sixty
setenta	seventy
ochenta	eighty
noventa	ninety
cien	one hundred
cento uno	one hundred one
doscientos	two hundred
quinientos	five hundred
mil	one thousand
mil uno	one thousand one
dos mil	two thousand
un million	one million
mil milliones	one billion
primero	first
segundo	second
tercero	third
cuarto	fourth
quinto	fifth
sexto	sixth
septimo	seventh
octavo	eighth
noveno	ninth
decimo	tenth
undecimo	eleventh
duodecimo	twelfth
ultimo	last

Conversation

¿Como esta usted?	How are you?
Bien, gracias, y usted?	Well, thanks, and you?
Buenas dias.	Good morning.
Buenas tardes.	Good afternoon.
Buenas noches.	Good evening/night.
Hasta la vista.	See you again.
Hasta luego.	So long.
¡Buen suerte!	Good luck!
Adios.	Goodbye.
Mucho gusto de conocerle.	Glad to meet you.
Felicidades.	Congratulations.
Muchas felicidades.	Happy birthday.
Feliz Navidad.	Merry Christmas.
Feliz Año Nuevo.	Happy New Year.
Gracias.	Thank you.
Por favor.	Please.
De nada/con mucho gusto.	You're welcome.
Perdoneme.	Pardon me.
¿Como se llama esto?	What do you call this?
Lo siento.	I'm sorry.
Permitame.	Permit me.
Quisiera...	I would like...

Adelante.	Come in.
Permitame presentarle...	May I introduce...
¿Como se llamo usted?	What is your name?
Me llamo...	My name is...
No se.	I don't know.
Tengo sed.	I am thirsty.
Tengo hambre.	I am hungry.
Soy norteamericano/a	I am an American.
¿Donde puedo encontrar...?	Where can I find...?
¿Que es esto?	What is this?
¿Habla usted ingles?	Do you speak English?
Hablo/entiendo un poco español.	I speak/understand a little Spanish
¿Hay alguien aqui que hable ingles?	Is there anyone here who speaks English?
Le entiendo.	I understand you.
No entiendo.	I don't understand.
Hable mas despacio por favor.	Please speak more slowly.
Repita por favor.	Please repeat.

Telling Time

¿Que hora es?	What time is it?
Son las...	It's...
... cinco.	... five o'clock.
... ocho y diez.	... ten past eight.
... seis y cuaro.	... quarter past six.
... cinco y media.	... half past five.
... siete y menos cinco.	... five of seven.
antes de ayer.	the day before yesterday.
anoche.	yesterday evening.
esta mañana.	this morning.
a mediodia.	at noon.
en la noche.	in the evening.
de noche.	at night.
a medianoche.	at midnight.
mañana en la mañana.	tomorrow morning.
mañana en la noche.	tomorrow evening.
pasado mañana.	the day after tomorrow.

Directions

¿En que direccion queda...?	In which direction is...?
Lleveme a... por favor.	Take me to... please.
Llevame alla... por favor.	Take me there please.
¿Que lugar es este?	What place is this?
¿Donde queda el pueblo?	Where is the town?
¿Cual es el mejor camino para...?	Which is the best road to...?
De vuelta a la derecha.	Turn to the right.
De vuelta a la isquierda.	Turn to the left.
Siga derecho.	Go this way.
En esta direccion.	In this direction.

¿A que distancia estamos de...?	How far is it to...?
¿Es este el camino a...?	Is this the road to...?
¿Es...	Is it...
... cerca?	... near?
... lejos?	... far?
... norte?	... north?
... sur?	... south?
... este?	... east?
... oeste?	... west?
Indiqueme por favor.	Please point.
Hagame favor de decirme donde esta...	Please direct me to...
... el telephono.	... the telephone.
... el excusado.	... the bathroom.
... el correo.	... the post office.
... el banco.	... the bank.
... la comisaria.	... the police station.

Accommodations

Estoy buscando un hotel....	I am looking for a hotel that's...
... bueno.	... good.
... barato.	... cheap.
... cercano.	... nearby.
... limpio.	... clean.
¿Dónde hay hotel, pensión, hospedaje?	Where is a hotel, pensión, hospedaje?
Hay habitaciones libres?	Do you have available rooms?
¿Dónde estçn los baños/ servicios?	Where are the bathrooms?
Quisiera un...	I would like a...
... cuarto sencillo.	... single room.
... cuarto con baño.	... room with a bath.
... cuarto doble.	... double room.
Puedo verlo?	May I see it?
Cuanto cuesta?	What's the cost?
Es demasiado caro!	It's too expensive!

Index

Additional Reading

from Hunter Publishing

INSIDER'S GUIDE TO WESTERN CANADA
$15.95, ISBN 1-55650-580-9, 205pp

".... The lively, sometimes whimsical text makes reading a pleasure... major sites and attractions are intelligently discussed; there's an emphasis on fine arts and performing arts, and culture...." *Travel Books Worldwide.*

INSIDER'S GUIDE TO EASTERN CANADA
$15.95, ISBN 1-55650-581-7, 256pp

"... text and abundant photographs [are] so outstanding.... This would make a fine addition to most libraries." *Library Journal.*

Filled with history, tour information, local museums and galleries, where to shop, where to eat, these are the most complete guides to Canada in the bookstores. Superb color photos and maps complement the text. Complete accommodation information, from the most luxurious hotels to places for the traveller on a shoestring budget. As with all the books in this series, a free pull-out color map makes planning your days easy.

Among other guides in this series:

FLORIDA $15.95, ISBN 1-55650-452-7, 256pp
HAWAII $15.95, ISBN 1-55650-495-0, 230pp
NEW ENGLAND $17.95, ISBN 1-55650-455-1, 256pp
MEXICO $18.95, ISBN 1-55650-454-3, 320pp
RUSSIA $17.95, ISBN 1-55650-558-2, 224pp
CALIFORNIA $14.95, ISBN 1-55650-163-3, 192pp
INDONESIA $15.95, ISBN 1-55650-453-5, 224pp
TURKEY $17.95, ISBN 1-55650-283-4, 209pp
INDIA $16.95, ISBN 1-55650-164-1, 360pp
NEW ZEALAND $15.95, ISBN 1-55650-624-4, 224pp

BEST DIVES OF THE CARIBBEAN
$15.95, ISBN 1-55650-644-9, 342pp

A unique guidebook written by experienced divers and snorklers – Joyce and John Huber. Covering the most well-known islands

such as Antigua and St. Maarten/St. Martin, and the more secluded ones like Anguilla and St. Eustatius. Sites are rated for
visibility and outstanding marine life and every skill level is considered. In addition, this book tells you where to find the most
diver-friendly resorts, the best restaurants, where to stay, and gives
contacts for equipment rental and English-speaking tour operators. Color photos and maps throughout.

BEST DIVES OF THE WESTERN HEMISPHERE
$17.95, ISBN 1-55650-250-8, 320pp

"... for serious underwater enthusiasts who want to get in as much
bottom time as possible... Best Dives is probably the only guidebook they'll need." *Caribbean Travel & Life Magazine.*
"... [Best Dives] opens a new world of discovery to anyone with a
facemask and a desire to look beneath the water's surface." *Pacific
Stock, Hawaii.*

Best-selling scuba and snorkeling guide to Florida, California, Hawaii, the Caribbean and Latin America. Over 200 sites listed. Color
photos and maps throughout. Also, restaurant recommendations,
money-saving tour packages, sightseeing. Dive in!

ADVENTURE GUIDE TO THE HIGH SOUTHWEST
$14.95, ISBN 1-55650-633-3, 384pp

"... a conscientious and beautifully written guide...."

Hiking, mountaineering, trail riding, cycling, camping, river running, ski touring, wilderness trips – a guide to enjoying the natural
attractions of the Four Corners area of Northwest New Mexico,
Southwest Colorado, Southern Utah, Northern Arizona, and the
Navajo Nation and Hopiland. Includes all practical details on
transportation, services, where to eat, where to stay and travel tips
on how to cope with the harsh terrain and climate. The most
adventurous guide to this region on the market. Maps.

ADVENTURE GUIDE TO COASTAL ALASKA &
THE INSIDE PASSAGE
$14.95, ISBN 1-55650-583-3, 288pp

How to travel the coast of Alaska on the state's official Marine
Highway. From Bellingham WA up to the Aleutians and Kodiak.
Color photos and maps.

Among other guides in the Adventure Guide series:

COSTA RICA 2nd Ed. $15.95, ISBN 1-55650-598-1, 470pp
PUERTO RICO 2nd Ed. $14.95, ISBN 1-55650-628-7, 304pp
CANADA $15.95, ISBN 1-55650-315-6, 320pp
VIRGIN ISLANDS 3rd Ed. $14.95, ISBN 1-55650-597-3, 280pp
EVERGLADES & THE FLORIDA KEYS $14.95,
  ISBN 1-55650-494-2, 192pp
BAJA CALIFORNIA $11.95, 1-55650-590-6, 280pp

THE GREAT AMERICAN WILDERNESS:
TOURING AMERICA'S NATIONAL PARKS
$11.95, ISBN 1-55650-567-1, 320pp

The 41 most scenic parks throughout the US including Acadia, the Great Smokey Mountains, Yellowstone, Hawaii Volcanoes, the Grand Canyon, Big Bend, the Everglades and many more. This tells you where to stay, where to eat, which roads are most crowded or most beautiful, how much time to allow, what you can safely skip and what you must not miss. Detailed maps of each park show all the surrounding access routes and special sections tell you how to make the most of your time if you only have a couple of hours.

CANADIAN ROCKIES ACCESS GUIDE 3rd Ed.
$15.95, ISBN 0-91943-392-8, 369pp

The ultimate guide to outdoor adventure from Banff to Lake Louise to Jasper National Park. This book covers walking and canoeing routes, climbs, cycling and hiking in one of the most spectacular regions on earth. Maps, photos and contact numbers.

WHERE TO STAY IN NEW ENGLAND
$11.95, ISBN 1-55650-602-3, 512pp

"... isn't just your usual B&B or hotel listing, but a selection of almost all hotels, motels, country houses, condos and cottages for rent in the region.... Highly recommended: much more comprehensive in scope than competitors." *Reviewer's Bookwatch.*

Over 5,000 places are listed in this all-inclusive guide. Brief descriptions are supplemented by address, phone number (toll-free when available) and prices. Special sections are dedicated to chain hotels and deals they offer to business travellers, school groups, government workers and senior citizens.

Among other guides in the *Where to Stay* series:

AMERICA'S EASTERN CITIES $11.95, ISBN 1-55650-600-7, 416pp
AMERICA'S WESTERN CITIES $11.95, ISBN 1-55650-420-9, 416pp
MID-ATLANTIC STATES $12.95, ISBN 1-55650-631-7, 446pp
AMERICA'S HEARTLAND $13.93, ISBN 1-55650-632-5, 572pp
SOUTHERN CALIFORNIA $12.95, ISBN 1-55650-573-6, 394pp
NORTHERN CALIFORNIA $12.95, ISBN 1-55650-572-8, 280pp

TRAVELER'S GUIDE TO THE GALAPAGOS ISLANDS 2nd Ed.
$15.95, ISBN 1-55650-640-6, 256pp

Comments on the 1st edition:
".... Boyce's excitement and knowledge mix to produce a comprehensive and responsible guide." *Booklist.*
".... An excellent resource both for exploring the archipelago and for trip preparation." *Great Expeditions.*
".... Just on the market and badly needed.... Boyce's effort is likely to be a definitive work." *San José Mercury News.*

Barry Boyce, a relentless adventure traveler, shares his knowledge and experience of travel in this amazing archipelago. Unlike any other book on the subject it orients the reader to various touring options on both yachts and cruise ships, from specialty tours such as photography and bird watching, to general tours covering history and sightseeing. Companies offering tours are described, analysed and price structures are included. Fax and toll-free numbers put you in direct contact to make planning easier.

ARIZONA, COLORADO & UTAH: A TOURING GUIDE
$11.95, ISBN 1-55650-656-2, 160pp

A compact guide written for those eager to see the unforgettable attractions of these three states. Driving tours begin in the state capital and cover the museums, parks, zoos and historical buildings in each city. They then lead the reader out into the fascinating land of giant arches, pinnacles, natural bridges, canyons and deserts for which the region is so well known. All the sights are described, along with the best routes to reach them whether on a daytrip or as part of a month-long tour. Accommodations and attractions are listed with opening times and fees. State and city maps make planning easy.

STATE PARKS OF THE SOUTH
$13.95, ISBN 1-55650-655-4, 224pp

This book takes you to 250 state parks in the states of Georgia, Alabama, Tennessee, Kentucky and Florida. From small ones that are largely undiscovered by the public, to others whose names you will recognize – each offers something unique. History, background on the ecosystem, lodges, camping facilities, local attractions, activities, maps and photos put this guide way above any other available in terms of practical tips and usability.

HUGO'S SPANISH FOR BUSINESS

If you're heading to Latin America for an important meeting, try our Spanish for Business course. Business courses are available in several languages and consist of four one-hour audio cassettes and a book, with the accent on commercial vocabulary and dialog. Real-life scenarios featuring native speakers teach the use of the language in a wide variety of business situations, from placing ads to handling a job interview to negotiating a loan.

CASSETTE & BOOK $39.95, ISBN 0-8585-208-8
BOOK ALONE (220pp) $9.95, ISBN 0-85285-207-0

HUGO'S LATIN-AMERICAN TRAVEL PACK
$14.95, ISBN 0-85285-219-3, 128pp

A new title in the series that is the perfect learning tool for those taking a vacation in a foreign country. These packs contain a 128-page phrasebook with mini-dictionary and menu guide, plus a 60-minute cassette with all the key phrases spoken by natives.

HUGO'S 3 MONTHS LANGUAGE COURSES

"Our personal favorites... Hugo actually teaches you the building blocks of the language so you have a fighting chance of participating in a real live conversation." *Conde Nast Traveller.*

Hugo's come in Three Months courses, At The Wheel courses, Business courses, Conversational courses, Travel Packs, Phrasebooks, Dictionaries and Verb books and something is available in all of the following languages:

ARABIC
CHINESE
CZECH
DANISH
DUTCH
EL INGLES/ENGLISH FOR SPANISH SPEAKERS
FRENCH
GERMAN
HEBREW
HUNGARIAN
INDONESIAN
ITALIAN
JAPANESE
L'ANGLAIS SIMPLIFIE/ENGLISH FOR FRENCH SPEAKERS
LATIN-AMERICAN SPANISH
NORWEGIAN
POLISH
PORTUGUESE
ROMANIAN
RUSSIAN
SERBO-CROAT
SPANISH
SWEDISH
THAI
TURKISH
YUGOSLAV

All of these titles plus thousands more are available from Hunter Publishing. To receive our free color catalog or to find out more about our books and maps, contact Hunter Publishing, 300 Raritan Center Parkway, Edison NJ 08818, or call (908) 225 1900.